ENGLISH
At Your Command!

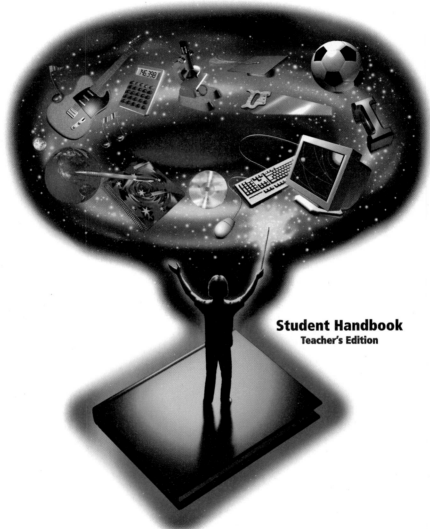

Student Handbook
Teacher's Edition

Curriculum Consultants

Nancy Alexander	Kristi Lichtenberg	Ellie Paiewonsky
Elizabeth Buckley	Lourdes Lopez	Wilma Ramirez

HAMPTON-BROWN

Hampton-Brown
P.O. Box 223220
Carmel, CA 93922
(800) 333-3510

Printed in the United States of America
0-7362-0194-7
99 00 01 02 03 04 9 8 7 6 5 4 3

ACKNOWLEDGMENTS
Every effort has been made to secure permission, but if any omissions
have been made, please let us know. We gratefully acknowledge
permission to reprint the following material:

Alphabet Font Copyright© 1996 Zaner-Bloser.

Illustrations:
Liseth, Dawn: p14T, p41T, p48T, 52T, p56T, p60T, p68T, p84T

Photographs:
Batista Moon Studio: p19T, p23T, p27T, p35T, p39T, p43T, p47T,
p55T, p59T, p63T (letter), p67T, p71T, 75T, p79T, p83T, 87T, 91T,
95T

PhotoDisc: p63T (girl gardening)

Acknowledgments continued on page 2 and pages 335–336.

Contents

Program Overview

Communication Projects

Contents, continued

Teacher Annotations in the Student Handbook

Program Overview

Components and Features

Welcome to **English At Your Command!** . . . a comprehensive language arts handbook specially designed for English learners and at-risk students. You can use the **Handbook** across several grade levels as an instructional tool and as an independent reference resource for students. Students will develop familiarity with the **Handbook** over time and will come to rely on it as a key resource for learning as they progress throughout the grades.

Student Handbook

- Five chapters to build vocabulary; promote the use of graphic organizers; and develop skills in writing, grammar, mechanics, and research
- Dateline U.S.A.™ to build familiarity with U.S. history and culture
- Contextualized explanations of skills with lots of examples, models, and visual support
- Multicultural, student-centered topics with content connections
- Grammar practice opportunities

Practice Book

- Independent practice for vocabulary, graphic organizers, grammar, mechanics, and research skills
- Writing frames plus revising and proofreading practice for Communication Projects
- Progress Test
- Self-Assessment Form
- Student Progress Form

Teacher's Edition for the Handbook

- Strategies to familiarize students with the **Handbook**
- Annotations on student pages for teaching and practice–plus multi-level strategies for varying language proficiencies
- Communication Projects to motivate students to use the skills and content in the **Handbook** for authentic purposes
- Assessment

Teacher's Edition for the Practice Book

- Answers to the exercises and tests
- Annotations for administering, scoring, and interpreting results of the Progress Test

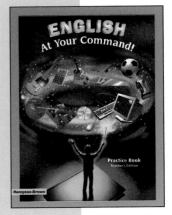

Strategies to Familiarize Students with the Handbook

If your students are using the **Handbook** for the first time, spend a few weeks familiarizing them with its content and organization. You may wish to present one chapter at a time using the following activities:

Chapter Preview Assign a span of pages within the chapter to each of several groups. Have them look through their pages and talk about the pictures and content. Then have each group write one or two sentences to tell what their section is mostly about and share them with the class.

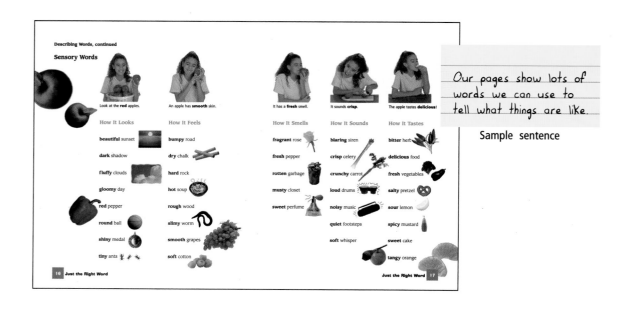

Our pages show lots of words we can use to tell what things are like.

Sample sentence

Favorite Pages Have students look through the pages in a chapter and choose a favorite page or a page that shows a picture, person, topic, or skill they are familiar with. Invite volunteers to share that page with the class and tell as much as they can about it.

Scavenger Hunt Have groups go on a scavenger hunt within a chapter, giving clues such as *You're going on a journey. Start on page 12 and find a color* (green). *Now find something on page 13 that is green* (the clock). *What shape does it have?* (circular). *Now go to page 14. Is there something green on this page?* (yes) *What is it?* (a watch, a watch band) *What time does the watch say?* (three o'clock), and so on.

Clue Hunt Provide partners with a list of page numbers and sentences to complete such as *The third step in the Writing Process is _____*. Partners search the pages in the chapter and fill in the blanks.

Finding Entries Chapters 1, 2, 3, and part of Chapter 5 present entries in alphabetical order. To help students access these entries, teach the section on alphabetical order on **Handbook** page 224. For practice, write the main entries from one of these chapters on separate slips of paper. Then give teams fifteen minutes to put the slips in order to match the order of entries in the chapter.

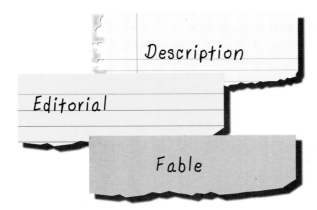

Orientation activities such as these will help students build a sense of where to turn in their **Handbooks** to find information they need. Gaining this overview will promote greater use of the **Handbook** in your classroom.

Teaching with the Handbook

You can use the **Handbook** for direct instruction in a variety of ways.

1 Presenting a Series of Lessons

You may wish to focus on one concept across multiple lessons and teach related pages in the **Handbook** in order. For example:

- To teach the research process, you can teach pages 220–233 of the **Handbook** across two weeks, covering each step of the process in one or two daily lessons. If you are conducting a six-week unit on research and reporting, continue to teach the rest of the chapter across that time, introducing each different reference resource.

- You can teach all of Chapter 4 in order, focusing on a different part of speech each week or two-week period. For example, the section on pronouns on pages 174–179 can be taught in 5 lessons.

Refer to the annotations on the **Handbook** pages in this **Teacher's Edition** to find strategies for introducing the skills and for multi-level practice. These annotations also reference pages in the student **Practice Book** for independent practice.

2 Pinpointing Skills for Reinforcement

As you observe students during daily instruction, make notes about any problem areas. Then group students with like needs and use appropriate pages in the **Handbook** as minilessons to reteach or review those skills. For example, if your students are having difficulty summarizing a story they've read, you might teach or review Story Maps in Chapter 2. Or, if students are having trouble with multiple-meaning words during a social studies or science lesson, you can review Multiple-Meaning Words on pages 21–27 in Chapter 1. As a follow-up, you can select practice activities provided in the annotations that are appropriate for your students' proficiency levels and/or assign **Practice Book** pages for independent practice.

**Practice Book page 10:
Multiple-Meaning Words**
The Practice Book includes independent practice for each skill taught in the Handbook.

3 Using the Communication Projects

Students acquire English most quickly and easily when they use it for meaningful communication. When you base your curriculum on purposeful, communicative activities, your students will be motivated to produce language and use the vocabulary as well as the patterns and structures they need to acquire. Pronunciation and fluency also develop naturally as students use language for purposeful activities.

English At Your Command! includes 24 Communication Projects on pages 14T–95T of this **Teacher's Edition**. These projects focus on oral language and writing. They promote the kind of interaction that generates authentic communication.

Each project involves using several different sections of the **Handbook** as individuals, partners, and groups participate in the oral language activities or undertake the different stages of the Writing Process. In Project 13: Personal Narrative, for example, students access the **Handbook** at several points:

- First, they go to page 131 in Chapter 3 to study the personal narrative as a writing form.

- Next, in **Prewriting**, they use page 63 in Chapter 2 for support in creating an Event Cluster that helps them organize ideas for writing.

- For **Drafting**, they use page 88 in Chapter 3 to find out how to write a first draft.

- Then students go to pages 89–91 in Chapter 3 for **Revising** guidelines, and to Describing Words on pages 12-19 in Chapter 1 for words they can use to add descriptive details to their narratives.

- For **Proofreading**, they turn to the guidelines on page 92 in Chapter 3; and study Pronouns on pages 174–179 and Capitalization of *I* on page 202 in Chapter 4 to help them fix any mistakes in their writing.

- Finally, for **Publishing**, students use the sharing idea for the project, or look on page 93 in Chapter 3 for other ways to share their writing.

Here are some recommendations for selecting projects for your students:

- For students at all grades, Projects 1–6

- For students using the **Handbook** for the first year, Projects 7–12; for the second year, Projects 13–18; and for the third year, Projects 19–24.

The **Practice Book** includes writing frames to support the Drafting step in each project and pages for revising and proofreading practice.

Using the Handbook as an Independent Resource

Once students are familiar with the contents and organization of the **Handbook**, they can use it as an independent resource for any skills they need help with. Display several copies at the Writing Center or have students keep a **Handbook** at their desks to use whenever they need help completing assignments. Invite students to use self-adhesive notes to mark pages that they use over and over again so that they can easily access words, models, or guidelines. Also send the **Handbook** home so students can use it as a reference tool for completing their homework.

Assessment

Progress Test

The **Practice Book** includes a test for assessing students' mastery of the skills taught in the **Handbook** which can be administered at the end of the year. Use the annotations in the **Teacher's Edition** for the **Practice Book** to administer and score the test, and record results on the Student Progress Form provided on the inside back cover of the student **Practice Book**.

Ongoing Assessment

Student participation in the Communication Projects also provides many opportunities for assessing students' growth in language proficiency. As you observe students presenting their products, check for their use of language functions as well as patterns and structures. The Observation Checklist on page 12T will help you monitor and track each student's progress.

Using Portfolios

Collect students' writing projects or have students create their own portfolios as described in the Good Writer Guide on **Handbook** page 157. Students' portfolios can provide meaningful information about their language use. To evaluate students' writing, look through the portfolios about six times a year and use the criteria on the Observation Checklist on page 12T to help you determine students' proficiency levels.

Self-Assessment

Give students an active role in the evaluation process by having them complete self-assessments of their writing at specified intervals throughout the year. Students can use the Self-Assessment Form provided at the end of the Progress Test in their **Practice Books** (page 16A) to guide their evaluation. Encourage students to keep the forms in their portfolios.

Observation Checklist for
name

Assessing Language Functions

Study the scoring rubric. In the box, write the proficiency level that corresponds to your observation of the student's behavior during the Project.

Scoring Rubric	Function	Evaluation Opportunities			
3 The student demonstrates the function using short phrases without connected discourse and with frequent errors.	Give Directions	Project 7 ☐			
	Ask for/Give Information	Projects 1 ☐	17 ☐	21 ☐	24 ☐
4 The student demonstrates the function with more detailed language in connected discourse and with fewer errors.	Describe	Projects 8 ☐	11 ☐	13 ☐	14 ☐
		19 ☐	20 ☐		
5 The student demonstrates the function with language comparable to native-speaker peers.	Persuade	Projects 3 ☐	10 ☐	17 ☐	22 ☐
	Retell a Story	Project 6 ☐			
	Tell an Original Story	Projects 12 ☐	15 ☐	23 ☐	

Assessing Language Functions

Record dates in the blanks to show when the student correctly uses each structure.

Pattern/Structure	Beginning	Consistent	Evaluation Opportunities
Statements			Projects 16, 17
Questions			Projects 1, 9, 14, 16, 21, 24
Commands			Projects 1, 7
Compound Sentences			Project 15
Nouns			Projects 9, 11, 17, 23
Pronouns			Projects 8, 13, 20
Adjectives			Projects 11, 18, 19
Prepositions			Project 19
Verbs			Projects 10, 14, 21, 24
Contractions			Project 12

Assessing Writing

Use the scoring rubric to evaluate the student's writing about six times per year. Record the date of your evaluation and the student's proficiency level.

Scoring Rubric	Date of Evaluation	Proficiency Level
3 The writing includes complete sentences with grammatical inaccuracies and awkwardness, but text tells about something, describes, compares, etc.; conventional spelling begins to appear.	1. _____	☐
	2. _____	☐
4 The writing includes connected text with conventional English spelling and more extensive vocabulary as well as few grammatical errors.	3. _____	☐
	4. _____	☐
5 The writing includes text comparable to that of native-speaker peers.	5. _____	☐
	6. _____	☐

3 Speech Emergence   **4** Intermediate Fluency   **5** Advanced Fluency/Fluent

Activities to Promote Language and Writing Through Authentic Communication

Dear Classroom Pal

Overview Students will talk about ways to ask for and clarify information, brainstorm problems and solutions, and then create an ongoing classroom advice column.

OBJECTIVES

Functions
• Ask for/Give Information

**RELATED PAGES
IN THE HANDBOOK**

Writing
• Advice Column ....**Writing Model**, page 94

Language Patterns and Structures
• Questions and Commands ....**Instruction and Practice**, pages 160–162,
page 305

Warm-Up

▶ **MATERIALS:** *chart paper*

Discuss Strategies Talk with students about ways to ask for help when you don't understand something or when you need to solve a problem.

Demonstrate a Problem Act out a problem such as misplacing your car or house keys while students try to guess what the problem is. Draw a set of keys and write the problem and a question. Have students offer suggestions for ways to solve the problem.

Explain the Project Goal Thank students for their advice, and then explain: *In your group, you'll write about a problem and ways to solve it. You'll add the information to a class book. Whenever you or your classmates need help with a problem, you can look in the class book.*

*I'm always losing my keys.
What should I do?*

1. *Always put your keys in the same place.*

2. *Get a really big key ring.*

Learn About Advice Columns

Discuss Characteristics Have students turn to the Advice Column on **Handbook** page 94. Use the annotations to introduce or review its characteristics. Ask volunteers to describe what an advice column is in their own words.

Write an Advice Column

▶ **MATERIALS:** *3-ring binder, shoe box*

Prewriting Brainstorm a title for the class advice column, such as *Dear Classroom Pal,* and grade-appropriate problems students' might have. Then form groups of varied proficiency levels. Have each group choose a problem (or make up a new one) and discuss possible solutions for it.

Drafting, Revising, Proofreading Use level-appropriate strategies to involve students of all proficiency levels in the writing process.

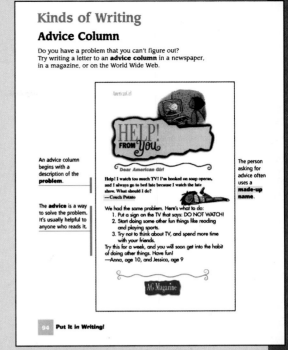

**Writing Model
Handbook page 94**

MULTI-LEVEL STRATEGIES

3 SPEECH EMERGENCE
Have these students use drawings, key words, or phrases to show a problem. Help them write a question at the end such as *What should I do?* or *Can you help me?*

4 5 INTERMEDIATE and ADVANCED FLUENCY/FLUENT
These students can write the advice for the problem.

Publishing When groups are pleased with their advice columns, collect them in a binder. Display the binder in the Reading Center. Whenever students need advice throughout the year, they can write a problem on a slip of paper and place it in a shoe box. Then groups can respond to each problem by writing new columns to add to the binder.

> Dear Classroom Pal:
>
> Sometimes I don't understand what the teacher is saying. What can I do?
> —Confused
>
> Dear Confused:
>
> Here are some things you might try:
> 1. Raise your hand and ask the teacher to say it again.
> 2. Tell the teacher "I don't understand."
> 3. Ask your partner to help you understand.
> — Classroom Pal

What a Book!

Overview Students will read books, and then write book reviews to share with the class.

OBJECTIVES

Functions
• Respond to Literature

Learning Strategies
• Summarize

**RELATED PAGES
IN THE HANDBOOK**

Writing
• Book Review ....**Writing Model,** page 98
• Capitalization: Titles ....**Instruction and Practice,** page 207, page 325

Write Book Reviews

Discuss Characteristics Use **Handbook** page 98 to introduce or review elements of a book review.

Read and Share Books Choose one of these activities depending on students' proficiency levels:

• Set up small group Book Clubs in which each student reads and discusses the same book. Afterward, students can work together to write a book review to post in the Reading Center.

• Have partners each read the same book, write a book review, and use it to make an illustrated book poster to persuade others to read it.

• Have students read as many books as they can in a month and choose a favorite to write about. Collect reviews in a binder organized by genre. Students can use it to select new books to read.

Book Review

Sometimes you read a book that you just have to talk about with someone. You can tell about it by writing a **book review**.

THE LOST LAKE

ALLEN SAY

The Lost Lake

In the first paragraph, tell the **title** of the book and the **author**. Then tell what the book is mostly about, or its **main idea**.

The Lost Lake by Allen Say is about a boy, Luke, who went to live with his father in New York for the summer. Luke was bored there because his dad was always too busy to spend time with him. One Saturday, Dad took Luke on a hiking trip to a secret "lost lake." The lake wasn't really secret, though, because lots of other people were there. So Luke and Dad looked for another lake. They hiked and talked all the next day. Then they found a place to camp and went to sleep. When they woke up, they saw a lake in front of them! No one else was around.

Next, tell how you **feel** about the book and why.

I like this book because it reminded me of camping trips with my family. I also like that the father and the son talked to each other more when they were out camping.

Finally, tell the **most important idea you learned** from the book.

This book shows how sometimes adults can get so busy that they forget to spend time with their kids. Maybe people should think about going somewhere else to help them remember what is important.

98 Put it in Writing!

**Writing Model
Handbook page 98**

Books for Varying Proficiency Levels

3 *I Want to be an Astronaut* by Byron Barton, *Vegetable Garden* by Douglas Florian

3 4 *The Wind Eagle* by Joyce McGreevy, *The Three Little Javelinas* by Susan Lowell

3 4 5 *Too Many Tamales* by Gary Soto, *Cinder-Elly* by Frances Minters, *Grandfather's Dream* by Holly Keller, *Grandfather's Journey* by Allan Say, *Dancing with the Indians* by Angela Medearis, *The Fox in the Moon* retold by Juan Quintana and Michael Ryall

3 What a Bargain!

Overview Students will talk about characters in books they've read and write advertisements for items those characters might want to sell or trade at a flea market.

OBJECTIVES

Functions
• Persuade

RELATED PAGES IN THE HANDBOOK

Writing
• Announcements and Advertisements ....**Writing Models,** pages 95–96

Write Advertisements

▶ **MATERIALS:** *large sheets of construction paper, 1 per group; crayons or markers*

Discuss Characteristics Use the annotations on **Handbook** pages 95–96 to introduce or review advertisements.

Make an Advertising Flyer Have groups choose a book they've read and talk about what the characters are like. Then:

• Prompt groups to brainstorm what the characters could sell or trade, what service they could offer, and so on.

• Have each student write an advertisement.

• Then have the group arrange and glue their advertisements on the construction paper.

• Use each group's flyer to create a display.

Writing Models
Handbook page 95

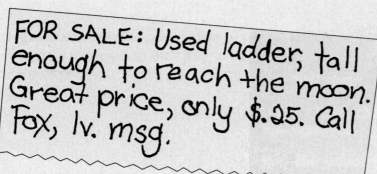

FOR SALE: Used ladder, tall enough to reach the moon. Great price, only $.25. Call Fox, lv. msg.

Listen to the Rhythm

Overview Students will choose a poem, practice reciting it, and then present their poems at a poetry recital.

OBJECTIVES

**RELATED PAGES
IN THE HANDBOOK**

Language Fluency
• Poems

Functions
• Recite

Speaking and Listening
• Poem ....**Poetry Models,** pages 134–137

Warm-Up

Build Background Recite your favorite poem or a poem from **Handbook** pages 134–137. Ask students to comment on the poem and what you did.

Explain the Project Goal Explain: *Now you can choose a poem to recite.* Recite *means to learn the words and say them from memory. You'll practice reciting your poem, and then present it to other classes.*

Choose a Poem

▶ **MATERIALS:** *poetry anthologies, student portfolios*

Encourage students to choose a poem from the **Handbook,** available anthologies such as *A Chorus of Cultures* (Hampton-Brown Books, 1993), or their writing portfolios. Have them record their choice on a sign-up sheet.

Plan the Performance

Model Ways to Recite Recite your poem again. This time model different ways to say it by saying certain lines loudly or softly, using gestures and sound effects, and so on. Have students think about the different ways to say their poem and decide which way they like best.

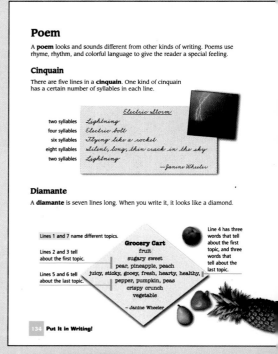

**Poetry Models
Handbook pages 134–137**

Think About Speaking and Listening Share the following tips with students, pointing out that they'll be helpful when students practice and present their poem.

As the Speaker
- Stand or sit up with your back straight.
- Look at your audience.
- Speak in a loud, clear voice.
- Introduce the poem and poet.
- Use expressions and movements that go with the poem.
- When you're done, say thank you and take a bow!

As the Listener
- Look at the performer.
- Listen carefully.
- Be quiet while the speaker is talking.
- Don't interrupt unless you need the speaker to talk louder.
- Wait until the speaker is done before clapping your hands.

Practice the Poem

Use level-appropriate strategies to involve all students in practicing for their recital.

MULTI-LEVEL STRATEGIES

3 SPEECH EMERGENCE
Have these students practice echoing the poem while you or a more fluent student reads it aloud. Repeat or do choral recitations until the poem is memorized.

4 5 INTERMEDIATE and ADVANCED FLUENCY/FLUENT
Have these students practice with a partner who follows along with the printed poem, provides forgotten words, and makes other suggestions for the performance.

Recite Poetry

▶ **MATERIALS:** *students' poems, audio recording equipment (optional)*

Present Poems Set aside a time for the poetry recital. You might want to prepare a program with a list of presentations and send invitations to students' families or students from other classes. After the recital, encourage the class to share their impressions of the event.

Matriarch
by Francisco X. Alarcón

my dark
grandmother

would brush
her long hair

seated out
on her patio

even ferns
would bow

to her splendor
and her power

5 It's Showtime!

Overview Students will write a class script based on a story they've read. In their groups, students will use the script to put on a play for the class.

OBJECTIVES

**RELATED PAGES
IN THE HANDBOOK**

Functions
• Dramatize

Writing
• Play ....**Writing Models,** pages 132–133
• Fable ....**Writing Model,** page 105

Concepts and Vocabulary
• Story Language ....**Instruction,** page 140

Warm-Up

Build Background Have students talk about plays they've seen at school. Encourage them to describe the characters and the plot.

Explain the Project Goal Tell students: *We are going to read a story, and then use that story to make up a play. You'll help me write a script that tells who the characters are and what happens in the play. Then your group will put on the play for the class.*

Learn About Plays

Discuss Characteristics Use the annotations on **Handbook** pages 132–133 to introduce or review plays and how to make a script.

**Writing Models
Handbook pages 132–133**

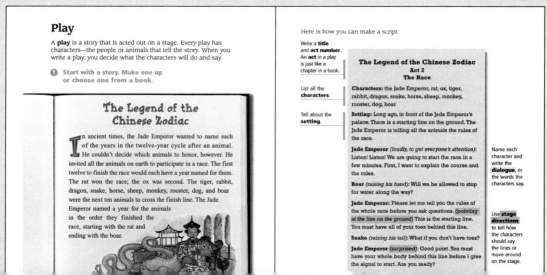

Play

A **play** is a story that is acted out on a stage. Every play has characters—the people or animals that tell the story. When you write a play, you decide what the characters will do and say.

❶ Start with a story. Make one up or choose one from a book.

The Legend of the Chinese Zodiac

In ancient times, the Jade Emperor wanted to name each of the years in the twelve-year cycle after an animal. He couldn't decide which animals to honor, however. He invited all the animals on earth to participate in a race. The first twelve to finish the race would each have a year named for them. The rat won the race; the ox was second. The tiger, rabbit, dragon, snake, horse, sheep, monkey, rooster, dog, and boar were the next ten animals to cross the finish line. The Jade Emperor named a year for the animals in the order they finished the race, starting with the rat and ending with the boar.

Here is how you can make a script.

Write a **title** and **act number.** An **act** in a play is just like a chapter in a book.

List all the **characters.**

Tell about the **setting.**

The Legend of the Chinese Zodiac
Act 2
The Race

Characters: the Jade Emperor, rat, ox, tiger, rabbit, dragon, snake, horse, sheep, monkey, rooster, dog, boar

Setting: Long ago, in front of the Jade Emperor's palace. There is a starting line on the ground. The Jade Emperor is telling all the animals the rules of the race.

Jade Emperor *(loudly, to get everyone's attention):* Listen! Listen! We are going to start the race in a few minutes. First, I want to explain the course and the rules.

Boar *(raising his hand):* Will we be allowed to stop for water along the way?

Jade Emperor: Please let me tell you the rules of the whole race before you ask questions. *(pointing at the line on the ground)* This is the starting line. You must have all of your toes behind this line.

Snake *(raising his tail):* What if you don't have toes?

Jade Emperor *(surprised):* Good point. You must have your whole body behind this line before I give the signal to start. Are you ready?

Name each character and write the **dialogue,** or the words the characters say.

Use **stage directions** to tell how the characters should say the lines or move around on the stage.

Write the Script

▶ **MATERIALS:** *chart paper*

Read the Story Have students read and discuss the fable on **Handbook** page 105. You may want to choose a different story from the **Handbook** or one students are familiar with.

Make a Script Prompt students to tell you the story title, name the characters, and describe the setting as you record responses. Continue, encouraging students to describe events and suggest what the characters say. Brainstorm how the characters might move around the stage, and then add stage directions to the script.

Put on the Play

▶ **MATERIALS:** *class script; props such as branches, grass, feathers, etc.; video camera and tape (optional)*

Assign Roles Form heterogenous groups of five. For each group, assign roles according to students' proficiency levels.

MULTI-LEVEL STRATEGIES

3 SPEECH EMERGENCE	**4** INTERMEDIATE FLUENCY	**5** ADVANCED FLUENCY/FLUENT
These students can gather and create props. You may also assign these students to any non-speaking roles in the play.	These students can be the supporting actors. Help them memorize their parts by having them echo as you read their lines aloud to them.	These students can play the leading role. You might also want to assign an advanced student to the role of director, who uses the script to help actors remember their lines.

Rehearse Arrange time for each group to use the class script to practice the play or distribute a copy of the script to each group.

Present Invite groups to take turns presenting their plays to the class. You may want to videotape the plays so students can evaluate their performances.

```
              The Birds Learn How to Build a Nest
                            Act 2
              The Phoenix Tries to Teach a Lesson

Characters: phoenix, hen, crow, sparrow, swallow
Setting: an ancient forest

Phoenix (sitting in front of all the other birds):
All right, you asked me how to build a nest, so I'll
tell you. To learn this skill, you have to listen
carefully. Hen, are you listening?

Hen (sleeping): Zzzzzzz

Crow (pointing at Hen): Ha-ha! Hen's asleep. Too bad
for you, Hen. Go ahead, Phoenix, we're listening.

Phoenix: As I was saying, first you have to find three
big branches. Then you have to stack them on top of
each other.

Crow (flapping his wings): Is that all? That's too
simple! (flies away)
```

Let's Tell It Again!

Overview Students will choose a story to retell and present their retelling to another class.

OBJECTIVES

**RELATED PAGES
IN THE HANDBOOK**

Functions
• Retell a Story

Learning Strategies
• Plan/Summarize ....**Story Map Model,** page 71

Writing
• Folk Tale/Fairy Tale................................**Writing Models,** pages 106–107

Concepts and Vocabulary
• Story Language ....**Instruction,** page 140

Warm-Up

Explain the Project Goal Ask students how they've shared stories or books they've read. Then explain: *One way to share a story with someone else is to tell it in your own words. Now you will choose a story to read, and then use what you know about the story to retell it to the class.*

Choose a Story Students can choose to retell *Stone Soup* or *Cinderella* on **Handbook** pages 106 and 107. Depending upon your students' proficiency levels, you may want to have them select a story from the list of books on page 16T.

**Writing Models
Handbook pages 106–107**

Folk Tales and Fairy Tales

Folk Tale

A **folk tale** is a story that people have been telling one another for many years.

The **characters** in a folk tale often have a problem to solve.

The **setting** is often a made-up place, long ago.

Stone Soup

ne day, three hungry men walked into a tiny village. Everyone told these travelers that there was no food. Really, the villagers were greedy and didn't want to share with the men.

"Oh well, there is nothing more delicious than a bowl of stone soup," one traveler said.

The villagers thought this was odd, but agreed to lend the men a huge soup pot. The men lit a fire, put three stones in the pot with some water, and waited.

A villager looked at the soup and thought, "Ridiculous! No soup is complete without some carrots." He went home, got a bunch of carrots, and put them in the pot.

Another villager looked at the soup and thought, "What that really needs is onions!" So she took a few onions and added them to the soup.

Soon, lots of people brought beef, cabbage, celery, potatoes— a little of everything that makes

Fairy Tale

A **fairy tale** is a special kind of folk tale. It often has royal characters like princes and princesses, and magical creatures like elves and fairies.

Cinderella

nce upon a time, there was a sweet, gentle girl named Cinderella, who wanted to go to the royal ball. Her mean stepmother told her to stay home and scrub the floor while she and her daughters went to the ball. Cinderella wept.

Suddenly, Cinderella's fairy godmother appeared. She waved her magic wand and turned Cinderella's ragged clothes into a sparkling gown and her shoes into glass slippers. She also turned a pumpkin into a coach and mice into horses. Now Cinderella could go to the ball! However, the fairy godmother warned Cinderella that if she wasn't home by midnight, her clothes would change into rags again.

When the prince saw Cinderella, he was overwhelmed by her beauty. All night, he refused to dance with anyone but her.

A fairy tale often begins with **Once upon a time.**

Plan the Retelling

▶ **MATERIALS:** *art supplies for making story props or real hats, scarves, soup pot, etc. (optional)*

Read and Map Have students read their story and complete a story map like the one on **Handbook** page 71 to show the characters, setting, and plot. Use level-appropriate strategies to involve all students in summarizing the story.

MULTI-LEVEL STRATEGIES

3 SPEECH EMERGENCE

Have students draw pictures to show the events. Ask yes/no questions about the pictures, record key words, and have students echo. *Are there three men?* (write *three men*) *Did they walk into a village?* (write *walked into village*) and so on.

4 **5** INTERMEDIATE and ADVANCED FLUENCY/FLUENT

Pair these students with a partner who has chosen the same story. After talking about the story, they can each complete a story map.

Create Props Some students may want to create simple props such as story boards, hats, a soup pot, magic wand, and so on to support their retelling or add drama.

Practice Have students use their story maps to help them rehearse their retelling with a partner. Before students begin, you may want to discuss the Speaking and Listening tips on page 19T.

Retell the Story

▶ **MATERIALS:** *students' story maps, story props (optional)*

Present Have students take turns retelling their stories for the class. Invite volunteers to tell their stories to other classes or to students attending the school library's story hour.

. . .and the fairy godmother turned Cinderella's shoes into glass slippers.

7 Step-by-Step

Overview Students will make a mask, talk about how they made it, and then write directions for making the mask. Students will use their directions to teach others how to make the mask.

OBJECTIVES

**RELATED PAGES
IN THE HANDBOOK**

Functions
• Give Directions

Learning Strategies
• Plan/Organize Information Graphically ....**Flow Chart Model,** page 81

Writing
• Directions ....**Writing Models,** pages 102–103
• Punctuation/Commas ....**Instruction and Practice,** pages 208–211,
                                                                                                       pages 326–327

Language Patterns and Structures
• Commands ....**Instruction and Practice,** pages 160, 208,
                                                                                                       page 305

Concepts and Vocabulary
• Number/Order Words ....**Word Lists,** pages 14–15
• Holidays ....**Dateline U. S. A.,** page 296

Warm-Up

▶ **MATERIALS:** *a variety of masks (or pictures of masks) from different cultures;
mask-making supplies such as large sheets of poster board,
paper plates, foil, yarn, glitter, glue, scissors, etc.*

Discuss Masks Display several kinds of masks or pictures of masks such as those worn during plays like Japanese Kabuki masks and for special holidays like Halloween or Carnival. You may want to read aloud page 296 in **Dateline U.S.A.** for background about Halloween. Briefly describe each mask by telling what it's made of and when or why someone might wear it.

Model Making a Mask Use the materials to demonstrate making a simple mask as you verbalize each step.

Explain the Project Goal Tell students: *You and your partner will make masks, and then write down what you did to make them. Then you will use your directions to teach someone else how to make the mask.*

Learn About Directions

Discuss Characteristics Use the annotations on **Handbook** pages 102–103 to introduce or review Directions. Have volunteers describe each type of directions in their own words. Then ask students which type of directions they would use to explain how to make a mask.

Write Directions

Prewriting

▶ **MATERIALS:** *art supplies listed for the Warm-Up on page 24T*

Make a Mask Have partners follow your model or brainstorm a different type of mask to make. Encourage them to think about each step as they do it.

Make a Flow Chart Have partners talk about how they made their masks. Ask them to record each step in a flow chart like the one on **Handbook** page 81. Involve students in a way that reflects their proficiency levels.

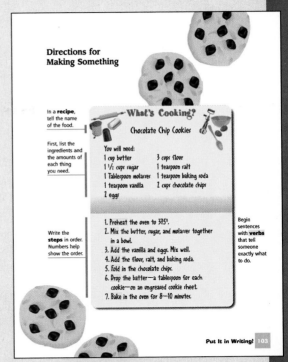

**Writing Model
Handbook page 103**

MULTI-LEVEL STRATEGIES

3 SPEECH EMERGENCE
Have students dictate the steps as you record key words in a flow chart. Prompt them with questions: *What did you do first? Then what did you do?*

4 5 INTERMEDIATE and ADVANCED FLUENCY/FLUENT
Ask these students to make a flow chart showing each step. As they complete the chart, encourage them to make a separate list of the materials they used.

How to Make a Kachina Mask

1. Cut poster board. → 2. The ends are stapled together. → 3. Decorate.

4. Put the shape over your head. → 5. Ask someone to mark where your eyes are. → 6. Take it off and cut out the eyes.

Flow Chart

Drafting

▶ **MATERIALS:** *Practice Book page 109*

Demonstrate how to elaborate on the details in the flow chart to write clear directions using commands, and how to add a title and list of materials.

How to Make a Kachina Mask

| 1. Cut poster board. | → | 2. The ends are stapled together. |

How to Make a Kachina Mask

You will need:

poster board, scissors, crayons or markers, glue, yarn, feathers, stapler

1. Cut a piece of poster board about 12 inches wide. Make it long enough to fit around your head.
2. Staple the ends of the poster board together to form a cylinder.

Involve students in the drafting stage of the writing process in a way that reflects their proficiency levels.

MULTI-LEVEL STRATEGIES

3 SPEECH EMERGENCE
Help students review their flow charts. Then partners can use their charts to help them complete the writing frame on **Practice Book** page 109.

4 5 INTERMEDIATE and ADVANCED FLUENCY/FLUENT
Have these students review Drafting on **Handbook** page 88, and then use their flow charts to write their drafts.

Revising

▶ **MATERIALS:** *Practice Book page 110*

After students have finished their drafts, talk about the different ways they can revise their writing to make sure their directions are clear and the steps are in order. Have students look on **Handbook** pages 89–91 for help with the revising steps of the writing process. Use level-appropriate strategies.

MULTI-LEVEL STRATEGIES

3 SPEECH EMERGENCE
Display **Practice Book** page 110 and model making revisions as you verbalize what you are doing. Circulate as students revise their drafts. Offer individual help as necessary.

4 INTERMEDIATE FLUENCY
Discuss Number and Order Words on **Handbook** pages 14–15. Point out how they help to make the steps and details in directions clear. Before students revise their drafts, you might assign **Practice Book** page 110 as practice for checking the order of the steps and adding specific details.

5 ADVANCED FLUENCY/FLUENT
Have students use the peer conferencing guidelines on **Handbook** page 90. Partners can read each other's directions for logical order and clarity. You might also assign **Practice Book** page 110 as practice for checking the order of the steps and adding specific details.

Proofreading

▶ **MATERIALS:** *Practice Book page 110*

Teach or review the use of commands and sentence punctuation on **Handbook** pages 160 and 208, and the use of commas in a series on page 209. These elements are the focus of the proofreading practice on **Practice Book** page 110. Also, review the Proofreading Marks on **Handbook** page 92. Then use level-appropriate strategies as students proofread their directions.

MULTI-LEVEL STRATEGIES

3 SPEECH EMERGENCE

Display **Practice Book** page 110. Correct the writing model as you verbalize: *Here it says "The paper plate goes up to your face." When we tell someone to do something, we use commands. A command begins with a verb so we need to add the verb* Put— *Put the paper plate up to your face.* Then assist students in proofreading their directions.

4 INTERMEDIATE FLUENCY

Point out errors on **Practice Book** page 110 and guide students in making the corrections: *How does a command begin? That's right. A command tells someone to do something so it starts with a verb. Add a verb to this sentence to make it a command.* Then have students proofread and correct their directions.

5 ADVANCED FLUENCY/FLUENT

Have these students complete **Practice Book** page 110 and then proofread their directions. Partners can check each other's work.

Publishing

▶ **MATERIALS:** *students' directions for making a mask, art supplies listed for the Warm-Up on page 24T*

Try Out the Directions Schedule a time for students to use their directions to teach students in another class how to make masks. Have students gather the materials, and then read their directions aloud to a partner who assembles the mask. Afterward, encourage your class to share how well their directions worked. Display all of the masks and directions in the Art Center.

8

The First Time I . . .

Overview Students will talk about the first time they experienced an event, write a personal narrative to describe the event, and present their memories on a poster.

OBJECTIVES

RELATED PAGES IN THE HANDBOOK

Functions
- Describe

Learning Strategies
- Relate to Personal Experience
- Plan/Organize Information Graphically ....**List Models,** page 87

Writing
- Personal Narrative...**Writing Model,** page 131
- Capitalization: Pronoun "I" ....**Instruction and Practice,** page 202, page 323

Language Patterns and Structures
- Pronouns...**Instruction and Practice,** pages 174–179, pages 311–313

Concepts and Vocabulary
- Describing Words ....**Word Lists,** pages 12–19

Warm-Up

▶ **MATERIALS:** *butcher paper for list*

Share Display a photo or other memento as you tell students about a "first" in your life, such as the first time you tried a new sport or won an award.

Make a Class List Invite students to brainstorm "firsts" in their lives as you record ideas.

Explain the Project Goal Review the class list with students, and then explain: *To share what you remember about the first time you did something, you can write a story. The story can tell about what happened and how you felt about it. You'll use your story to make a* **"first-time"** *poster.*

The first time I . . .

went camping
met my best friend
hit a home run
got e-mail
went swimming
rode a bike

Class List

Learn About Personal Narratives

Discuss Characteristics Have students turn to the Personal Narrative on **Handbook** page 131. Use the annotations to introduce or review its characteristics. After students find more order words and describing words in the model, encourage volunteers to describe in their own words what a personal narrative is like.

Write Personal Narratives

Prewriting

▶ **MATERIALS:** *large sheets of construction paper, 1 per student; crayons or markers*

Choose an Event Ask students to review the events on the class list and choose one they are familiar with as their topic.

Draw a Picture Have students think about the event, and then draw a picture on construction paper to show what happened.

List Details Students can use their picture to help them write a list of key words that tell about the event. Use level-appropriate strategies to encourage responses.

Personal Narrative

When you write a **personal narrative**, you tell a story about something that happened to you. Because the story is about you, you'll write it in the first person. That means you'll use the words *I, me,* and *my* a lot.

The **beginning** tells what the event is all about.

The **middle** tells more about the event.

The **end** tells what finally happened.

A Good Luck Valentine

I'll never forget my first Valentine's Day. When I got to school, I was surprised to find some bright red envelopes on my desk.

At first, I thought they were gifts for Chinese New Year. Each new year my family gives me money in red envelopes to wish me good luck. But when I opened the little envelopes, I only found some paper hearts.

Then my teacher explained what happens on Valentine's Day. The notes in the envelopes were valentines. Now when I look at my valentines, I feel just as wonderful as when I get gifts for the new year!

A personal narrative has **order words** that tell when something happened.

It has **describing words** that tell what things were like and how you felt.

Dateline U.S.A. on pages 264–301 for more information about Valentine's Day and other special days and holidays.

Put It in Writing! 131

**Writing Model
Handbook page 131**

MULTI-LEVEL STRATEGIES

3 SPEECH EMERGENCE
Comment on students' drawings as you record key words: *I see you are on your bike* (write *bike*) *and there are training wheels* (write *training wheels*), and so on. Have students write the words and say them aloud.

4 INTERMEDIATE FLUENCY
Point to elements of these students' drawings as you ask open-ended questions: *What is happening here? Who is this?* Help students identify the key words from their responses that they should write on their lists.

5 ADVANCED FLUENCY/FLUENT
Have partners ask each other questions about their pictures and work together to list the key words.

Get Organized Have students review their lists and ask themselves what happened first, next, and so on. Then they can number the details to show the order.

List

Topic: the first time I went swimming

1. Dad took me swimming at the lake
4. lifted my feet up
5. I floated!
2. at first was nervous
3. water warm, no waves

29T

Drafting

▶ **MATERIALS:** *Practice Book page 111*

Demonstrate for students how to turn the details from their lists into sentences and write the details in a logical order.

Topic: the first time I went swimming

1. Dad took me swimming at the lake

When I was six, Dad took me swimming at the lake. I was nervous at first, but I really wanted to try to swim.

Involve students in the drafting stage of the writing process in a way that reflects their proficiency levels.

MULTI-LEVEL STRATEGIES

3 SPEECH EMERGENCE
Students can use Practice Book page 111 as a writing frame for their drafts.

4 5 INTERMEDIATE and ADVANCED FLUENCY/FLUENT
Have these students review Drafting on Handbook page 88, and then use their lists to write their drafts.

Revising

▶ **MATERIALS:** *Practice Book page 112*

After students have finished their drafts, talk about the different ways they can revise their writing to say exactly what they want. Encourage students to look on **Handbook** pages 89–91 for help with the revising steps of the writing process. Use the following level-appropriate strategies.

MULTI-LEVEL STRATEGIES

3 SPEECH EMERGENCE
Display Practice Book page 112 and model making revisions as you verbalize what you are doing. Circulate as students revise their drafts. Offer individual help as necessary.

4 INTERMEDIATE FLUENCY
Talk about the Describing Words on Handbook pages 12–19 and help students choose words to use in revising their personal narratives. Before students revise their drafts, you may wish to assign Practice Book page 112 as practice for adding descriptive details.

5 ADVANCED FLUENCY/FLUENT
Refer students to the peer conferencing guidelines on Handbook page 90. Partners can read aloud each other's drafts and suggest revisions. You might assign Practice Book page 112 as practice for adding descriptive details.

Proofreading

▶ **MATERIALS:** *Practice Book page 112*

Teach or review the use of pronouns on **Handbook** pages 174–179 and capitalization of the pronoun "I" on page 202. These elements occur naturally in personal narratives and are the focus of the proofreading practice on **Practice Book** page 112.

Also, review the Proofreading Marks on **Handbook** page 92. Then use level-appropriate strategies as students proofread their own personal narratives.

MULTI-LEVEL STRATEGIES

3 SPEECH EMERGENCE
Display **Practice Book** page 112. Correct the writing model as you verbalize: *Here it says "Last year I won the school Spelling Bee. They was not easy to win." The writer is talking about the Spelling Bee so we need to change* They *to* It*. Whenever you talk about a thing use the pronoun* It*. Then assist students in proofreading their narratives.*

4 INTERMEDIATE FLUENCY
Point out errors on **Practice Book** page 112 and guide students in making the corrections: *When you talk about a thing, what pronoun should you use? That's right,* it*. Change* They *to* It *because this sentence is talking about the Spelling Bee.* Then have students proofread and correct their narratives.

5 ADVANCED FLUENCY/FLUENT
Have these students complete **Practice Book** page 112, and then proofread their personal narratives. Partners can check each other's work.

Publishing

▶ **MATERIALS:** *students' drawings and narratives, glue*

Complete and Share the Posters Have students make a final copy of their narratives and glue them under their drawings on the construction paper. Encourage students to add titles and sign their names. Display students' posters around the room. Invite students to take turns presenting their creations to the class.

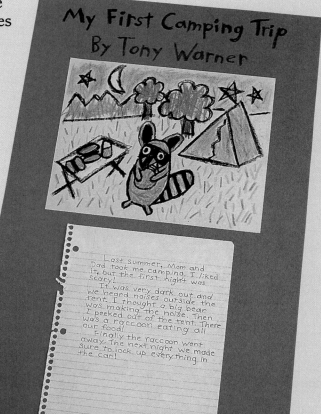

My First Camping Trip
By Tony Warner

Last summer, Mom and Dad took me camping. I liked it, but the first night was scary!

It was very dark out and we heard noises outside the tent. I thought a big bear was making the noise. Then I peeked out of the tent. There was a raccoon eating all our food!

Finally the raccoon went away. The next night we made sure to lock up everything in the car!

Yours Truly

Overview Students will write a friendly letter, address an envelope, and mail the letter.

OBJECTIVES

**RELATED PAGES
IN THE HANDBOOK**

Functions
• Express Feelings, Needs, Opinions

Learning Strategies
• Plan/Organize Information Graphically ....**Chart Model,** page 78

Writing
• Friendly Letter/Envelope ....**Writing Models,** pages 114 and 119
• Capitalization/Punctuation..................................**Instruction and Practice,** pages 203–206, 208–209, pages 323–326

Language Patterns and Structures
• Questions...**Instruction and Practice,** pages 161–162, page 305

• Proper Nouns ....**Instruction and Practice,** page 167, page 307

Warm-Up

▶ **MATERIALS:** *friendly letter and envelope, butcher paper for chart*

Build Background Share with students a friendly letter you have received. Tell about the person who sent you the letter: *This letter is from my friend Carol. Carol and I went to school together. We write letters to each other several times a year to share what's going on in our lives.*

Make a Class Chart Have students brainstorm people they might write to and why. Record responses.

Who	*Why*
friends and family	*to share special news about your life and to ask how they are doing*
pen pals	*to tell about where you live and what you like to do*
school workers, teachers, or parent volunteers you know	*to thank them for the special things they do and for helping you learn*

Class Chart

Explain the Project Goal Review the class chart with students. Then explain: *You will choose someone and write a friendly letter to that person. Then you'll use an envelope to mail the letter.*

Learn About Friendly Letters

Discuss Characteristics Have students turn to the Friendly Letter on **Handbook** page 114. Use the annotations to introduce or review the five parts. Encourage volunteers to name each part and describe in their own words what it's like. Repeat the procedure for the Envelope on **Handbook** page 119.

Write Friendly Letters

Prewriting

Choose Whom to Write To Ask each student to review the class chart and to choose a person from one of the groups to write to. Have them write the name of the person on their papers.

Think About the Person and the Message Ask students what they want to tell or ask the person and make a list of key words. Use a variety of strategies to help students at all proficiency levels participate.

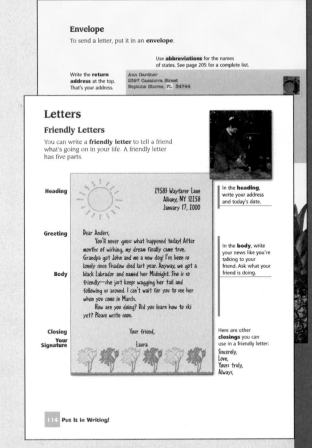

**Writing Models
Handbook pages 114, 119**

MULTI-LEVEL STRATEGIES

3 SPEECH EMERGENCE
Have these students draw a picture to show what they want to say in their letter. Comment on their pictures as you record key words on the paper: *This looks like the aquarium* (write *aquarium*). *I remember that we went on a field trip there* (write *field trip*). Have students write and say the words aloud.

4 INTERMEDIATE FLUENCY
Ask these students open-ended questions as you record key words from their responses: *How did Mrs. Miller help us last week? What do you want to ask her?*

5 ADVANCED FLUENCY/FLUENT
Have individuals list their key words, then go over their lists with a partner.

Get Organized Students can make a chart to help them group their key words and ideas.

Mrs. Miller	
Tell about	Ask about
What I liked about the aquarium	What she liked
How she helped us	Another field trip

Student Chart

Drafting

▶ **MATERIALS:** *Practice Book page 113*

Remind students to include a heading and greeting for their letters. Then demonstrate how to use their charts to form complete sentences for the body.

Mrs. Miller	
Tell about	Ask about
What I liked about the aquarium How she helped us	What she liked Another field trip

Thank you for taking us to the aquarium. I really liked the shark exhibit. What was your favorite part?

Involve students in the drafting stage of the writing process in a way that reflects their proficiency levels.

MULTI-LEVEL STRATEGIES

3 SPEECH EMERGENCE
Students can use **Practice Book** page 113 as a writing frame for their drafts.

4 5 INTERMEDIATE and ADVANCED FLUENCY/FLUENT
Have these students review the Drafting guidelines on **Handbook** page 88, and then use their charts to write drafts.

Revising

▶ **MATERIALS:** *Practice Book page 114*

Have students check their drafts to be sure they included all five parts of a friendly letter. Then encourage students to use **Handbook** pages 89–91 to help them revise the body of their letters. Use level-appropriate strategies to involve students in the revising stage of the writing process.

MULTI-LEVEL STRATEGIES

3 SPEECH EMERGENCE
Display **Practice Book** page 114 and model making revisions as you verbalize what you are doing. Circulate as these students revise their drafts. Offer individual help as necessary.

4 INTERMEDIATE FLUENCY
Talk about the Questions on **Handbook** pages 161–162 and help students form questions to use in revising their letters. You may wish to assign **Practice Book** page 114 as practice for adding questions.

5 ADVANCED FLUENCY/FLUENT
Refer these students to the peer conferencing guidelines on **Handbook** page 90. Have partners read each other's drafts aloud and make suggestions for revisions. You may also wish to assign **Practice Book** page 114 as practice for adding questions.

Proofreading

▶ **MATERIALS:** *Practice Book page 114*

Teach or review Proper Nouns on **Handbook** page 167, and capitalization and punctuation marks used in parts of a letter on pages 203–206 and 208–209. These elements occur naturally in friendly letters and are the focus of the proofreading practice on **Practice Book** page 114.

Also, review the Proofreading Marks on **Handbook** page 92. Then use level-appropriate strategies as students proofread their own friendly letters.

MULTI-LEVEL STRATEGIES

3 SPEECH EMERGENCE

Display **Practice Book** page 114. Correct the writing model as you verbalize: *Here I see that the name of the street isn't capitalized. The names of special places and things should begin with capital letters, so we need to make the o in oak Street a capital letter.* Then assist students in proofreading their letters.

4 INTERMEDIATE FLUENCY

Point out errors on **Practice Book** page 114 and guide students in making the corrections: *Look at the heading. Do the names of streets, cities, and states start with lowercase letters or capital letters? Yes, the first letters should be capitalized.* Then have students proofread and correct their friendly letters.

5 ADVANCED FLUENCY/FLUENT

Have these students complete **Practice Book** page 114, and then proofread their letters. Encourage partners to check each other's work.

Publishing

▶ **MATERIALS:** *students' letters; envelopes and stamps, 1 per student*

Address Envelopes and Mail After students have made clean copies of their letters, help them use **Handbook** page 119 to address envelopes and add a stamp. Collect the letters and mail them. Invite volunteers to share any responses they receive.

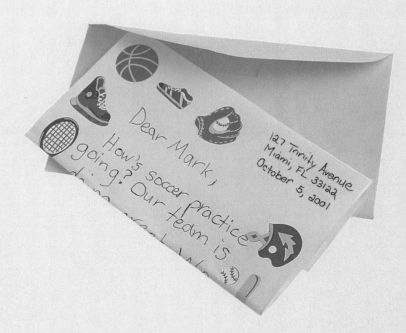

10 See It My Way

Overview Students will brainstorm school issues, write a persuasive paragraph, and then present their paragraph to the appropriate school staff.

OBJECTIVES

**RELATED PAGES
IN THE HANDBOOK**

Functions
• Persuade

Learning Strategies
• Plan/Organize Information Graphically ....**Main Idea Cluster Model,** page 64

Writing
• Persuasive Paragraph ....**Writing Model,** page 130

Language Patterns and Structures
• Action and Linking Verbs/Helping Verbs ....**Instruction and Practice,** pages 186–187, page 316

Concepts and Vocabulary
• Persuasive Words

Warm-Up

▶ **MATERIALS:** *butcher paper for chart*

Build Background Talk with students about an issue at your school such as repairing the playground equipment or needing more computers, and how they feel about it

Explain the Project Goal Tell students: *To share how you feel about something that's important to you, you can write a paragraph. The paragraph will tell what you want changed or what you want someone to do. You'll use your paragraph to try to get the librarian, principal, or other school staff to agree with you.*

Make a Chart Have students brainstorm issues and who might be able to do something about the issue. Record their ideas.

Issue	Who to Tell
new playground equipment	principal
fix vegetarian lunches	cafeteria staff
get more computers	PTA
show our work in library	librarian
school uniforms	PTA, principal

Class Chart

Learn About Persuasive Paragraphs

Discuss Characteristics Have students turn to the Persuasive Paragraph on **Handbook** page 130. Use the annotations to introduce or review its characteristics. Ask volunteers if they agree with the writer and why.

Write Persuasive Paragraphs

Prewriting

Choose an Issue Form small groups of students and have each group choose an issue from the class chart. Explain that each member of the group will write a paragraph about that issue.

Think About the Issue Have students think about the issue and make a list of key words that state the issue, their opinion, and what they want someone to do about the issue. Involve students in the prewriting stage of the writing process in a way that reflects their proficiency levels.

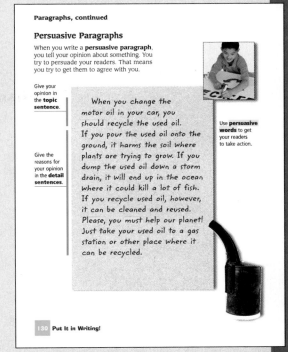

Paragraphs, continued

Persuasive Paragraphs

When you write a **persuasive paragraph**, you tell your opinion about something. You try to persuade your readers. That means you try to get them to agree with you.

Give your opinion in the **topic sentence**.

Give the reasons for your opinion in the **detail sentences**.

Use **persuasive words** to get your readers to take action.

> When you change the motor oil in your car, you should recycle the used oil. If you pour the used oil onto the ground, it harms the soil where plants are trying to grow. If you dump the used oil down a storm drain, it will end up in the ocean where it could kill a lot of fish. If you recycle used oil, however, it can be cleaned and reused. Please, you must help our planet! Just take your used oil to a gas station or other place where it can be recycled.

130 Put It in Writing!

**Writing Model
Handbook page 130**

MULTI-LEVEL STRATEGIES

3 SPEECH EMERGENCE
Have students draw a picture to show the issue. Make comments and ask questions as you record key words from their responses: *I see a computer on every desk. Do you think we need more computers?* (Write *need more computers*.) *If we had more computers, could everyone learn to use one?* (Write *so everyone can learn*.) Have students echo as you read the key words aloud.

4 INTERMEDIATE FLUENCY
Ask these students yes/no questions followed by an open-ended question to help them formulate their opinion: *Should students have to wear school uniforms? Why or why not?* Record key words from their responses.

5 ADVANCED FLUENCY/FLUENT
Have these students ask each other questions about the group's topic. After these interviews, students can record key words individually.

Get Organized Students can use their key words to help them group ideas, and then make a Main Idea Cluster like the one on **Handbook** page 64.

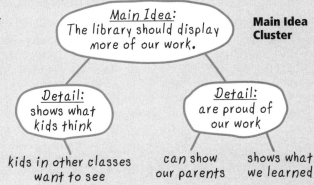

Main Idea Cluster

Main Idea:
The library should display more of our work.

Detail:
shows what kids think

Detail:
are proud of our work

kids in other classes want to see

can show our parents

shows what we learned

Drafting

▶ **MATERIALS:** *Practice Book page 115*

Demonstrate for students how to state the main idea as an opinion in the topic sentence, form sentences from the details in their clusters, and write the details in a logical order.

Involve students in the drafting stage of the writing process in a way that reflects their proficiency levels.

MULTI-LEVEL STRATEGIES

3 SPEECH EMERGENCE
Students can use **Practice Book** page 115 as a writing frame for their drafts.

4 5 INTERMEDIATE and ADVANCED FLUENCY/FLUENT
Have these students review Drafting on **Handbook** page 88, and then use their clusters to write their drafts.

Revising

▶ **MATERIALS:** *Practice Book page 116*

After students have finished their drafts, talk about the different ways they can revise their writing to convince others to take action. Encourage students to look on pages 89–91 of the **Handbook** for help with the revising steps of the writing process. Use level-appropriate strategies.

MULTI-LEVEL STRATEGIES

3 SPEECH EMERGENCE
Display **Practice Book** page 116 and model making revisions as you verbalize what you are doing. Circulate as students revise their drafts. Offer individual help as necessary.

4 INTERMEDIATE FLUENCY
Talk with students about the persuasive words and the reasons for the writer's opinion in the paragraph on **Handbook** page 130. Then have students revise their drafts. Before they begin, you may wish to assign **Practice Book** page 116 as practice for adding persuasive words and giving reasons for their opinions.

5 ADVANCED FLUENCY/FLUENT
Refer students to the peer conferencing guidelines on **Handbook** page 90. You may also wish to assign **Practice Book** page 116 as practice for adding persuasive words and giving reasons for their opinions. After these students revise their drafts, they can assist other students with revisions.

Proofreading

▶ **MATERIALS:** *Practice Book page 116*

Use **Handbook** pages 186–187 to teach or review Action and Linking Verbs, and Helping Verbs. These verbs are the focus of the proofreading practice on **Practice Book** page 116.

Also, review the Proofreading Marks on **Handbook** page 92. Then use level-appropriate strategies as students proofread their persuasive paragraphs.

MULTI-LEVEL STRATEGIES

3 SPEECH EMERGENCE
Display **Practice Book** page 116. Correct the writing model as you verbalize: *Listen: Our school not have enough computers. This sentence has a main verb, but it needs a helping verb. Let's add the helping verb* does. (Repeat the sentence.) *That's better. In some sentences, we need to use a helping verb to help tell about an action or what something has.* Then assist students in proofreading their paragraphs.

4 INTERMEDIATE FLUENCY
Point out errors on **Practice Book** page 116. Guide students in making corrections: *Is something missing between the subject and main verb in the first sentence? Which helping verb should go there? That's right,* does. *Our school* does *not have enough computers.* Then have students proofread and correct their paragraphs.

5 ADVANCED FLUENCY/FLUENT
Have these students complete **Practice Book** page 116 and then proofread their persuasive paragraphs. Partners can check each other's work.

Publishing

▶ **MATERIALS:** *students' persuasive paragraphs*

Present the Paragraphs After students prepare final copies of their paragraphs, help them display their work in the school office or library. You might also arrange for students to read their paragraphs aloud to the appropriate school staff.

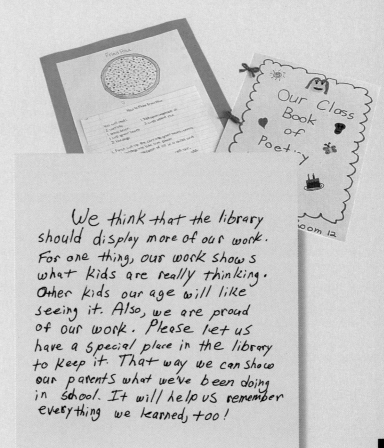

Class Poets

Overview Students will talk about a poem, write a poem, and present it as part of an illustrated Big Book of Poems for a younger class.

OBJECTIVES

**RELATED PAGES
IN THE HANDBOOK**

Functions
• Describe

Learning Strategies
• Plan/Organize Information Graphically ....**Word Web Model,** page 62

Writing
• Poem..**Writing Models,** pages 134–137

Language Patterns and Structures
• Adjectives..**Instruction and Practice,** pages 180–185,
pages 313–315
• Plural Nouns...**Instruction and Practice,** pages 168–169, page 308

Concepts and Vocabulary
• Describing Words ....**Word Lists,** pages 12–19

Warm-Up

▶ **MATERIALS:** *butcher paper for web*

Choose a Type of Poetry In advance, choose one type of poetry from **Handbook** pages 134–137 for the writing project. Then use or adapt the following procedures.

Recite the Poem Ask students what they know about lightning, and then read aloud the cinquain on **Handbook** page 134. Recite the poem again, having students chime in.

Explain the Project Goal Explain that the poem tells what lightning is like—what it looks like and how it sounds. Then say: *Now you will write your own poem to tell what something is like. We'll use all of our poems to make a Big Book of Poems for a class of younger students.*

Make a Class Web Begin a web with general writing topics and have students brainstorm specific topics like favorite places, animals, and so on.

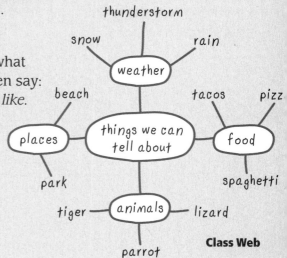

Class Web

Learn About Poems

Discuss Characteristics Use the annotations to introduce or review the characteristics of the cinquain on **Handbook** page 134. Define syllables and use your fingers to count them as you repeat each line. Afterward, encourage students to describe the poem's characteristics.

Write a Descriptive Poem

Prewriting

Choose a Topic Have students choose a topic for their poem from the class web.

Make a Word Web Have students list details about their topics. You may want to review Adjectives on **Handbook** pages 180–185 to help students think of descriptive details. Then use level-appropriate strategies to encourage responses.

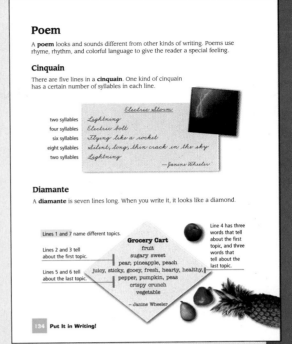

**Writing Model
Handbook page 134**

MULTI-LEVEL STRATEGIES

3 SPEECH EMERGENCE
Have these students draw a picture of their topic. Ask yes/no questions and questions with embedded answers and record the answers as details for their web: *Is this a parrot or a robin?* (Write *parrot.*) *Is it colorful?* (Write *colorful.*) Have students say the details aloud.

4 INTERMEDIATE FLUENCY
Use open-ended questions to prompt descriptive details students can add to their webs: *What do tacos look like? What other things do they remind you of? Where do you see them?*

5 ADVANCED FLUENCY/FLUENT
Have partners collaborate by suggesting details to add to each other's webs.

Word Web

Drafting

▶ **MATERIALS:** *Practice Book page 117*

Demonstrate for students how to form sentences and phrases using the details from their webs. Explain that not all cinquains have to have a certain number of syllables in each line, but they are always five lines long.

long, black stripes

quiet

quick

tiger

sharp teeth

dangerous

strong

Tiger

Tiger
Crouching, quiet
Long, black stripes and sharp teeth
Quick, strong, and oh so dangerous
Tiger.

Involve students in the drafting stage of the writing process in a way that reflects their proficiency levels.

MULTI-LEVEL STRATEGIES

3 SPEECH EMERGENCE
Students can use **Practice Book** page 117 as a writing frame for their drafts.

4 5 INTERMEDIATE and ADVANCED FLUENCY/FLUENT
Have these students review Drafting on **Handbook** page 88, and then use their word webs to write their drafts.

Revising

▶ **MATERIALS:** *Practice Book page 118*

After students have finished their drafts, talk about the different ways they can revise their poems to say exactly what they want. Encourage students to look on **Handbook** pages 89–91 for help with the revising steps of the writing process. Use level-appropriate strategies.

MULTI-LEVEL STRATEGIES

3 SPEECH EMERGENCE
Display **Practice Book** page 118 and model making revisions as you verbalize what you are doing. Circulate as students revise their drafts. Offer individual help as necessary.

4 INTERMEDIATE FLUENCY
Have these students turn to Describing Words on **Handbook** pages 12–19 and help them choose words to use in revising their poems. Before students begin, you may wish to assign **Practice Book** page 118 as practice for adding sensory words and other descriptive details.

5 ADVANCED FLUENCY/FLUENT
Refer students to the peer conferencing guidelines on **Handbook** page 90. Partners can read each other's poems aloud and make suggestions for revisions. You may also wish to assign **Practice Book** page 118 as practice for adding sensory words and other descriptive details.

Proofreading

▶ **MATERIALS:** *Practice Book page 118*

Teach or review Plural Nouns on **Handbook** pages 168–169. Plurals are the focus of the proofreading practice on **Practice Book** page 118.

Also, review the Proofreading Marks on **Handbook** page 92. Then use level-appropriate strategies as students proofread their descriptive poems.

MULTI-LEVEL STRATEGIES

3 SPEECH EMERGENCE
Display **Practice Book** page 118. Correct the writing model as you verbalize: *Here the writer is telling about more than one slice of pizza so we need to add an -s. We add an -s to many nouns to make them plural.* Then assist students in proofreading their poem.

4 INTERMEDIATE FLUENCY
Point out spelling errors on **Practice Book** page 118 and guide students in making corrections: *When a noun ends in e, what do you do to make it tell about more than one? That's right, you add -s.* Then have students proofread and correct their poems.

5 ADVANCED FLUENCY/FLUENT
Have these students complete **Practice Book** page 118, and then proofread their descriptive poems. Partners can check each other's work.

Publishing

▶ **MATERIALS:** *students' poems; large sheets of construction paper or poster board, 1 per student; markers or crayons; binding materials*

Make the Pages Have students copy their poems onto the paper and illustrate them. Help them bind all their pages into a book with a cover.

Present the Big Book Arrange a time for students to present the poems to a class of first- or second-graders. Encourage each student to read aloud his or her contribution.

Philippines
Tropical islands
Palm trees with coconuts
White sandy beaches with cool, clear water
Philippines

—Dana Leonard

12 It Could Really Happen

Overview Students will talk about story elements, brainstorm story ideas, and then write a realistic fiction story for a class anthology.

OBJECTIVES

**RELATED PAGES
IN THE HANDBOOK**

Functions
• Tell an Original Story

Learning Strategies
• Plan/Organize Information Graphically ....**Problem-and-Solution Map Model,** page 73

Writing
• Realistic Fiction ....**Writing Model,** page 141
• Dialogue...**Instruction and Practice,** page 213,
                                                                                             page 327

Language Patterns and Structures
• Contractions...**Instruction and Practice,** page 193,
                                                                                             page 320

Concepts and Vocabulary
• Parts of a Story..**Instruction,** page 140

Warm-Up

▶ **MATERIALS:** *realistic fiction stories, butcher paper for list*

Activate Prior Knowledge Invite students to share their favorite stories, encouraging them to describe the characters, setting, and plot. You may also want to read aloud and discuss several realistic fiction stories such as *Too Many Tamales* by Gary Soto, *At the Beach* by Huy Voun Lee, or *Subway Sparrow* by Leyla Torres.

Brainstorm and List Story Ideas Ask students if any of the events in the stories they discussed have happened to them or someone they know. Use their responses to list possible story ideas.

Explain the Project Goal Explain: *Now you can use these ideas to make up a story of your own. You'll decide who is in the story, where the story happens, and what happens. We'll put all our stories together into a class book.*

> ## What We Could Write About
> helping an animal
> winning a contest
> losing a ring
> going to a new place
> hitting a home run
> learning something new

Class List

Learn About Realistic Fiction

Discuss Characteristics Have students turn to the Realistic Fiction story on **Handbook** page 141. Use the annotations to introduce or review the characteristics of realistic fiction. After students have identified all of the characteristics, encourage volunteers to describe in their own words what realistic fiction is like.

Write Realistic Fiction

Prewriting

Choose a Story Idea Have students choose an idea from their class list or use the Good Writer Guide on **Handbook** pages 148–149 for other writing ideas.

Think About the Story Have students think about their story, make up characters, and make a list of key words to help them remember story details. Use level-appropriate strategies.

Realistic Fiction

Some stories have characters that seem like people you know. They happen in a place that seems real. These stories are called **realistic fiction** because they tell about something that could happen in real life.

Another Saturday Morning

The **characters** are like people you know.

Mom and I were eating breakfast Saturday morning when a woman knocked on the door to our apartment.

"Hello," she said. "I'm from Bikes and Stuff and we're having a drawing for a mountain bike. Would you be interested in signing up?" Mom agreed and filled out a form for me.

"Come by this afternoon to see if you have won," the woman said.

"Anything is possible, but don't count on winning the bike, Alex," Mom said when the woman left.

So I forgot all about the bike and started playing video games. Before I knew it, mom came in the room and said it was time to go to the bike store.

When I walked in, the first thing I saw was a huge sign that said: *Mountain bike winner: Alex Sanchez!* I couldn't believe it!

They put my name and photograph in the newspaper in an ad for Bikes and Stuff. That was the day I learned anything is possible on a Saturday morning.

The events in the **plot** could really happen.

The **setting** is in a place and a time you know.

The **dialogue** sounds real.

Put It in Writing! 141

**Writing Model
Handbook page 141**

MULTI-LEVEL STRATEGIES

3 SPEECH EMERGENCE
Have these students draw pictures to show the story elements and events. Comment on each picture and record key words: *Who is this?* (Write the name.) *He/She is the character in your story. Where is he?* (Write the name of the place.) *That's the setting,* and so on.

4 INTERMEDIATE FLUENCY
Have these students record key words in response to your prompts: *Who are your characters? Where are they? What happens to the characters?*

5 ADVANCED FLUENCY/FLUENT
These students can discuss the elements of their story with a partner and then work together to list key words.

Get Organized Have students use their story idea and key words to make a story map like the one on **Handbook** page 73.

Problem-and-Solution Map

Characters: Sam and his dad
Setting: at Sam's house on Monday morning

↓

Problem: Sam can't find his school books and homework.

↓

Event 1: Sam rushes to get ready for school.
Event 2: He tries to grab his books and homework on his desk, but they're not there.
Event 3: Dad says it's too late, Sam will have to go without them.
Event 4: Sam throws on his backpack—it feels heavy.

↓

Solution: Sam forgot that he put his books and homework there last night so he wouldn't forget.

Communication Projects 45T

Drafting

▶ **MATERIALS:** *Practice Book page 119*

Use a student's story map to demonstrate how to use the details to form sentences and add dialogue.

Characters: Sam and his dad
Setting: at Sam's house on Monday morning

Problem: Sam can't find his school books and homework.

Event 1: Sam rushes to get ready for school.
Event 2: He tries to grab his books and homework on his desk, but they're not there.

Last Monday, Sam was in a big hurry. He was almost late for school. When he went to grab his homework on his desk, it wasn't there!
"Oh, no!" he thought, "I'm in big trouble."

Involve students in the drafting stage of the writing process in a way that reflects their proficiency levels.

MULTI-LEVEL STRATEGIES

3 SPEECH EMERGENCE
Students can use **Practice Book** page 119 as a writing frame for their drafts.

4 5 INTERMEDIATE and ADVANCED FLUENCY/FLUENT
Have these students review Drafting on **Handbook** page 88, and then use their story maps to write their drafts.

Revising

▶ **MATERIALS:** *Practice Book page 120*

Before students revise their drafts, talk about ways to make their writing more interesting by adding details and dialogue. Encourage students to look on **Handbook** pages 89–91 for help with the revising steps of the writing process. Use level-appropriate strategies.

MULTI-LEVEL STRATEGIES

3 SPEECH EMERGENCE
Display **Practice Book** page 120 and model making revisions as you verbalize what you are doing. Circulate as students revise their drafts. Offer individual help as necessary.

4 INTERMEDIATE FLUENCY
Talk about Parts of a Story on **Handbook** page 140 and help students create realistic dialogue for their characters. Before they begin you may wish to assign **Practice Book** page 120 as practice for adding dialogue and other details.

5 ADVANCED FLUENCY/FLUENT
Refer students to the peer conferencing guidelines on **Handbook** pages 89–90. Have partners read aloud each other's drafts and suggest revisions. You might assign **Practice Book** page 120 as practice for adding dialogue and other details

Proofreading

▶ **MATERIALS:** *Practice Book page 120*

Teach or review forming contractions on **Handbook** page 193 and showing dialogue on page 213. These elements are the focus of the proofreading practice on **Practice Book** page 120.

Also, review the Proofreading Marks on **Handbook** page 92. Then use level-appropriate strategies as students proofread their own stories.

MULTI-LEVEL STRATEGIES

3 SPEECH EMERGENCE
Display **Practice Book** page 120. Correct the writing model as you verbalize: *Here it says,* I don't want school to be over. *That must be Carlo speaking, so I'll put quotation marks at the beginning and at the end of this sentence. When you want to show a speaker's exact words, use quotation marks.* Then help students in proofreading their stories.

4 INTERMEDIATE FLUENCY
Point out errors on **Practice Book** page 120 and guide students in making the corrections: *How can you show that Carlo is the speaker? That's right, add quotations marks before* I *and after the word* over. *That way we'll know exactly what that character says.* Then have students proofread and correct their stories.

5 ADVANCED FLUENCY/FLUENT
Have these students complete **Practice Book** page 120, and then proofread their stories. Partners can check each other's work.

Publishing

▶ **MATERIALS:** *students' stories, drawing paper, crayons or markers, 2 sheets of poster board or construction paper, stapler or 3-hole punch, 3 brads*

Present and Collect Stories for an Anthology
Have students make final copies of their stories, add titles, and illustrate them. Before binding the stories together, invite each student to share his or her story in an Author's Chair.

I Remember When . . .

Overview Students will talk about special days and holidays, write a personal narrative about a celebration they have experienced, and present their memories as an illustrated filmstrip.

OBJECTIVES

**RELATED PAGES
IN THE HANDBOOK**

Functions
• Describe

Warm-Up

▶ **MATERIALS:** *butcher paper for web*

Build Background Read aloud several pages of Dateline U.S.A. on **Handbook** pages 263–303. You may also want to share with students books like *Celebrations* by Anabel Kindersley.

Make a Class Web Have students brainstorm celebrations and write or draw details that characterize them.

Explain the Project Goal Review the class web with students, then explain: *To share what you remember about an event, you can write a story. The story can tell about one thing that happened to you on that day. You'll use your story to make an* **"I remember when"** *filmstrip.*

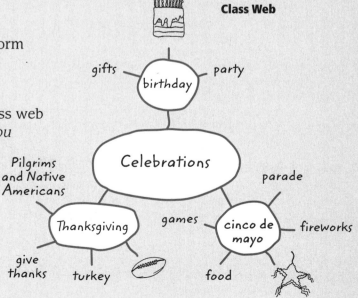

Class Web

Learn About Personal Narratives

Discuss Characteristics Have students turn to the Personal Narrative on **Handbook** page 131. Use the annotations to introduce or review its characteristics. After students find more order words and describing words in the model, encourage volunteers to describe in their own words what a personal narrative is like.

Write Personal Narratives

Prewriting

Choose a Celebration Ask students to review the celebrations on the class web and choose one celebration they have participated in as the topic for the writing project.

Think About the Event Have students think about something that happened to them during that celebration and make a list of key words to help them remember the ideas and details. Use level-appropriate strategies to encourage responses.

Personal Narrative

When you write a **personal narrative**, you tell a story about something that happened to you. Because the story is about you, you'll write it in the first person. That means you'll use the words *I, me,* and *my* a lot.

The **beginning** tells what the event is all about.

The **middle** tells more about the event.

The **end** tells what finally happened.

A Good Luck Valentine

I'll never forget my first Valentine's Day. When I got to school, I was surprised to find some bright red envelopes on my desk.

At first, I thought they were gifts for Chinese New Year. Each new year my family gives me money in red envelopes to wish me good luck. But when I opened the little envelopes, I only found some paper hearts.

Then my teacher explained what happens on Valentine's Day. The notes in the envelopes were valentines. Now when I look at my valentines, I feel just as wonderful as when I get gifts for the new year!

A personal narrative has **order words** that tell when something happened.

It has **describing words** that tell what things were like and how you felt.

Go To Dateline U.S.A. on pages 264–301 for more information about Valentine's Day and other special days and holidays.

Put It in Writing! 131

Writing Model
Handbook page 131

MULTI-LEVEL STRATEGIES

3 SPEECH EMERGENCE
Have these students draw a picture of the event. Comment on each picture as you record key words on the paper: *This looks like your birthday party* (write *birthday*). *I see some gifts* (write *gifts*) and so on. Have students write the words and say them aloud.

4 INTERMEDIATE FLUENCY
Ask these students open-ended questions as you record key words from their responses: *What happened to you during cinco de mayo? Tell me about the funny thing that happened during your birthday.*

5 ADVANCED FLUENCY/FLUENT
Have partners ask each other questions about an event and work together to list the key words.

Get Organized Students can use their key words to help them group their ideas, then make an Event Cluster like the one on **Handbook** page 63.

Event Cluster

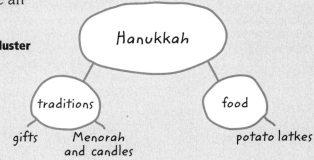

Drafting

▶ **MATERIALS:** *Practice Book page 121*

Demonstrate for students how to form sentences from the details in their clusters and write the details in a logical order:

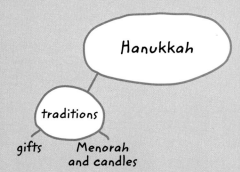

During Hanukkah, we celebrate with important traditions. Mom lights candles in the Menorah on each night of Hanukkah. We give gifts to each other.

Involve students in the drafting stage of the writing process in a way that reflects their proficiency levels.

MULTI-LEVEL STRATEGIES

3 SPEECH EMERGENCE
Students can use **Practice Book** page 121 as a writing frame for their drafts.

4 5 INTERMEDIATE and ADVANCED FLUENCY/FLUENT
Have these students review Drafting on **Handbook** page 88, and then use their clusters to write their drafts.

Revising

▶ **MATERIALS:** *Practice Book page 122*

After students have finished their drafts, talk about the different ways they can revise their writing to say exactly what they want. Encourage students to look on **Handbook** pages 89–91 for help with the revising steps of the writing process. Use level-appropriate strategies.

MULTI-LEVEL STRATEGIES

3 SPEECH EMERGENCE
Display **Practice Book** page 122 and model making revisions as you verbalize what you are doing. Circulate as students revise their drafts. Offer individual help as necessary.

4 INTERMEDIATE FLUENCY
Talk about the Describing Words on **Handbook** pages 12-19 and help students choose words to use in revising their personal narratives. Before students revise their drafts, you may wish to assign **Practice Book** page 122 as practice for adding descriptive details.

5 ADVANCED FLUENCY/FLUENT
Refer students to the peer conferencing guidelines on **Handbook** page 90. Partners can read aloud each other's drafts and suggest revisions. You might assign **Practice Book** page 122 as practice for adding descriptive details.

Proofreading

▶ **MATERIALS:** *Practice Book page 122*

Teach or review the use of pronouns on **Handbook** pages 174–179 and capitalization of the pronoun "I" on page 202. These elements occur naturally in personal narratives and are the focus of the proofreading practice on **Practice Book**, page 122.

Also, review the Proofreading Marks on **Handbook** page 92. Then use level-appropriate strategies as students proofread their own personal narratives.

MULTI-LEVEL STRATEGIES

3 SPEECH EMERGENCE
Display **Practice Book** page 122. Correct the writing model as you verbalize: *Here it says, "Dad bought a piñata. She bought it for my birthday party."* It was Dad who bought the piñata so we need to change She to He. *When you talk about a boy or a man, use the pronoun He.* Then assist students in proofreading their narratives.

4 INTERMEDIATE FLUENCY
Point out errors on **Practice Book** page 122 and guide students in making the corrections: *What pronoun do you use for a boy or a man? That's right,* he. *Change* She *to* He *because this sentence is talking about Dad.* Then have students proofread and correct their narratives.

5 ADVANCED FLUENCY/FLUENT
Have these students complete **Practice Book** page 122 and then proofread their narratives. Partners can check each other's work.

Publishing

▶ **MATERIALS:** *students' personal narratives, long strips of paper, pencils or markers*

Make and Share the Filmstrips Have students turn their personal narratives into a filmstrip by copying their final stories onto the frames and adding illustrations. Create a display of students' filmstrips. Invite volunteers to share their work in an Author's Chair.

14 Guess Who?

Overview Students will talk about ways to describe a person, write a character sketch about a classmate without naming him or her, and have the class guess who is being described.

OBJECTIVES

Functions
• Describe

RELATED PAGES
IN THE HANDBOOK

Learning Strategies
• Plan/Organize Information Graphically ....**Character Map Model,** page 62

Writing
• Character Sketch ....**Writing Model,** page 100
• Subject–Verb Agreement.....................................**Instruction and Practice,** pages 186–189,
pages 316–318

Language Patterns and Structures
• Verbs ....**Instruction and Practice,** pages 186–194,
pages 316–320

• Questions ....**Instruction and Practice,** pages 160–162,
page 305

Concepts and Vocabulary
• Describing Words ....**Word Lists,** pages 12–19

Warm-Up

► **MATERIALS:** *butcher paper for web, pictures of three famous people or characters*

Build Background Show students pictures of three people or characters familiar to all students. Describe one of the pictured people in detail and ask students to identify the person being described.

Make a Class Character Map Have students choose a person and brainstorm details about him or her. Invite students to add words, details, or drawings to the map.

Explain the Project Goal Review the class map with students, then explain: *To tell what someone is like, you can write a character sketch. The sentences in your character sketch will tell what one of your classmates looks like, likes to do, and how he or she is special. We'll all read your sketch, and then guess which classmate you are describing.*

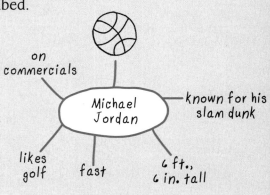

Class Character Map

Learn About Character Sketches

Discuss Characteristics Have students turn to the Character Sketch on **Handbook** page 100. Use the annotations to introduce or review its characteristics. Have students point to and say all the describing words they find. Then invite volunteers to explain in their own words what a character sketch is like.

Write Character Sketches

Prewriting

Choose a Classmate Have students write their names on slips of paper and put the slips into a small container. Then have each student draw a name.

Make Observations Give students time to observe their subjects and ask you or other classmates about them. You may want to review kinds of questions on **Handbook** pages 161–162 before they begin. Have students list key words from the answers. Use level-appropriate strategies.

Description

A **description** uses words to help you picture in your mind what someone or something is like.

Character Sketch

One kind of description is a **character sketch.** It describes a real or an imaginary person.

Name the person in the **topic sentence.**

My Friend Germukh

Germukh is my best friend at school. He has dark brown hair and dark eyes. Germukh is shorter than most of the kids in our class, but that doesn't bother him.

Germukh is a great artist. He can draw creepy outer space creatures with antennae and bug eyes. Actually, his creatures are kind of cute!

Germukh is shy when there are a lot of people around, but he talks a lot when just the two of us work together on a project. Germukh always helps me with my English. Once we had to give an oral report, and Germukh stayed inside during recess to help me practice for it.

Give **examples** of what the person does that makes him or her special.

Use **describing words** and other details that tell what the person looks like and how the person acts.

100 **Put It in Writing!**

**Writing Model
Handbook page 100**

MULTI-LEVEL STRATEGIES

3 SPEECH EMERGENCE
Assist these students in writing key words and talking to other classmates: *You are writing about Jorge. He is a friend of Manuel's. Ask Manuel: Does Jorge like to play baseball or soccer?* Help students write the answers and say them aloud.

4 INTERMEDIATE FLUENCY
Help these students form questions, then encourage them to write down key words from the answers: *Does Lenora like to tell jokes or listen to them? Do you know how many languages Mai speaks? How can you ask her?*

5 ADVANCED FLUENCY/FLUENT
Have these students share their questions with you, then ask classmates questions and record the answers.

Get Organized Students can use their key words and details to make a Character Map like the one on **Handbook** page 62.

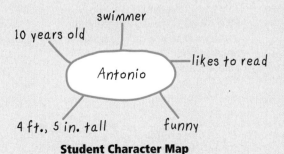

Student Character Map

Drafting

▶ **MATERIALS:** *Practice Book page 123*

Demonstrate for students how to use the details from their character maps to write sentences and give examples of what makes the person special.

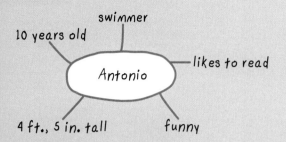

This person is a fantastic swimmer. He has been on swim teams for four years and has won many ribbons and medals. Someday, my friend wants to swim on the Olympic team.

Use level-appropriate strategies to involve students in the drafting stage of the writing process.

MULTI-LEVEL STRATEGIES

3 SPEECH EMERGENCE
Students can use **Practice Book** page 123 as a writing frame for their drafts.

4 5 INTERMEDIATE and ADVANCED FLUENCY/FLUENT
Have these students review Drafting on **Handbook** page 88, and then use their character maps to write their drafts.

Revising

▶ **MATERIALS:** *Practice Book page 124*

After students have finished their drafts, talk about the ways they can revise their writing to give a clear description of the person. Encourage students to look on **Handbook** pages 89–91 for help with the revising steps of the writing process. Use strategies appropriate to students' proficiency levels.

MULTI-LEVEL STRATEGIES

3 SPEECH EMERGENCE
Have these students follow along on **Practice Book** page 124 as you model making revisions and verbalize what you are doing. Offer individual help as necessary.

4 INTERMEDIATE FLUENCY
Talk about the Describing Words on **Handbook** pages 12–19 and help students choose words to use in revising their sketches. Before students begin, you might assign **Practice Book** page 124 as practice for adding descriptive details and examples.

5 ADVANCED FLUENCY/FLUENT
Refer students to the peer conferencing guidelines on **Handbook** page 90. Partners can read each other's drafts and suggest revisions. You might assign **Practice Book** page 124 as practice for adding descriptive details and examples.

Proofreading

▶ **MATERIALS:** *Practice Book page 124*

Use **Handbook** pages 186–189 to teach or review subject–verb agreement. This skill is the focus of the proofreading practice on **Practice Book** page 124.

Also, review the Proofreading Marks on **Handbook** page 92. Then use level-appropriate strategies as students proofread their character sketches.

MULTI-LEVEL STRATEGIES

3 SPEECH EMERGENCE

Display **Practice Book** page 124. Correct the writing model as you verbalize: *The subject of this sentence is* She. She *tells about one person so we need to change the verb from* are *to* is. *She is a very happy person. When the subject of a sentence is* he, she, *or* it, *we use* has *and* is *and verbs that end in* -s. Then assist students in proofreading their character sketches.

4 INTERMEDIATE FLUENCY

Point out errors on **Practice Book** page 124, and guide students in making the corrections: *If the subject of a sentence tells about one person, do you use the verb* is *or* are? *That's right—*is. *Change* are *to* is *because this sentence tells about one girl.* Then have students proofread and correct their character sketches.

5 ADVANCED FLUENCY/FLUENT

Have these students complete **Practice Book** page 124, and then proofread their character sketches. Partners can check each other's work.

Publishing

▶ **MATERIALS:** *students' character sketches, tape, blank sheet for guesses, blue ribbon (optional)*

Guess the Classmate After students read aloud their final sketches, have them add the sketches to a class display. Then attach a separate blank sheet to each sketch. Have the class guess who is being described by recording a name. You may want to give the student writer with the highest number of correct guesses a special award.

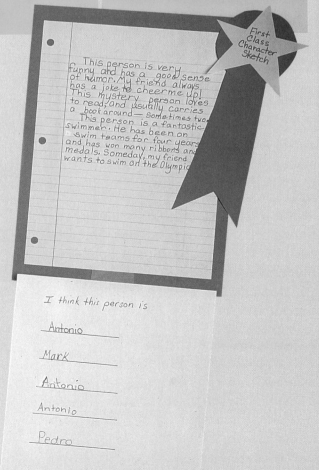

An Unbelievable Story!

Overview Students will write a tall tale with a partner, and then tell the tale to a class of younger children.

OBJECTIVES

RELATED PAGES
IN THE HANDBOOK

Functions
- Tell an Original Story

Learning Strategies
- Plan/Organize Information Graphically ....**Character Map Model,** page 62
  Goal-and-Outcome Map Model, page 74

Writing
- Tall Tale...**Writing Model,** page 146

Language Patterns and Structures
- Compound Sentences...**Instruction and Practice,** page 166,
  page 307

Concepts and Vocabulary
- Describing Words ....**Word Lists,** pages 12–19
- Synonyms...**Word Lists,** pages 33–37
- Tall Tale Characters..**Dateline U.S.A.,** page 275

Warm-Up

▶ **MATERIALS:** *butcher paper for web, several tall tales or collections*

Build Background Read aloud several tall tales from collections such as *Tall Tale America* by Walter Blair or *American Tall Tales* by Mary Pope Osborne. Invite students to share any tall tales they know.

Make a Class Web Have students brainstorm tall tale characters and write or draw details that characterize them. Students can look on **Handbook** pages 162–166 and 275 for details about Paul Bunyan, Pecos Bill, and John Henry.

Explain the Project Goal Review the class web with students, and then explain: *You will work with a partner to write a funny story called a tall tale. You can make up your own character or make up a new adventure for one of the characters we talked about. Then you will tell your tall tale to a class of younger children.*

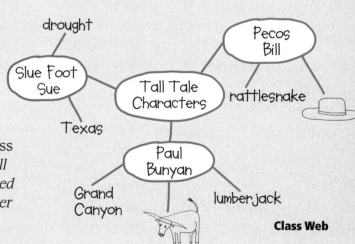

Class Web

Learn About Tall Tales

Discuss Characteristics Have students turn to the Tall Tale on **Handbook** page 146. Use the annotations to introduce or review its characteristics. Point out that tall tales often explain something in nature (for example, how Paul Bunyan "dug" the Great Lakes). Then have partners tell each other what a tall tale is like.

Write Tall Tales

Prewriting

Brainstorm a Character and Situation Assign partners and have them brainstorm a new character or choose one from the class web. Encourage students to draw and label a scene showing the character and what he or she might do.

Make a Story Map Have students use their scene to help them complete a Goal-and-Outcome Map like the one on **Handbook** page 74 to plan the story events. Involve students in a way that reflects their proficiency levels.

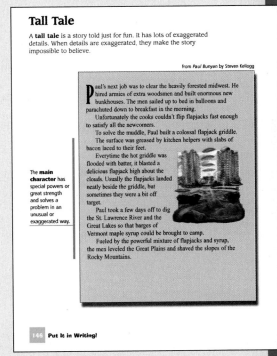

Tall Tale

A **tall tale** is a story told just for fun. It has lots of exaggerated details. When details are exaggerated, they make the story impossible to believe.

from *Paul Bunyan* by Steven Kellogg

Paul's next job was to clear the heavily forested midwest. He hired armies of extra woodsmen and built enormous new bunkhouses. The men sailed up to bed in balloons and parachuted down to breakfast in the morning.

Unfortunately the cooks couldn't flip flapjacks fast enough to satisfy all the newcomers.

To solve the muddle, Paul built a colossal flapjack griddle. The surface was greased by kitchen helpers with slabs of bacon laced to their feet.

The **main character** has special powers or great strength and solves a problem in an unusual or exaggerated way.

Everytime the hot griddle was flooded with batter, it blasted a delicious flapjack high about the clouds. Usually the flapjacks landed neatly beside the griddle, but sometimes they were a bit off target.

Paul took a few days off to dig the St. Lawrence River and the Great Lakes so that barges of Vermont maple syrup could be brought to camp.

Fueled by the powerful mixture of flapjacks and syrup, the men leveled the Great Plains and shaved the slopes of the Rocky Mountains.

146 Put It in Writing!

**Writing Model
Handbook page 146**

MULTI-LEVEL STRATEGIES

3 SPEECH EMERGENCE
Ask students questions about their pictures as you record key words from their responses in appropriate places in the map: *Who is this? What does* (character's name) *want to do? What does* (character's name) *do first?* and so on.

4 5 INTERMEDIATE and ADVANCED FLUENCY/FLUENT
Have partners discuss their picture with another pair of students. Then they can complete the story map.

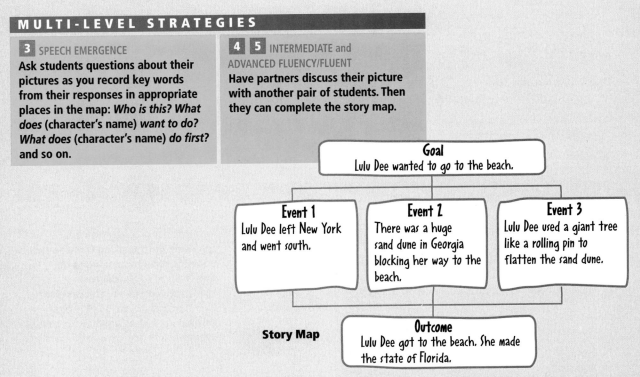

Goal
Lulu Dee wanted to go to the beach.

Event 1
Lulu Dee left New York and went south.

Event 2
There was a huge sand dune in Georgia blocking her way to the beach.

Event 3
Lulu Dee used a giant tree like a rolling pin to flatten the sand dune.

Outcome
Lulu Dee got to the beach. She made the state of Florida.

Story Map

Drafting

▶ **MATERIALS:** *Practice Book page 125*

Use one or two student story maps to demonstrate how to use the details to form sentences and paragraphs for a tall tale.

Involve students in the drafting stage of the writing process in a way that reflects their proficiency levels.

MULTI-LEVEL STRATEGIES

3 SPEECH EMERGENCE
Have each student use **Practice Book** page 125 as a writing frame for their drafts. Afterward, encourage partners to choose one of their drafts to use for their tall tale.

4 5 INTERMEDIATE and ADVANCED FLUENCY/FLUENT
Have these students review Drafting on **Handbook** page 88, and then use their map to collaborate on writing a draft.

Revising

▶ **MATERIALS:** *Practice Book page 126*

After groups have finished their drafts, talk about the different ways they can revise their writing to make it entertaining and impossible to believe. Encourage students to look on pages 89–91 of the **Handbook** for help with the revising steps of the writing process. Use level-appropriate strategies.

MULTI-LEVEL STRATEGIES

3 SPEECH EMERGENCE
Display **Practice Book** page 126 and model making revisions as you verbalize what you are doing. Then circulate as partners revise their drafts. Assist students as necessary.

4 INTERMEDIATE FLUENCY
Talk about Synonyms on **Handbook** pages 33–37 and help students choose words to use in revising their tales. Before students begin, you may wish to assign **Practice Book** page 126 as practice for using synonyms.

5 ADVANCED FLUENCY/FLUENT
Refer students to the peer conferencing guidelines on **Handbook** page 90. Have partners read the drafts aloud to another pair of students who can suggest revisions. You may wish to assign **Practice Book** page 126 as practice for using synonyms.

Proofreading

▶ **MATERIALS:** *Practice Book page 126*

Teach or review Compound Sentences on **Handbook** page 166. Compound sentences are the focus of the proofreading practice on **Practice Book** page 126.

Also, review the Proofreading Marks on **Handbook** page 92. Use level-appropriate strategies as partners proofread their tall tales.

MULTI-LEVEL STRATEGIES

3 SPEECH EMERGENCE

Display **Practice Book** page 126. Correct the writing model as you verbalize: *Here are two short sentences. The ideas are a lot alike. To make the sentences more interesting to read, we can put them together. Let's add a comma and the word and.* Then assist partners in proofreading their tall tale.

4 INTERMEDIATE FLUENCY

Point out sentences on **Practice Book** page 126. Guide students in making the corrections: *What's one way we can make sentences more interesting to read? Yes, we can put two short sentences together. Add a comma and the word and to make a compound sentence.* Then have partners proofread and correct their tall tale.

5 ADVANCED FLUENCY/FLUENT

Have each student complete **Practice Book** page 126. Then partners can proofread their tall tale.

Publishing

▶ **MATERIALS:** *students' tall tales, drawings, props (optional)*

Tell the Tale Encourage partners to take turns reading or telling parts of their final tall tales to a younger class. They may want to create story boards or a backdrop, use props, or dress up like the character for their presentation.

16 Dear Sir or Madam

Overview Students will brainstorm and choose an environmental improvement project, and then write and mail business letters requesting the materials they need to complete it.

OBJECTIVES

**RELATED PAGES
IN THE HANDBOOK**

Functions
• Express Social Courtesies

Writing
• Business Letter/Envelope...**Writing Models,** pages 116 and 119
• Capitalization/Punctuation...................................**Instruction and Practice,** pages 202–213,
  pages 323–327

Language Patterns and Structures
• Statements and Questions ....**Instruction and Practice,** pages 160–163,
  page 305

Concepts and Vocabulary
• Earth Day ....**Dateline U.S.A.,** page 276
• Formal/Informal Language

Warm-Up

▶ **MATERIALS:** *butcher paper for web*

Build Background Share books with a conservation theme like *Tanya's Big Green Dream* by Linda Glaser or *A River Ran Wild* by Lynne Cherry. If you choose to do this project for Earth Day, read aloud the information on **Handbook** page 276.

Make a Class Web Have students brainstorm projects and write or draw items they'll need to carry it out. Then have them choose one project to do.

Explain the Project Goal Review the project students chose, then explain:
To do our project, first we need to gather the materials or equipment. Sometimes businesses in our community will give us, or donate, materials. We will write letters to those businesses to ask them for the materials.

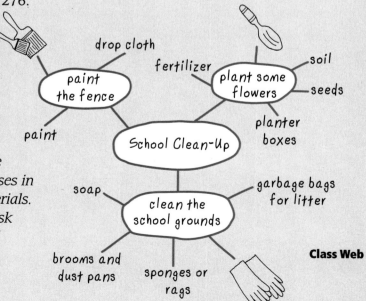

Class Web

Learn About Business Letters

Discuss Characteristics Have students look at the Business Letter on **Handbook** page 116. Point out the purpose and call attention to the formal writing style. Ask volunteers to describe in their own words what a business letter is like. Repeat the procedure with the Envelope on **Handbook** page 119.

Write Business Letters

Prewriting

Decide Whom to Write To Help students select local businesses to write to for the materials and provide their addresses. Depending on their proficiency levels, some students may be able to find possible donors in the telephone directory or on the Internet.

Plan the Letter Have students make a chart to record the details they want to include in their letters. Use level-appropriate strategies.

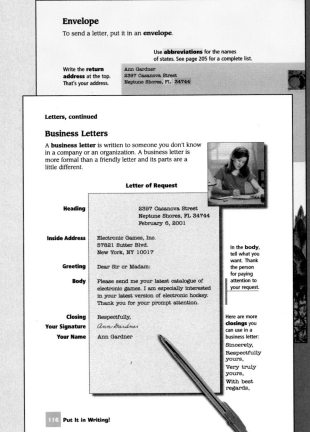

**Writing Models
Handbook pages 116, 119**

MULTI-LEVEL STRATEGIES

3 SPEECH EMERGENCE
Have these students copy the address. Then have them draw and label pictures to show the project and what materials they need.

4 5 INTERMEDIATE and ADVANCED FLUENCY/FLUENT
These students can copy the address, and then brainstorm with a partner the details to include in their charts.

Who am I writing to?	Why am I writing?	What do I want?
Garden Supply 582 E. Oak Phoenix, AZ 85069	to tell about our project to ask for things we need to plant flowers	planter boxes soil

Chart

Drafting

▶ **MATERIALS:** *Practice Book page 127*

Demonstrate writing a heading and inside address for a business letter. Then show students how to form sentences from the details in their charts and arrange them logically in the body of the letters.

Why am I writing?	What do I want?
to tell about our project	planter boxes

Dear Sir or Madam:

I am a student at Walnut Lane School. Our class wants to plant some flowers at the front entrance to our school. Would you be able to donate one or two wooden planter boxes?

Involve students in the drafting stage of the writing process in a way that reflects their proficiency levels.

MULTI-LEVEL STRATEGIES

3 SPEECH EMERGENCE
Students can use **Practice Book** page 127 as a writing frame for their drafts.

4 5 INTERMEDIATE and ADVANCED FLUENCY/FLUENT
Have these students review Drafting on **Handbook** page 88, and then use their charts to write their drafts.

Revising

▶ **MATERIALS:** *Practice Book page 128*

After students have finished their drafts, talk about the differences between formal and informal language. Then have students revise their writing to be sure they've used formal language. Encourage students to look on **Handbook** pages 89–91 for help with the revising steps of the writing process. Use level-appropriate strategies.

MULTI-LEVEL STRATEGIES

3 SPEECH EMERGENCE
Display **Practice Book** page 128 and model making revisions as you verbalize what you are doing. Then circulate as students revise their drafts. Offer individual help as necessary.

4 INTERMEDIATE FLUENCY
Have students compare their drafts with the model on **Handbook** page 116, to be sure they've included all the parts; and have used formal language, statements, and questions in the body of the letter to make their requests clear. You may wish to assign **Practice Book** page 128 as practice before they begin.

5 ADVANCED FLUENCY/FLUENT
Refer students to the peer conferencing guidelines on **Handbook** page 90. Have partners read each other's drafts aloud and make suggestions for revisions. You may also wish to assign **Practice Book** page 128 as practice for using formal language, statements, and questions in the body of a letter to make requests clear.

Proofreading

▶ **MATERIALS:** *Practice Book page 128*

Teach or review capitalization and punctuation used in letters on **Handbook** pages 205–206 and 209–211. These elements are the focus of the proofreading practice on **Practice Book** page 128.

Also, review the Proofreading Marks on **Handbook** page 92. Then use level-appropriate strategies as students proofread their own business letters.

MULTI-LEVEL STRATEGIES

3 SPEECH EMERGENCE
Display **Practice Book** page 128. Correct the writing model as you verbalize: *Here's the inside address. Look at the w. When you write the abbreviation of a place name, use a capital letter. Let's show that the lowercase w should be a capital letter.* Then assist students in proofreading their letters.

4 INTERMEDIATE FLUENCY
Point out errors on **Practice Book** page 128 and guide students in making the corrections: *Which parts of the inside address should have capital letters? That's right, abbreviations for special place names should be capitalized. Mark the letters that should be capitalized.* Then have students proofread their own letters.

5 ADVANCED FLUENCY/FLUENT
Have these students complete **Practice Book** page 128, and then proofread their business letters. Partners can check each other's work.

Publishing

▶ **MATERIALS:** *students' letters; stationery (optional); business size envelopes and stamps, 1 of each per student*

Write and Mail the Letter After students write or type their final letters, have them address an envelope and mail their letters. When students receive all the donations, plan and implement the project. Afterward, encourage students to write thank-you letters to the donors.

634 Hillcrest Road
Garland, TX 75042
October 3, 2000

Sunbright Nursery
2110 West Fifth Street
Garland, TX 75042

Dear Sir or Madam:

I am in fourth grade at Garland Elementary School. Our school project this year is to make our school look more beautiful. Some of the classes are picking up trash and others are painting. Our class would like to plant flowers around the school, but we need gardening tools. Can you help us?

Sincerely,
Tara Brolin
Tara Brolin

63T

Extra! Extra!

Overview Students will talk about newspapers, and then write editorials, news stories, or advertisements for a class newspaper.

OBJECTIVES

**RELATED PAGES
IN THE HANDBOOK**

Warm-Up

▶ **MATERIALS:** *school and local newspapers, butcher paper for web*

Build Background Show students several local and school newspapers or newsletters. Invite volunteers to share what they know about newspapers, and then talk about the different sections—news, sports, comics, classified ads, and so on.

Make a Class Web Brainstorm with students topics that might be covered in the different sections. Record their ideas.

Explain the Project Goal Explain: *We will create a class newspaper. In our newspaper, we'll have advertisements, news stories, and editorials. You will work in your group to write one part of the newspaper. We will put all the parts together to create a newspaper to share with other classes.*

Class Web

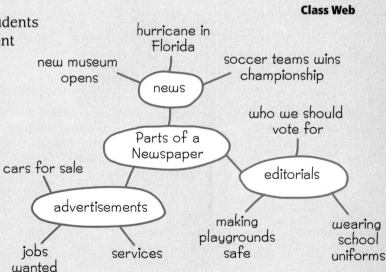

Learn About Advertisements, Editorials, and News Stories

Discuss Characteristics Have students look at each writing model in turn as you use the annotations to introduce or review their characteristics: Announcements and Advertisements on **Handbook** page 95, Editorial on page 104, and News Story on page 121.

Ask students questions to help them compare the models: *To sell something, would you write an advertisement or a news story? What could you write to tell how you feel about something? Do you tell your opinion in a news story?* and so on.

Write Sections for a Class Newspaper

Prewriting

Assign Groups and Choose Topics Group students by proficiency level and have each group review the class web. Then assist each group as necessary to brainstorm school topics and list details for their writing.

News Story

A **news story** tells about an event that really happened. It includes only **facts**.

Editorial

An **editorial** is a newspaper or magazine article that is written to persuade people to believe the same way you do. When you write an editorial, tell how you feel about something. That's your...

Announcements and Advertisements

An **announcement** is a short message that tells about an event.

Advertisements (or ads) tell about services you might need or special products you can buy.

River School's Spring Fair

Saturday, April 15
10–4 at the school
Come for food, games, prizes!

Bicycle Repair
It's Time for Spring Cleaning!

Complete bike repair and cleaning for road and mountain bikes.
Nathan's Bike Shop
796 Mission Fields Center
Alton, IL 60381   555-0099

A company's **name**, **address**, and **telephone number** is given so you can get in touch with them.

Show Your School Spirit!

Ads often show pictures of what you can buy.

A description tells you more about the item.

Your school's name and mascot can be on this 100% cotton shirt. Available in an assortment of colors.
Sizes: ☐ S ☐ M ☐ LG ☐ XL
SD143-714 . . . . $15.00
Mail your order to:
School Colors International
P.O. Box 683
New York, NY 11021
or call : 1-800-555-3671

A **code number** identifies the item. You use that code on the order form.

Put It in Writing! 95

Writing Models
Handbook pages 95, 104, 121

MULTI-LEVEL STRATEGIES

3 SPEECH EMERGENCE
Have these students write ads. Have them draw pictures of what they'd like to buy, sell, or trade. Help students record key words: *These look like balloon animals. Would you like to sell some of these to raise money for our class party? (Write Balloon animals for sale.)*

4 INTERMEDIATE FLUENCY
These students can write the news stories. Ask open-ended questions to help them identify a current local or school event to write about: *When was the bake sale? How many people came? Where did it happen?* and so on.

5 ADVANCED FLUENCY/FLUENT
Ask these students to write editorials. Have students brainstorm a list of topics they feel strongly about. Guide them to choose topics they know the most about and make a list of reasons to support their opinion.

Get Organized Students can use a web like the one on **Handbook** page 62 to group their ideas.

over 100 came   PTA   Saturday

bake sale   gym

cookies, cupcakes   need money for painting school

Student Web

Drafting

▶ **MATERIALS:** *Practice Book page 129*

Create Layouts You may want to give each group a page layout for their part of the newspaper to help guide their writing. You might also arrange for groups to work on computers.

Demonstrate Circulate and demonstrate for students how to form sentences from the details in their clusters and write them in a logical order.

over 100 came   PTA   Saturday

bake sale — gym

cookies, cupcakes   need money for painting school

On Saturday afternoon in the school gym, the PTA held a bake sale to help raise money to paint the school.

Involve students in the drafting stage of the writing process in a way that reflects their proficiency levels.

MULTI-LEVEL STRATEGIES

3 SPEECH EMERGENCE
Students can use **Practice Book** page 129 to help them create an advertisement.

4 5 INTERMEDIATE and ADVANCED FLUENCY/FLUENT
Have these students review Drafting on **Handbook** page 88, and then use their clusters to write drafts of their news stories and editorials.

Revising

▶ **MATERIALS:** *Practice Book page 130*

After students have finished their drafts, talk about the ways they can revise their work to include the important details and facts. Encourage students to look on **Handbook** pages 89–91 for help with the revising steps of the writing process. Use level-appropriate strategies.

MULTI-LEVEL STRATEGIES

3 SPEECH EMERGENCE
Use one student's advertisement to model making revisions as you verbalize what you are doing. Circulate as students revise their drafts. Offer individual help as necessary.

4 INTERMEDIATE FLUENCY
Talk about important details and facts that answer the questions *who, what, when, where, why,* and *how* and prompt students to add details to their writing. Before students begin, you may wish to assign **Practice Book** page 130 as practice.

5 ADVANCED FLUENCY/FLUENT
Refer students to the peer conferencing guidelines on **Handbook** page 90. Partners can read aloud each other's drafts and make sure their editorials contain opinions, important details, and facts. You might assign **Practice Book** page 130 as practice before they begin.

Proofreading

▶ **MATERIALS:** *Practice Book page 130*

Teach or review the use of nouns and plurals on **Handbook** pages 167–173 and capitalization of proper nouns on pages 203–207. These elements are the focus of the proofreading practice on **Practice Book** page 130.

Also, review the Proofreading Marks on **Handbook** page 92. Then use level-appropriate strategies as students proofread their work.

MULTI-LEVEL STRATEGIES

3 SPEECH EMERGENCE

Display **Practice Book** page 130. Correct the writing model as you verbalize: *Here's the name of a particular person—Cata. Cata is a proper noun so it should start with a capital letter. Whenever you name a particular person, place, or thing, use a capital letter.* Then assist students in proofreading their advertisements.

4 INTERMEDIATE FLUENCY

Point out errors on **Practice Book** page 130 and guide students in making the corrections: *Did just one child participate in Make-a-Difference Day? What word should we use to show more than one child? That's right,* children. *Remember that nouns change in different ways to show more than one.* Then have students proofread and correct their own news stories.

5 ADVANCED FLUENCY/FLUENT

Have these students complete **Practice Book** page 130, and then proofread their editorials. Partners can check each other's work.

Publishing

▶ **MATERIALS:** *students' advertisements, news stories, and editorials; page layouts on large sheets of white paper; glue*

Create and Assemble Pages Have each group glue their final advertisements or articles onto the pages. Invite the class to decide how to put the pages together and to give the newspaper a name. Call on a volunteer to add the name to the first page.

Distribute Make several copies of students' pages, staple, and distribute a copy of the completed newspaper to other classes. Also encourage students to take a copy home to share with their families.

March 3, 2002

ROOM 24 REPORTS

Aquarium Diver Visits Room 24

Last Wednesday, an aquarium diver came to visit our class. Her name is Maya Mazzi and she works at the Bayside Aquarium. She came to talk to us about sharks and other sea life. We learned a lot from Maya and we really enjoyed her visit. If your class would like to have Ms. Mazzi visit, you can contact her at the Bayside Aquarium.

5th Annual International Day—A Big Success

On Sunday, the 5th Annual International Day was held at Oak Grove Park. There were a lot of different kinds of foods from all over the world. People could buy arts and crafts and watch clowns do magic tricks. There were also dancers who did dances from different countries. Dominik Pomorze, from room 24, and his brother and father did a traditional Polish folk dance called Goralski. Everyone had tons of fun at this year's International Day.

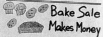 **Bake Sale Makes Money**

On Saturday afternoon, the PTA held a bake sale in the gym. The sale helped raise money to paint the school.

67T

Reporting the Facts

Overview Students will talk about objects in outer space, choose two objects to research, and then write a report that compares and contrasts their objects for a space exhibit.

OBJECTIVES

**RELATED PAGES
IN THE HANDBOOK**

Warm-Up

▶ **MATERIALS:** *butcher paper for web*

Build Background Have students look through **Handbook** pages 220–233 and **Dateline U.S.A.** page 288 and comment on the content and pictures.

Make a Class Web Have students brainstorm objects in outer space and write or draw their ideas.

Explain the Project Goal Review the class web with students, and then explain: *You will choose two objects and do research to find out what they are like. Then you will write a report to show how the two objects are alike and how they are different. We'll use our reports to make a space exhibit.*

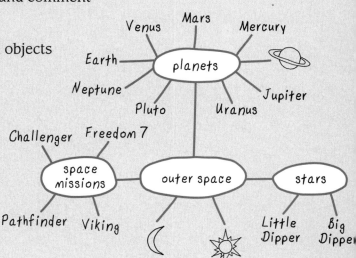

Class Web

Learn About Reports

Discuss Characteristics Ask students to turn to the Report on **Handbook** pages 232–233. Use the annotations to introduce or review its characteristics. After students have identified the parts of a report, have them describe a report in their own words.

Write Reports

Prewriting

▶ **MATERIALS:** encyclopedias, almanac, books about the solar system, notecards

Choose Objects Have students choose two objects from the class web to use for their writing topic.

Do Research Remind students that they will be looking for how the two objects are alike and how they are different. You may want to work through **Handbook** pages 128–129 with students before they begin. Use level-appropriate strategies to involve all students in the research process.

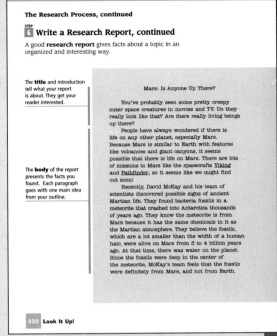

The Research Process, continued

STEP
6 Write a Research Report, continued

A good **research report** gives facts about a topic in an organized and interesting way.

The **title** and introduction tell what your report is about. They get your reader interested.

The **body** of the report presents the facts you found. Each paragraph goes with one main idea from your outline.

Mars: Is Anyone Up There?

You've probably seen some pretty creepy outer space creatures in movies and TV. Do they really look like that? Are there really living beings up there?

People have always wondered if there is life on any other planet, especially Mars. Because Mars is similar to Earth with features like volcanoes and giant canyons, it seems possible that there is life on Mars. There are lots of missions to Mars like the spacecrafts Viking and Pathfinder, so it seems like we might find out soon!

Recently, David McKay and his team of scientists discovered possible signs of ancient Martian life. They found bacteria fossils in a meteorite that crashed into Antarctica thousands of years ago. They know the meteorite is from Mars because it has the same chemicals in it as the Martian atmosphere. They believe the fossils, which are a lot smaller than the width of a human hair, were alive on Mars from 3 to 4 billion years ago. At that time, there was water on the planet. Since the fossils were deep in the center of the meteorite, McKay's team feels that the fossils were definitely from Mars, and not from Earth.

232 Look It Up!

**Writing Models
Handbook pages 232–233**

MULTI-LEVEL STRATEGIES

3 SPEECH EMERGENCE
Help students form questions for their research such as *How big is the sun (moon)? How far away is the sun (moon) from Earth?* Have them copy the research questions onto notecards, and then help them find answers to their questions in an encyclopedia. Record key words on their notecards.

4 INTERMEDIATE FLUENCY
Pair these students with a partner who has chosen the same two objects to research. Have them work together to write research questions, look up the information in an encyclopedia, and take notes.

5 ADVANCED FLUENCY/FLUENT
Have these students review The Research Process on **Handbook** pages 220–233, and then take notes on notecards from two sources.

Make an Outline Use students' notecards to model how to turn notes and details into an outline. Circulate to assist students as necessary as they write their outlines.

Two Shining Objects in the Sky

I. Different sizes
  A. Sun 400 times bigger
  B. Moon looks big because is closer to Earth
II. What they're made of
  A. Sun
    1. Ball of hot gases
    2. Helium and hydrogen
  B. Moon
    1. Gray rock
    2. Craters

69T

Drafting

▶ **MATERIALS:** *Practice Book page 131*

Demonstrate for students how to turn the main ideas and details in their outlines into topic sentences and paragraphs.

> ### Two Shining Objects in the Sky
>
> I. Different sizes
>   A. Sun 400 times bigger
>   B. Moon looks big because is closer to Earth

> *It's easy to think that the moon and the sun are the same size, but actually they are different sizes. The sun is 400 times bigger than the moon. The moon just looks as big as the sun because it's closer to Earth.*

Involve students in the drafting stage of the writing process in a way that reflects their proficiency levels.

MULTI-LEVEL STRATEGIES

3 SPEECH EMERGENCE
Students can use **Practice Book** page 131 as a frame for writing their drafts.

4 5 INTERMEDIATE and ADVANCED FLUENCY/FLUENT
Have these students review Drafting on **Handbook** page 88, and then use their outlines to write drafts.

Revising

▶ **MATERIALS:** *Practice Book page 132*

After students have finished their drafts, talk about ways they can revise their report to present the facts in an organized and interesting way. Encourage students to look on **Handbook** pages 89–91 for help with the revising steps of the writing process. Use level-appropriate strategies.

MULTI-LEVEL STRATEGIES

3 SPEECH EMERGENCE
Display **Practice Book** page 132 and model making revisions as you verbalize what you are doing. Circulate as students revise their drafts. Offer individual help as necessary.

4 INTERMEDIATE FLUENCY
Review with students the parts of a report and how to write topic sentences. Before students revise their reports, you may wish to assign **Practice Book** page 132 as practice for checking the organization and topic sentences.

5 ADVANCED FLUENCY/FLUENT
Refer students to the peer conferencing guidelines on **Handbook** page 90. Have partners read each other's drafts aloud and make suggestions for revisions. You may also wish to assign **Practice Book** page 132 as practice for checking the organization and topic sentences.

Proofreading

▶ **MATERIALS:** *Practice Book page 132*

Teach or review the use of adjectives on **Handbook** pages 180–185. Comparative adjectives are the focus of the proofreading practice on **Practice Book** page 132.

Also, review the Proofreading Marks on **Handbook** page 92. Then use level-appropriate strategies as students proofread their own reports.

MULTI-LEVEL STRATEGIES

3 SPEECH EMERGENCE
Display **Practice Book** page 132. Correct the writing model as you verbalize: *Here it says, "Each group has seven stars, but the Big Dipper is bright than the Little Dipper." We need to change* bright *to* brighter. *When we compare two things, we need to add -er to the end of the adjective.* Then assist students in proofreading their reports.

4 INTERMEDIATE FLUENCY
Point out the errors on **Practice Book** page 132 and guide students in making the corrections: *What do we add to adjectives to show that we are comparing two or more things? That's right, -er or -est. We need to change* bright *to* brighter *because we are comparing two things.* Then have students proofread and correct their reports.

5 ADVANCED FLUENCY/FLUENT
Have these students complete **Practice Book** page 132, and then proofread their reports. Partners can check each other's work.

Publishing

▶ **MATERIALS:** *students' reports, binding materials or folders, art supplies for making models (optional)*

Make a Space Exhibit After students prepare and bind their final reports, encourage them to illustrate or make models of their objects. Then students can use their reports and models to create a space exhibit. Invite other classes to "tour" the exhibit, encouraging volunteers to read aloud their reports and describe their contributions.

PROJECT 19

DESCRIPTION OF A PLACE

And to Your Right . . .

Overview Students will talk about familiar places and write a spatial description to add to a class guide for visitors or newcomers.

OBJECTIVES

RELATED PAGES IN THE HANDBOOK

Functions
- Describe

Learning Strategies
- Plan/Organize Information Graphically ....**Diagram Model,** page 65

Writing
- Description of a Place..**Writing Model,** page 101

Language Patterns and Structures
- Adjectives..**Instruction and Practice,** pages 182–183, pages 314–315
- Prepositions ....**Instruction and Practice,** pages 198–199, pages 321–322

Concepts and Vocabulary
- Describing Words ....**Word Lists,** pages 12–19
- Similes...**Word List,** page 28

Warm-Up

Activate Prior Knowledge Ask students to tell about their favorite places to go, or talk about places they've visited with their families or on school field trips. Make a list of students' responses on the chalkboard.

Explain the Project Goal Review the list with students, and then explain: *You will each choose a place you know well and then draw a picture of it. You'll use your picture to help you tell what the place is like. We will put all of the pictures and descriptions together to make a book for visitors or newcomers to our area.*

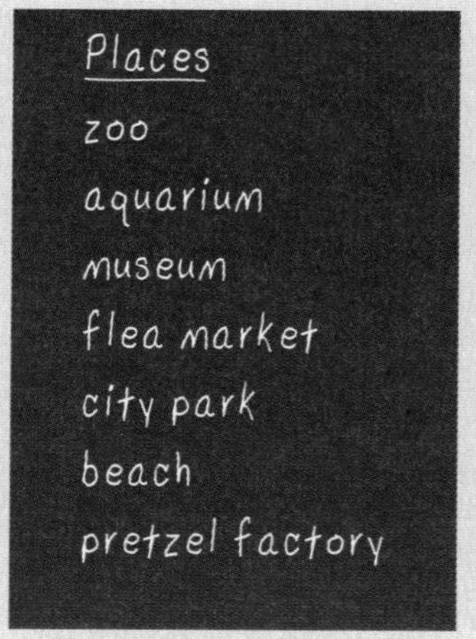

Places
zoo
aquarium
museum
flea market
city park
beach
pretzel factory

Class List

Learn About Descriptions

Discuss Characteristics Have students turn to the Description of a Place on **Handbook** page 101. Use the annotations to introduce or review its characteristics. After students have identified the sensory words, direction words, and similes, have partners think of a new example of each to share with the class.

Write Descriptions

Prewriting

Choose a Place Have students choose a familiar place to describe. Help them narrow the topic to one specific area, such as the playground area of a park or the first floor of a museum.

Make a Diagram Have students think about where things are in a place, and then make a diagram like the one on **Handbook** page 65. Students can also include illustrations to help them recall specific details.

Discuss the Diagram Have students use their diagram to describe the place. Use level-appropriate strategies to help students decide on the space order for their description.

Description of a Place

When you describe a place, use lots of details to help your readers imagine that they are there!

Name the subject in the **topic sentence**.

Write the details in **space order**. That means to tell what you see in order from left to right, near to far, or top to bottom.

A Market in Vietnam

The outdoor market in Vietnam is jammed full with food and people. Closest to the street, you'll see a row of square wicker or plastic containers filled with parsley, pineapples, apples, taro, and waterlilies as white as clouds. In the next row up are large round bowls of fresh beans, bean sprouts, and a special kind of meat piled high like pyramids. Above the bowls, the seller lies in a hammock to free up space for more things to sell. Just above the seller, plastic bags for carrying the food hang down from the wooden beams of the stall.

Use **direction words** and phrases to tell where things are.

Use **sensory words** that tell how things look, sound, feel, smell, or taste.

Use **similes** to help the reader imagine what's being described.

Go Sensory Words on pages 16 and 17 for more words you can use in a description.

Diary
See *Journal Entry.*

Put It in Writing! 101

**Writing Model
Handbook page 101**

MULTI-LEVEL STRATEGIES

3 SPEECH EMERGENCE
Ask questions about students' diagrams: *What place is this? If you start walking here* (point to a position on the diagram) *and go in this direction, what do you see first? Is it to the left or to the right of the soccer field?*

4 5 INTERMEDIATE and ADVANCED FLUENCY/FLUENT
Ask students where they'll begin to describe the place and have them point to that position. Prompt them to use direction words to tell where things are as they point to and move their fingers left to right, bottom to top, and so on.

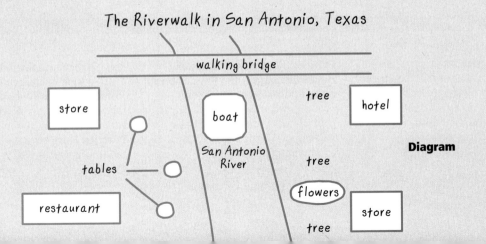

The Riverwalk in San Antonio, Texas

walking bridge

store

boat

tree

hotel

San Antonio River

tables

tree

Diagram

restaurant

flowers

store

tree

Drafting

▶ **MATERIALS:** *Practice Book page 133*

Demonstrate for students how to use their diagrams as a guide for writing sentences and for adding details and direction words:

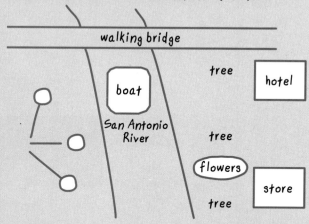

The Riverwalk in San Antonio, Texas

walking bridge

boat

San Antonio River

tree   hotel

tree

flowers

store

tree

The Riverwalk in San Antonio, Texas, is a shady, wonderful place. If you stand on the walking bridge and look straight ahead, you'll see the San Antonio River flowing like a golden-brown ribbon through the middle of the area.

Involve students in the drafting stage of the writing process in a way that reflects their proficiency levels.

MULTI-LEVEL STRATEGIES

3 SPEECH EMERGENCE
Students can use **Practice Book** page 133 as a writing frame for their drafts.

4 5 INTERMEDIATE and ADVANCED FLUENCY/FLUENT
Have these students review Drafting on **Handbook** page 88, and then use their diagrams to write their drafts.

Revising

▶ **MATERIALS:** *Practice Book page 134*

After students have finished their drafts, talk about ways to revise their writing to give their readers a clear picture of the place. Encourage students to look on **Handbook** pages 89–91 for help with the revising steps of the writing process. Use level-appropriate strategies.

MULTI-LEVEL STRATEGIES

3 SPEECH EMERGENCE
Display **Practice Book** page 134 and model adding descriptive details and direction words as you verbalize what you are doing. Circulate as students revise their drafts. Offer individual help as necessary.

4 INTERMEDIATE FLUENCY
Talk about Describing Words on **Handbook** pages 12–19 and Similes on **Handbook** page 28. Before students begin revising their drafts, you may wish to assign **Practice Book** page 134 as practice for adding descriptive details.

5 ADVANCED FLUENCY/FLUENT
Refer students to the peer conferencing guidelines on **Handbook** page 90. Partners can read aloud each other's drafts and suggest revisions. You might assign **Practice Book** page 134 as practice for adding descriptive details.

Proofreading

▶ **MATERIALS:** *Practice Book page 134*

Teach or review the use of comparative adjectives on **Handbook** pages 182–183 and prepositions on **Handbook** pages 198–199. These elements are the focus of the proofreading practice on **Practice Book** page 134.

Also, review the Proofreading Marks on **Handbook** page 92. Then use level-appropriate strategies as students proofread their descriptions.

MULTI-LEVEL STRATEGIES

3 SPEECH EMERGENCE
Display **Practice Book** page 134. Correct the writing model as you verbalize: *Here, it says "There are four theaters in town, but the Galaxy is the nicer." The writer is comparing four theaters so we need to change* nicer *to* nicest. *When we compare three or more things, we add* -est *to the adjective.* Then assist students in proofreading their descriptions.

4 INTERMEDIATE FLUENCY
Point out errors on **Practice Book** page 134. Guide students in making corrections. *When we compare three or more things, what should we add to an adjective? That's right,* -est. *Change* nicer *to* nicest *to show that we are comparing more than two things.* Then have students proofread and correct their descriptions.

5 ADVANCED FLUENCY/FLUENT
Have these students complete **Practice Book** page 134, and then proofread their descriptions. Partners can check each other's work.

Publishing

▶ **MATERIALS:** *students' diagrams and descriptions, book-binding materials or three-ring binder*

Make and Share a Guide Book After each student has shared his or her description with the class, help students compile their diagrams and descriptions into a guide book. Invite volunteers to create a table of contents and title page. You may wish to have students send a copy of the book to the local library or the Chamber of Commerce.

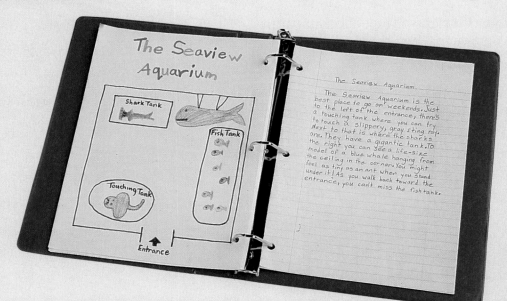

It Happened to Me

Overview Students will talk about what they've discovered about the school grounds or staff, write a personal narrative to describe events leading up to the discovery, and present their narratives as helpful tips for new students.

OBJECTIVES

**RELATED PAGES
IN THE HANDBOOK**

Functions
• Describe

Learning Strategies
• Plan/Organize Information Graphically ....**List Model,** page 87

Writing
• Personal Narrative..**Writing Model,** page 131
• Capitalization: Pronoun "I" ....**Instruction and Practice,** page 202, page 323

Language Patterns and Structures
• Pronouns..**Instruction and Practice,** pages 174–179,
pages 311–313

Concepts and Vocabulary
• Describing Words ....**Word Lists,** pages 12–19

Warm-Up

Build Background Share something non-academic you discovered about school equipment or staff such as finding the best pencil sharpener or learning about the P.E. coach's artistic abilities. Explain how you found out about it.

Make a Class List Have students brainstorm discoveries they've made at school and record their ideas.

Explain the Project Goal Review the class list with students, and then explain: *To help new students know about things at school, we'll use our ideas to make a class book of tips. You'll each write a helpful tip, and then write a story to tell how you found out about it.*

Discoveries About School

where the best pencil sharpener is

how to use the water fountain without getting wet

getting the best equipment during recess

who to ask for help with homework

what to do after school

what happens on April Fool's Day

Class List

Learn About Personal Narratives

Discuss Characteristics Have students turn to the Personal Narrative on **Handbook** page 131. Use the annotations to introduce or review its characteristics. Then have volunteers describe a personal narrative in their own words.

Write Personal Narratives

Prewriting

Choose a Tip Ask students to review the ideas on the class list and choose one as their writing topic.

Think About the Experience Allow time for students to think about the events that lead up to their discovery. Then have students make a list of key words to help them remember the details. Involve students in the prewriting stage of the writing process in a way that reflects their proficiency levels.

Personal Narrative

When you write a **personal narrative**, you tell a story about something that happened to you. Because the story is about you, you'll write it in the first person. That means you'll use the words *I*, *me*, and *my* a lot.

The beginning tells what the event is all about.

The middle tells more about the event.

The end tells what finally happened.

A Good Luck Valentine

I'll never forget my first Valentine's Day. When I got to school, I was surprised to find some bright red envelopes on my desk.

At first, I thought they were gifts for Chinese New Year. Each new year my family gives me money in red envelopes to wish me good luck. But when I opened the little envelopes, I only found some paper hearts.

Then my teacher explained what happens on Valentine's Day. The notes in the envelopes were valentines. Now when I look at my valentines, I feel just as wonderful as when I get gifts for the new year!

A personal narrative has **order words** that tell when something happened.

It has **describing words** that tell what things were like and how you felt.

Dateline U.S.A. on pages 264–301 for more information about Valentine's Day and other special days and holidays.

Put It in Writing! 131

**Writing Model
Handbook page 131**

Get Organized Have students review their lists and use numbers to put their details in order.

TIP: Remember that April 1 is April Fool's Day!

4. studied during morning recess
1. last April on my way to school
2. friend asked about spelling test
5. no test—it was a trick!
3. I thought I forgot

Student List

Drafting

▶ **MATERIALS:** *Practice Book page 135*

Demonstrate for students how to form sentences from the details
in their lists and write the details in a logical order:

TIP: Remember that April 1
is April Fool's Day!

4. studied during morning
   recess
1. last April on my way to
   school
2. friend asked about
   spelling test

Tip: Remember that April 1 is
April Fool's Day!
 I was walking to school one
day last April with my friend
Paul. He asked me if I was
ready for our spelling test.
 "Oh, no, I forgot," I said.

Involve students in the drafting stage of the writing process in
a way that reflects their proficiency levels.

MULTI-LEVEL STRATEGIES

3 SPEECH EMERGENCE
**Have these students use Practice
Book page 135 as a writing frame
for their drafts.**

4 5 INTERMEDIATE and
ADVANCED FLUENCY/FLUENT
**These students can review Drafting
on Handbook page 88, and then use
their lists to write drafts.**

Revising

▶ **MATERIALS:** *Practice Book page 136*

After students have finished their drafts, talk about the different ways
they can revise their writing to say exactly what they want. Encourage
students to look on **Handbook** pages 89-91 for help with the revising
steps of the writing process. Use level-appropriate strategies.

MULTI-LEVEL STRATEGIES

3 SPEECH EMERGENCE
**Display Practice Book page 136
and model making revisions as you
verbalize what you are doing.
Circulate as students revise their
drafts. Offer individual help as
necessary.**

4 INTERMEDIATE FLUENCY
**Talk about the Describing Words on
Handbook pages 12-19 and help
students choose words to use in
revising their narratives. Before
students revise their drafts, you
might have them complete Practice
Book page 136 as practice for
adding descriptive details.**

5 ADVANCED FLUENCY/FLUENT
**Have students review the peer
conferencing guidelines on
Handbook page 90, and then work
with a partner to revise their drafts.
You may wish to assign Practice
Book page 136 as practice for
adding descriptive details.**

Proofreading

▶ **MATERIALS:** *Practice Book page 136*

Teach or review the use of pronouns on **Handbook** pages 174-179 and capitalization of the pronoun "I" on page 202. These elements occur naturally in personal narratives and are the focus of the proofreading practice on **Practice Book** page 136.

Also, review the Proofreading Marks on **Handbook** page 92. Then use level-appropriate strategies as students proofread their narratives.

MULTI-LEVEL STRATEGIES

3 SPEECH EMERGENCE
Display **Practice Book** page 136. Correct the writing model as you verbalize: *Here it says, "Her and I didn't know there were things to do after school." Because we're talking about a girl in the* **subject** *of a sentence, we need to change* Her *to* She. Then assist students in proofreading their narratives.

4 INTERMEDIATE FLUENCY
Point out errors on **Practice Book** page 136 and guide students in making the corrections: *Which pronouns do you use to talk about a girl in the* **subject** *of a sentence? That's right—she. Change* Her *to* She. Then have students proofread and correct their narratives.

5 ADVANCED FLUENCY/FLUENT
Have these students complete **Practice Book** page 136, and then proofread their narratives. Partners can check each other's work.

Publishing

▶ **MATERIALS:** *students' personal narratives, crayons or markers, binding materials*

Share Experiences When students are pleased with their work, have them add illustrations and share their narratives with the class.

Make a Book of Tips Collect students' work into a class book. You may want to have students present their book to another class or leave it in the classroom or school office to share with new students.

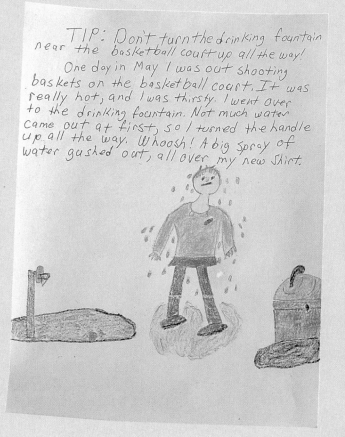

TIP: Don't turn the drinking fountain near the basketball court up all the way!
One day in May I was out shooting baskets on the basketball court. It was really hot, and I was thirsty. I went over to the drinking fountain. Not much water came out at first, so I turned the handle up all the way. Whoosh! A big spray of water gushed out, all over my new shirt.

Getting to Know You

Overview Students will prepare for a classroom guest, ask the guest questions about his or her job or career, and then write a career biography about that person.

OBJECTIVES

RELATED PAGES IN THE HANDBOOK

Functions
• Give Information

Learning Strategies
• Plan/Organize Information Graphically ....**KWL Chart Model,** page 80

Writing
• Biography..**Writing Model,** page 97

Language Patterns and Structures
•Past-Tense Verbs...**Instruction and Practice,** pages 190–191, pages 318–319

•Questions ....**Instruction and Practice,** pages 160–162, page 305

Concepts and Vocabulary
• Dates and Sequence Words

Warm-Up

Build Background Briefly share with students details about your life and career as a teacher. Encourage students to ask questions about your background.

Make a Class List Ask students what other jobs or careers they are curious about and record responses on the chalkboard. If students know people who work in those career areas, add their names to the list.

Explain the Project Goal Review the list with students, and then explain: *We are going to invite a person on this list to come in and talk to us about his or her life and job. We'll use what he or she says to write a true story about his or her experiences.*

Jobs
computer expert — Mr. Chung
banker
nurse —Ms. Raines
pilot
artist
astronaut
waitress — Mrs. Taylor
carpenter

Class List

Learn About Biographies

Discuss Characteristics Have students turn to the Biography on **Handbook** page 97. Use the annotations to introduce or review its characteristics. Ask students to point out examples of facts, dates, and sequence words as they discuss the biography.

Write Biographies

Prewriting

▶ **MATERIALS:** *KWL charts*

Arrange for a Guest Speaker Have students choose a person from the class list, and then arrange for him or her to visit the class. You may want to invite several different speakers over a period of months.

Start KWL Charts Before the guest's visit, model completing the *K* and *W* sections of a KWL chart like the one on **Handbook** page 80. Use level-appropriate strategies to help students begin their own charts.

Biography

A **biography** is the true story of a person's life. When you write a biography, you tell about the most important events and people in another person's life.

Circus Ponies
by María Izquierdo

A biography has **facts** that tell about the person and what he or she did.

It has **dates** and **sequence words** that tell when things happened.

María Izquierdo

María Izquierdo was born in 1902 in San Juan de los Lagos, Mexico. Her mother and father died when she was a child, so María lived with her grandmother and aunt. When she was a teenager, she married and moved to Mexico City.

In Mexico City, María attended art classes at the Academia de San Carlos. It was there that a famous Mexican painter, Diego Rivera, saw and liked her paintings. He helped her show them for the first time.

María became very famous for her paintings of the people and landscapes of Mexico and for her pictures of the circus. In 1929, she showed her paintings in New York City. She was the first Mexican woman to have an exhibit that included only her paintings. María painted for the rest of her life until her death in 1955.

Put It in Writing! 97

**Writing Model
Handbook page 97**

MULTI-LEVEL STRATEGIES

3 SPEECH EMERGENCE
Help students form and write W-H questions in their charts: *Do you want to know where Mrs. Taylor was born? We can write the question this way: Where were you born?* Have students write and then say the questions aloud.

4 5 INTERMEDIATE and ADVANCED FLUENCY/FLUENT
Pair up Level 4 students with Level 5s to write questions. You may want to have them look on **Handbook** pages 161–162 for help.

Interview the Guest
Invite students to ask the questions from the *W* columns of their charts and record key words or sentences from the guest's responses in the *L* columns. You may want to compile students' questions and give them to the guest ahead of time.

KWL Chart

Guest: Mrs. Taylor		
K What I Know	**W** What I Want to Know	**L** What I Learned
• She works hard. • She likes people. • She works at the Old Town Cafe.	• When were you born? Where were you born? • How long have you been a waitress? • Why did you become a waitress? • What is your day like?	• She was born in 1960 in Chicago, Illinois. • She started when she was about 23 right in her hometown. • She needed to earn some money for her family. Once she started, she really liked it a lot. • Her day is very busy. She gets to meet a lot of different people.

Drafting

▶ **MATERIALS:** *Practice Book page 137*

Demonstrate for students how to form sentences from the details on their KWL charts and write the details in time order:

| W
What I Want to Know | L
What I Learned |
|---|---|
| • When were you born? Where were you born?

• How long have you been a waitress? | • She was born in 1960 in Chicago, Illinois.

• She started when she was about 23 right in her hometown. |

> *Mrs. Taylor was born in 1960 in Chicago, Illinois. She started waiting on tables when she was twenty-three. Her first job was in her hometown of Chicago.*

Involve students in the drafting stage of the writing process in a way that reflects their proficiency levels.

MULTI-LEVEL STRATEGIES

3 SPEECH EMERGENCE
Students can use **Practice Book** page 137 as a writing frame for their drafts.

4 5 INTERMEDIATE and ADVANCED FLUENCY/FLUENT
Have these students review Drafting on **Handbook** page 88, and then use the information on their KWL charts to write their drafts.

Revising

▶ **MATERIALS:** *Practice Book page 138*

After students have finished their drafts, talk about ways to show time order and to check their writing for facts. Have them look on **Handbook** pages 89–91 for help with the revising steps of the writing process. Use level-appropriate strategies.

MULTI-LEVEL STRATEGIES

3 SPEECH EMERGENCE
Display **Practice Book** page 138 and model making revisions as you verbalize what you are doing. Circulate as students revise their drafts. Offer individual help as necessary.

4 INTERMEDIATE FLUENCY
Help students check the facts and choose sequence words they can use in revising their biographies. You may want to assign **Practice Book** page 138 as practice before students revise their drafts.

5 ADVANCED FLUENCY/FLUENT
Refer students to the peer conferencing guidelines on **Handbook** page 90. Have students read their drafts aloud to a partner and make revisions. You may also wish to assign **Practice Book** page 138 as practice for checking the facts and adding sequence words.

Proofreading

▶ **MATERIALS:** *Practice Book page 138*

Teach or review Past-Tense Verbs on **Handbook** pages 190–191. Past-tense verbs occur naturally in a biography and are the focus of the proofreading practice on **Practice Book** page 138.

Also, review the Proofreading Marks on **Handbook** page 92. Then use level-appropriate strategies as students proofread their biographies.

MULTI-LEVEL STRATEGIES

3 SPEECH EMERGENCE

Display **Practice Book** page 138. Correct the writing model as you verbalize: *The first sentence says "Tamara Lewis is born in 1958 in California." Is Tamara little now? No, she was little. When we tell about an action that happened in the past, we use a past-tense verb so we need to change the verb* is *to* was. Then assist students in proofreading their biographies.

4 INTERMEDIATE FLUENCY

Point out errors on **Practice Book** page 138 and guide students as they make corrections: *What verb tense do we use to tell about an action that already happened? That's right—the past tense. Change the verb* is *to* was *because this sentence is talking about an action that happened in the past.* Then have students proofread and correct their biographies.

5 ADVANCED FLUENCY/FLUENT

Have these students complete **Practice Book** page 138, and then proofread their biographies. Partners can check each other's work.

Publishing

▶ **MATERIALS:** *students' career biographies, large envelope and stamps (optional)*

Share Biographies Display students' final biographies and invite volunteers to read their biographies aloud to the class. You may want to have students present or mail all the biographies to the guest speaker along with a thank-you letter.

Learning About Mr. Chung

Meet Mr. Chung

Mr. Chung was born in Taiwan in 1952. He lived there until he finished high school. Then he moved to the United States and went to the University of Austin.

Mr. Chung started to learn English in the sixth grade. He took a special English course in college to help with science and computer words. After he finished college, he became a U. S. citizen.

Now Mr. Chung owns a business called Chung's Computer Services. He fixes computers. Mr. Chung likes his work very much.

What's Your Opinion?

Overview Students will brainstorm issues they are concerned about, and then write and mail a persuasive business letter to express their opinions.

OBJECTIVES

**RELATED PAGES
IN THE HANDBOOK**

Functions
• Persuade

Writing
• Persuasive Letter/Envelope.................................**Writing Models,** pages 118 and 119
• Persuasive Paragraph ....**Writing Model,** page 130
• Capitalization/Punctuation..................................**Instruction and Practice,** pages 205, 208–211,
                                                                     pages 323–327

Language Patterns and Structures
• Sentences..**Instruction and Practice,** pages 160–166,
                                                                     pages 305–307

Concepts and Vocabulary
• Persuasive/Opinion Words

Warm-Up

▶ **MATERIALS:** *butcher paper for web*

Build Background Talk with students about local issues you are concerned about. You might also read aloud several newspaper editorials to familiarize students with local issues and persuasive language.

Make a Class Web Have students brainstorm issues and write or draw details that characterize them.

Explain the Project Goal Review the class web with students, and then explain: *When you want something to be changed, you can write a letter to someone who can help make the change. You will write a letter to tell how you feel about something, why you feel that way, and what you want someone to do about the problem.*

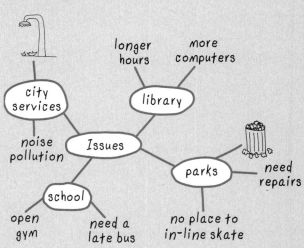

Class Web

Learn About Persuasive Business Letters

Discuss Characteristics Have students turn to the Persuasive Letter on **Handbook** page 118. Use the annotations to introduce or review its characteristics. Ask volunteers to describe the parts of a persuasive business letter. Follow the same procedure for the Envelope on **Handbook** page 119.

Write Persuasive Business Letters

Prewriting

Choose an Issue and an Audience After students review the class web, have them choose an issue that matters to them as the topic for their letters. Help them use the telephone directory or other resources to find the name and address of an appropriate person or group.

Think About the Issue Use level-appropriate strategies to help students list their opinions and reasons, and what they want someone to do.

Envelope
To send a letter, put it in an **envelope**.

Use **abbreviations** for the names of states. See page 205 for a complete list.

Write the **return address** at the top. That's your address.

Ann Gardner
2397 Casanova Street
Neptune Shores, FL 34744

Letters, continued

Sometimes you'll write a business letter to persuade someone to do something.

Persuasive Letter

349 Olympic Blvd.
Los Angeles, CA 90064
May 10, 2002

Parent and Teacher Association (PTA)
Valley School
562 North Cañon Drive
Los Angeles, CA 90064

Dear PTA Members:

Give your **opinion** in the first paragraph.

I think that the PTA should vote to keep a gym teacher for our school. I know that it costs more money to have a teacher who teaches only physical education, but I think it's worth it.

Next, give **reasons** for your opinion.

Most of the kids in my class love gym, and our teacher, Mrs. Richards, is really great. If Mrs. Richards doesn't teach us physical education, our homeroom teacher will have to, and he already has too much to do. Also, Mrs. Richards helps us learn how to work in a team and be good sports. Isn't that an important part of our education?

Finally, tell what action you want people to take.

We must have a gym teacher in our school. Please vote "yes" when you meet with the Valley School Board.

Use **opinion words** to tell how you feel. Other ways to begin an opinion are:
I feel that
I believe
My opinion is

Use **persuasive words** to get people to think the way you do.

Sincerely,
Andy Brown
Andy Brown

118 Put It in Writing!

**Writing Models
Handbook pages 118-119**

MULTI-LEVEL STRATEGIES

3 SPEECH EMERGENCE
Have these students draw the issue and a solution. Comment on the pictures and have students repeat the key words as you write captions: *The streetlights in this picture are broken* (write *broken streetlights*). *In this picture it looks like the streetlights work. Do you want someone to fix the streetlights?* (write *fix the streetlights*).

4 INTERMEDIATE FLUENCY
Ask questions to encourage students to elaborate on their issue as you record key words: *How can the city make the parks better? What do you want the Senator to do about the environment?*

5 ADVANCED FLUENCY/FLUENT
Have partners ask each other questions about their issue, reasons, and solutions and then collaborate on writing a list of key words.

Get Organized Students can use their key words to help them construct a chart.

Opinion	Reasons	Solution
Arroyo Grande library hours are too short on weekends	1. kids want more time to read books 2. parents work during week 3. need more time for research	keep it open until 5 P.M. on Saturday

Student Chart

85T

Drafting

▶ **MATERIALS:** *Practice Book page 139*

Demonstrate for students how to state an opinion, form sentences from the details in their charts, and write the sentences in a logical order. Before students begin their drafts, you may also wish to review the different kinds of sentences on **Handbook** pages 160–163 that they can use to get their ideas across.

Opinion	Reasons
Arroyo Grande library hours are too short on weekends	1. kids want more time to read books 2. parents work during week

Dear Friends of the Library:

The Arroyo Grande Library is only open until noon on Saturdays. In my opinion, the library's hours are too short on weekends.

Involve students in the drafting stage of the writing process in a way that reflects their proficiency levels.

MULTI-LEVEL STRATEGIES

3 SPEECH EMERGENCE
Students can use **Practice Book** page 139 as a writing frame for their drafts.

4 **5** INTERMEDIATE and ADVANCED FLUENCY/FLUENT
Have these students review Drafting on **Handbook** page 88, and then use their charts to write their drafts.

Revising

▶ **MATERIALS:** *Practice Book page 140*

After students have finished their drafts, talk about the ways they can revise their letters to clearly express their opinions and persuade someone to take action. Encourage students to look on **Handbook** pages 89–91 for help with the revising steps of the writing process. Use level-appropriate strategies.

MULTI-LEVEL STRATEGIES

3 SPEECH EMERGENCE
Display **Practice Book** page 140 and model making revisions as you verbalize what you are doing. Circulate as students revise their drafts. Offer individual help as necessary.

4 INTERMEDIATE FLUENCY
Talk about the persuasive words and other details in the letter on **Handbook** page 118 and the paragraph on page 130. Then help students choose words to use in revising their letters. Before students begin, you might assign **Practice Book** page 140 as practice for adding persuasive words and details.

5 ADVANCED FLUENCY/FLUENT
Refer students to the peer conferencing guidelines on **Handbook** page 90. Have partners read each other's drafts aloud and make suggestions for revisions. You may also wish to assign **Practice Book** page 140 as practice for adding persuasive words and details.

Proofreading

▶ **MATERIALS:** *Practice Book page 140*

Because business letters contain many special mechanics rules, teach or review capitalization, punctuation, and the use of abbreviations on **Handbook** pages 205 and 208–211. These elements are the focus of the proofreading practice on **Practice Book** page 140.

Also, review the Proofreading Marks on **Handbook** page 92. Then use level-appropriate strategies as students proofread their own letters.

MULTI-LEVEL STRATEGIES

3 SPEECH EMERGENCE
Display **Practice Book** page 140. Correct the writing model as you verbalize: *Here's the inside address. It shows an abbreviation for a state, but the a in Ca should be a capital letter. When you use abbreviations for states, use capital letters.* Then assist students in proofreading their letters.

4 INTERMEDIATE FLUENCY
Point out errors on **Practice Book** page 140 and guide students in making the corrections: *Where do you use a colon in a business letter? That's right—there should be a colon after the greeting. Change the comma to a colon.* Then have students proofread and correct their own letters.

5 ADVANCED FLUENCY/FLUENT
Have these students complete **Practice Book** page 140, and then proofread their persuasive business letters. Partners can check each other's work.

Publishing

▶ **MATERIALS:** *students' persuasive letters; stationery (optional); business-size envelopes and stamps, 1 per student*

Mail the Letters After students make final copies of their letters, have them address envelopes and mail the letters. Encourage students to share any responses they receive.

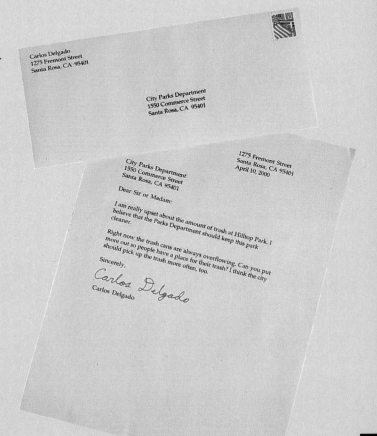

23 A Story About the Past

Overview Students will talk about historical periods, choose one event from a period, and then write a historical fiction story based on the event.

OBJECTIVES

RELATED PAGES IN THE HANDBOOK

Functions
- Tell an Original Story/Conduct Research

Learning Strategies
- Plan/Organize Information Graphically ....**Map for Rising/Falling Action Model,** page 75

Writing
- Historical Fiction......................................**Writing Model,** page 142
- Punctuation/Dialogue.................................**Instruction and Practice,** pages 208–213, pages 325–326

Language Patterns and Structures
- Plural Nouns..**Instruction and Practice,** pages 168–169, page 308

Concepts and Vocabulary
- Historical Figures and Events ....**Dateline U.S.A.,** pages 263–301

Warm-Up

▶ **MATERIALS:** *social studies or history books, butcher paper for web*

Build Background Have students follow along as you point out the different periods in history in **Dateline U.S.A.** on **Handbook** pages 263–301. You may want to focus on the periods and events your students are familiar with or are currently studying.

Make a Class Web Record historical periods, and then prompt students to name or describe specific events during each period.

Explain the Project Goal Review the class web, and then explain: *You'll choose an event from one time in history and find out what it was like to live during that time. You'll use the details you find to make up a story about the event.*

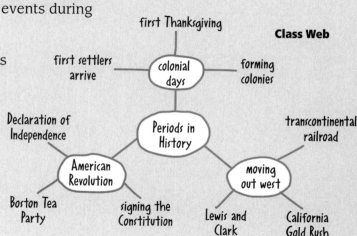

Class Web

Learn About Historical Fiction

Discuss Characteristics Have students turn to the Historical Fiction excerpt on **Handbook** page 142. Use the annotations to introduce or review its characteristics. Point out that it takes place during the American Revolution. You might also share and discuss with students other historical fiction stories like *Roses Sing on New Snow* by Paul Yee and Harvey Chan.

Write Historical Fiction

Prewriting

▶ **MATERIALS:** *social studies textbooks, encyclopedias, picture books about historical events, etc.*

Choose an Event Have students review the class web and choose an event to use as their topic.

Conduct Research Have students research their event. Help them make a list of details and name or describe people who lived during that time. Use strategies appropriate to students' proficiency levels.

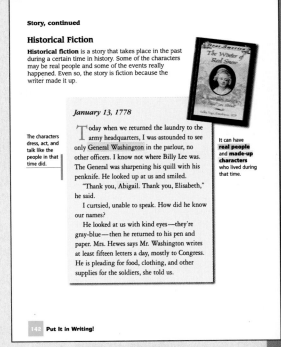

**Writing Model
Handbook page 142**

MULTI-LEVEL STRATEGIES

3 SPEECH EMERGENCE	**4** INTERMEDIATE FLUENCY	**5** ADVANCED FLUENCY/FLUENT
Have students find pictures in **Dateline U.S.A.** or in their social studies texts that show their event. Comment on the pictures as you record key words: *These look like Pilgrims* (write *Pilgrims*). *Look at their bonnets and long dresses* (write *bonnets and long dresses*).	Pair these students with a partner who has chosen the same event. Have them work together to each record details about the people who lived during that time and their way of life.	These students can follow The Research Process on **Handbook** pages 220–227 to help them locate and record details about their event.

Get Organized Students can use their key words to plan their story. They might make a story map like the one on **Handbook** page 75.

3. George signed the Constitution with a quill, then gave it to Ben Franklin.

2. George Washington told them about the Constitution.

4. Delegates went home.

1. Delegates came to Philadelphia.

5. States agreed to follow the rules.

Setting:
Independence Hall
Philadelphia, 1787

Characters:
George Washington, Ben Franklin, other delegates

Story Map

Drafting

▶ **MATERIALS:** *Practice Book page 141*

Demonstrate for students how to turn the details in their story map into a story with dialogue.

3. George signed the Constitution with a quill, then gave it to Ben Franklin.

2. George Washington told them about the Constitution.

4. Delegates went home.

1. Delegates came to Philadelphia.

5. States agreed to follow the rules.

Setting:
Independence Hall
Philadelphia, 1787

All the delegates had arrived in Philadelphia, some by foot and some by horseback or coach. George stood up.

"Hear, hear," he said. "Welcome to this historical event. I have in front of me a plan to help us organize our new country. It's called the Constitution."

Involve students in the drafting stage of the writing process in a way that reflects their proficiency levels.

MULTI-LEVEL STRATEGIES

3 SPEECH EMERGENCE
Students can use **Practice Book** page 141 as a writing frame for their drafts.

4 5 INTERMEDIATE and ADVANCED FLUENCY/FLUENT
Have these students review Drafting on **Handbook** page 88, and then use their story maps to write their drafts.

Revising

▶ **MATERIALS:** *Practice Book page 142*

After students have finished their drafts, talk about the ways they can revise their writing to include details about their time period to make it more realistic. Encourage students to look on **Handbook** pages 89–91 for help with the revising steps of the writing process. Use level-appropriate strategies.

MULTI-LEVEL STRATEGIES

3 SPEECH EMERGENCE
Display **Practice Book** page 142 and model replacing modern details with details more appropriate to the time period as you verbalize what you are doing. Circulate as students revise their drafts. Offer individual help as necessary.

4 INTERMEDIATE FLUENCY
Talk about the way that historical fiction uses real and accurate details to help the reader "see" and "feel" the time period. Help students choose details to make their stories more authentic. Before students revise their drafts, you may wish to assign **Practice Book** page 142 as practice for adding authentic details.

5 ADVANCED FLUENCY/FLUENT
Refer students to the peer conferencing guidelines on **Handbook** page 90. Have partners read each other's drafts aloud and make suggestions for revisions. You may also wish to assign **Practice Book** page 142 as practice for adding authentic details.

Proofreading

▶ **MATERIALS:** *Practice Book page 142*

Teach or review how to form plurals on **Handbook** pages 168–169, and how to use commas and quotation marks in dialogue on **Handbook** pages 209–213. These elements are the focus of the proofreading practice on **Practice Book** page 142.

Also, review the Proofreading Marks on **Handbook** page 92. Then use level-appropriate strategies as students proofread their own historical fiction stories.

MULTI-LEVEL STRATEGIES

3 SPEECH EMERGENCE
Display **Practice Book** page 142. Correct the writing model as you verbalize: *I know that someone is saying something because here's a quotation mark. Yes, it's Robert Smith who's talking. We need to add a quotation mark after the question mark to show where the speaker's exact words stop.* Then assist students in proofreading their stories.

4 INTERMEDIATE FLUENCY
Point out errors on **Practice Book** page 142 and guide students in making the corrections: *If a noun ends with x what do you do to make it tell about more than one? That's right—add -es. Change* tax *to* taxes *to make the noun plural.* Then have students proofread their own stories.

5 ADVANCED FLUENCY/FLUENT
Have these students complete **Practice Book** page 142, and then proofread their stories. Partners can check each other's work.

Publishing

▶ **MATERIALS:** *students' historical fiction stories, props (optional)*

Share Stories After students have written their final copies, call on volunteers to share their stories in an Author's Chair. Students may want to use props or dress as a person who lived during that time. You might also want to invite small groups to choose one of their stories to act out for the class.

> It was 1848 in the hills of California. Gus and I stopped by a stream to look for gold. I was taking out my metal pan from the saddlebags on my horse when I heard Gus shout.
>
> "Yippee! I think we've found gold. Look at that gold nugget shining there in the water," he said.

My Next Question Is . . .

Overview Students will plan and conduct an interview with a community volunteer, and then write a report based on the interview.

OBJECTIVES

**RELATED PAGES
IN THE HANDBOOK**

Functions
• Listen Actively/Ask for Information

Learning Strategies
• Gather Information/Take Notes

Writing
• Interview ....**Process and Writing Model,** pages 110–111
• Questions and Answers ....**Instruction and Practice,** pages 160–162,
pages 305–306

• Sentence Punctuation/Quotation Marks ....**Instruction and Practice,** pages 208, 213,
pages 325, 327

Language Patterns and Structures
• Present-Tense Verbs ....**Instruction and Practice,** pages 188–189,
pages 317–318

Warm-Up

▶ **MATERIALS:** *local newspaper, telephone directory, butcher paper for chart*

Build Background Ask students if they know anyone who does special things for their neighborhood or community. Name some volunteer agencies and adults or students you know who do volunteer work, and discuss the roles of volunteers.

Make a Class Chart Record the names of community volunteers, what they do, and organizations they support.

Explain the Project Goal Review the class chart with students, and then explain: *You can help others learn how these volunteers make our community a better place. First you'll choose a volunteer and write questions to ask him or her. Then you'll meet with the person and ask your questions. You'll use what you find out to write a report that we'll put in a book to keep in the library.*

Class Chart

Name	Job/Service	Organization
John Rey	sings and plays guitar	Harbor View Convalescent Home
Mrs. Cortez	delivers meals to seniors	Meals on Wheels
Ms. Johnson	builds houses	Habitat for Humanity
Diane Hollis	helps with animals	Humane Society

Learn About Interviews

Discuss Characteristics Have students turn to the Interview process on **Handbook** pages 110–111. Use the annotations to introduce or review the interview process and how to share the results. Encourage volunteers to tell when the questions are written (before the interview) and how the answers are written (using the person's exact words).

Conduct Interviews and Write Reports

Prewriting

▶ **MATERIALS:** *tape recorder (optional)*

Choose Volunteers Have partners choose a volunteer from the class chart to interview. Make a list to ensure each pair interviews a different volunteer.

Arrange for Interviews Schedule interviews with the volunteer one at a time over a period of weeks, or have an "interview day" in which all the interviews take place on the same day.

Make a List of Questions Review how to form questions on **Handbook** pages 161–162. Then use level-appropriate strategies to involve all students in writing questions.

❸ **Share the results of the interview.**
- Look over your notes and listen to the tape.
- Choose the information you want to share.
- Decide how you want to share it. You might write an editorial, a description, or an article like this one.

Interview

A good way to find out more about someone is to conduct, or set up, an **interview**. An interview is a meeting where one person asks another person questions to get information.

❶ **Prepare for the interview.**
- Read any information you can find about the person you want to interview.
- Call or write the person to plan a time when the two of you can meet.
- Make a list of questions that you want to ask.

Questions to ask Wynton Marsalis

How old were you when you started playing the trumpet?

How did you feel about practicing when you were a kid?

❷ **Conduct the interview.**
- Be sure you have your questions, a pencil, and some paper to make any notes. Try to have a tape recorder with you. You can play the tape later to help you remember what was said.
- Greet the person you are interviewing.
- Ask the questions you planned and others that come up during the interview.
- Thank the person when you are done.

110 **Put It in Writing!**

**Writing Models
Handbook pages 110–111**

MULTI-LEVEL STRATEGIES

3 SPEECH EMERGENCE
Suggest questions students can ask the volunteer: *How many hours a week do you volunteer? Is it hard work? What do you like best about it?* Encourage students to copy the questions and read them aloud.

4 INTERMEDIATE FLUENCY
Assist as necessary while students make a list. Remind them to start questions with *who, what, when, where, why* , and *how.*

5 ADVANCED FLUENCY/FLUENT
These students can complete their lists independently, and then assist Level 3 or 4 students.

Conduct Interviews and Take Notes Have partners ask their questions and record the answers. Some students may want to record the interview. Remind students to thank the person when they are done.

Questions to Ask John Rey

What kind of volunteer work do you do at the Harbor View Convalescent Home?

   play guitar and sing

How often do you go there?

   at least once a week

What do you like about your work?

   "I love to sing, and it makes me feel good to know that my music makes other people happy, too."

Drafting

▶ **MATERIALS:** *Practice Book page 143*

Demonstrate for students how to use their notes from the interview to write a report in a Q and A format or in paragraph form.

> Questions to Ask John Rey
>
> What kind of volunteer work do you do at the Harbor View Convalescent Home?
>
>   play guitar and sing
>
> How often do you go there?
>
>   at least once a week

> In Tune with John Rey
>
>   Singing and playing guitar is what John Rey loves to do. He shares his love of music with people recovering from illnesses at the Harbor View Convalescent Home.

Involve students in the drafting stage of the writing process in a way that reflects their proficiency levels.

MULTI-LEVEL STRATEGIES

3 SPEECH EMERGENCE

Students can use **Practice Book** page 143 as a writing frame for their drafts.

4 5 INTERMEDIATE and ADVANCED FLUENCY/FLUENT

These students can review Drafting on **Handbook** page 88, and then use their notes to write their drafts. After they finish, they can assist Level 3 students.

Revising

▶ **MATERIALS:** *Practice Book page 144*

After students have finished their drafts, talk about how they can revise their reports to accurately present the questions asked and facts given by the person interviewed. Encourage students to look on pages 89–91 of the **Handbook** for help with the revising steps of the writing process. Use level-appropriate strategies.

MULTI-LEVEL STRATEGIES

3 SPEECH EMERGENCE

Display **Practice Book** page 144 and model making revisions as you verbalize what you are doing. Circulate as students work with partners to revise their drafts. Offer individual help as necessary.

4 INTERMEDIATE FLUENCY

Ask students questions about their reports to help them focus on the accuracy of the details: *Is this the question you asked John Rey? What was his answer? Does this show exactly what he said?* Before students revise their reports, you may wish to assign **Practice Book** page 144.

5 ADVANCED FLUENCY/FLUENT

Refer students to the peer conferencing guidelines on **Handbook** page 90. Have partners collaborate with another pair of students to read and discuss their drafts and suggest revisions. You might assign **Practice Book** page 144 as practice before they begin.

Proofreading

▶ **MATERIALS:** *Practice Book page 144*

Teach or review Present-Tense Verbs on **Handbook** pages 188–189 and the use of quotation marks and end punctuation on **Handbook** pages 208 and 213. These elements are the focus of the proofreading practice on **Practice Book** page 144.

Also, review the Proofreading Marks on **Handbook** page 92. Then use level-appropriate strategies as students proofread their reports.

MULTI-LEVEL STRATEGIES

3 SPEECH EMERGENCE
Display **Practice Book** page 144. Correct the writing model as you verbalize: *Here it says "Why do you volunteer." This sentence sounds like a question, not a statement. We need to change the period to a question mark.* Then assist students in proofreading their reports.

4 INTERMEDIATE FLUENCY
Point out errors on **Practice Book** page 144. Guide students in making corrections: *Does this sentence talk about something that happens all the time? Yes, it does. We need to change* volunteered *to the present-tense verb* volunteers. Then have students proofread and correct their reports.

5 ADVANCED FLUENCY/FLUENT
You may want to have these students complete **Practice Book** page 144, and then proofread their own reports. When they are done, encourage students to assist Level 3 and 4 students.

Publishing

▶ **MATERIALS:** *students' reports, presentation binder*

Share Reports Have partners share the results of their interview and their reports with the class, encouraging the class to ask them questions about the volunteer and his or her work.

Make a Book Volunteers can make a cover page and a table of contents, and then assemble all of the reports in a presentation binder. Present a copy of the book to the school media center or the community library. You might also wish to submit some or all of the reports to the editor of the local newspaper's lifestyle section.

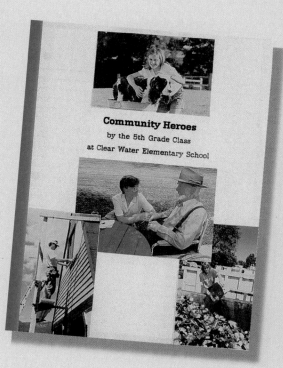

Community Heroes
by the 5th Grade Class
at Clear Water Elementary School

Curriculum Consultants

Nancy Alexander   Kristi Lichtenberg   Ellie Paiewonsky

Elizabeth Buckley   Lourdes Lopez   Wilma Ramírez

HAMPTON-BROWN

About the Curriculum Consultants

Nancy Alexander
ESL Teacher, Grades 6, 7, 8
Nichols Middle School
Community Consolidated SD 65
Evanston, Illinois

Elizabeth M. Buckley
ESL Teacher, Grades K–8
Lincoln, Emerson, Whittier,
Mann Schools
Oak Park SD 97
Oak Park, Illinois

Kristi M. Lichtenberg
Bilingual 3rd Grade Teacher
Williams Elementary School
Garland ISD
Garland, Texas

Lourdes A. Lopez
ESOL Grade 3 Teacher
Citrus Grove Elementary School
Miami-Dade County Public Schools
Miami, Florida

Ellie Paiewonsky
Director, Nassau BOCES BETAC
Bilingual/ESL Technical
Assistance Center
Seaford, New York

Wilma Ramírez
Instructional Coach for
Curriculum-Based ELD
Alisal Community and Chavez
Elementary Schools/Alisal USD
Salinas, California

Hampton-Brown
P.O. Box 223220
Carmel, California 93922
(800) 333-3510

Printed in the United States of America
Softbound: 0-7362-0192-0
Casebound: 0-7362-0894-1
99 00 01 02 03 04 9 8 7 6 5 4 3 2

ACKNOWLEDGMENTS

Every effort has been made to secure permission, but if any omissions have been made, please let us know. We gratefully acknowledge permission to reprint the following material:

Alphabet Font Copyright © 1996 Zaner-Bloser
p71, From CINDER-ELLY by Frances Minters. Copyright © 1994 by Frances Minters, text. Used by permission of Viking Penguin, a division of Penguin Putnam Inc.
p72, RICHIE'S ROCKET by Joan Anderson. Illustrations by George Ancona. Text Copyright © 1993 by Joan Anderson. Illustrations Copyright © 1993 by George Ancona. Used by permission of Morrow Jr. Books, a division of William Morrow & Company, Inc.
p73, Cover illustration from SUBWAY SPARROW by Leyla Torres. Copyright © 1993 by Leyla Torres. Reprinted by permission of Farrar, Straus & Giroux, Inc.
pp76–77, From TOAD IS THE UNCLE OF HEAVEN by Jeanne M. Lee, © 1985 by Jeanne M. Lee. Reprinted by permission of Henry Holt and Company, Inc.
p94, Courtesy of Pleasant Company Publications
p97, Used by permission of Galeria de ArteMexicano.
p98, Cover, from THE LOST LAKE by Allen Say.

Copyright © 1989 by Allen Say. Reprinted by permission of Houghton Mifflin Co. All rights reserved.
pp99 and **105**, Extensive unsuccessful attempts were made to contact the copyright holder of these works.
pp99, **11**, and **135** Copyright © 1997 by Highlights for Children, Inc., Columbus, Ohio.
p113, Adapted excerpt from THE INNER WORLD OF THE IMMIGRANT CHILD (p89) by Christina Igoa, 1995. New York: St. Martin's Press. Copyright 1995 by St. Martin's Press, Inc. Adapted by permission of Lawrence Erlbaum Assoc., Inc.
p115, Copyright 1998 American Online, Inc. All Rights Reserved.
p124, Reprinted with permission of the publisher, Children's Book Press, San Francisco, CA.
p136, From SNAKE POEMS by Francisco Alarcón. © 1992. Published by Chronicle Books, San Francisco.
p137, "Today is Very Boring" from THE NEW KID ON THE BLOCK by Jack Prelutsky. Copyright © 1984 by Jack Prelutsky. By permission of Greenwillow Books, a division of William Morrow & Company, Inc.
p142, Adapted from DEAR AMERICA: THE WINTER OF RED SNOW, THE REVOLUTIONARY WAR DIARY OF ABIGAIL STEWART VALLEY

FORGE PENNSYLVANIA, 1977 by Kristiana Gregory. Copyright © by Kristiana Gregory. Reprinted by permission Scholastic Inc. DEAR AMERICA is a trademark of Scholastic Inc.
p143, Excerpt from JUMANJI by Chris Van Allsburg. Copyright © 1981 by Chris Van Allsburg. Reprinted by permission of Houghton Mifflin Co. All rights reserved.
p144, © 1997 Time Inc. Reprinted by permission. Photo from Reuters/Stringer/ Archive Photos.
p146, From PAUL BUNYAN by Steven Kellogg. Copyright © 1984 by Steven Kellogg by permission of Morrow Jr. Books, a division of William Morrow and Company, Inc.
p194, "Icy", from STORIES TO BEGIN ON by Rhoda W. Bacmeister. Copyright 1940 by E.P. Dutton, renewed © 1968 by Rhoda W. Bacmeister. Used by permission of Dutton Children's Books, a division of Penguin Putnam Inc.
pp218, **222**, and **247**, Map © 1998 by Rand McNally R.L. #98-S-90.
pp218, **223**, **225**, and **244–245**, Reprinted with permission from THE WORLD ALMANAC FOR KIDS 1998. Copyright © 1997 PRIMEDIA Reference Inc. All rights reserved.

Acknowledgments continued on pages 335–336.

Welcome!

In this book, you'll find all kinds of ways to communicate what you're thinking, feeling, and imagining. You can use this book to find out just what you want to know about words and writing. You'll learn how to organize your ideas and how English works. You can also learn how to do research—not just in the library, but on the Internet, too! At the back, you'll find fascinating facts about life in the U.S.A.

Whenever you have a question about English, you can look here first. This book will put **English At Your Command!**

Table of Contents

Chapter 2
Picture It!

Chapter 3
Put It in Writing!

The Good Writer Guide

Chapter 4
Grammar Made Graphic 158

Chapter 5
Look It Up!

Chapter 1

Just the Right Word

shiny

spectacular

hundreds

enormous

like gold

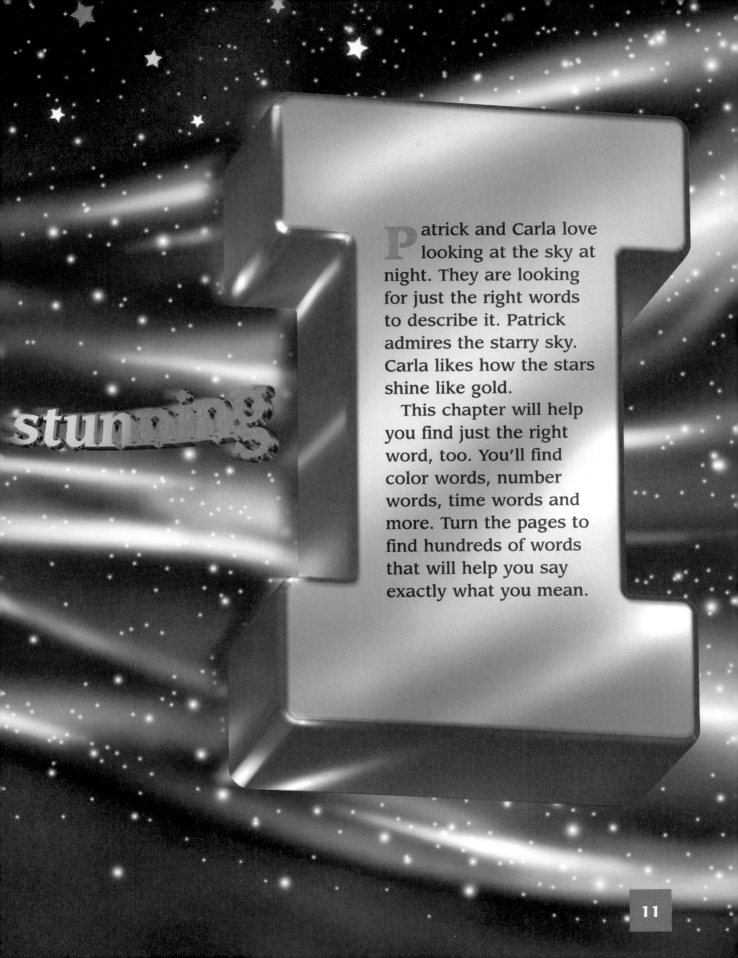

stunning

Patrick and Carla love looking at the sky at night. They are looking for just the right words to describe it. Patrick admires the starry sky. Carla likes how the stars shine like gold.

This chapter will help you find just the right word, too. You'll find color words, number words, time words and more. Turn the pages to find hundreds of words that will help you say exactly what you mean.

Describing Words

Some **describing words** tell what something is like. Others tell how many, how you or someone else feels, or where something is.

Teach:
Read aloud the introduction as you create this cluster:

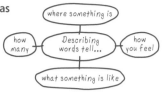

Then describe the mask and add the following words to the cluster: *colorful, 2 eyes and thirteen teeth, scared, in our books.*

Color Words

● red	● blue
● pink	● turquoise
● crimson	● teal
● purple	● royal blue
● lavender	● sky blue
● maroon	● navy blue
	● green
	● lime green
	● forest green
	● emerald green
	● yellow
	● gold
	● orange
	● brown
	● tan
	● black
	● gray
	● silver
	○ white

This cat mask has **red** lips and **white** teeth.

Color Words Practice:

3 Point to the cat mask and read aloud the caption. Have students use the sentence pattern to describe the mask or dolls on page 12 and classroom objects.

4 Use a prism to create a color spectrum on the wall or display a picture of a rainbow. Ask students to describe the color bands from top to bottom or bottom to top.

5 Have students look at the pictures on pages 64, 97, and 120; choose one; and write a descriptive paragraph that includes the colors of the objects. Students can find an example of a descriptive paragraph on page 101.

Size Words

small

medium

large

 Synonyms on pages 33 and 35 to find more size words.

Shape Words

 This is a **circle**.
The clock has a **circular** shape.
It has a **round** face.

This is a **square**.
The window is **square**.

Here is a **rectangle**.
The gift box is **rectangular**.

This is a **triangle**.
The hanger has a **triangular** shape.

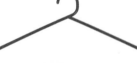

This is a **star**.
This starfish has a **star-like** shape.

This is an **oval**.
An egg has an **oval** shape.

Here is a **line**.
This line is **straight**. ———
This line is **curved**. ⌒

 The sign has a **diamond** shape.

Size Words Practice:

3 Display three erasers, pencils, or pieces of chalk in different sizes. Have students arrange the objects in order from small to large as they say the size words.

4 Have each student draw an object or animal in three sizes: small, medium, and large. Then have partners exchange pictures and write captions using complete sentences: *This is a small dog. This is a medium dog. This is a large dog.*

5 Have each student in a group name from three to five animals. Then the group can draw, label, and display a chart of all the animals, categorizing them by size: small, medium, and large. Students can refer to page 78 for a model of a chart.

Shape Words Practice:

3 Have students point to appropriate pictures on the page in response to your prompts: *Show me something that is square.* As students point to the picture, encourage them to repeat the shape word, and then name something else that has the shape.

4 Encourage partners to take turns asking and answering questions about the shapes. Have one student secretly choose an object and ask a question: *What shape does the hanger have?* Have the partner use a complete sentence to answer: *The hanger is triangular.*

5 Ask partners to create a floor plan for their classroom using different shapes to represent the furniture, display areas, and so on. Students can find an example of a floor plan on page 65. Show students how to make a key showing what each shape represents. Then have them display the floor plan and key, and describe them.

➤ Practice Book page 3

Describing Words, continued

Number Words

0	zero	**26**	twenty-six
1	one	**27**	twenty-seven
2	two	**28**	twenty-eight
3	three	**29**	twenty-nine
4	four	**30**	thirty
5	five	**40**	forty
6	six	**50**	fifty
7	seven	**60**	sixty
8	eight	**70**	seventy
9	nine	**80**	eighty
10	ten	**90**	ninety
11	eleven	**100**	one hundred
12	twelve	**500**	five hundred
13	thirteen	**1,000**	one thousand
14	fourteen	**5,000**	five thousand
15	fifteen	**10,000**	ten thousand
16	sixteen	**100,000**	one hundred thousand
17	seventeen	**500,000**	five hundred thousand
18	eighteen	**1,000,000**	one million
19	nineteen		
20	twenty		
21	twenty-one		
22	twenty-two		
23	twenty-three		
24	twenty-four		
25	twenty-five		

Number Words Practice:
3 Give word cards to one student and numeral cards to a partner. Have pairs match words to numerals by playing a variation of "Go Fish."
4 Give teams 15 minutes to write sentences that use number words and describe the class or classroom: *There are twenty-one students in our class. There are two computers*. The team with the most correct sentences wins.
5 Have partners estimate the number of students in their school. Encourage them to write a paragraph explaining the results and how they came up with the total.

➤ **Practice Book page 4**

She came in **first** to win the race.

14

Order Words

1st	first
2nd	second
3rd	third
4th	fourth
5th	fifth
6th	sixth
7th	seventh
8th	eighth
9th	ninth
10th	tenth
11th	eleventh
12th	twelfth
13th	thirteenth
14th	fourteenth
15th	fifteenth
16th	sixteenth
17th	seventeenth
18th	eighteenth
19th	nineteenth
20th	twentieth
21st	twenty-first
22nd	twenty-second
23rd	twenty-third
24th	twenty-fourth
25th	twenty-fifth
26th	twenty-sixth
27th	twenty-seventh
28th	twenty-eighth
29th	twenty-ninth
30th	thirtieth
40th	fortieth
50th	fiftieth
60th	sixtieth
70th	seventieth
80th	eightieth
90th	ninetieth
100th	one hundredth

More Words That Tell How Many

a **pair** of eggs

a **couple** of eggs

a **few** eggs

several eggs

some eggs

a **lot** of eggs

many eggs

Order Words Practice:

3 Line up a group of objects like pencils or books. Give students directions using ordinals: *Pick up the fifth book.* As students carry out the instruction have them confirm the choice by saying: *This is the fifth book.*

4 Have each student interview at least five classmates to find out their birthdates and record the results. Students can then use complete sentences to share the results with the class.

5 Have students choose a president from the list on page 265. They can then use order words to describe the details about him: *President Clinton is the forty-second president. He began his term in nineteen-hundred and ninety-three.*

all the eggs

More Words That Tell How Many Practice:

3 Give one student manipulatives like pencils or paper clips. Have the partner use indefinite number words to request an amount: *Give me a few pencils. Give me a lot of pencils.* Students can switch roles and repeat.

4 Have groups create their own version of the list on page 15. After brainstorming what they want to draw, students can create a poster that shows a picture and a caption for each word.

5 Have students use indefinite number words to describe their favorite daily meals: *For breakfast, I like to eat a couple of eggs, some toast, and a glass of milk.*

▶ **Practice Book page 5**

Describing Words, continued

Sensory Words

Look at the **red** apples.

An apple has **smooth** skin.

How It Looks

beautiful sunset

dark shadow

fluffy clouds

gloomy day

red pepper

round ball

shiny medal

tiny ants

How It Feels

bumpy road

dry chalk

hard rock

hot soup

rough wood

slimy worm

smooth grapes

soft cotton

3 Speech Emergence **4** Intermediate Fluency **5** Advanced Fluency/Fluent

It has a **fresh** smell.

It sounds **crisp**.

The apple tastes **delicious**!

How It Smells

fragrant rose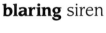

fresh pepper

rotten garbage

musty closet

sweet perfume

Sensory Words Practice:
3 Bring in objects like a red pepper, soft cotton balls, and so on. Have students point to and describe each object using appropriate sensory words.
4 Have partners use the sense and sensory words to ask and answer each other's questions about the objects on the page: *How does a worm feel? It feels slimy.*
5 Have partners talk about the menu on page 120. Ask one student to choose a meal and use sensory words to persuade the partner to order it. Have the partner persuade the first student <u>not</u> to order it. Have students reverse roles and repeat for a different meal.

How It Sounds

blaring siren

crisp celery

crunchy carrot

loud drums

noisy music

quiet footsteps

soft whisper

How It Tastes

bitter herb

delicious food

fresh vegetables

salty pretzel

sour lemon

spicy mustard

sweet cake

tangy orange

Describing Words, continued

Feeling Words

Feeling Words Practice:

3 Give partners word cards with feeling words. Have one student pick a card and act out the feeling while the partner guesses the word. Students reverse roles and repeat.

4 Have students choose a feeling word and write a journal entry like the one on page 113 that tells about a time they felt that way.

5 Have students elaborate on why the boy is afraid, sad, angry, and happy. Then have them choose synonyms from pages 33, 35, and 36 for those words and write new captions for the photos.

▶ **Practice Book page 7**

Jason is **afraid** of the bee.

Is Jason **bored**?

Jason is **sad**.

Jason is **angry**.

He's **puzzled**.

What is Jason **happy** about?

Jason is **surprised**.

Words That Tell Where

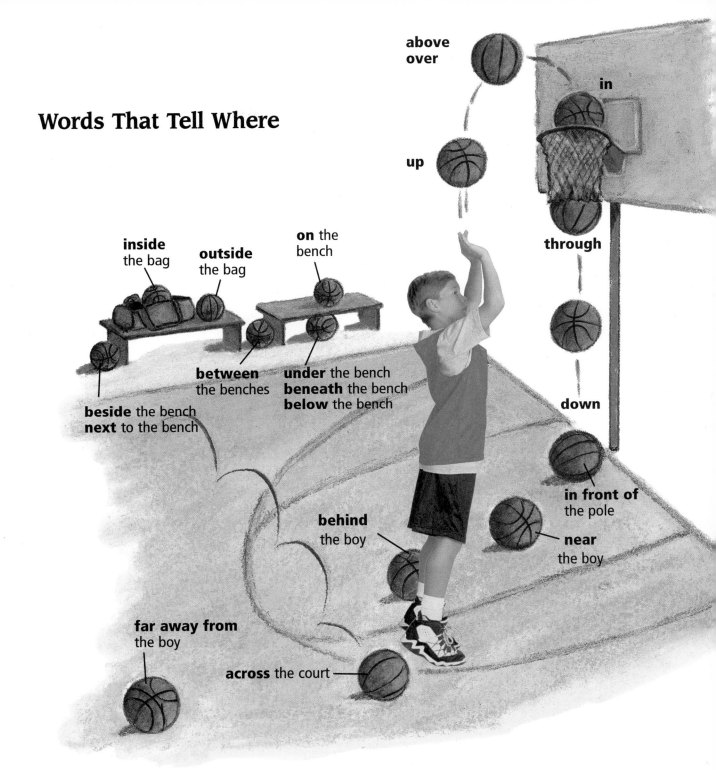

above
over

in

up

through

inside
the bag

outside
the bag

on the
bench

down

between
the benches

under the bench
beneath the bench
below the bench

beside the bench
next to the bench

in front of
the pole

behind
the boy

near
the boy

far away from
the boy

across the court

Words That Tell Where Practice:

3 Duplicate the basketball scene with a real ball, bag, bench, and improvised basket (perhaps a student with arms forming a circle). Have partners give and follow each other's directions: *Hold the ball over the basket, in front of the bench*, and so on.

4 Have students brainstorm action verbs that describe the movement of a basketball such as *bounce, hit, roll*. Then ask them to use the verbs and "words that tell where" to write complete sentences: *The basketball bounces across the court. It rolls near the boy.*

5 Ask partners to describe the scene as you elaborate on how the game of basketball is played. Then ask students to write a script for a sportscast of the scene. Have one student role-play the player while the partner announces the scene for the class.

▶ **Practice Book page 8**

Greetings and Good-byes

There are many ways to say **hello** and **good-bye.** When you say hello and good-bye to your friends, you can be informal. When you say hello and good-bye to teachers and other adults, you need to be formal.

Teach:
With a volunteer, role-play greeting someone and saying good-bye. Then read aloud the paragraph. Talk about each photograph, then read aloud the list of hellos and good-byes. Point out the differences between formal and informal language.

Informal

Formal

Hello

Hi!
Hi, there!
Hello, there!
Hey!
Howdy!
How's it going?
What's up?
What's new?
What's happening?

Good-bye

Bye!
Bye-bye!
See you later!
See you later, alligator.
So long!
Take care!
Take it easy!

Greetings and Good-byes Practice:
3 Have partners role-play greeting and saying good-bye to each other, using the informal greetings. Then have them try out the formal greetings as they role-play greeting and saying good-bye to you.
4 Give examples of times when you use formal language such as at doctor's office and informal language such as talking on the telephone with a friend. Then describe a situation and have students choose and say an appropriate greeting and good-bye from the lists.
5 Have partners write the names of friends, teachers, and adults they know on cards. Have them each take a card, then make up a conversation the two people might have. Remind students to begin and end the conversation with appropriate greetings and good-byes.

Hello

Good morning!
Good afternoon!
Good evening!
How are you?
It's nice to see you.

Good-bye

It was nice talking to you.
Good night!
Good-bye!
Have a good day.
I hope you have a good afternoon.
It was good to see you.

3 Speech Emergence **4** Intermediate Fluency **5** Advanced Fluency/Fluent

Multiple-Meaning Words

Multiple-meaning words look the same but have different meanings. They can have two or more different meanings.

Teach:
Read aloud the introduction and work through the entries on page 21 to illustrate the concept. Depending on the proficiency levels of your students, plan to introduce one, a few, or a group of multiple-meaning words each day or week.

address

noun
1. My **address** is 231 South Elm Street.

verb
2. The speaker will give a report today.
He will **address** the group.

bark

noun
1. A dog makes a short, loud sound called a **bark**.

noun
2. Bark covers the outside of a tree trunk.

You may wish to:
- assign a multiple-meaning word to each student who can teach it to the rest of the class.
- have a multiple-meaning word contest in which teams alternate explaining the different meanings of a given word.
- display a multiple-meaning word and its part of speech each day and have partners write as many sentences as they can using that meaning.

bat

noun
1. Use a **bat** to hit a baseball.

noun
2. A **bat** is a small, flying animal.

country

noun
1. The United States of America is a big **country**.

noun
2. Farms are found in the **country**.

Multiple-Meaning Words, continued

current

adjective
1. When something is **current**, it is happening now.

noun
2. Strong winds and the ocean **current** moved the sailboat farther out to sea.

directions

noun
1. The **directions** on a test tell you what to do to answer the questions.

> Directions:
> Please fill in the space next to the correct answer.

noun
2. The **directions** on a map are north, south, east, and west.

fair

noun
1. A **fair** is a place that has rides and games.

adjective
2. You're being **fair** if you treat everyone the same way.

adjective
3. When the weather is clear and sunny, it's **fair**.

fan

noun
1. They love sports. They are sports **fans**.

noun
2. Turn on the **fan** to make the air move.

float

noun
1. Our **float** for the parade was colorful.

verb
2. An inner tube can **float** in water.

foot

noun
1. Put the shoe on your **foot**.

noun
2. A **foot** is 12 inches long.

ground

noun
1. The corn is growing in the **ground**.

adjective
1. Use **ground** corn to make tortillas.

jam

noun
1. Jam is a sweet food. It is made with fruit and sugar.

verb
2. I tried to **jam** too many clothes into my small suitcase.

key

noun
1. Press the delete **key** to erase a word.

noun
2. You need a **key** to open the lock.

Multiple-Meaning Words Practice:
3 Read aloud the entries that have a picture for each meaning. After you read each meaning, have students point to the picture that shows the meaning. Then make up a new sentence using each meaning and have students point to the correct picture.
4 Have one student pantomime one of the meanings for a word for a partner to guess. For a correct answer, the partner must name the word, tell its part of speech, and say the meaning.
5 Copy an entry on a large sheet of paper, leaving space between each numbered meaning for additional sentences. Have partners discuss the different meanings of the word. Then ask each student to write a new sentence for each meaning. Repeat for two more entries.

Multiple-Meaning Words, continued

last

adjective
1. The person at the end of the line is **last**.

verb
2. If you take good care of something, it will **last** a long time.

left

verb
1. He is not here. He has **left** the room.

adjective
2. Part of the cookie is **left**.

adjective
3. She wore a ring on her **left** hand.

Multiple-Meaning Words Practice:
3 Draw a word web on the chalkboard, writing a multiple-meaning word in the center. Say the word and have students locate the entry on the page. Call on different students to add to the web by drawing pictures to show the word's different meanings. Repeat for other words.
4 Play "I Spy" with groups. Choose a word and give students clues: *I spy a word that has three meanings. It can be a noun that means a place where people work. What word is it?*
5 Make a set of cards with one word and a part of speech on each card. Have students in a group take turns drawing a card, reading the word and its part of speech, and then using the correct meaning of the word in a sentence. You may want to review the definitions of nouns, adjectives, and verbs on pages 167, 180, and 186 before students begin.

➜ **Practice Book page 9**

letter

noun
1. My friend wrote me a **letter**.

noun
2. The first **letter** in the English alphabet is <u>A</u>.

light

Aa Bb Cc

adjective
1. Something that is not heavy is **light**.

noun
2. Turn on the **light** so you can see.

miss

verb
1. When my mother is gone, I **miss** her.

verb
2. When you don't hit your target, you **miss** it.

noun
3. She is called **Miss** Kratky because she is not married.

pen

noun
1. A **pen** is a fenced-in area for animals.

noun
2. You can write a letter with a **pen**.

pitcher

noun
1. The **pitcher** is a baseball player who throws the ball to a catcher.

noun
2. Mix the juice in a **pitcher**. Then pour some into a glass.

plant

noun
1. My dad works at the **plant**.

noun
2. A tree is one kind of green **plant**.

verb
3. Plant tomato seeds two inches apart.

Multiple-Meaning Words, continued

point

verb
1. Point to the place on the map.

A

noun
2. A **point** is a dot on a line.

noun
3. She made a good **point** in the debate.

pupil

pupil

noun
1. The **pupil** is the center part of the eye.

noun
2. Another word for *student* is **pupil**.

pound

noun
1. The vegetables weigh one **pound**.

verb
2. Use a hammer to **pound** a nail into wood.

ring

noun
1. A **ring** is a piece of jewelry. You wear it on your finger.

verb
2. When you hear the telephone **ring**, someone is calling you.

noun
3. Draw a **ring**, or a circle, around the answer.

Multiple-Meaning Words Practice:

3 Make picture cards for *bat, key, letter, pen,* and *table* and distribute to students. Say a word and read the sentence for one meaning aloud. Have the student with the picture for that meaning hold up the card and repeat the sentence. Continue until all the cards have been shown.

4 Have partners choose several words that have two meanings. Encourage them to write one sentence for each word, using the word twice to show each meaning:
*I heard him **state** that he was from the **state** of Illinois.*

5 Have each student use a dictionary to look up three of the words and write their definitions. Refer students to pages 250–253 for how to use a dictionary.

➤ **Practice Book page 10**

scale

noun
1. You can use a **scale** to find out how much something weighs.

noun
2. A map **scale** shows how many inches on the map are equal to real miles.

noun
3. Each **scale** on a fish's body is thin and flat.

space

noun
1. Words in a sentence are separated by a blank **space**.

noun
2. An astronaut works in outer **space**.

state

noun
1. Illinois is a **state** in the United States.

verb
2. I heard him **state** that he wanted to go to Illinois.

table

noun
1. I use a multiplication **table** in math class.

$$3 \times 1 = 3$$
$$3 \times 2 = 6$$

noun
2. We put our food on the **table**.

Similes

A **simile** compares one thing to another. Sometimes it uses the word *as*. Other times it uses the word *like*.

Similes Practice:
3 Read each sentence aloud, pausing to have students say the simile to complete the sentence. They can then copy the sentences changing the subject to something else for which the simile is appropriate. For example: *The glass was as cold as ice.*
4 Display sets of three incomplete sentences. Have students use the photographs and pictures to write the describing word and the simile: *His hands were* (cold). *Ice is* (cold). *His hands were* (as cold as ice).

1. His hands were **as cold as ice**.

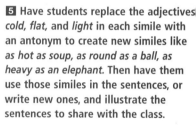

2. Dad's hat is **as flat as a pancake**.

3. My sister can sing **like a bird**.

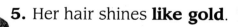

4. That balloon is **as light as a feather**.

5. Her hair shines **like gold**.

6. Cora and Tara are **like two peas in a pod**.

Sound Words

How does a bee sound? What sound do you hear when a person sneezes? To name those sounds, you can use **sound words**.

Teach:
Read aloud the first sentence, make a buzzing sound, and then show students how to represent the sound as the word *buzz*. Read the rest of the paragraph, invite students to make the sneezing sound, and show them the word *ah-choo*. Then talk about each group of sounds, encouraging students to compare sound words from their first languages to the English words. Also point out appropriate social behaviors in American culture, such as covering your mouth when you sneeze.

Animal Sounds

baa

buzz

cock-a-doodle-do

meow

moo

neigh

oink

quack

woof

People Sounds

ah-choo

ha-ha

hmmm

ooh

waa

whee

yum

Machine Sounds

beep

clang

r-r-ring

tick-tock

zoom

Hitting Sounds

boom

crash

splat

splash

Sound Words Practice:
3 Have one student make a sound from the list. Have the partner say and write the word for the sound.
4 Read aloud this story, pausing for students to add the sound words: *I went to a movie, but I couldn't hear anything! A man was eating popcorn. All I heard was* (crunch). *A baby cried and I heard* (waa). *When someone spilled a drink I heard* (splash).

More Sounds

crackle

crunch

fizz

glug

pop

sizzle

whoosh

zip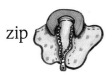

Then someone's watch alarm went (r-r-ring). *After that a bee got caught inside the theater. Then all I heard was* (buzz).
5 Have students use sound words to write a paragraph about morning at home or lunch in the cafeteria. Have students read their paragraph aloud, replacing the sound words with sound effects.

Sound-Alike Words

Many words like *flour* and *flower* sound alike, but have different spellings and different meanings. Be sure to choose the right meaning for the word you want to use.

flour   **flower**

ant
noun
An **ant** is a tiny insect.

aunt
noun
My **aunt** is my mother's sister.

ate
verb
I **ate** a sandwich.

eight
noun
The number **eight** comes after seven.

be
verb
What time will you **be** there?

bee
noun
A **bee** is an insect that makes honey.

blew
verb
The girl **blew** out the candles.

blue
noun
Her shirt is **blue**.

buy
verb
When you **buy** something, you pay money for it.

by
preposition
The ball is **by** the paddle.

noun
cent A penny is one **cent**.

noun
scent When something smells, it has a **scent**.

verb
sent She **sent** a letter to her cousin in Peru.

preposition
for What's **for** dinner?

noun
four The number **four** comes after three.

verb
hear You **hear** with your ears.

adverb
here Please come **here**.

noun
hour One **hour** is sixty minutes.

adjective
our She took **our** picture.

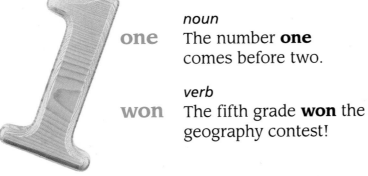

noun
one The number **one** comes before two.

verb
won The fifth grade **won** the geography contest!

Sound-Alike Words, continued

pair
noun
A **pair** is two of something.

pare
verb
When you **pare** an apple, you peel it.

pear
noun
A **pear** is a kind of fruit.

read
verb
We **read** that book last year.

red
noun
Red is a bright color.

right
adjective
Right is the opposite of left.

write
verb
Write your name on the paper.

see
verb
Glasses help you **see** better.

sea
noun
The **sea** is home for lots of fish.

threw
verb
She **threw** a ball across the field.

through
preposition
I like to walk **through** the woods.

Sound-Alike Words Practice:
3 Have students make a set of word cards for several of the sound-alike pairs. Display one pair at a time, such as *ant* and *aunt*. Ask students questio such as *Which word names an insect? Which word names a person?* Have students point to the correct card, sa the word, and spell it aloud. They can then add illustrations to the car to show the meaning of each word. Keep the cards at the Writing Center.
4 Have students choose two entries and write new sentences for each word. Ask them to use a different col to write the sound-alike words. Then have students exchange papers with partner. The partner can check if the correct word was used.
5 Have students write a paragraph t explain what they learned about soun alike words. Encourage them to use word entries from pages 30–32 as examples for their paragraph. Before students begin, have them look at the paragraph model on page 126.

➤ **Practice Book page 12**

Synonyms and Antonyms

Synonyms

A **synonym** is a word that has the same or almost the same meaning as another word.

Teach:
Read aloud the definition. Then read aloud the first entry, pointing out how the synonyms are listed in order of degree: *frightened* and *scared* mean *afraid*, but *alarmed* and *terrified* mean _really_ afraid. Have partners choose a few other sets and talk about times they would use words toward the beginning of each list and times when the words at the end would be more appropriate. Ask partners to share with the class and compare their ideas.

afraid

The cat is **afraid** of the dog.

frightened
scared
fearful
alarmed
terrified

big

What a **big** dinosaur!

large
huge
enormous
gigantic
colossal

cold

It's **cold** today.

chilly
brisk
frosty
wintry
icy
freezing

bad

A monster!
Is it **bad**?

mean
naughty
unkind
awful
terrible
horrible
rotten
cruel

brave

The **brave** dog saved its puppy from drowning.

courageous
fearless
heroic

cry

Don't **cry**.
You'll be okay.

weep
whimper
whine
sob
bawl
wail

Synonyms, continued

eat

How many cookies did you **eat**?

nibble on
bite into
chew up
dine on
consume
gobble up
feast on
devour

go

Come on! Let's **go**!

Ways to go fast:
run
scamper
scurry
gallop
jog
hurry
rush
dash
race
scramble
sprint

Ways to go slow:
walk
meander
stroll
ramble
trudge
hobble

Other ways to go:
crawl
hop
jump
leap
march
skip

good

That was **good**!

fine
pleasing
enjoyable
delightful
agreeable
wonderful
great
super
excellent
marvelous
terrific
awesome
splendid
top-notch
perfect
tremendous
spectacular

3 Speech Emergence **4** Intermediate Fluency **5** Advanced Fluency/Fluent

3 Say synonyms for a key word and have students point to the correct picture as they repeat the word. For example, say *hurry* and *race* and have students point to the picture for the key word *go*.

4 Give students a list of five key words (*afraid, big,* and so on) and have them write a sentence for each word. Then ask them to trade papers with a partner. The partner can rewrite each sentence replacing the key word with a synonym.

happy

We're so **happy**! We won!

glad
pleased
cheerful
joyful
delighted
thrilled

like

They **like** their grandmother.

enjoy
appreciate
admire
adore
love
cherish
treasure

mad

Why is he **mad**?

annoyed
cranky
irritated
cross
upset
angry
furious
enraged

laugh

My little brother likes to **laugh** when he's happy.

smile
grin
giggle
chuckle
cackle
howl

little

The flea is **little**.

small
slight
tiny
wee
miniature
minute
microscopic

noisy

Oh! That's too **noisy**!

loud
clamorous
shrill
booming
blaring
thunderous

5 Have students write a fantasy like the one on page 143 about a dinosaur or other creature. When students are done, have them revise their writing by replacing the adjectives and verbs with synonyms.

Synonyms, continued

pretty

What a **pretty** rainbow.

attractive
lovely
beautiful
gorgeous
stunning

sad

He's **sad**. His toy is broken.

unhappy
blue
down
cheerless
disappointed
gloomy
miserable

talk

Everyone's **talking**!

Ways to talk loudly:
cheering
calling out
crying out
shouting
hollering
yelling
screaming

Ways to talk softly:
murmuring
whispering
mumbling

Ways to say said:
added
answered
asked
blurted
declared
exclaimed
explained
inquired
replied
reported
responded
stated
suggested
told

quiet

This is such a **quiet** place.
I can't hear a thing.

still
hushed
tranquil
silent
soundless

strong

The elephant is **strong**.

sturdy
tough
powerful
mighty
brawny

ugly

Ugh! All the trash on the beach is **ugly**!

homely
unattractive
unappealing
unsightly
disgusting

warm

Boy! It's **warm** today!

hot
roasting
steaming
scorching
sweltering
sizzling
boiling

worried

You're late.
I was **worried**.

uneasy
concerned
upset
troubled
fretful
anxious
disturbed
distressed

wet

My shoes are **wet**.

damp
moist
soggy
soaked
drenched

Synonyms Practice:
3 Use gestures as you say the sentence under each picture. For example, wipe your forehead as you say *Boy! It's **warm** today!* Then have students follow your model, but use a synonym for the key word as they repeat the sentence: *Boy! It's **boiling** today!*
4 Have each student in a group use a synonym for *go* and *laugh* to finish a sentence: *I like to (jog), I like to (giggle).* Encourage students to compare their sentences and count how many different synonyms for each word they used.
5 Have students write the dialogue for a recent conversation they've had with their friends or family, or heard on TV. Encourage them to choose synonyms from the list for ***talk*** to tell exactly how the people talked.

➤ **Practice Book page 14**

Antonyms

Antonyms are words that have opposite meanings. All kinds of words can have antonyms.

Teach:
Open and close the door as you verbalize what you are doing. Explain that each action is the opposite of the other, so the words *open* and *close* are antonyms. Then read aloud the definition. As you discuss each antonym pair, have the group create a context sentence that shows their opposite meanings. For example: *If you break a vase, get some glue and fix it!*

Nouns

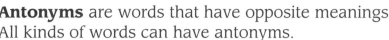

| whole | part | | male | female |

Verbs

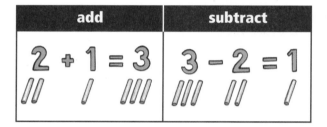

| add | subtract |

| float | sink |

| give | receive |

| enter | exit |

Antonyms Practice:

3 Have partners use a strip of paper to cover up the box on the left for each pair of boxes on pages 38 and 39. One partner then chooses one of the words in the boxes still visible, and the other gives its antonym. Then students can cover up the right boxes and repeat.

| start | finish |

Adjectives

wild | tame

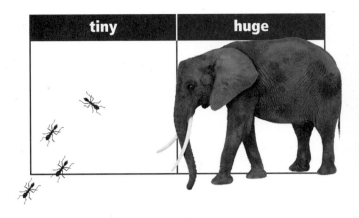

tiny | huge

clean | dirty

empty | full

broken | fixed

beautiful | ugly

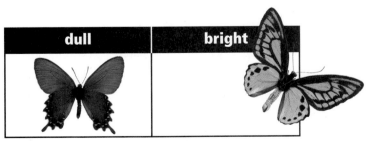

dull | bright

Antonyms Practice, continued:

4 Have one student use a word in a sentence. Ask the partner to use its antonym in a sentence. Have students continue until each pair has been used.

5 Ask groups to brainstorm other antonym pairs such as:

above/below	*back/front*	*before/after*
big/little	*day/night*	*fast/slow*
loud/soft	*tall/short*	*top/bottom*

Have students write and illustrate their antonym pairs to display in the Writing Center.

➤ **Practice Book page 15**

Time and Measurement Words

Time words tell you when things happen.
Measurement words tell how much of something you have.

calendar

Instruments Used for Measuring Time

wristwatch

hourglass

sundial

stopwatch

timer

clock

alarm clock

Teach:
Read the introduction aloud. Then discuss each group of words. If possible, provide real time instruments and challenge students to point out the similarities and differences in the objects and how they are used. For other groups, model a sentence and ask for a response that involves students in using the words: *At midday* on Saturdays, *I go running. What do you do at* **midday**?

Words for Telling Time on a Clock

o'clock

second

minute

hour

half hour
half past

quarter hour
quarter past

3 Speech Emergence **4** Intermediate Fluency **5** Advanced Fluency/Fluent

Short Periods of Time

instant   moment   second   nanosecond   split-second

Time and Measurement Practice:
3 Ask questions with embedded answers: *Is a ten-year period a* **decade** *or a* **century**? *Would you eat your first meal of the day at* **sunrise** *or at* **dusk**?
4 Have students describe their daily schedules using as many time words as they can: *Every* **morning** *my mom gets me up at* **half past seven**. *It takes me fifteen* **minutes** *to get dressed.*

Long Periods of Time

5 Have partners solve problems such as how many quarter hours in 6 hours or how many sunsets there are in a decade or a score. Encourage each student to write sentences explaining how they solved each problem.
➤ **Practice Book page 16**

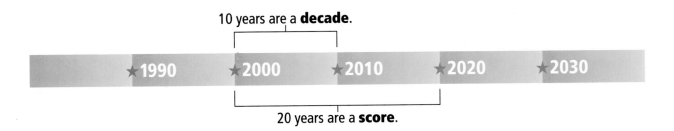

10 years are a **decade**.

★1990   ★2000   ★2010   ★2020   ★2030

20 years are a **score**.

100 years are a **century**.

★1900 ★2000   ★3000

1000 years are a **millennium**.

Times of the Day

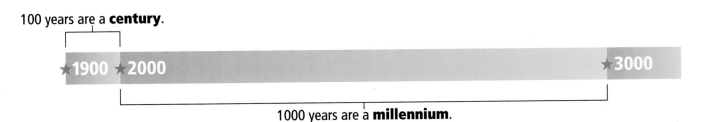

12:00 p.m.
noon
midday

dawn
daybreak
sunrise
sunup

morning afternoon evening night

a.m. p.m.

sunset
dusk
sundown

12:00 a.m.
midnight

Time and Measurement, continued

Seasons and Months of the Year

Time and Measurement Practice:

3 Display a calendar. Have students find the month of their birthday and record their name on the correct date, along with a colorful drawing. After the calendar is complete, ask questions to prompt use of the vocabulary: *What month is Rigoberto's birthday What day of the week is it on?* Involve students in making cookies for one of the birthdays to review other vocabulary on the page.

fall or **autumn**	**winter**	**spring**	**summer**
September	December	March	June
October	January	April	July
November	February	May	August

Days of the Week

Sunday   Monday   Tuesday   Wednesday   Thursday   Friday   Saturday

More Words That Tell When

first

next

then

finally

last

never

once in awhile

sometimes

occasionally

frequently

always

before

daily — every day

weekly — every week

biweekly — every two weeks

monthly — every month

quarterly — four times in a year

semiannually — two times in a year

annually — one time in a year

after

4 Provide a yardstick or ruler to one group, and a scale to another group. Have each group measure or weigh objects in the classroom and use complete sentences to record the results. Then groups exchange measuring instruments and repeat. Have them compare their results and reconcile discrepancies.

5 Have groups grow beans, sweet peas, or a plant from an avocado seed. Each group can use a calendar or create an observation log (similar to the ones on page 124) to record their observations over a week or a month. Encourage students to record the dates and times of day they observe the plant, and use measurement words to describe the plant's growth.

► **Practice Book page 17**

Length

inch

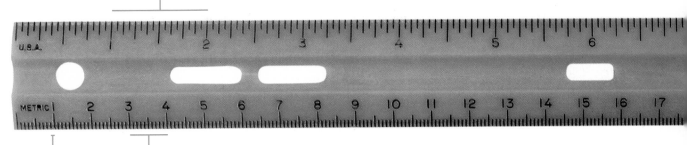

millimeter **centimeter**

12 inches	=	1 foot	10 millimeters	=	1 centimeter
3 feet	=	1 yard	100 centimeters	=	1 meter
5,280 feet	=	1 mile	1,000 meters	=	1 kilometer

Weight

ounce
pound
ton

milligram
centigram
gram
kilogram

Volume

teaspoon   tablespoon   cup

pint   quart   gallon

Word Building

Word building is what you do when you make new words.

Compound Words

You can put two or more small words together to make one word. The new word is called a **compound word**.

backpack =
back + pack

fingernail =
finger + nail

backyard =
back + yard

flashlight =
flash + light

basketball =
basket + ball

headphones =
head + phones

bathtub =
bath + tub

houseboat =
house + boat

bookshelf =
book + shelf

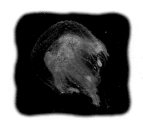

jellyfish =
jelly + fish

keyboard =
key + board

seashells =
sea + shells

lighthouse =
light + house

shoelaces =
shoe + laces

motorcycle =
motor + cycle

sunflower =
sun + flower

pineapple =
pine + apple

sweatshirt =
sweat + shirt

popcorn =
pop + corn

toothbrush =
tooth + brush

rainbow =
rain + bow

videocassette =
video + cassette

Compound Words Practice:

3 Play "Compound Concentration." Have students copy each root word on page 45 on a separate card. Turn the cards face down in a 6-card x 4-card grid. Students turn up a pair of words and keep them if they make up a compound word. The student with the most pairs wins.

4 Give a set of cards with compound word equations to groups. Have students take turns drawing a card and saying a sentence using the compound word formed from the words.

5 Give each team a set of cards with compound word parts, one small word per card. Explain that they have 15 minutes to put the words together to make up the compound words. The first team to finish wins.

➤ **Practice Book page 18**

Word Building, continued

Suffixes

Teach:
Write *pack, backpack* and *packer* on the chalkboard. Review how compound words are formed. Then explain how some new words are formed by adding a word part to the end of a word as you circle the *-er* in *packer*. Explain that *-er* means "a person who," so a *packer* is a person who packs. Read aloud the introduction and explain that the *-er* in *packer* is a suffix. Talk about how it changes the meaning of the root word and how *-er* does not make sense by itself. Then read the definitions of each suffix, discuss the examples, and help students build other words with suffixes:

A **suffix** is a word part that comes at the end of a word. When you add a suffix, you change the word's meaning.

-able, -ible	
comfortable	convertible
washable	sensible

-en	
harden	frighten
lengthen	weaken

-able, -ible means "can be"

A **breakable** vase can be broken.

-er	
builder	teacher
painter	writer

-ful	
careful	playful
helpful	thankful

A **reversible** coat can be reversed, or turned inside out.

-less	
careless	priceless
helpless	sleepless

-ward	
eastward	southward
northward	westward

-en means "to make" or "made of"

She **sharpens** the pencil to make the point sharp.

Is the mask made of wood?
Yes, it is **wooden**.

-er means "a person who"

A **runner** is a person who runs in a race.

A **baker** is a person who bakes.

3 Speech Emergence **4** Intermediate Fluency **5** Advanced Fluency/Fluent

-ful means "full of"

Some spider bites can be **harmful.**

An umbrella can be **useful**.

-less means "without"

A butterfly is **harmless.**

A broken umbrella is **useless**.

-ward means "in the direction of"

To go **forward** means to go in the direction in front of you.

To go **backward** means to go in the direction in back of you.

Suffixes Practice:

3 Have students point to and say the word you describe: *This word has the suffix* -less. *The word means "without harm." Which word is it?*

4 Have partners make suffix charts listing all the words they can think of that have the suffixes *-able/-ible, -en, -er, -ful,* and *-less.* See the list on page 46 for some possibilities.

5 Provide a paragraph containing several words with suffixes. Have students circle each word with a suffix, write the word, then write its definition. For example: *My brother and sister are* helpless *when it's time to clean our house. I'm the best* cleaner *in our family! When I dust the table, I move anything* breakable *out of the way. Then I use a* washable *rag to wipe the table going* forward *then* backward *several times. When I'm done, our* wooden *table looks* beautiful!

Word Building, continued

Prefixes

A **prefix** is a word part that comes at the beginning of a word. When you add a prefix, you change the word's meaning.

Teach:
Display the words *pack*, *backpack*, *packer*, and *repack*. Review how compound words an words with suffixes are formed. Read aloud the introduction and show how to build *repack* by adding the prefix *re-* to *pack*. Explain that *re-* means "again," so *repack* mean to *pack again*. Contrast the meanings of *packer* and *repack* noting that the suffix *-er* in *packer* and the prefix *re-* in *repack* account for the change in meaning. Then read the definitions of each prefix, discuss the examples, and help students build other words with these prefixes:

bi-
    bifocals   bicentennial

dis-
    disappear   disagree
    dishonest   dislike

bi- means "two" or "twice"

A **bicycle** has two wheels.

im-, in-
    impatient   incomplete
    impossible   incorrect

mini-
    minibus   minicam

re-
    reappear   reread
    reattach   rewash

pre-
    preplan   preview
    prepay   precook

A **biplane** has two sets of wings.

dis- means "the opposite of"

First she connected the cars.
Then she **disconnected** them.

semi-
    semiannual   semipreciou
    semifinal   semiprivate

im-, in- mean "not"

Imperfect clothes are not completely right. These sneakers have holes in them.

Inexpensive items are ones that do not cost a lot.

mini- means "small" or "little"

The little globe is called a **miniglobe**.

pre- means "before"

I **precut** the vegetables before putting them in the soup.

re- means "again" or "back"

When you use something again, you **reuse** it.

When you put something back in its place, you **replace** it.

semi- means "half"

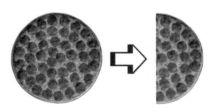

A **semicircle** is half of a circle.

Prefixes Practice:

3 Give partners a set of cards with prefixes and root words. Have them match the prefixes to the root words and say the words.

4 Give students clues to the words with prefixes and have them chime in with the word that finishes the sentence: *The opposite of connect is* (disconnect). *A cycle with two wheels is a* (bicycle), and so on. Later, have one team of students make up their own clues for another team to guess.

5 Provide a paragraph containing words with prefixes. Have students circle each word with a prefix, write the word, then write its definition. *The final baseball game is today. We won the semifinal so now we'll replay the Bears for the championship. Some fans think it will be impossible for us to win. We disagree. We say "Bring your minicam! You'll want pictures of your team getting the championship trophy!"*

Words Used in Special Ways

Idioms

Idioms are colorful ways to say something. Usually, a few words combine, or go together, to make up an idiom. In combination, these words mean something different from what the words mean by themselves.

Teach:
Read aloud the introduction and use one of the illustrated examples to clarify the concept. To establish the concept of idioms, have students with the same home language form buzz groups and share idioms in their language. Then, depending on proficiency levels of your students, plan to introduce on a few, or a group of idioms each day or wee

You may wish to:
- assign an idiom to each student, who takes responsibility for teaching to the rest of the class.
- have partners illustrate some idioms showing the literal and figurative mean ings. Post the illustrations an idiom gallery.
- set up a competition wher students try to "sell" their favorite idiom to the class A vote determines the winner.

What you say:

Skating is **a piece of cake**.

I'm **all thumbs**.

Stop **beating around the bush**.

What you mean:

Skating is easy.

I'm clumsy.

Stop talking about things that don't matter.

Pam always **bends over backwards**.

Pam always does whatever she can to help.

Don't **blow your top**.

Break a leg!

Juan is as **cool as a cucumber**.

That car **costs an arm and a leg**.

Cut it out.

My friend is **down in the dumps**.

Mr. Meyers is **down to earth**.

I'll **drop you a line**.

It's as **easy as pie**.

Don't get angry.

Good luck!

Juan is very calm.

That car is very expensive.

Stop what you're doing.

My friend is feeling very sad.

Mr. Meyers is easy to talk to.

I'll write you a letter.

It's very simple.

What you say:	What you mean:
I had to **eat my words**.	I had to say, "I'm sorry."
My **eyes were bigger than my stomach**.	I took more food than I could eat.
Now you have to **face the music**.	Now you have to take responsibility for what you did.
She **gave him the cold shoulder**.	She didn't pay any attention to him.
I'll **give it my best shot**.	I'll try my hardest.
Give me a break!	That's ridiculous!
Go fly a kite!	Go away!
I **got cold feet**.	I became unsure about doing something.
Tim **got up on the wrong side of the bed today**.	Tim is in a bad mood today.
Mom has a **green thumb**.	Mom is a good gardener.
Hang on.	Wait.

Daniel **has a heart of gold**.

Daniel is kind and generous.

I need to **hit the books**.	I need to study.
My mom **hit the ceiling**.	My mom got mad.

Idioms Practice:

3 Describe yourself using idioms and have students use words or short phrases to tell what you really mean: *Today, I'm all thumbs. That means that I'm* (clumsy).

4 Ask students to illustrate three idioms and their meanings. Have them write captions for each picture and display them in the Writing Center.

5 Have partners write a conversation between two characters. Encourage them to include at least four idioms in the dialogue. Ask students to role play the conversation for the class, pausing at appropriate places to tell what the idiom means.

Idioms, continued

What you say:	**What you mean:**
Hold your horses.	Wait a minute.
I am walking around **in a fog**.	I am confused.
I'm **in a jam**.	I'm in trouble.
My brother's **in hot water**.	My brother's in trouble.
Don't **jump down my throat**.	Don't yell at me.
Keep your shirt on.	Wait a minute. Be patient.
Knock it off!	Stop it!

Will you **lend me a hand**?

Will you help me?

Her car runs **like clockwork**.	Her car runs smoothly.
We'd better **make tracks**.	We'd better hurry.
You're **off the hook**.	You're out of trouble.
My dad is **out of shape**.	My dad needs to exercise.
You're **out of the woods**.	You're safe.
Don't be a **pain in the neck**.	Don't bother me.
Pat yourself on the back.	Tell yourself you did a good job.

What you say:

He's **playing with fire**.

Stop **pulling my leg**.

I always **put my best foot forward**.

Let's **put our heads together**.

We don't **see eye to eye**.

My dog is as **smart as a whip**.

Please don't **spill the beans**.

Don't **spread yourself too thin**.

That car can **stop on a dime**.

I **turned the room upside down**.

Jasmine is **under the weather**.

You bet!

What you mean:

He's doing something dangerous.

Stop kidding me.

I always do my best.

Let's work together.

We don't agree with each other.

My dog is very quick and clever.

Please don't tell my secret.

Don't try to do too much.

That car can stop quickly.

I looked everywhere in the room.

Jasmine is not feeling well.

Yes, I agree!

Zip your lips!

Be quiet!

Idioms Practice:
3 Prepare sentence strips with idioms and display a list of their meanings. Have partners match the idioms to the meanings.
4 Give partners a list of brief sentences such as *I'm sad, It's easy,* and *I'm in trouble*. Have them write the idioms that are related to those meanings.
5 Teams can play an idiom game. Read a sentence with an idiom. Team 1 decides what it means and has one minute to answer. Read another sentence and have Team 2 answer, and so on. Teams score a point for each correct answer.

▶ **Practice Book page 22**

Two-Word Verbs

Sometimes a little word like *in*, *up*, or *out* can make a big difference in meaning. A **two-word verb** often includes one of these little words. Look at how they change a verb's meaning.

Teach:
Review what students know about verbs, then read aloud the introduction and work through the entries for *break* and *bring* to illustrate the concept. Divide the class into five multi-level groups and assign one page from pages 55–59 to each group. Students should study the entries on their page and create at least five more sentences for each two-word verb. Then across the next week or two, invite each group to present the verb and their sentences to the class.

break

1. break — *to split into pieces*
Don't drop the plate! It will **break**.

2. break down — *to stop working*
My old car **breaks down** every week.

3. break up — *to come apart*
The ice on the lake will **break up** in the spring.

bring

1. bring — *to take or carry something with you*
Bring a salad to the picnic.

2. bring out — *to take out things you have in another place*
She **brings out** the pies.

3. bring up — *to suggest*
She **brings up** the idea to her friends.

check

1. **check** — *to make sure what you did is right*
Always **check** your work.

2. **check in** — *to stay in touch with someone*
My grandmother phones to **check in** with me every week.

3. **check off** — *to mark off a list*
Tom **checked off** the chores he had done.

4. **check up** — *to see if everything is okay*
The cowboy **checks up** on the cattle.

fill

1. **fill** — *to put as much as possible into a container or space*
Fill the pail with water.

2. **fill in** — *to color or shade in a space*
Please **fill in** the circle

3. **fill out** — *to complete*
Marcos **fills out** a form to order a book.

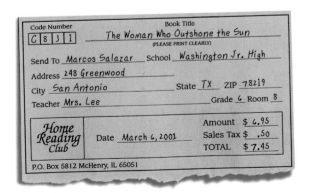

Code Number	Book Title
C 8 3 1	*The Woman Who Outshone the Sun*

(PLEASE PRINT CLEARLY)

Send To _Marcos Salazar_   School _Washington Jr. High_
Address _248 Greenwood_
City _San Antonio_   State _TX_   ZIP _78219_
Teacher _Mrs. Lee_   Grade _6_ Room _8_

Home Reading Club   Date _March 6, 2001_

Amount	$ 6.95
Sales Tax $	.50
TOTAL	$ 7.45

P.O. Box 5812 McHenry, IL 65051

Two-Word Verbs Practice:

3 Use the definitions to ask questions that can be answered with two-word verbs: *What happens when a car stops working? It breaks down. What can you do to mark off chores on a list? Check off the chores.*

4 Write the first word in each two-word verb on a card and distribute one to a student. Make another set of cards with the words *across, back, down, for, in, off, on, out, over,* and *up,* and place face down in a pile. Turn the cards over one at a time and have students write a sentence using their word and the word in the pile if it forms a two-word verb. The student with the most correct sentences wins.

5 Have students use as many two-word verbs for *check* and *fill* as they can to write a paragraph describing a visit to a doctor or dentist. Repeat for other pairs and scenarios, such as *get* and *pick* to describe a trip to a shopping mall.

▶ **Practice Book page 23**

Two-Word Verbs, continued

get

Two-Word Verbs Practice:
3 Act out two-word verbs such as *fill in, fill out, go back, look out,* and *look up,* as you verbalize. Then have students follow your model as they act out and say the verbs.
4 Ask open-ended questions and have students elaborate on their answers: *Did you* **get through** *your homework last night? What do you* **look forward** *to every year? Do you ever* **go out** *to the movies?*
5 Have students use two-word verbs to write persuasive want ads or announcements. Direct them to pages 95 and 96 for examples.

➤ **Practice Book page 24**

1. get — *to go after something*
Get the keys, please.

2. get through — *to finish*
I can **get through** this book tonight.

3. get ahead — *to go beyond what is expected of you*
She worked hard to **get ahead** in her math class.

4. get out — *to leave*
The students **get out** at the bus stop.

5. get over — *to feel better*
She'll **get over** her cold soon.

give

1. give — *to hand someone something*
I will **give** you some cake.

2. give back — *to return*
She **gives back** the CD she borrowed.

3. give up — *to quit*
Never **give up**!
Practice until you get it right!

3 Speech Emergence **4** Intermediate Fluency **5** Advanced Fluency/Fluent

go

1. go — *to move from one place to another*
I will **go** to the movies on Saturday.

2. go away — *to leave*
Tomorrow the rain will **go away**.

3. go back — *to return*
Every spring, the geese **go back** north.

4. go on — *to keep happening*
I hope the music will **go on** forever.

5. go out — *to go someplace special*
They like to **go out** to breakfast.

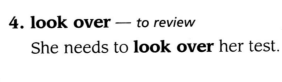

look

1. look — *to see or watch*
Look at the stars.

2. look forward — *to be excited about something that will happen*
I **look forward** to the parade every year.

3. look out — *to watch for danger*
Look out! The ball is coming right at you!

4. look over — *to review*
She needs to **look over** her test.

5. look up — *to hunt for and find*
You can **look up** a word in the dictionary.

Two-Word Verbs, continued

pick

1. pick — *to choose*
I always **pick** red clothes.

2. pick on — *to bother or tease*
If you **pick on** someone, you're asking for trouble.

3. pick out — *to choose*
I always **pick out** red clothes.

4. pick up — *to gather*
My class project is to **pick up** trash.

5. pick up — *to go faster*
When the wind **picks up**, you'll need your jacket.

run

1. run — *to move quickly on foot*
He had to **run** to catch the bus.

2. run into — *to see someone you know when you weren't expecting it*
Sometimes I **run into** my neighbor on the street.

3. run out — *to suddenly have nothing left*
If you use all of the milk, we'll **run out**.

Two-Word Verbs Practice:
3 Ask yes/no questions and questions with embedded answers: *Do you* **run out** *of milk or* **run into** *it? When you give books back to the library, do you* **turn over** *the books or* **turn in** *the books?*
4 Have partners choose five two-word verbs and alternate saying sentences using the words.
5 Have students use two-word verbs to make a list of things they did before they got to school this morning: *Got up at 7 a.m.,* **picked out** *my clothes, ate breakfast, caught the bus,* **ran into** *John at the bus stop,* and so on. If students need help with past-tense verbs, direct them to pages 190–191.
▶ **Practice Book page 25**

stand

1. **stand** — *to be in a straight up and down position*
   We **stand** in line to buy movie tickets.

2. **stand for** — *to represent*
   The stars on the U.S. flag **stand for** the 50 states.

3. **stand in** — *to take the place of*
   While our team pitcher is gone, Jerry will **stand in** for him.

4. **stand out** — *to make easier to see*
   Highlight the words so they **stand out**.

turn

1. **turn** — *to change direction*
   Turn right at the next corner.

2. **turn in** — *to give back*
   She has to **turn in** her library book before it is due.

3. **turn off** — *to stop using*
   Please **turn off** the lights when you leave.

4. **turn up** — *to appear*
   I lost my favorite socks. I hope they **turn up.**

5. **turn over** — *put something on its opposite side*
   He **turns over** the pot.

Chapter 2

Picture It!

Janet has a lot of bright ideas. She's using a story map to help her "picture" some of them before she starts to write a story. This chapter has all kinds of useful ways to picture ideas and details in clusters, story maps, graphs, time lines, and more. You can use these graphic organizers to make a picture of things you've read and to get organized before you write.

1985 1995 2005

Clusters

Teach:
Read aloud the paragraph, then demonstrate drawing a cluster: *First, write the topic in the middle of the paper. Then, draw a circle around it. Next, write the details around the topic. Finally, draw lines to connect the topic to the details.* Afterward, read aloud the description for each graphic. Point to and name the topic, and explain how the details relate to it.

A **cluster** is a picture that shows how words or ideas go together. Sometimes a cluster is called a **map**. Sometimes it is called a **web** because it looks a little like a spider web! Here are some examples.

Word Web

This **word web** groups words related to baseball.

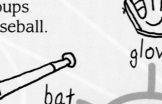

Word Web Practice:

3 Start a new web on the chalkboard. Have students draw pictures of other items related to baseball. As volunteers add the pictures to the web, write the names. Vocalize each name as you write it. Repeat for other categories.

4 Have students use the baseball word web to write sentences that explain how the words are related.

5 Have partners make word webs about two of the following: sports, restaurants, solar system, communication, fun things to wear. As volunteers display their webs, have them explain how the words are related.

Character Map

A **character map** shows what a person in a story is like.

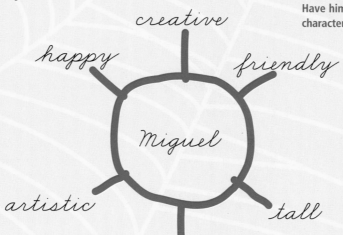

Character Map Practice:

3 Display a picture of a character students are familiar with. Ask students to describe the character as you create a character map. Have students echo as you "read" the completed map back to them: *Miguel is a happy person, Miguel is a friendly person,* and so on.

4 Ask each student to make a map that tells about a character in a story the class has read. Have him or her cover up the name of the character, then share the map with a partner. Can the partner guess the name of the character?

5 Have partners make up a story character and make a map that tells about the character. Have them use the map to write a character sketch. Encourage students to use the model of a character sketch on page 100 for help.

➤ Practice Book page 26

Event Cluster

The girl who made this **event cluster** was getting ready to write about a special celebration. She organized her ideas so she could tell what happened.

rice cakes

taro soup

foods

fruit

Circle Dance

Farmer's Dance

dances

Festival of the Harvest Moon

honored ancestors

family activities

at night looked at full moon

visited relatives

Main Idea Cluster

This **cluster** shows how details are related to a main idea.

very sharp
claws, can
be four
inches long

special
eyelids keep
eyes clean

large eyes

Detail:
strong claws
hooked beaks

Detail:
good
eyesight

beaks good for
tearing prey

Main Idea:
Eagles are strong predators.

prey is too
slow to
get away

Detail:
fly fast
and high

prey can't see
the eagle
coming

Main Idea Cluster Practice:
3 Draw a blank cluster on the chalkboard. Ask students to point to and tell you where to write the main idea and details. As you confirm their answers, explain why the main idea goes in the middle (it's the most important idea) and why the details go around it (each detail explains why eagles are strong predators).
4 Encourage students to write the sentence from the cluster that tells the main idea. Then have them choose one set of details and write sentences to tell more about the main idea.
5 Have students use the cluster to write a paragraph. Encourage them to use the model of a paragraph on page 125 for help.

➤ **Practice Book page 27**

Diagrams

A **diagram** is a drawing that shows where things are, how something works, or when something happens. Most diagrams have words, or labels, that tell more about the drawing. Look at these examples.

Floor Plan

A **floor plan** is a diagram that shows where things are in a room or in a building. It shows what a room looks like as if you were above it looking down. Here is a floor plan for a museum.

Teach:
Talk with students about any diagrams posted in your classroom or school such as an emergency exit plan or science posters and describe what they show. Then read aloud the paragraph and the description for each diagram. Point out how the diagrams use shapes, pictures, and labels to give information.

Floor Plan Practice:
3 Use position and direction words to describe the location of each "exhibit." Have students point to the area on the floor plan and repeat your description.

Museum of Kites from Around the World

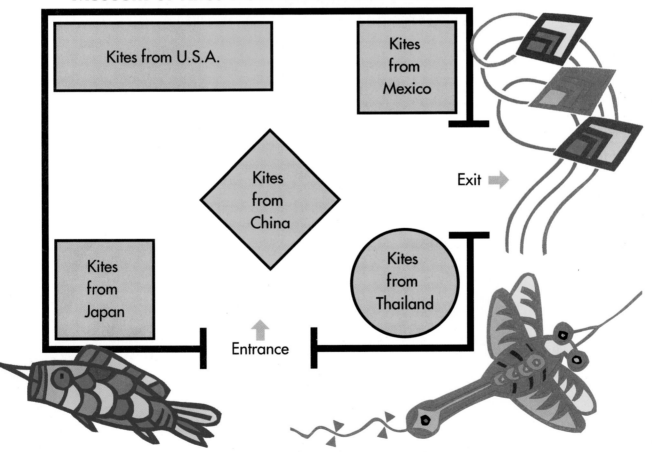

4 Have partners write as many sentences as they can that use direction words and describe the floor plan: *This is the entrance. It's across from the kites from China.* Remind students that they can find words that tell where on page 19.
5 Have partners brainstorm furniture and equipment in the classroom or school building. Then students can draw and label a floor plan. Encourage students to display their floor plan and explain it to the class.

Diagrams, continued

Parts Diagram

Parts Diagram Practice:
3 Display a guitar and talk about what the parts do. Then ask students questions with embedded answers: *Does the **bridge** or the **sound hole** keep the strings tight?*
4 Brainstorm familiar objects with students like a car or a bicycle. Each student can choose one object, and draw and label its parts. Volunteers can describe their diagrams to the class.
5 Have partners make up an invention such as a machine to do their homework or clean their room. Have them draw their invention, label its parts, and write a paragraph to describe it.
➤ **Practice Book page 28**

This diagram helps you know how a guitar works.

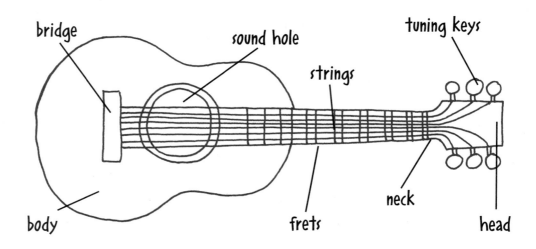

Scientific Diagram

Scientific Diagram Practice:
3 Have students point to the pictures and labels as you elaborate on the stages: *The female beetle lays **eggs**. Each egg hatches into a **larva**. The larva sheds its skin and becomes a **pupa**. The pupa splits open and an **adult beetle** crawls out.*
4 Have students use order words to write sentences about how a beetle grows: *First there are eggs. Next an egg becomes a larva,* and so on.
5 Talk with students about the life cycle of a butterfly (egg, caterpillar, pupa, butterfly) or frog (egg, tadpole, frog). Have partners create a diagram with pictures, labels, and sentences that describe each stage of the process.

Follow the arrows in this diagram to see how a beetle grows and changes over time.

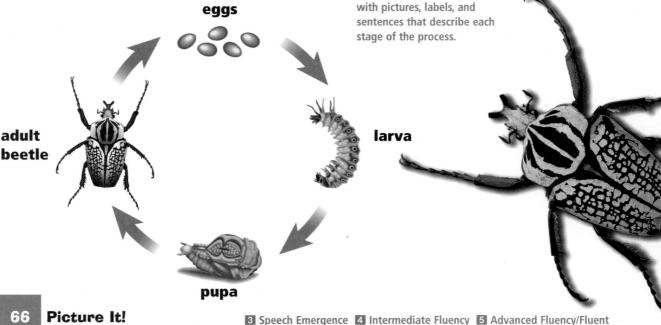

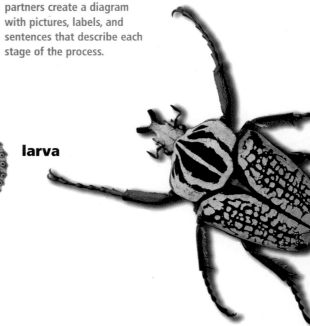

3 Speech Emergence **4** Intermediate Fluency **5** Advanced Fluency/Fluent

Venn Diagram Practice:
3 Start a new diagram on the chalkboard. Use complete sentences to compare and contrast the 4th of July and Cinco de Mayo, having students point to or tell where you should write the key words.
4 Discuss celebrations with students such as birthdays and New Years, and other cultural events. Have partners choose two celebrations and create a Venn diagram to compare them.

Venn Diagram

A **Venn diagram** compares and contrasts two things. It shows how two things are the same and how they are different.

Tell about one thing here.   **Tell about the other thing here.**

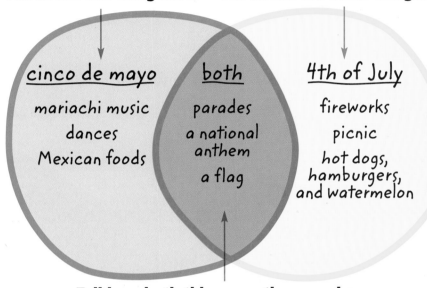

cinco de mayo
mariachi music
dances
Mexican foods

both
parades
a national
anthem
a flag

4th of July
fireworks
picnic
hot dogs,
hamburgers,
and watermelon

Tell how both things are the same here.

5 Ask students to turn the key words in the diagram into sentences and write a comparison and a contrast paragraph. Have them look on pages 128 and 129 for models.

Main Idea Diagram Practice:
3 Provide props such as a small U.S. flag, kitchen utensils, paper plates, and napkins, and have three students role-play the details in the diagram. Then have students dictate the details and main idea to help you complete a main idea diagram.

Main Idea Diagram

This diagram shows how details are related to a main idea.

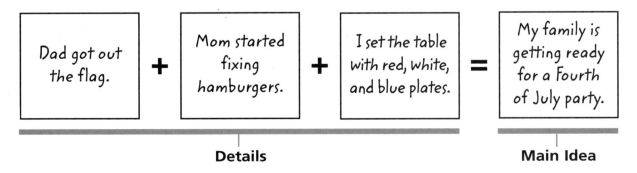

Dad got out the flag.

+

Mom started fixing hamburgers.

+

I set the table with red, white, and blue plates.

=

My family is getting ready for a Fourth of July party.

Details   **Main Idea**

4 Talk with students about special events they have experienced such as birthday parties or trips to visit relatives. Ask what they did to prepare for the event. Then have students help you create a main idea diagram. Call on volunteers to write the details and main idea.
5 Have each student choose a special day or holiday from **Dateline U.S.A.** on pages 264–301 and use the information to create a main idea diagram. Encourage students to add other details they know about the holiday.

Graphs

Teach:
Have students look at each graph as you point out its shape, the numbers, bars, lines, and labels. Explain that graphs show a lot of information in one picture. Then read aloud the definition and description for each graph.

A **graph** is a picture that compares mathematical information, or data.

Bar Graph

One kind of graph has bars that go from left to right or up and down to give information. That's why it's called a **bar graph**.

- Each bar shows one kind of information.

- The length or height of the bar shows another kind of information.

In this graph, look at the bars to see which family sold the most tickets.

Bar Graph Practice:
3 Ask students questions about the graph, encouraging them to point to appropriate parts of the graph as they respond. *What is the graph all about? Where does it show the number of tickets?* and so on.
4 Ask partners to survey how many students in the class have a blue notebook, a red notebook, and so on. Then model how to make a bar graph to show the data. Have partners use their data to make a graph.
5 Have partners brainstorm a list of three or four sports or games. Have them use the list to ask classmates to vote for their favorite sport, and then use the results to make a bar graph. Encourage students to display the graph and explain the results.

➤ Practice Book page 30

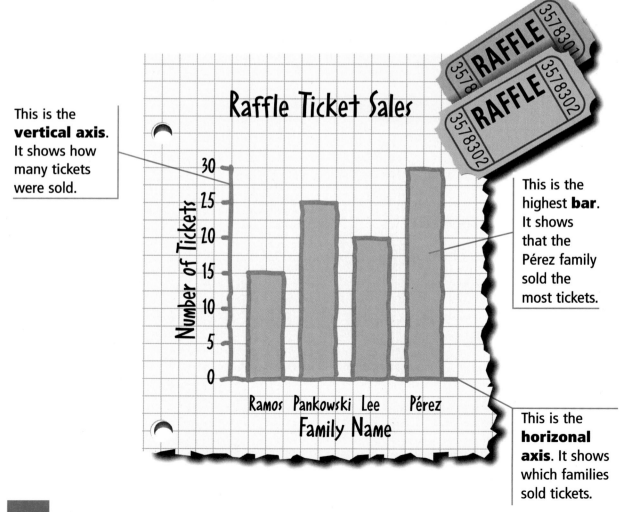

This is the **vertical axis**. It shows how many tickets were sold.

Raffle Ticket Sales

Number of Tickets
30
25
20
15
10
5
0

Ramos Pankowski Lee Pérez
Family Name

This is the highest **bar**. It shows that the Pérez family sold the most tickets.

This is the **horizonal axis**. It shows which families sold tickets.

Line Graph

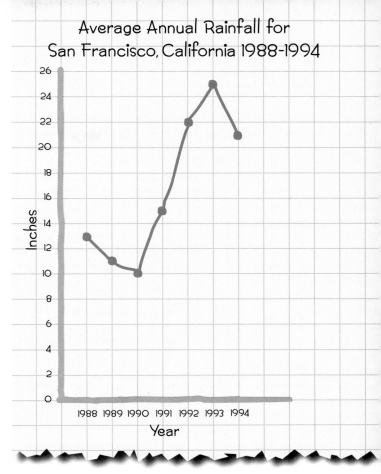

This kind of graph has points, or dots, that show the data. It's called a **line graph** because lines are used to connect the points.

Line Graph Practice:

3 Demonstrate how to read the graph going up from the horizontal axis to a point, then left to the vertical axis as you verbalize. Have students follow your model to find the data and answer questions: *How many inches of rain did San Francisco have in 1990? In which year did San Francisco have the most rain?*

4 Have students select three consecutive years on the graph. Ask them to write sentences that compare the years: *There was less rain in 1990 than in 1989. However, there was more rain in 1991 than in 1990.*

5 Provide students with data of typical weather patterns in your area. Have groups of students plot the points and draw a line graph onto a large sheet of paper. Have the groups use their graphs to present the information to the class: *In 1988, there were seven inches of snow. A year later, there were...,* and so on.

Pie Graph

A **pie graph** looks a lot like a pie! It has a circular shape and is divided into parts. Each part of a pie graph is a percentage of the whole circle. All parts added together equal 100 percent.

Pie Graph Practice:

3 Recreate the pie graph on a sheet of paper and cut it apart. Tape one section on the board and distribute the others to students. Explain: *This is one part of the whole circle. It shows that Italy won 6 percent of all the medals.* Then have each student add to the graph as they say the country's name and percentage.

4 Have partners ask and answer questions about the pie graph: *What percentage of medals did Finland win? They won 8 percent of the medals.*

5 Have students use the data in the pie graph to write a paragraph. Have them use the model on page 126 for help.

➜ **Practice Book page 31**

Medals Won by the Top 10 Countries in the 1998 Winter Olympics

Outlines

Teach:
Read aloud the paragraph. Describe and discuss the content of the outline with students, then point to and explain each feature: Roman numerals, letters, and numbers.

An **outline** uses words to show the most important information about a topic. It groups the main ideas and details related to the topic.

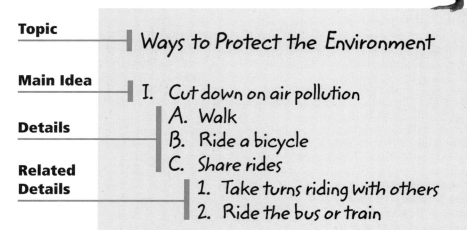

Topic

Ways to Protect the Environment

Main Idea

I. Cut down on air pollution

Details

  A. Walk
  B. Ride a bicycle
  C. Share rides

Related Details

    1. Take turns riding with others
    2. Ride the bus or train

II. Reduce garbage
  A. Reuse
    1. Use paper and plastic bags more than once
    2. Share your newspaper with a neighbor
  B. Recycle

III. Save water
  A. Turn off the water while brushing teeth
  B. Fill the bathtub less than halfway when you take a bath
  C. Use less water when you wash your car
  D. Water the grass only in the morning or evening on every other day

Outlines Practice:
3 Have students point to the topic as you read it aloud. Repeat for the main idea, details, and related details. Then ask students yes/no questions: *Is "Reuse" a main idea? Is "Use less water when you wash your car" a detail?*
4 Have these students write a paragraph using one of the main ideas and details from the model.
5 Have partners brainstorm a new main idea about a way to protect the environment such as *Don't Litter* or *Save Energy* and write section IV to add to the outline.

Story Maps

Teach:
Have students tell about stories they've read. Then read aloud the paragraph. After reading aloud each story map description, work through the map explaining how it organizes and summarizes the details and events.

A **story map** is a picture that tells what happens in a story. There are many different kinds of story maps because there are so many different kinds of stories. You can use a story map to plan a story you will write or to show what happened in a story you read.

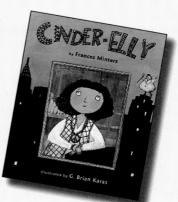

Beginning, Middle, and End

This kind of story map tells what happens in each main part of a story.

Beginning, Middle, and End Practice:
3 Create picture cards to show the events in *Cinder-Elly* such as tickets, a cane, a basketball, and glass shoes; and distribute them to students. Create a new map on the board and call on students to add the pictures to the map as you record the events.
4 5 Have Level 4 students join Level 5 students to talk about a story they have recently read in class. Ask each group to make a beginning, middle, and end map to show what happened in the story. Level 4 students can write the events for the beginning and end. Level 5 students can write the events for the middle in the correct sequence.

➤ **Practice Book page 32**

Title: Cinder-Elly

Author: Frances Minters

Beginning
Cinder-Elly and her sisters won free tickets to a basketball game. Elly's mean sisters and her mother wouldn't let her go.

Middle
1. Elly's godmother helped Elly. She used a magic cane to give Elly glass shoes, new clothes, and a bike.
2. Elly went to the basketball game and met Prince Charming.
3. Elly stayed too late so her new clothes and bike disappeared. She lost a glass shoe.
4. Prince Charming tried to find Elly, but he only found her shoe.
5. Prince Charming wrote a note asking the shoe's owner to call him.

End
Elly's mean sisters tried on the glass shoe, but it didn't fit. It only fit Elly.
The sisters said they were sorry for being mean.
Cinder-Elly and Prince Charming lived happily ever after.

Circular Story Map

Sometimes a story ends at the same place it begins.
Use a **circular story map** for this kind of story.

Event 6:
Richie's rocket landed safely on the roof of his apartment building.

Event 1:
Richie was in his home-made rocket on the roof when it blasted off into outer space.

Richie's Rocket
Author: Joan Anderson

Event 5:
The rocket soared back through space toward Earth.

Event 2:
Richie met some astronauts from another spacecraft. They towed his rocket to the moon.

Event 4:
The astronauts came back. Their spacecraft lifted Richie's rocket off the moon.

Event 3:
The rocket landed on the moon. Richie walked on the moon and wrote his name in moon dust.

Circular Story Map Practice:
3 Have students point to each event as you read it aloud. Then ask students to point to and use one- or two-word responses to answer questions: *Where does the story begin? Does it end at the same place? Where does it show the third event?* and so on.
4 Have each student recreate the circular story map using him- or herself as the main character. Students can use pictures and labels to show the events.
5 Ask students to make up a story about a space adventure. Have them create a map, and then write the stories. Students can use the story models on pages 141 and 143 for help. Invite volunteers to read their stories aloud to the class.

3 Demonstrate a problem-and-solution situation as you verbalize. Look around like something's wrong: *Oh no! I've lost my pencil!* Then pick up a pencil and smile: *I found it!* Then ask students to point to and describe the problem-and-solution in the story map.

Problem-and-Solution Map

In some stories, there is a problem that has to be solved. A **problem-and-solution map** will help you show the problem, the ways the characters try to solve it, and the solution.

4 Have students share stories they've read or seen on TV or in movies. As they offer details and events, clarify the problem and solution. Ask students to choose one story to map.

5 Have students read or reread a problem/solution story like *Too Many Tamales* by Gary Soto and Ed Martinez or *The Great Kapok Tree* by Lynne Cherry. Have them create problem-and-solution maps for the story.

The **problem** gets the story started.

The **events** tell what happens.

The **solution** tells how the problem is solved.

Title: Subway Sparrow

Author: Leyla Torres

Characters: Four passengers on a subway train

Setting: Atlantic Avenue subway station in Brooklyn, New York

Problem: A sparrow flies inside a subway car. The doors close and the bird can't get out.

Event 1: A girl tries to catch the sparrow, but it flies away from her.

Event 2: A man tries to help by catching the sparrow with his hat, but he misses.

Event 3: A boy wants to help, too, but he's afraid that he might hurt the sparrow.

Event 4: The man starts to use an umbrella to catch the bird, but a woman stops him. She's afraid the umbrella will hurt the bird.

Event 5: Finally, the sparrow lands on the floor of the train and the woman covers it gently with her scarf.

Solution: The girl picks up the sparrow and takes it out of the subway car. Outside the station, the four passengers watch the bird fly away.

Story Maps, continued

Goal-and-Outcome Map

Some stories tell what characters do to get what they want, or to reach their goals. Use a **goal-and-outcome map** for these stories.

Goal-and-Outcome Map Practice:

3 Read aloud each part of the map as students follow along. Pause after each part to ask questions. For example, after reading the definition of goal and the story text ask *What does Spider want?* and confirm responses *Spider wants to go to both feasts. That's the goal.*

4 Create a large version of the map on butcher paper and have groups work together to illustrate and label each part. Have them glue their illustrations in appropriate sections on the map. Call on volunteers to read the label and describe the illustration in each part.

5 Have students read the story on page 107 and create a goal-and-outcome map.

Title: _How Spider Got His Thin Middle_

The **goal** tells what the character in a story wants.

> **Goal**
> Two villages were having feasts at the same time. Spider, who loved to eat, wanted to go to both of them.

The **events** tell what happens.

> **Event 1**
> Spider stood in the forest between the villages. He tied a rope around his middle.

> **Event 2**
> He gave one end of the rope to a friend who was going to one feast. Then he asked him to pull the rope when the feast began.

> **Event 3**
> He gave the other end to a friend who was going to the other feast and asked him to do the same thing.

> **Event 4**
> Both friends started pulling on the rope at the same time. The rope kept getting tighter and tighter.

The **outcome** tells if the character gets what he or she wants.

> **Outcome**
> Spider didn't get to go to either feast. Spider's middle became thin, and that's how he is today.

3 Explain that rising and falling action in a story is like running up and over the top of a hill and then down. Then read aloud the story map, using your voice and pointing to events on the map to emphasize the rising and falling action. Have students follow your model, using one or two words to describe the events.

Map for Rising and Falling Action

This kind of story map looks like a mountain. The most important part of a story, or the **climax**, is at the top of the mountain. Follow the arrows to find out what happens before and after the climax.

4 Distribute self-adhesive notes with key words for each event: *hurricane watch, emergency supplies, leave home,* and so on. Draw the map on the board. Have students add the notes to the map in order as they retell what happens.

5 Provide several rising and falling action stories for students to read. Ask them to map the action. Volunteers can retell the story to the class, using their maps as props.

Caught in a Hurricane!

4. The hurricane hits! Wind, rain, and waves pound the town.

3. The Center announces a hurricane warning. Rosa and her family leave their house.

5. The electricity and phones go out.

2. Rosa's family hangs storm shutters and gathers emergency supplies.

6. Finally, the storm passes. Over the radio, people hear they can return home.

1. The National Hurricane Center announces a hurricane watch.

7. Rosa and her family go home to check for damage.

8. The people of the town begin to clean up after the storm.

Setting:
Early morning in a small town in Florida

Characters:
Rosa and her grandparents, Hector and Inez Santos, are eating breakfast.

Story Staircase Map

This story map looks like the steps in a staircase. Start at the bottom "step" and move up to the top to show when things happen.

"Toad Is the Uncle of Heaven"
A Vietnamese Folk Tale retold and
illustrated by Jeanne M. Lee

The toad tried to ask for rain, but the King ordered his guards to capture the toad. The bees stung the guards.

When the animals found the King, the toad jumped into his lap by mistake. That made the King angry.

A very thirsty tiger joined them.

A sad rooster joined the toad and the bees.

There was a drought on Earth, so a toad went to see the King to ask for rain.

Some bees decided to go with the toad.

The King
ordered rain.
He said that
anytime Earth
needed rain,
all the toad
had to do
was croak.

The King asked
"Uncle Toad"
to save his
hound. The
toad stopped
the tiger
because the
King treated
the toad
with respect
by calling
him "Uncle."

The toad tried
to ask again,
but the King
told the
Thunder God
to make the
toad be quiet.
The rooster
screeched and
scared the
Thunder God.

The King's
hound tried
to scare the
toad, bees,
and rooster
away. The
tiger fought
the hound.

Then the toad
asked the King
for rain.

The toad is a symbol of
rain in Vietnam. When
Uncle Toad croaks, rain
will soon follow.

Story Staircase Map Practice:
3 Have students use the pictures to
retell the story in their own words.
4 Start a new map on the chalkboard
and have groups of students write one-
or two-word labels to show the events.
When they are done, encourage students
to take turns pointing to an event to
retell the story.
5 Have partners make up a story. After
students brainstorm a list of events, have
them draw a story staircase and write
sentences to describe each event.

▶ **Practice Book page 33**

Tables and Charts

Teach:
Read aloud the first paragraph. Then briefly preview pages 78–81 having students talk about what they see. Point out how each graphic organizes information using boxes, rows, and columns. Then use the first table to model how to read across the rows and down the columns to find information. Afterward, read aloud the description and content for each table or chart.

Tables and **charts** present information in rows and columns. Read across the rows and down the columns to compare information.

Number of Books Read During the October Read-a-thon

The **rows** go from left to right ➡.

	Class 1	Class 2	Class 3
Grade 1	47	35	62
Grade 2	33	85	102
Grade 3	75	95	88
Grade 4	78	93	82
Grade 5	96	96	95
Grade 6	102	107	65

The **columns** go from top to bottom ⬇.

Comparison Tables

Some tables show how two things are the same and how they're different.

Life in the United States and Russia

These tell how Russia and the U.S. are the same.

Life in the United States	Life in Russia
go to school Monday through Friday	go to school Monday through Friday
participate in many different sports	participate in many different sports
don't learn to swim at school	learn to swim at school in Kindergarten
cable television with hundreds of channels	television with only a few channels
can learn another language	must learn another language

These tell how Russia and the U.S. are different.

Comparison Tables Practice:
3 Read aloud each row in the table and ask students if the two things are the same or if they are different. Then call on volunteers to name one thing that is the same and one thing that is different.
4 Model a sentence that compares and one that contrasts. Then have students use the chart to write compare and contrast sentences: *In both the United States and in Russia, students go to school Monday through Friday.*
5 Ask partners to talk about how life is the same and how it is different in their two countries of origin. Have them create a comparison table and then write a compare or contrast paragraph. Students can find paragraph models on pages 128 and 129.

3 Speech Emergence **4** Intermediate Fluency **5** Advanced Fluency/Fluent

3 Create a cause-and-effect chart of a natural occurrence students are familiar with, such as an earthquake, snowstorm, or hurricane. State the causes, asking volunteers to offer the effects.

4 Talk about how volcanoes erupt. Have students cover the effect side of the chart with a blank sheet of paper. Ask them to read each cause and write the corresponding effect. Repeat for the cause side of the chart.

5 Have students use the chart to write a cause-and-effect paragraph. Tell them to look at page 127 for an example.

Cause-and-Effect Chart

This chart shows how one event can cause another event to happen. That's why it's called a **cause-and-effect chart**.

How a Volcano Erupts

Cause	Effect
The temperature is very hot below the earth's surface.	The rock melts to form a pool of magma in a magma chamber.
Solid rock around the magma chamber puts pressure on the magma.	The hot magma makes a conduit, or tunnel, up through the earth.
The magma forces its way out of the conduit.	The volcano erupts!

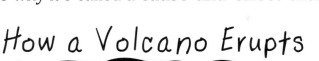

eruption

gases and water vapor

volcano

conduit

magma

magma chamber

cracks

KWL Chart

A **KWL Chart** helps you think about something you are studying. Read the question at the top of each column. It tells you how to complete the chart.

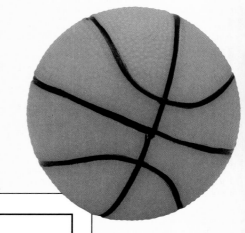

Topic: Basketball		
K **What Do I Know?**	**W** **What Do I Want to Learn?**	**L** **What Did I Learn?**
• It takes two teams to play a game. • Each team tries to throw the ball into the basket. • The team that makes the most baskets wins.	• How many players are on each team? • How many points are given for a basket? • How long does the game last?	• There are 5 players on a team. • A basket can count as 1, 2, or 3 points. • A game is 32 minutes long. • The game is played in two parts. Each part takes 16 minutes. • Basketball began in the U.S. in 1891.

KWL Chart Practice:
3 Tell students that you want to know about soccer or another topic familiar to students. Begin a new **KWL** chart. Verbalize as you write in a detail for the **K** and the **W** section, and then ask students to supply an answer for the **L** section. Continue having students tell you where you should write each detail.
4 Give each student a **KWL** chart. Have them choose a sport and fill in the first two columns. Students can ask classmates their questions and use the responses to finish the last column.
5 Provide students with a topic from an article of interest to them. Have them complete the first two columns of a **KWL** chart. Distribute the article and have them read it to complete the last column. Ask them to present to the class what they learned.

3 Speech Emergence **4** Intermediate Fluency **5** Advanced Fluency/Fluent

Flow Chart

Flow Chart Practice:

3 Create several sets of illustrated cards with labels for each step in the flow chart. Distribute a set to each pair of students and have them put the cards in order.

4 Help students recall a recent class or school project. Create a flow chart for the project as students dictate the steps.

5 Encourage students to create illustrated flow charts for hobbies such as building model airplanes or making jewelry. Have them present their flow charts to the class along with the finished product.

▶ **Practice Book page 34**

A **flow chart** shows the steps in a process. Arrows show the order of the steps.

How Jeans Are Made

Draw a picture of the jeans. → Use the picture to make a pattern.

Use the pattern to cut the denim fabric.

Sew the pieces of denim together.

Add buttons, rivets, zippers, and labels.

Wash the jeans to make the fabric feel softer or look worn.

Deliver the jeans to the stores for sale.

Time Lines

A **time line** shows a series of important events.
It tells about each event and when it happened.

Horizontal Time Line

This time line tells about special events in a
person's life. It's called a **horizontal time line**
because the line goes from left to right ➡.

Age 4	Age 5	Age 7	Age 9	Age 12
My family left the Philippines and moved to the United States.	I started kindergarten at a school in Los Angeles, California.	My family opened a restaurant.	We went back to the Philippines to visit relatives.	I won 1st place at the National Spelling Bee.

Vertical Time Line

This time line goes from top to bottom ⬇. That's why it's called a **vertical time line**.

Dr. Franklin Chang-Díaz has spent over 1,033 hours in space.

Dr. Chang-Díaz: Astronaut

1950
Born in San José, Costa Rica

1969
Graduated from Hartford High School in Hartford, Connecticut

1973
Graduated from the University of Connecticut

1977
Graduated from the Massachusetts Institute of Technology

1981
Became an astronaut for the National Aeronautics and Space Administration (NASA)

1986
6-day space shuttle <u>Columbia</u> mission during which he participated in the deployment of the SATCOM KU satellite

1989
5-day space shuttle <u>Atlantis</u> mission during which the crew deployed the Galileo spacecraft on its journey to Jupiter

1992
8-day space shuttle <u>Atlantis</u> mission during which the crew deployed the European Retrievable Carrier satellite

1994
First joint U.S./Russian space shuttle mission

1996
15-day space shuttle mission

Time Line Practice:
3 Have students create a time line of their life. They can draw pictures and write one- or two-word labels to describe each event.
4 Have partners make time lines about their lives. One student can describe events in his or her life while the partner records the information on a time line. Then have students reverse roles.
5 Have students read the biography about María Izquierdo on page 97. Ask them to use the details to make a time line for her life.
➤ **Practice Book page 35**

Chapter 3
Put It in Writing!

Danny and Aisha love to write! They know that writing is a good way to share ideas with others and to express their own personal thoughts and feelings.

How can you be a spectacular writer? Just look in this chapter and you'll find out! You'll learn how to put your own ideas in writing and how to write everything from letters and reports to stories and even tongue twisters!

The Writing Process

Writing is a great way to express yourself! The five steps in the **Writing Process** will help you plan, create, improve, and publish your work.

Teach:
Plan to spend a day introducing **The Writing Process** before students begin work on the Communication Projects described on pages 24T–95T. Read aloud each step, elaborate on the models, and then have volunteers describe the step in their own words.

Depending on your students' proficiency levels, you may also want to plan an additional day or two to introduce **The Good Writer Guide** on pages 148–157 (see those pages for additional teaching strategies). Then, as students work on their writing projects, remind them to refer to **The Writing Process** pages and the **The Good Writer Guide** whenever they need help.

STEP
1 **Prewriting**

Prewriting is what you do before you write. That's when you decide what to write about and organize your ideas.

Brainstorm Ideas and Choose a Topic

An idea is all you need to get started! Try collecting ideas in a writing file. Then, when it's time to write, just find one in your file. You can also brainstorm ideas and jot down those that interest you.

Think about your ideas. Which ideas do you know the most about? Which one means something special to you? Circle one idea. That will be your **topic**.

 The Good Writer Guide on pages 148–149 for tips on collecting ideas.

Writing Ideas

facts about Port-au-Prince, Haiti

what I do after school

what my uncle sells in his store

my first day of school in the United States

Plan Your Writing

■ **Ask yourself questions about your topic. The answers will help you decide which kinds of details to include.**

Three important questions are:

1. **Why** am I writing? This will be your **purpose** for writing. For example, you might want to describe to your friends where you used to live or go to school.

2. **Who** is going to read my writing? Your **audience**, or readers, can be your family, classmates, or someone you don't know.

3. **What** am I going to write? This will be the **kind of writing** you'll do like a letter, report, or personal narrative.

 The Good Writer Guide on pages 150–152 for tips on writing for a specific purpose and audience.

■ Collect the details.

List details about your topic. Talk about your topic with others. They might give you even more details to add. Here are some ways to show your details.

Make a cluster.

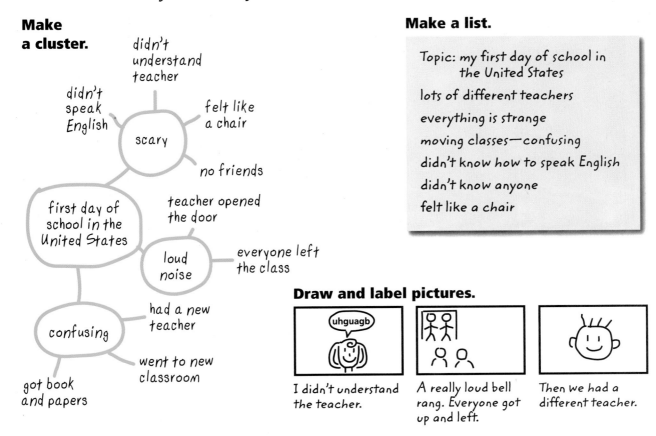

Make a list.

Topic: my first day of school in the United States

lots of different teachers

everything is strange

moving classes—confusing

didn't know how to speak English

didn't know anyone

felt like a chair

Draw and label pictures.

I didn't understand the teacher.

A really loud bell rang. Everyone got up and left.

Then we had a different teacher.

■ Organize the details.

Are the details about your topic in order? Sometimes you can organize the details as you write them down. Other times, you may need to put your details in order. One way to do that is to use numbers to show the order.

 Go To **Picture It!** on pages 62–83 to find more ways to organize your details.

Topic: my first day of school in the United States

6. lots of different teachers

1. everything is strange

5. moving classes—confusing

2. didn't know how to speak English

3. didn't know anyone

4. felt like a chair

The Writing Process, continued

2 Drafting

Now you're ready to write your **first draft**. That's when you write quickly just to get your ideas down on paper. Turn your details into sentences and paragraphs, but don't worry about making mistakes. Just write!

Details

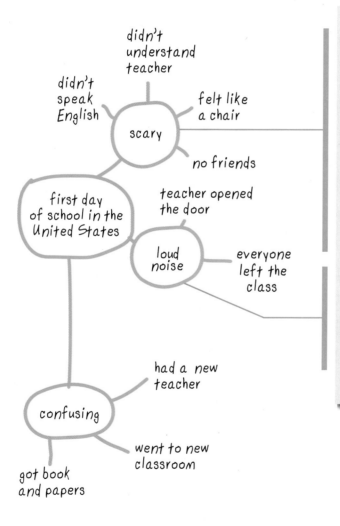

Sentences and Paragraphs

My first day of school in the United States was very scary and I didn't speak English and I didn't know how I was going to talk to people. I didn't have any friends. I felt like a chair. I tried to understand the teacher, but I couldn't.

Suddenly, a very loud bell rang. The teacher opened the door, and all the kids stood up and left the room.

3 Revising

Revise means to make changes. When you revise your writing, you change it to make it clear for your readers. You also make changes to be sure that it says what you want it to say.

Read Your Draft

Ask yourself questions about your writing.

- ❏ Is my writing interesting?

- ❏ Did I say what I wanted to say?

- ❏ Did I include all the details? Should I take any out? Should I add some?

- ❏ Did I stick to the topic?

- ❏ Is my writing clear?

- ❏ Does my writing make sense? Are the sentences, details, and events in the best order?

- ❏ Are there any words I should change to make my writing clearer?

The Writing Process, continued

Have Someone Else Read Your Draft

Have the person who reads your draft follow these steps to give you ideas for making your writing better. Discussing your writing like this is called a **peer conference**.

The Reader's Role in a Peer Conference

1 Read the writing at least two times.

2 Try summarizing it in one sentence. What is the main idea?

> This story (report) is all about ____.

3 Tell which part you liked best. Why?

> I really liked how you ____. The beginning (ending) is really good because ____.

4 Tell which part you liked least. Why?

> The beginning (ending) didn't get my attention because ____. I didn't like ____ because ____.

5 Tell if any parts confused you.

> I didn't understand the part where ____.
>
> I was surprised to read that ____.

6 Tell how to make it better. Be specific.

> This would be better if ____.
>
> You might try adding (or taking out) ____.

Mark Your Changes

Now **edit**, or mark your changes using the **editing marks**.

Editing Marks	Meaning
∧	Add.
↻	Move to here.
↖	Replace with this.
⌣	Take out.

I used "and" too many times in this sentence.

My first day of school in the United States was very scary
                    because
~~and~~ I didn't speak English ~~and~~ ⊙
I didn't know how I was going to talk to people. I didn't have any friends. (I felt like a chair.) I tried to understand the teacher, but I couldn't. ←

Suddenly, a very loud bell rang. The teacher opened the
                              jumped
door, and all the kids ~~stood~~ up
         rushed out the door.
and ~~left the room.~~

Ingrid said it would be better if I put how I felt last.

These changes will give my readers a better picture of what happened.

 The Good Writer Guide on pages 153–156 for tips on improving your writing.

The Writing Process, continued

STEP
4 Proofreading

After revising your draft, **proofread** it. That means to look for mistakes in capitalization, spelling, and punctuation. Use the **proofreading marks** to show what you need to fix.

Proofreading Marks	Meaning
∧	Add.
⋏	Add a comma.
⊙	Add a period.
≡	Capitalize.
◯	Check spelling.
/	Make lowercase.
¶	Start a new paragraph.
⌠	Take out.

Why was everyone leaving? In Haiti⋏ we stayed in the same C̲lassroom all day. I followed the class⋏ and we went into a new room. A stranger gave me a book and some papers. I was really puzzled. Fortunately, the man spoke some Creole and explained that he was my science teacher.¶ Finally⋏ i̲ understood. In a̲merica, there are special teachers for science, music⋏ and gym. Students also move to new classrooms. At first⋏ it was very confusing⋏ but now I like having different (diferent) teachers for my subjects⊙

Go To Pages 202-217 for capitalization, punctuation, and spelling tips.

STEP

5 Publishing

Publishing is the best part of the writing process! Now you can make a clean copy of your writing and share it. Here are some ideas for publishing your writing.

- Send it to a magazine or newspaper.

- E-mail it to your friend in Singapore.

- Put it in a notebook with other students' work and make it a reference book for next year's class.

- Read it out loud to your class.

- Turn it into a book.

- Read it out loud on a stage with music playing in the background.

- Make a home video of you reading it.

- Fax it to your mom at her office.

My First Day in an American School

by Marco Quezada

My first day of school in the United States was very scary because I didn't speak English. I didn't know how I was going to talk to people. I didn't have any friends. I tried to understand the teacher, but I couldn't. I felt like a chair.

Suddenly, a very loud bell rang. The teacher opened the door, and all the kids jumped up and rushed out the door.

Why was everyone leaving? In Haiti, we stayed in the same classroom all day. I followed the class, and we went into a new room. A stranger gave me a book and some papers. I was really puzzled. Fortunately, the man spoke some Creole and explained that he was my science teacher.

Finally, I understood. In America, there are special teachers for science, music, and gym. Students also move to new classrooms. At first, it was very confusing, but now I like having different teachers for my subjects.

Kinds of Writing

Advice Column

Do you have a problem that you can't figure out? Try writing a letter to an **advice column** in a newspaper, in a magazine, or on the World Wide Web.

AmericanGirl

HELP! FROM you

Dear *American Girl*

An advice column begins with a description of the **problem**.

Help! I watch too much TV! I'm hooked on soap operas, and I always go to bed late because I watch the late show. What should I do?
—Couch Potato

The person asking for advice often uses a **made-up name**.

The **advice** is a way to solve the problem. It's usually helpful to anyone who reads it.

We had the same problem. Here's what to do:
1. Put a sign on the TV that says: DO NOT WATCH!
2. Start doing some other fun things like reading and playing sports.
3. Try not to think about TV, and spend more time with your friends.

Try this for a week, and you will soon get into the habit of doing other things. Have fun!
—Anna, age 10, and Jessica, age 9

AG Magazine

Announcements and Advertisements

An **announcement** is a short message that tells about an event.

Advertisements (or ads) tell about services you might need or special products you can buy.

River School's Spring Fair

Saturday, April 15 10—4 at the school Come for food, games, prizes!

Bicycle Repair

It's Time for Spring Cleaning!

Complete bike repair and cleaning for road and mountain bikes.

Nathan's Bike Shop 756 Mission Fields Center Alton, IL 60381

555-0099

A company's **name**, **address**, and **telephone number** is given so you can get in touch with them.

Ads often show pictures of what you can buy.

A description tells you more about the item.

Show Your School Spirit!

OAK GROVE SCHOOL

Your school's name and mascot can be on this 100% cotton shirt. Available in an assortment of colors.

Sizes: ☐ S   ☐ M   ☐ LG   ☐ XL
5D143-714 . . . . $15.00

Mail your order to:
School Colors International
P.O. Box 683
New York, NY 11021
or call : 1-800-555-3671

A **code number** identifies the item. You use that code on the order form.

Announcements and Advertisements, continued

Classified ads are short notices that are classified, or put into groups. For example, the "New Today" section groups those items that are appearing for the first time. Look at these ads.

Help Wanted

New Today

DOGGY DAY CARE: Wanted dog lover w/ time to care for energetic puppy 2-3 days per week. 555-1759, lv. msg.

For Sale

UNICYCLE: Brand new! We can't ride it! $80 obo. Call 555-2521.

Wanted to Buy

WANTED: Used longboard, 8 ft. or longer. Call Marc 555-8653 pgr.

People pay for classified ads by the line, so they use **abbreviations**, or shortened words, to keep the ad brief.

w/ = with
lv. msg. = leave message
obo. = or best offer
ft. = feet
pgr. = pager

Advertisements Practice:
Use Communication Project 3 on page 17T and Project 17 on pages 64T–67T to involve students in writing advertisements (service, catalog, and classified ads).

Autobiography

An **autobiography** is the true story of your life, written by you.

My Haiti
I am from Haiti, a country in the Caribbean Sea. I was born on a hot December day there in 1987.
Every day is warm in Haiti. In fact, until I was ten years old and moved to Boston, I had no idea what snow was like...

Biography

Teach:
If possible, display prints or art books that contain María Izquierdo's paintings. Have students talk about the paintings or describe the one on this page. Explain that María Izquierdo was a real person and to tell about her life, you can write a biography. Then read aloud the introduction and the writing model. Ask students questions about the facts: *When was María Izquierdo born? Why was she famous?*

A **biography** is the true story of a person's life. When you write a biography, you tell about the most important events and people in another person's life.

Circus Ponies
by María Izquierdo

A biography has **facts** that tell about the person and what he or she did.

It has **dates** and **sequence words** that tell when things happened.

Biography Practice:
Use Communication Project 21 on pages 80T–83T to involve students in writing a biography.

María Izquierdo

María Izquierdo was born in 1902 in San Juan de los Lagos, Mexico. Her mother and father died when she was a child, so María lived with her grandmother and aunt. When she was a teenager, she married and moved to Mexico City.

In Mexico City, María attended art classes at the Academia de San Carlos. It was there that a famous Mexican painter, Diego Rivera, saw and liked her paintings. He helped her show them for the first time.

María became very famous for her paintings of the people and landscapes of Mexico and for her pictures of the circus. In 1929, she showed her paintings in New York City. She was the first Mexican woman to have an exhibit that included only her paintings. María painted for the rest of her life until her death in 1955.

Book Review

Sometimes you read a book that you just have to talk about with someone. You can tell about it by writing a **book review**.

Teach:
Hold up a book that students are familiar with and say that you haven't read it. Call on volunteers to tell you whatever they can about the book. Explain how the information they gave can help you decide whether or not to read the book. Define *book review*, and then read aloud the introduction above. As you work through the page, have students find and name the book's title, author, and so on.

In the first paragraph, tell the **title** of the book and the **author**. Then tell what the book is mostly about, or its **main idea**.

Next, tell how you **feel** about the book and why.

Finally, tell the **most important idea you learned** from the book.

The Lost Lake

The Lost Lake by Allen Say is about a boy, Luke, who went to live with his father in New York for the summer. Luke was bored there because his dad was always too busy to spend time with him. One Saturday, Dad took Luke on a hiking trip to a secret "lost lake." The lake wasn't really secret, though, because lots of other people were there. So Luke and Dad looked for another lake. They hiked and talked all the next day. Then they found a place to camp and went to sleep. When they woke up, they saw a lake in front of them! No one else was around.

I like this book because it reminded me of camping trips with my family. I also like that the father and the son talked to each other more when they were out camping.

This book shows how sometimes adults can get so busy that they forget to spend time with their kids. Maybe people should think about going somewhere else to help them remember what is important.

Book Review Practice:
Use Communication Project 2 on page 16T to involve students in writing a book review.

Cartoons and Comic Strips

Cartoons and **comic strips** are drawings that show funny situations. Which of these makes you laugh the most?

"I'm calling it a surprise cake because I lost my bubble gum in the batter."

Character Sketch

See *Description*.

Description

Teach:
Out of students' sight, choose two classroom objects. Have students close their eyes while you use describing words and sensory words to tell about one object. Have students open their eyes, identify the object you described, and tell how they knew. Then read aloud the introduction. Work through the two types of descriptions in different sessions. As you teach **Character Sketch**, call on volunteers to find and read aloud the sentences, details, or words in the model that illustrate each characteristic.

A **description** uses words to help you picture in your mind what someone or something is like.

Character Sketch

One kind of description is a **character sketch**. It describes a real or an imaginary person.

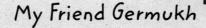

Name the person in the **topic sentence**.

My Friend Germukh

Germukh is my best friend at school. He has dark brown hair and dark eyes. Germukh is shorter than most of the kids in our class, but that doesn't bother him.

Give **examples** of what the person does that makes him or her special.

Germukh is a great artist. He can draw creepy outer space creatures with antennae and bug eyes. Actually, his creatures are kind of cute!

Germukh is shy when there are a lot of people around, but he talks a lot when just the two of us work together on a project. Germukh always helps me with my English. Once we had to give an oral report, and Germukh stayed inside during recess to help me practice for it.

Use **describing words** and other details that tell what the person looks like and how the person acts.

Character Sketch Practice:
Use Communication Project 14 on pages 52T–55T to involve students in writing a character sketch.

Description of a Place

When you describe a place, use lots of details to help your readers imagine that they are there!

Teach, continued:
As you teach **Description of a Place**, have students work as partners: one reads the description while the other tracks the position of the items in the photo. Help students summarize that the description starts at the front and moves back, then up to the hammock and to the top of the photo. Ask students to find other phrases that cue the positions (*Above the bowls, Just above the seller*). Then have students study the photo and suggest more descriptive details that could be added to the paragraph.

Name the subject in the **topic sentence**.

Write the details in **space order**. That means to tell what you see in order from left to right, near to far, or top to bottom.

A Market in Vietnam

The outdoor market in Vietnam is jammed full with food and people. Closest to the street, you'll see a row of square wicker or plastic containers filled with parsley, pineapples, apples, taro, and waterlilies as white as clouds. In the next row up are large round bowls of fresh beans, bean sprouts, and a special kind of meat piled high like pyramids. Above the bowls, the seller lies in a hammock to free up space for more things to sell. Just above the seller, plastic bags for carrying the food hang down from the wooden beams of the stall.

Use **direction words** and phrases to tell where things are.

Use **sensory words** that tell how things look, sound, feel, smell, or taste.

Use **similes** to help the reader imagine what's being described.

Go To **Sensory Words** on pages 16 and 17 for more words you can use in a description.

Description of a Place Practice:
Use Communication Project 19 on pages 72T–75T to involve students in writing a spatial description.

Diary
See *Journal Entry.*

Directions

Directions tell how to play a game, how to get somewhere, or how to make something. When you write directions, the most important thing to do is to put the steps in order.

Game Directions

Tell how many people can play.

Tell how to play the game.

Tell how to win the game.

Rock, Paper, Scissors

Number of Players: 2

How to Play: First make a fist with one hand. Next move your fist up and down three times as you say *rock, scissors, paper*. After you say *paper*:
 – keep a fist for rock
 – put two fingers out for scissors
 – put your palm down for paper.
Finally, look at your hands to see who wins.

Who Wins:
Rock beats scissors, scissors beats paper, and paper beats rock. Play again if both players have the same hand position.

Use **time** and **order words** to show the steps.

Directions to a Place

Use **direction words** to tell people which way to go.

To get to the theater, turn left out of the parking lot. Go four blocks, past the school, to Citrus Street. Turn right. The theater is on the left. It's a yellow building with a big, white sign.

Use **describing words** to help someone find the correct place.

3 Speech Emergence **4** Intermediate Fluency **5** Advanced Fluency/Fluent

Directions for Making Something

In a **recipe**, tell the name of the food.

First, list the ingredients and the amounts of each thing you need.

What's Cooking?

Chocolate Chip Cookies

You will need:

1 cup butter	3 cups flour
1 1/2 cups sugar	1 teaspoon salt
1 Tablespoon molasses	1 teaspoon baking soda
1 teaspoon vanilla	2 cups chocolate chips
2 eggs	

Write the **steps** in order. Numbers help show the order.

1. Preheat the oven to 375°.
2. Mix the butter, sugar, and molasses together in a bowl.
3. Add the vanilla and eggs. Mix well.
4. Add the flour, salt, and baking soda.
5. Fold in the chocolate chips.
6. Drop the batter—a tablespoon for each cookie—on an ungreased cookie sheet.
7. Bake in the oven for 8–10 minutes.

Begin sentences with **verbs** that tell someone exactly what to do.

Directions for Making Something Practice:
Use Communication Project 7 on pages 24T–27T to involve students in writing directions.

Editorial

Teach:
Tell students about an issue you feel strongly about such as wearing seat belts or clean air. Ask students what you could do to share your opinions. Point out that one way a newspaper tells a lot of people about its opinion is by writing an editorial.

An **editorial** is a newspaper or magazine article that is written to persuade people to believe the same way you do. When you write an editorial, tell how you feel about something. That's your **opinion**. Give **facts** to support your opinion.

Teach, continued:
Read aloud the introduction and the editorial, pausing after each paragraph to clarify vocabulary and point out the specific details that illustrate each characteristic.

Give your **opinion** about the subject in the first paragraph.

Next, give **facts** that explain why you feel the way you do.

At the end, tell what people can do to help, and state your opinion again.

February 6, 2001

Save the Gentle Manatees

Our manatees need protection from speeding boats. If we don't keep boat speeds slow, more and more of these gentle beasts will die.

A few members of the City Council want to pass a law that will increase boat speeds in some waterways where manatees live. When boats go too fast, the manatees can't get out of the way of the dangerous boat propellers in time.

We need to tell the City Council that saving the manatees is important to us. Increasing boat speeds is not. You can take action no matter where you live. Call, write, fax, or e-mail City Council members. Ask them to support protection for manatees and their home, and to *keep existing slow speed zones in our waters*! Any type of letter or call helps!

Editorial Practice:
Use Communication Project 17 on pages 64T–67T to involve students in creating a class newspaper that includes advertisements, news stories, and editorials.

Fable

A **fable** is a story written to teach a lesson. It often ends with a moral that states the lesson.

The **beginning** tells what the story is all about.

The **middle** tells about the events and what the characters do.

The **end** tells what finally happens.

The Birds Learn How to Build a Nest
adapted from Tung Chung-ssu

In the ancient forest, the phoenix knew best how to build a nest. Other birds wanted to learn, so they went to see him.

The phoenix said, "To learn this skill, you must listen carefully." The hen fell asleep.

The phoenix said, "If you want to make a good nest, you must first choose three big branches and then stack them on top of each other." The crow said, "Now I know how to do it!" He flew away. But the phoenix continued, "The best nest is under the eaves of someone's house where it is safe from wind and rain." The sparrow thought that was all and flew away. The phoenix said more: "Make the nest with layers of mud mixed with grass." Only the swallow heard these last words.

Today the hen does not know how to make a nest and has to be fed by people. The crow's nest is not very sturdy. The sparrow builds his nest beneath the eaves of people's homes. Only the swallow's nest is sturdy and safe from wind and rain.

Moral: Be like the swallow and listen to everything someone has to say. To learn, we must be patient.

A fable often has **talking animals**.

A fable has a **moral** that tells what you can learn from the story.

Fable Practice:
Depending on the proficiency levels of your students:
• Have partners work together to make a beginning, middle, and end story map like the one on page 71, and add a section for the moral. Encourage partners to display their map as they retell the fable.
• Read other fables like Aesop's "The Crow and the Pitcher" or "The Lion and the Mouse" and record the morals on the chalkboard. Then have groups choose a moral and make up a new fable to go with it. You may want to have students create a story map for their fable, then use the Writing Process on pages 86–93 to write it.

3 Speech Emergence 4 Intermediate Fluency 5 Advanced Fluency/Fluent

Folk Tales and Fairy Tales

Folk Tale

A **folk tale** is a story that people have been telling one another for many years.

Teach:
Depending on the proficiency levels of your students, plan to introduce one story a day or week. After reading aloud the folk tale, invite students to share any stories that their parents and grandparents have told them or any folk tales they know of from their native countries.

The **characters** in a folk tale often have a problem to solve.

The **setting** is often a made-up place, long ago.

The **ending** is usually a happy one.

Stone Soup

 ne day, three hungry men walked into a tiny village. Everyone told these travelers that there was no food. Really, the villagers were greedy and didn't want to share with the men.

"Oh well, there is nothing more delicious than a bowl of stone soup," one traveler said.

The villagers thought this was odd, but agreed to lend the men a huge soup pot. The men lit a fire, put three stones in the pot with some water, and waited.

A villager looked at the soup and thought, "Ridiculous! No soup is complete without some carrots." He went home, got a bunch of carrots, and put them in the pot.

Another villager looked at the soup and thought, "What that really needs is onions!" So she took a few onions and added them to the soup.

Soon, lots of people brought beef, cabbage, celery, potatoes— a little of everything that makes a soup good.

When the stone soup was done and everyone tasted it, they all agreed that they hadn't ever had anything so delicious! And imagine, a soup from stones!

3 Speech Emergence **4** Intermediate Fluency **5** Advanced Fluency/Fluent

Fairy Tale

Teach, continued:
After reading aloud the fairy tale, have students look at the story map for *Cinder Elly* on page 71. Talk about how the story is a more modern version of the tale. You may also want to share with students other variations such as *Yeh-Shen* by Ai-Ling Louie, *Mufaro's Beautiful Daughters* by John Steptoe, *Sidney Rella and the Glass Sneaker* by Bernice Myers, and *The Korean Cinderella* by Shirley Climo.

A **fairy tale** is a special kind of folk tale. It often has royal characters like princes and princesses, and magical creatures like elves and fairies.

Folk Tale and Fairy Tale Practice:
Use Communication Project 6 on pages 22T–23T to involve students in retelling a story. Students may want to choose one of the stories on pages 106 and 107 to retell.

Cinderella

Once upon a time, there was a sweet, gentle girl named Cinderella, who wanted to go to the royal ball. Her mean stepmother told her to stay home and scrub the floor while she and her daughters went to the ball. Cinderella wept.

Suddenly, Cinderella's fairy godmother appeared. She waved her magic wand and turned Cinderella's ragged clothes into a sparkling gown and her shoes into glass slippers. She also turned a pumpkin into a coach and mice into horses. Now Cinderella could go to the ball! However, the fairy godmother warned Cinderella that if she wasn't home by midnight, her clothes would change into rags again.

When the prince saw Cinderella, he was overwhelmed by her beauty. All night, he refused to dance with anyone but her. At the stroke of midnight, Cinderella ran away so quickly that she lost a glass slipper, and her clothes turned back into rags. The broken-hearted prince chased her but found only the slipper.

The next day, the prince asked every woman to try on the tiny slipper. No one could squeeze into it except Cinderella. Then the prince knew that he had found the woman of his dreams. Cinderella and the prince were soon married, and they lived happily ever after.

A fairy tale often begins with **Once upon a time.**

It usually has a happy ending.

107

Greetings

Cards

Is your cousin having a birthday? Is your aunt in the hospital? Do you want to send Kwanzaa greetings to your friend? All of these are reasons to send a **greeting card**.

Hurry up and feel better.

HAPPY BIRTHDAY

KWANZAA IS A CELEBRATION OF ONE ANOTHER.

Jeffrey Dibrell
1836 Hamlin Road
Washington, D.C. 20017

MAY ALL THE JOY OF KWANZAA BE YOURS THROUGHOUT THE YEAR.

Happy Kwanzaa
Jeffrey,
Love, Chloe

Greeting Cards Practice:
Ask students who they would like to send greeting cards to and why. Provide materials such as heavy paper, markers, and stickers for them to use to design their own cards and create envelopes. Students can also use their own artwork or clip art from a computer file. Have students write greetings on their cards, address the envelopes, and mail them.

 Dateline U.S.A. on pages 264–301 for special days to send greetings.

3 Speech Emergence **4** Intermediate Fluency **5** Advanced Fluency/Fluent

Postcards

When you go on a trip, you can send greetings to a friend. Just write a postcard!

Write your **message** here.

September 10, 2002

Dear Marc,

Chicago is amazing! O'Hare airport is huge—even bigger than the one in Los Angeles. Can you believe that Sears Tower is 110 stories tall? I walked along Lake Michigan yesterday and found out why Chicago's nickname is "The Windy City."

I'm having a great time. I can't wait to show you my pictures when I get back.

Your friend,
Felipe

Don't forget to add a **stamp**!

Write your friend's **name and address**.

Marc Rountree
347 Driscol Street
Los Angeles, CA 90064

Postcards Practice:

Contact a teacher at another school and arrange to exchange postcards between your classes. Provide (or have students create) enough postcards for the entire class. Explain to students that they are going to write and send postcards to pen pals. Then have the class brainstorm details about where they live and what they like to do to include in their postcards. Have each student write a message on a postcard, address it, and give it to you to be mailed. Distribute the postcards from the class's pen pals and encourage volunteers to read the return messages aloud.

Interview

Teach:
Invite students to name someone they admire or a favorite sports or entertainment personality such as Michael Jordan or Pelé. Then, call on a volunteer to pretend to be that person as you ask him or her questions as if you were conducting an interview. Then read aloud the introduction. After working through each step, have students tell in their own words how to prepare, conduct, or share the results of an interview.

A good way to find out more about someone is to conduct, or set up, an **interview**. An interview is a meeting where one person asks another person questions to get information.

① Prepare for the interview.

■ Read any information you can find about the person you want to interview.

■ Call or write the person to plan a time when the two of you can meet.

■ Make a list of questions that you want to ask.

Questions to ask Wynton Marsalis:

How old were you when you started playing the trumpet?

How did you feel about practicing when you were a kid?

② Conduct the interview.

■ Be sure you have your questions, a pencil, and some paper to make any notes. Try to have a tape recorder with you. You can play the tape later to help you remember what was said.

■ Greet the person you are interviewing.

■ Ask the questions you planned and others that come up during the interview.

■ Thank the person when you are done.

❸ Share the results of the interview.

■ Look over your notes and listen to the tape.

■ Choose the information you want to share.

■ Decide how you want to share it. You might write an editorial, a description, or an article like this one.

Name the person you interviewed in the title.

List the questions (**Q**) you asked and the answers (**A**).

The answers are exact words spoken by the person you interviewed.

Talking Jazz with Wynton Marsalis
by Judy Burke

Q: How old were you when you started playing the trumpet?

A: I was six. Now, I don't want to give you the impression that I could play. I was just holding the horn, basically. My father was known by all the musicians, and they would say, "Let Ellis's son play."

After they heard me play, they would ask me, "Are you sure you're Ellis's son?"

Q: Did your father give you any advice?
A: He said, "The ability to play has a direct relationship to the amount of hours you practice."

Q: How did you feel about practicing when you were a kid?
A: Oh, I hated it. Just like everybody else. Nobody wants to practice.

Interview Practice:
Use Communication Project 24 on pages 92T–95T to involve students in conducting an interview and incorporating the responses into a written report.

Invitations

To invite people to come to a party or other special event, send them an **invitation**!

Tell **what** the event is all about.

Tell **when** and **where** the event will take place.

Come to a Party!

Shhhh!
It's a Surprise Birthday Party!

For: Alma

Date: Saturday, March 19

Time: 3 p.m. (Don't be late, please.)

Place: 263 Newland Street

R.S.V.P. 555-8301 (Ask for Casandra, not Alma.)

R.S.V.P. stands for _respondez-vous s'ils vous plâit_ in French. That means "Please respond." Write your telephone number if you want people to call you to let you know they are coming.

Journal Entry

Teach:
Read aloud the introduction and the journal entry. Discuss with students how the writer of the entry feels about learning Chinese. Point out that you can write about anything you want in a journal entry and that journal entries can be good places to look for writing ideas. You might also mention that because journal entries tell about personal thoughts and feelings, the writer can decide whether or not to share his or her journal entries with others.

A **journal** is a lot like a diary. Begin each **journal entry** with the date. Then tell about your thoughts and feelings, and things that happen to you.

Day Wednesday, May 3, 2002

A couple of days ago I was thinking, I really hope to go into one of the Chinese classes during my years in college. I believe that since that's my original background and that's the language of my ancestors and also my parents and relatives— most of my relatives do not speak English at all — I think it's really important to keep the communication going. Also, when we travel, I think it would be hard to communicate if I didn't know any Chinese. I am an American citizen now, but I still have that feeling, that strong feeling, that I want to know about my background.

Letters

For **Friendly Letters**, read aloud the introduction and the letter. Point to each part as you name it and clarify its content and position: *Here is the* **heading.** *The heading comes first in a letter. The heading in a friendly letter has the writer's address and the date.* Have students read aloud the part you describe.

Friendly Letters

You can write a **friendly letter** to tell a friend what's going on in your life. A friendly letter has five parts.

Heading

29583 Wayfarer Lane
Albany, NY 12258
January 17, 2000

In the **heading**, write your address and today's date.

Greeting

Dear Anders,

Body

You'll never guess what happened today! After months of wishing, my dream finally came true. Grandpa got John and me a new dog! I've been so lonely since Shadow died last year. Anyway, we got a black Labrador and named her Midnight. She is so friendly—she just keeps wagging her tail and following us around. I can't wait for you to see her when you come in March.

How are you doing? Did you learn how to ski yet? Please write soon.

In the **body**, write your news like you're talking to your friend. Ask what your friend is doing.

Closing

Your friend,

Your Signature

Laura

Here are other **closings** you can use in a friendly letter:

Sincerely,
Love,
Yours truly,
Always,

Friendly Letter Practice:
Use Communication Project 9 on pages 32T–35T to involve students in writing a friendly letter.

3 Speech Emergence **4** Intermediate Fluency **5** Advanced Fluency/Fluent

Electronic Mail

Teach, continued:
For **Electronic Mail**, plan time with another teacher, librarian, or staff member to receive and respond to e-mail messages. Begin the lesson by reading aloud the introduction and working through the model with students. Then demonstrate sending an e-mail letter as you verbalize what you are doing. Have partners send brief messages and read aloud any responses.

You can use e-mail to send a letter to a friend. E-mail is short for **electronic mail** that is sent by a computer. You can send letters to or receive messages from anyone in the world who has an e-mail address. Here's one kind of computer "mailbox" you might use.

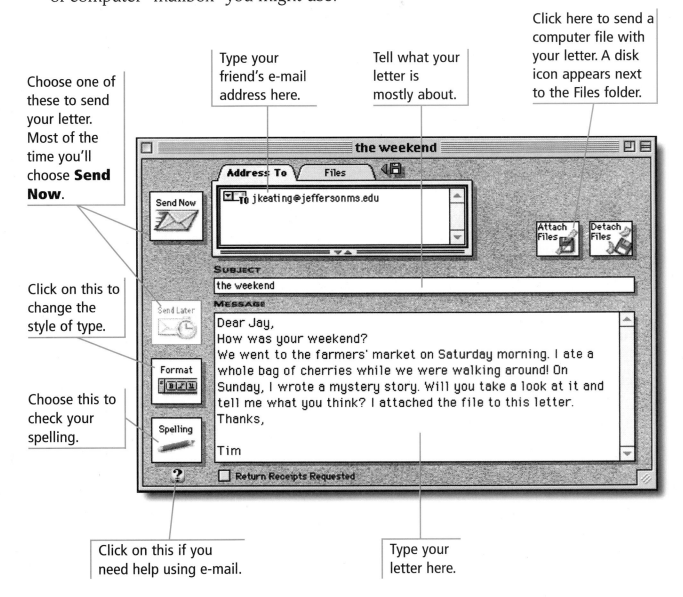

Click here to send a computer file with your letter. A disk icon appears next to the Files folder.

Type your friend's e-mail address here.

Tell what your letter is mostly about.

Choose one of these to send your letter. Most of the time you'll choose **Send Now**.

Click on this to change the style of type.

Choose this to check your spelling.

Click on this if you need help using e-mail.

Type your letter here.

Electronic Mail Practice:
Find keypals for your students by asking teachers from other schools or trying these Internet resources:
- epals.com Classroom Exchange (www.epals.com)
- Dave's ESL E-mail Connection (www.pacificnet.net/~sperling/guestbook.html)
- Keypal Opportunities for Students (www.ling.lancs.ac.uk/staff/visitors/kenji/keypal.htm)

Encourage students to write often to their new keypals. About once a month, ask students to share any experience or news from their correspondence.

Put It in Writing! 115

Letters, continued

Business Letters

Teach, continued:
Briefly review the characteristics of a friendly letter, then read aloud the introduction and the **Letter of Request**. As you work through the model, point out the addition of the inside address and the formal language used in the body and the closing. Have students tell in their own words why the girl wrote the letter. Then discuss how business letters and friendly letters are different.

A **business letter** is written to someone you don't know in a company or an organization. A business letter is more formal than a friendly letter and its parts are a little different.

Letter of Request

Heading	2397 Casanova Street Neptune Shores, FL 34744 February 6, 2001
Inside Address	Electronic Games, Inc. 57821 Sutter Blvd. New York, NY 10017
Greeting	Dear Sir or Madam:
Body	Please send me your latest catalogue of electronic games. I am especially interested in your latest version of electronic hockey. Thank you for your prompt attention.
Closing	Respectfully,
Your Signature	*Ann Gardner*
Your Name	Ann Gardner

In the **body**, tell what you want. Thank the person for paying attention to your request.

Here are more **closings** you can use in a business letter:

Sincerely,

Respectfully yours,

Very truly yours,

With best regards,

Letter of Request Practice:
Use Communication Project 16 on pages 60T–63T to involve students in writing a letter of request.

Sometimes you'll write a business letter to complain about something.

Letter of Complaint

2397 Casanova Street
Neptune Shores, FL 34744
June 30, 2001

Electronic Games, Inc.
57821 Sutter Blvd.
New York, NY 10017

Dear Sir or Madam:

I purchased your electronic game, "Invaders from the Purple Planet," on May 30, 2001, at the store Games, Games, Games in Neptune Shores. After playing with it for just three weeks, the button that you press to move the spaceship to the right stopped working. Since your product is warrantied for one year, I am requesting a replacement game. Enclosed is the broken one.

Respectfully,

Ann Gardner

Ann Gardner

Tell why you aren't happy with the product. Tell what you want the company to do about the problem.

Letters, continued

Sometimes you'll write a business letter to persuade someone to do something.

Persuasive Letter

349 Olympic Blvd.
Los Angeles, CA 90064
May 10, 2002

Parent and Teacher Association (PTA)
Valley School
562 North Cañon Drive
Los Angeles, CA 90064

Dear PTA Members:

Give your opinion in the first paragraph.

    I think that the PTA should vote to keep a gym teacher for our school. I know that it costs more money to have a teacher who teaches only physical education, but I think it's worth it.

Next, give reasons for your opinion.

    Most of the kids in my class love gym, and our teacher, Mrs. Richards, is really great. If Mrs. Richards doesn't teach us physical education, our homeroom teacher will have to, and he already has too much to do. Also, Mrs. Richards helps us learn how to work in a team and be good sports. Isn't that an important part of our education?

Finally, tell what action you want people to take.

    We must have a gym teacher in our school. Please vote "yes" when you meet with the Valley School Board.

Sincerely,

Andy Brown

Andy Brown

Use **opinion words** to tell how you feel. Other ways to begin an opinion are:

I feel that
I believe
My opinion is

Use **persuasive words** to get people to think the way you do.

Persuasive Business Letter Practice:
Use Communication Project 22 on pages 84T–87T to involve students in writing a persuasive business letter.

Envelope

To send a letter, put it in an **envelope**.

Envelope Practice:
Use the following Communication Projects to involve students in creating an envelope for their letters: Project 9, pages 32T–35T; Project 16, pages 60T–63T; and Project 22, pages 84T–87T.

Use **abbreviations** for the names of states. See page 205 for a complete list.

Write the **return address** at the top. That's your address.

Ann Gardner
2397 Casanova Street
Neptune Shores, FL 34744

Write the **mailing address** in the middle. That's the address of the person you are writing to.

Electronic Games, Inc.
57821 Sutter Blvd.
New York, NY 10017

Include the **ZIP code**. This number helps the post office deliver your letter quickly.

List Practice:
Talk with students about more reasons to write a list such as to remember homework assignments, to make sure they get all their chores done, to prepare to write a paragraph, and so on. Have students create and save lists for a week or two. Then have them share their lists and tell how the lists were useful.

List

What foods does your family need at the store? What chores do you need to do today? You can write a quick **list** to help you remember things.

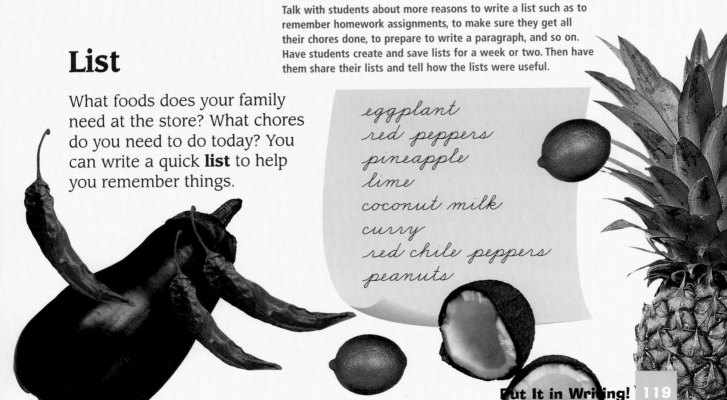

eggplant
red peppers
pineapple
lime
coconut milk
curry
red chile peppers
peanuts

Menu

A **menu** lists the food that a restaurant serves and tells its price. It usually gives a description of the meals.

World Café
DINNER MENU

MAIN DISHES

Shrimp Rice Bowl
Shrimp, red chiles and garden-fresh vegetables, served over rice . . . **$6.50**

Risotto Italian rice dish with chicken and cheese . . . **$7.95**

Southwestern-Style Burrito
Refried beans, beef, and cheddar cheese wrapped in a flour tortilla . . . **$5.75**

Tafelspitz Beef cooked in its own broth with horseradish . . . **$7.25**

Hawaiian Pizza
Thin slices of ham, pineapple, and extra mozzarella cheese . . . **$6.75**

SALADS

Caesar Salad Romaine lettuce with home-made croutons and our own Caesar dressing . . . **$3.95**

Oriental Chicken Salad
All breast meat, spices, almonds, celery, fried wontons, lettuce, and soy sauce dressing . . . **$5.95**

Garden Salad
Lettuce, tomatoes, cucumbers, mushrooms, carrots, onions, and your choice of dressing . . . **$2.50**

DRINKS

Soft Drinks . . . **$1.50**
Iced Tea . . . **$1.00**
Coffee . . . **$1.00**

Messages

See *Notes*.

News Story

A **news story** tells about an event that really happened. It includes only **facts**.

Teach:
Display a recent newspaper article about an event of interest to your students. Describe the event. Ask students to share any recent news they've heard or read about. Then read aloud the introduction. Define *fact* and talk about how facts are different from opinions. Then work through the news story. Afterward, have volunteers use the lead paragraph to answer the W-H questions.

The **headline** uses important words from the story to give a quick idea of what the story is about.

The **lead paragraph** answers the questions *who, what, when, where, why,* and sometimes *how* something happened.

The **body** gives more facts about the event.

Kids Rescue Puffins–Again

By Evelyn Davis
Banner News Service

VESTMANNAEYJAR, Iceland— Last night many of the children of Vestmannaeyjar were out rescuing birds. Pufflings, or young puffins, have wandered into the towns again this year. The children stayed awake to capture them and take them back to the ocean where they belong.

Pufflings were everywhere under bushes and cars, in the streets, on the grass. The six-week-old birds aren't old enough to fly well and are a bit disoriented. The birds went looking for open water but ended up in the city, far from the ocean.

In preparation, the children gathered cardboard boxes all last week. Then, this week, they stayed up and walked around the city with their boxes and flashlights to look for stray birds. The children say that they listen for the sound of flapping wings to lead them to the little birds.

In the early hours this morning, the kids took their boxes of birds to the ocean and let the birds go. The puffins, and the kids, should be back again next year.

News Story Practice:
Use Communication Project 17 on pages 64T–67T to involve students in writing a news story for a class newspaper.

3 Speech Emergence **4** Intermediate Fluency **5** Advanced Fluency/Fluent

Notes

A **note** is a short written message.

Telephone Message

When someone calls your mom and she isn't home, what can you do? Write a note, of course. This kind of note is called a **telephone message**.

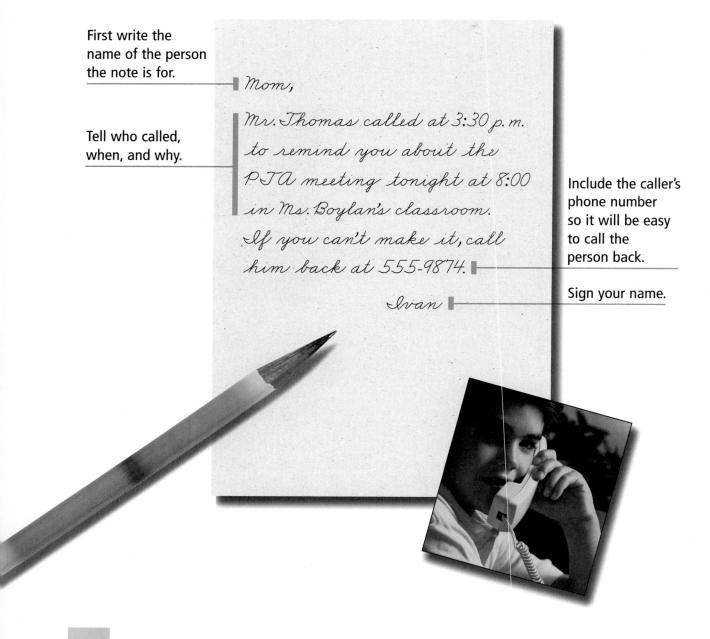

First write the name of the person the note is for.

Tell who called, when, and why.

Mom,

Mr. Thomas called at 3:30 p.m. to remind you about the PTA meeting tonight at 8:00 in Ms. Boylan's classroom. If you can't make it, call him back at 555-9874.

Ivan

Include the caller's phone number so it will be easy to call the person back.

Sign your name.

Teach:
Talk with students about times they were thankful for something. Then read aloud the definition. Call on a volunteer to read the note, and then ask individuals to find and read aloud the part you name. Invite students to say a new sentence for the thank-you note using the other ways to say "thank you."

Thank-you Note

A **thank-you note** thanks someone for doing something or for giving you a gift. It's a lot like a friendly letter.

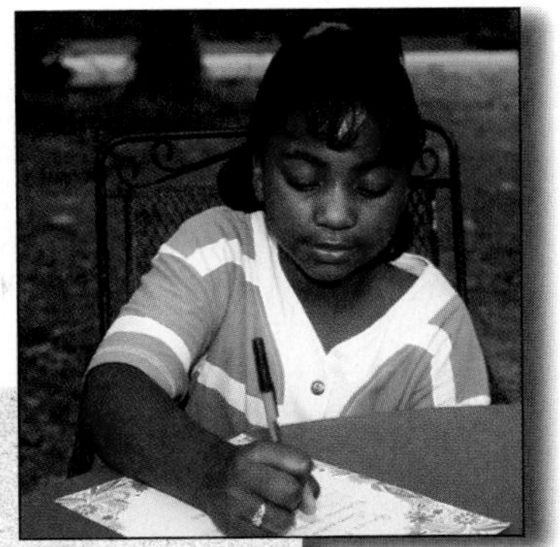

Write the **date**.

October 31, 2002

Write a **greeting**.

Dear Grandma and Grandpa,

Thank you so much for the game. It is so fun that my friend Sonia and I play every afternoon after school. Sometimes I win and sometimes she wins. I am so glad that you showed me how to play when I was at your house last summer. I hope that we can play again together soon—this time I might beat Grandpa!

In the **body**, say "thank you" and name the gift. Tell why you like it or how you are using it.

Love,
Liz

Write a **closing** and sign your name.

Here are some other ways to say *thank you*:

Many thanks...
I really appreciate...
Thanks a million...
You are so thoughtful...
I'm so grateful...

Observation Log

An **observation log** is a written record of things you see, or observe. It's a good idea to show dates for your notes to help you remember and carefully study what you saw.

Observations: Growing a Plant
Week 1: Brown dirt, no plant
Week 2: See a tiny, green shoot
Week 3: Shoot is now about
1/2 inch tall
Leaf starting to grow
Week 4: Plant taller
See two leaves
Week 5: Plant bigger
Leaves are reaching
for the sun

Heat and Water

	Temperature	Water Level
Monday	70°	5 inches
Tuesday	95°	4 inches
Wednesday	90°	3 inches
Thursday	77°	2 1/2 inches
Friday	73°	2 inches

Conclusion: Water evaporates faster in hot temperatures.

Order Form

To order something from a catalog or a magazine, you can use an **order form**. Be sure to include all the information about the item and where to send it.

THE WOMAN WHO OUTSHONE THE SUN

La mujer que brillaba aún más que el sol

From a poem by Alejandro Cruz Martínez

Pictures by Fernando Olivera

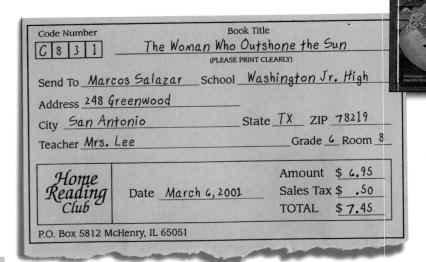

Code Number
C 8 3 1

Book Title
The Woman Who Outshone the Sun
(PLEASE PRINT CLEARLY)

Send To Marcos Salazar   School Washington Jr. High
Address 248 Greenwood
City San Antonio   State TX   ZIP 78219
Teacher Mrs. Lee   Grade 6 Room 8

Home Reading Club

Date March 6, 2001

Amount $ 6.95
Sales Tax $ .50
TOTAL $ 7.45

P.O. Box 5812 McHenry, IL 65051

Paragraphs

Teach:
Read aloud the definition and the first paragraph. Begin a cluster on the chalkboard, writing the topic sentence in the center. Then reread each detail sentence and ask students to help you record the details. Repeat for the second paragraph, using a main idea diagram like the one on page 67.

A **paragraph** is a group of sentences that all tell about the same idea. One sentence gives the main idea of the paragraph. The other sentences give details that support the main idea.

Sometimes the paragraph begins with the main idea.

The **topic sentence** tells the main idea of the paragraph.

The **details** in these sentences tell more about the main idea.

> There are so many treasures to see at the beach! Tiny shells, shaped like fans, are everywhere. Colorful rocks sparkle on the soft, warm sand. A little, pink crab shell sits in the middle of a log that has washed up on the sandy shore.

Indent the first sentence of a paragraph. *Indent* means to leave a space before you start to write.

Sometimes the main idea comes at the end of a paragraph.

These sentences give the **details**.

> Tiny shells, shaped like fans, are everywhere. Colorful rocks sparkle on the soft, warm sand. A little, pink crab shell sits in the middle of a log that has washed up on the sandy shore. There are so many treasures to see at the beach!

The **topic sentence** that tells the main idea is last.

Paragraphs Practice:
Give partners topic sentences for a paragraph such as *There is so much to do at the park, A garden is filled with living creatures,* and so on. Have them use the models to help them write one paragraph with the topic sentence at the beginning and one with the topic sentence at the end.

 Main Idea Diagram on page 67. It shows how to make a picture of your main idea and details before you write a paragraph.

Paragraphs with Examples

In some paragraphs, the detail sentences give **examples** that go with the main idea.

The **topic sentence** tells the main idea.

Stamps are little works of art that show something about a country. Some stamps from Australia show the country's shape. Others show native Australian animals like a fish and a wombat. In Brazil, there are stamps of Brazilian festivals, like Carnival. Stamps from Botswana or Senegal may have pictures of birds. There are lots of colorful birds in both countries. People in colorful traditional clothing are on some stamps from Ecuador.

Each detail sentence gives an **example** of one type of stamp.

Paragraph with Examples Practice:
Partners can use the ideas generated from the class discussion about stamps to write a new paragraph or add detail sentences with examples for one of these main ideas: *There are many different tools you can use for writing. There is a lot to do at a carnival.*

Cause-and-Effect Paragraphs

In a cause-and-effect paragraph, you tell what happens and why. An **effect** is what happens. The **cause** is why it happened.

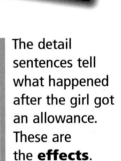

The topic sentence tells the **cause**.

Last week, my father started giving me a weekly allowance. Now, when I go to the store or the movies with my friends, I have my own money. Also, I can save some of my allowance every week to buy something nice for my sister's birthday. My allowance isn't a lot of money, but it is special to me.

The detail sentences tell what happened after the girl got an allowance. These are the **effects**.

Cause-and-Effect Paragraphs Practice:
Ask students what might happen if they got an allowance. Brainstorm the effects and have them help you rewrite the paragraph.

Paragraphs, continued

Paragraphs That Compare

Some paragraphs tell how two people, places, things, or ideas are alike. This paragraph compares alligators and crocodiles.

Teach:
Depending on the proficiency level of your students, you may want to introduce each type of paragraph during separate sessions or teach them together during one session. For **Paragraphs That Compare**, have students describe the pictures of the alligator and the crocodile. Then read aloud the introduction and the paragraph, pointing out details in the model that illustrate each characteristic. Draw a Venn diagram on the chalkboard. Ask students how the animals are the same and record the details in the middle of the diagram. Save the diagram so you can add to it when you teach **Paragraphs That Contrast**.

The **topic sentence** names the two things you are comparing.

The **detail sentences** tell how the things are the same.

It's easy to confuse an alligator with a crocodile because these two very large reptiles are a lot alike. Both live in marshes and swamps. They look similar, too. Both have tough skin, short legs, and long tails. Their large jaws have many sharp teeth. Alligators and crocodiles have the same kind of large eyes that stick up above their heads. When they swim, their eyes stay above the water so they always know where they're going!

Special words help you signal that the two things are alike.

Alligator

3 Speech Emergence **4** Intermediate Fluency **5** Advanced Fluency/Fluent

Paragraphs That Contrast

Some paragraphs tell how two people, places, things, or ideas are different. This paragraph contrasts alligators and crocodiles.

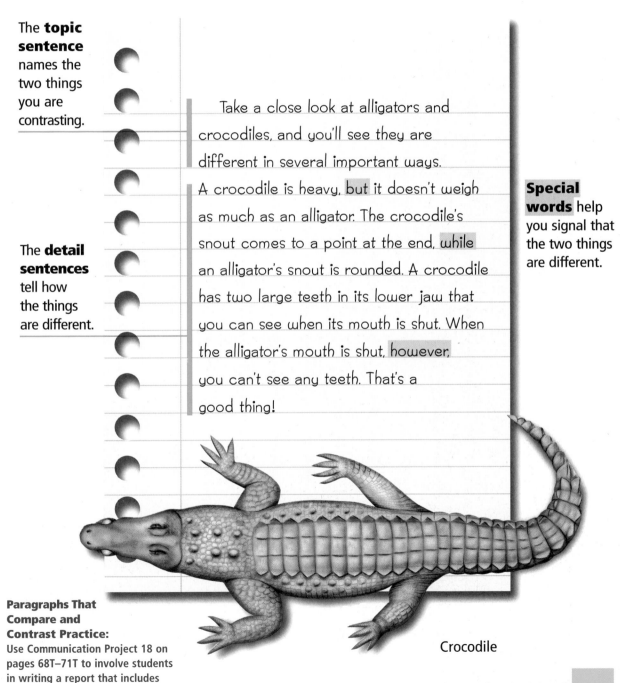

The **topic sentence** names the two things you are contrasting.

The **detail sentences** tell how the things are different.

Take a close look at alligators and crocodiles, and you'll see they are different in several important ways. A crocodile is heavy, but it doesn't weigh as much as an alligator. The crocodile's snout comes to a point at the end, while an alligator's snout is rounded. A crocodile has two large teeth in its lower jaw that you can see when its mouth is shut. When the alligator's mouth is shut, however, you can't see any teeth. That's a good thing!

Special words help you signal that the two things are different.

Crocodile

Paragraphs That Compare and Contrast Practice:
Use Communication Project 18 on pages 68T–71T to involve students in writing a report that includes compare and contrast paragraphs.

Paragraphs, continued

Persuasive Paragraphs

Teach:
Read aloud the introduction and work through the model, pointing out details in the paragraph that illustrate each characteristic. Then involve students in writing a class paragraph about something else that should be recycled. Prompt them to use persuasive words and give reasons for their opinions.

When you write a **persuasive paragraph**, you tell your opinion about something. You try to persuade your readers. That means you try to get them to agree with you.

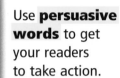

Give your opinion in the **topic sentence**.

Give the reasons for your opinion in the **detail sentences**.

> When you change the motor oil in your car, you should recycle the used oil. If you pour the used oil onto the ground, it harms the soil where plants are trying to grow. If you dump the used oil down a storm drain, it will end up in the ocean where it could kill a lot of fish. If you recycle used oil, however, it can be cleaned and reused. Please, you must help our planet! Just take your used oil to a gas station or other place where it can be recycled.

Use **persuasive words** to get your readers to take action.

Persuasive Paragraphs Practice:
Use Communication Project 10 on pages 36T–39T to involve students in writing a persuasive paragraph.

3 Speech Emergence **4** Intermediate Fluency **5** Advanced Fluency/Fluent

Personal Narrative

When you write a **personal narrative**, you tell a story about something that happened to you. Because the story is about you, you'll write it in the first person. That means you'll use the words *I*, *me*, and *my* a lot.

The **beginning** tells what the event is all about.

The **middle** tells more about the event.

The **end** tells what finally happened.

A Good Luck Valentine

I'll never forget my first Valentine's Day. When I got to school, I was surprised to find some bright red envelopes on my desk.

At first, I thought they were gifts for Chinese New Year. Each new year my family gives me money in red envelopes to wish me good luck. But when I opened the little envelopes, I only found some paper hearts.

Then my teacher explained what happens on Valentine's Day. The notes in the envelopes were valentines. Now when I look at my valentines, I feel just as wonderful as when I get gifts for the new year!

A personal narrative has **order words** that tell when something happened.

It has **describing words** that tell what things were like and how you felt.

Personal Narrative Practice:
Use the following Communication Projects to involve students in writing a personal narrative: Project 8, pages 28T–31T; Project 13, pages 48T–51T; and Project 20, pages 76T–79T.

 Dateline U.S.A. on pages 264–301 for more information about Valentine's Day and other special days and holidays.

Play

Teach:
Talk about plays or musicals you've seen or participated in and invite students to share their experiences. Then read aloud the introduction, the sentences for each step, and the models. Have students look back at the story. Ask them who the characters are, and then have them find the list of characters in the script. Repeat for the setting. Talk about the story's plot, and then point out the dialogue in the script. Explain that because a play is a story that is seen and heard, the characters tell the events through their dialogue. Encourage large groups to use the script to perform the play for the class.

A **play** is a story that is acted out on a stage. Every play has characters—the people or animals that tell the story. When you write a play, you decide what the characters will do and say.

1 **Start with a story. Make one up or choose one from a book.**

The Legend of the Chinese Zodiac

In ancient times, the Jade Emperor wanted to name each of the years in the twelve-year cycle after an animal. He couldn't decide which animals to honor, however. He invited all the animals on earth to participate in a race. The first twelve to finish the race would each have a year named for them. The rat won the race; the ox was second. The tiger, rabbit, dragon, snake, horse, sheep, monkey, rooster, dog, and boar were the next ten animals to cross the finish line. The Jade Emperor named a year for the animals in the order they finished the race, starting with the rat and ending with the boar.

2 **Turn the story into a script.**

The script names the characters. It tells the setting, or when and where the story takes place, and it describes what the characters say and do.

Here is how you can make a script.

Write a **title** and **act number**. An **act** in a play is just like a chapter in a book.

The Legend of the Chinese Zodiac
Act 2
The Race

List all the **characters**.

Characters: the Jade Emperor, rat, ox, tiger, rabbit, dragon, snake, horse, sheep, monkey, rooster, dog, boar

Tell about the **setting**.

Setting: Long ago, in front of the Jade Emperor's palace. There is a starting line on the ground. The Jade Emperor is telling all the animals the rules of the race.

Name each character and write the **dialogue**, or the words the characters say.

Jade Emperor *(loudly, to get everyone's attention)*: Listen! Listen! We are going to start the race in a few minutes. First, I want to explain the course and the rules.

Boar *(raising his hand)*: Will we be allowed to stop for water along the way?

Jade Emperor: Please let me tell you the rules of the whole race before you ask questions. *(pointing at the line on the ground)* This is the starting line. You must have all of your toes behind this line.

Use **stage directions** to tell how the characters should say the lines or move around on the stage.

Snake *(raising his tail)*: What if you don't have toes?

Jade Emperor *(surprised)*: Good point. You must have your whole body behind this line before I give the signal to start. Are you ready?

❸ Perform the play.

Choose people to play the characters. Have them use the script to practice. Then put on the play.

Play Practice:
Use Communication Project 5 on pages 20T–21T to involve students in putting on a play.

Poem

Teach:
Depending on the proficiency levels of your students, plan to introduce one type of poetry every few days or each week. During the first session, read aloud a favorite poem and ask students how it makes them feel. Then read aloud the introduction. Elaborate on the meaning of rhyme, rhythm, and colorful language. Next, read aloud the definition for **Cinquain** and the model. Talk about how this kind of poem builds from one word to several, uses adjectives and verbs to describe an object, and repeats the name of the object at the end.

A **poem** looks and sounds different from other kinds of writing. Poems use rhyme, rhythm, and colorful language to give the reader a special feeling.

Cinquain

There are five lines in a **cinquain**. One kind of cinquain has a certain number of syllables in each line.

	Electric Storm
two syllables	*Lightning*
four syllables	*Electric bolt*
six syllables	*Flying like a rocket*
eight syllables	*Silent, long, thin crack in the sky*
two syllables	*Lightning*
	—*Janine Wheeler*

Diamante

Teach, continued:
For **Diamante**, read aloud the introduction and the poem. Then have groups choral read the poem. Read the poem again, using the characteristics to point out how the words lead from one topic to the next.

A **diamante** is seven lines long. When you write it, it looks like a diamond.

Lines 1 and 7 name different topics.

Lines 2 and 3 tell about the first topic.

Lines 5 and 6 tell about the last topic.

Line 4 has three words that tell about the first topic, and three words that tell about the last topic.

Grocery Cart
fruit
sugary sweet
pear, pineapple, peach
juicy, sticky, gooey, fresh, hearty, healthy,
pepper, pumpkin, peas
crispy crunch
vegetable

– Janine Wheeler

Concrete Poem

A **concrete** poem is written so the words make
a picture of what they are describing.

Oak

(a poem to be read from the bottom up)

this great oak
into the coming night
its capillary ends
its garbled limbs
against the hazy light
now stretches
to stand winter and the wind
from wells far underground

with strength
girthed itself
upon a trunk
upon a branch
upon a sprig
once a leaf
spring by spring
a century ago
from under land
this tree unrolled
Simple as a flower

Poem Practice:
Use Communication Project 4 on pages 18T–19T or Project 11 on pages 40T–43T to involve students in reciting or writing a poem. Students can choose a poem from pages 134 or 135 to recite or they can use one of the poems as a model for writing.

—Dawn Watkins

A Poem in Free Verse

Free verse is a kind of poetry that doesn't have a regular rhythm. Sometimes a poem written in free verse can have rhyming words, but it doesn't have to.

Teach, continued:
For **A Poem in Free Verse**, read aloud the introduction and the poem. Ask students what the poem is about and how the poet feels about his grandmother. Then define *rhythm* and read the poem again at a different rate to demonstrate how a poem in free verse doesn't have a regular rhythm.

MATRIARCH

my dark
grandmother

would brush
her long hair

seated out
on her patio

even ferns
would bow

to her splendor
and her power

—Francisco X. Alarcón

Haiku

A **haiku** is three lines long and has a specific number of syllables in each line. A haiku is often about nature.

Teach, continued:
For **Haiku**, read aloud the definition and the haiku, clapping out the syllables for each line. Read it again, having students chime in. Ask students what the haiku is about and how they think the poet feels about flying a kite.

Dragon Song

five syllables — *Upon the blue sky*
seven syllables — *the dragon kite writes a song.*
five syllables — *Ah, my heart sings it!*

— *Shirleyann Costigan*

A Rhyming Poem

Teach, continued:
For **A Rhyming Poem**, record the rhyming word pairs from the poem on the chalkboard: *day, say; head, bed; through, do; sword, bored; yawn, lawn;* and *away, day*. Say each pair and have students echo you. Then read aloud the introduction. Stop after the second sentence to point out the rhyming word pairs on the board. Continue reading the last line and the poem. Ask students to listen especially for rhyming words. Assign a group for each verse and have each group choral read their assigned verse.

In a **rhyming poem**, some of the words at the end of the lines rhyme. That means the words have the same ending sounds. The rhyming words help give the poem a special rhythm, or beat.

Today is Very Boring

Today is very boring,
it's a very boring day,
there is nothing much to look at,
there is nothing much to say,
there's a peacock on my sneakers,
there's a penguin on my head,
there's a dormouse on my doorstep,
I am going back to bed.

Today is very boring,
it is boring through and through,
there is absolutely nothing
that I think I want to do,
I see giants riding rhinos,
and an ogre with a sword,
there's a dragon blowing smoke rings,
I am positively bored.

Today is very boring,
I can hardly help but yawn,
there's a flying saucer landing
in the middle of my lawn,
a volcano just erupted
less than half a mile away,
and I think I felt an earthquake,
it's a very boring day.

—*Jack Prelutsky*

Poem Practice:
Use Communication Project 4 on pages 18T–19T or Project 11 on pages 40T–43T to involve students in reciting or writing a poem. Students can choose one of the poems on pages 136 or 137 to recite, or they can use one as a writing model.

3 Speech Emergence **4** Intermediate Fluency **5** Advanced Fluency/Fluent   **Put It in Writing!** 137

Report

Teach:
Brainstorm what students know about reports. Record their ideas in a word web and add any missing characteristics. Read aloud the introduction and remind students that facts are statements that can be proven. Then work through the report. Ask students to find and read aloud the parts in the model you describe.

A **report** presents facts about a topic. You can gather facts by reading books, interviewing people, searching for information on the Internet, and doing other kinds of research. Then you can organize the information you find and write the report.

The **title** and **introduction** tell what your report is all about. They get your reader interested.

Each **topic sentence** tells one main idea about your topic.

Types of Fossils

Have you ever wondered about the creatures that roamed the earth thousands of years ago? Take a look at fossils! They can tell us a lot about what those creatures were like.

Long ago, dead plants and animals were buried under the earth or the ocean. For many years, materials like dirt, sand, and oil covered their remains. As the materials hardened, they trapped the remains inside to make fossils. There are many kinds of fossils.

The most common fossils are mold and cast fossils. In a mold fossil, rock hardened around the remains. However, parts of the plant or animal dissolved or disappeared, and left just an outline shape in the rock. In a cast fossil, minerals fill up an empty space left by an animal's body. It looks like a whole animal buried in the rock.

A trace fossil is another type of fossil. It shows the activities of an animal. An example is a dinosaur footprint in mud that later hardened into rock. Other trace fossils show animal trails or burrows.

True form fossils are the actual animals or parts of animals, such as teeth, bones, and shells. An ant caught in tree sap which hardened into amber is a true form fossil. A woolly mammoth frozen in a block of ice and a saber-toothed tiger stuck in a sticky tar pit are also true form fossils.

Fossils come in many forms. They may be in rock, tar, ice, or amber. They are all evidence of animals from long ago.

The **body** of the report has all the facts you found.

The last paragraph is the **conclusion**. It sums up your report.

Report Practice:
Use Communication Project 18 on pages 68T–71T and Project 24 on pages 92T–95T to involve students in writing a report.

Go To The Research Process on pages 220–233 to find out how to do research.

Story

Writers use their imaginations and make up different kinds of **stories** to entertain their readers. They decide where a story will happen, who will be in it, and what will happen.

Parts of a Story

Every story happens in a place at some time. That place and time are called the **setting**.

Saturday morning in our apartment

The people or animals in a story are called the **characters**. In most stories, the characters speak. Their words are called the **dialogue**.

Come by this afternoon to see if you have won.

woman from the bike store

Anything is possible, but don't count on winning the bike, Alex.

Alex and his mom

The things that happen in a story are the events. The order, or **sequence of events**, is called the **plot**.

1. Mom filled out a form for the bike drawing.

2. We went to the bike store.

3. I saw a huge sign that said that I won!

Realistic Fiction

Teach, continued:
For **Realistic Fiction**, read aloud the introduction and the story. Have students take turns naming an event that could happen in real life. Point out that the quotation marks show that a character is speaking. Have a volunteeer read aloud the dialogue and ask the class if it sounds like something a real person would say.

Some stories have characters that seem like people you know. They happen in a place that seems real. These stories are called **realistic fiction** because they tell about something that could happen in real life.

Another Saturday Morning

The **characters** are like people you know.

The events in the **plot** could really happen.

Mom and I were eating breakfast Saturday morning when a woman knocked on the door to our apartment.

"Hello," she said. "I'm from Bikes and Stuff and we're having a drawing for a mountain bike. Would you be interested in signing up?" Mom agreed and filled out a form for me.

"Come by this afternoon to see if you have won," the woman said.

"Anything is possible, but don't count on winning the bike, Alex," Mom said when the woman left.

So I forgot all about the bike and started playing video games. Before I knew it, mom came in the room and said it was time to go to the bike store.

When I walked in, the first thing I saw was a huge sign that said: *Mountain bike winner: Alex Sanchez!* I couldn't believe it!

They put my name and photograph in the newspaper in an ad for Bikes and Stuff. That was the day I learned anything is possible on a Saturday morning.

The **setting** is in a place and a time you know.

The **dialogue** sounds real.

Realistic Fiction Practice:
Use Communication Project 12 on pages 44T–47T to involve students in writing a realistic fiction story.

Story, continued

Teach, continued:
Review with students familiar historical figures they've studied such as George Washington and Abraham Lincoln, and the times in which they lived. Explain: *Sometimes writers use history to come up with story ideas. Because the stories writers make up are based on real people, places, and events in the past, they are called* **historical fiction**. Read aloud the introduction and the model. Define *parlour* and *quill* and explain that the writer uses those details to show that the story takes place in colonial days. Have students find other details that indicate the past.

Historical Fiction

Historical fiction is a story that takes place in the past during a certain time in history. Some of the characters may be real people and some of the events really happened. Even so, the story is fiction because the writer made it up.

January 13, 1778

The characters dress, act, and talk like the people in that time did.

Today when we returned the laundry to the army headquarters, I was astounded to see only General Washington in the parlour, no other officers. I know not where Billy Lee was. The General was sharpening his quill with his penknife. He looked up at us and smiled.

It can have **real people** and **made-up characters** who lived during that time.

"Thank you, Abigail. Thank you, Elisabeth," he said.

I curtsied, unable to speak. How did he know our names?

He looked at us with kind eyes—they're gray-blue—then he returned to his pen and paper. Mrs. Hewes says Mr. Washington writes at least fifteen letters a day, mostly to Congress. He is pleading for food, clothing, and other supplies for the soldiers, she told us.

Historical Fiction Practice:
Use Communication Project 23 on pages 88T–91T to involve students in writing an historical fiction story.

3 Speech Emergence **4** Intermediate Fluency **5** Advanced Fluency/Fluent

Teach, continued:
Invite students to talk about superheroes like Superman and Wonder Woman described in **Dateline U.S.A.** on page 274, or others they've read about or seen on TV and in movies. Ask students if the characters could really do the things they do. Then read aloud the introduction and the model. Ask volunteers to retell the episode and have the class identify the events that could really happen and those that could never happen.

Fantasy

A **fantasy** is a story that tells about events that couldn't possibly happen in real life. Here is part of a fantasy about some children playing a very unusual board game.

Fantasy Practice:
You may want to share the entire story of *Jumanji* with students and use Communication Project 6 on pages 22T–23T to involve them in retelling a favorite part or the entire story.

from *Jumanji* by Chris Van Allsburg

The **characters** can be like real people.

At home, the children spread the game out on a card table. It looked very much like the games they already had.

"Here," said Judy, handing her brother the dice, "you go first."

Peter casually dropped the dice from his hand.

"Seven," said Judy.

Peter moved his piece to the seventh square.

"'Lion attacks, move back two spaces,'" read Judy.

"Gosh, how exciting," said Peter, in a very unexcited voice. As he reached for his piece he looked up at his sister. She had a look of absolute horror on her face.

"Peter," she whispered, "turn around very, very slowly."

Some of the **events** could never happen in real life.

The boy turned in his chair. He couldn't believe his eyes. Lying on the piano was a lion, staring at Peter and licking his lips. The lion roared so loud it knocked Peter right off his chair. The big cat jumped to the floor. Peter was up on his feet, running through the house with the lion a whisker's length behind. He ran upstairs and dove under a bed. The lion tried to squeeze under, but got his head stuck. Peter scrambled out, ran from the bedroom, and slammed the door behind him. He stood in the hall with Judy, gasping for breath.

"I don't think," said Peter in between gasps of air, "that I want...to play...this game... anymore."

"But we have to," said Judy as she helped Peter back downstairs. "I'm sure that's what the instructions mean. That lion won't go away until one of us wins the game."

Put It in Writing! 143

Teach:
Help students recall that in a book review you don't write the entire story, you just tell about the most important ideas. Explain that a summary of an article is a lot like a book review. Then read aloud the introduction. Read each paragraph of the article, pausing to ask students W-H questions. As you read steps 1 and 2, direct students' attention to the article and the notes as appropriate to clarify where the notes came from and how to decide which ideas are unimportant.

Summary

In a **summary**, you write the most important ideas in something you have read or seen. Read this magazine article. Then follow the steps to see how to write a summary for it.

The first supersonic car, Thrust SSC, set a record at 763 miles per hour in Nevada's Black Rock Desert last week.

The World's Fastest Car
Thrust SSC zips through the sound barrier

WHOOSH! KABOOM! For Andy Green, a Royal Air Force pilot, that was the sound of success. Last Wednesday, Green rocketed into the history books by becoming the first person to drive a car faster than the speed of sound. His average speed: **763 miles per hour!**

Green was not driving an ordinary car. He was driving the Thrust SSC (for **S**uper **S**onic **C**ar), which has twin jet engines like those used on Phantom fighter planes. The car packs as much power as 1,000 Ford Escorts. It needs parachutes to help it stop.

Green had been building up speed for more than a month out in Nevada's Black Rock Desert. He had competition from American driver Craig Breedlove. But Breedlove's car couldn't keep up. On September 25, Green blasted away the old land-speed record of 633 miles per hour. His new record: 714 miles per hour.

Richard Noble, Green's fellow Englishman who set the old record in 1983, didn't mind seeing it bite the dust. Noble owns the Thrust SSC, so he was rooting for Green.

The ultimate dream for Noble and Green was to see their car travel faster than sound. The speed of sound varies, depending on weather conditions and altitude. In the Black Rock Desert, it is around 750 m.p.h.

Noble and Green finally saw their dream come true on October 15. When a plane or car reaches the speed of sound, people for miles around hear an explosive noise called a sonic boom. Each time the car broke through the sound barrier, a sonic boom thundered across the Black Rock Desert, announcing Green's amazing feat.

"We have achieved what we set out to do," he said. "We are finished." ∎ REUTERS

1 **Make a list of the most important ideas in the article.**

Look for the important ideas in the title or at the beginning of the paragraphs. In some articles, you can find important details in **bold** letters or *italics*.

2 **Read through your list and cross out details that are not important.**

A detail is important if it answers one of these questions: Who? What? When? Where? Why? How?

3 **Use your own words to turn your notes into sentences.**

world's fastest car
~~Whoosh! Kaboom!~~
Andy Green
first person to drive a car faster than the speed of sound
763 miles per hour
Thrust SSC (Super Sonic Car)
~~1,000 Ford Escorts~~
Nevada's Black Rock Desert
October 15— had been trying for more than a month
~~speed of sound in desert: about 750 m.p.h.~~

On October 15, Andy Green became the first person to break the sound barrier in a car. After trying for over a month, he successfully drove the world's fastest car, the Thrust SSC (Super Sonic Car), 763 miles per hour in Nevada's Black Rock Desert.

Summary Practice: Use the steps on this page to have students create a class summary for the news story on page 121.

Tall Tale

Teach:
Have students talk about the picture and explain that it shows a scene from an entertaining kind of story called a *tall tale*. Then read aloud the introduction and the model. Ask students who the hero of the story is, what the problems were, and how he solved the problems. Reinforce the meaning of *exaggeration* by commenting on students' responses: *That couldn't really happen, could it? That's an exaggeration.*

A **tall tale** is a story told just for fun. It has lots of exaggerated details. When details are exaggerated, they make the story impossible to believe.

from *Paul Bunyan* by Steven Kellogg

Paul's next job was to clear the heavily forested midwest. He hired armies of extra woodsmen and built enormous new bunkhouses. The men sailed up to bed in balloons and parachuted down to breakfast in the morning.

Unfortunately the cooks couldn't flip flapjacks fast enough to satisfy all the newcomers.

To solve the muddle, Paul built a colossal flapjack griddle.

The surface was greased by kitchen helpers with slabs of bacon laced to their feet.

The **main character** has special powers or great strength and solves a problem in an unusual or exaggerated way.

Everytime the hot griddle was flooded with batter, it blasted a delicious flapjack high about the clouds. Usually the flapjacks landed neatly beside the griddle, but sometimes they were a bit off target.

Paul took a few days off to dig the St. Lawrence River and the Great Lakes so that barges of Vermont maple syrup could be brought to camp.

Fueled by the powerful mixture of flapjacks and syrup, the men leveled the Great Plains and shaved the slopes of the Rocky Mountains.

Tall Tale Practice:
Use Communication Project 15 on pages 56T–59T to involve students in writing a tall tale.

Telephone Message

See *Notes.*

Thank-you Note

See *Notes.*

Teach:
Read aloud the introduction and the tongue twisters. Point out that most of the words in a tongue twister begin with or have the same sound. Invite volunteers to choose a tongue twister to say. Have them start out by saying the sentence slowly, then faster and faster. Encourage students to make up tongue twisters as you record them on the chalkboard.

Tongue Twister

A tongue twister is a phrase that is so difficult to say your tongue gets all twisted! Tongue twisters usually don't make much sense—they're just for fun.

Don't light a night-light on a light night like tonight.

Surely Shawn should show Sherry Shawna's shoes.

Chuck chews cherries by the cheekful.

What noise annoys an oyster most? A noisy noise annoys an oyster most.

The Good Writer Guide

A skater can't skate without skates, and a writer can't write without ideas. To be a good writer, first you need to collect ideas. Then, put them to use! Just like skaters, writers get better and better with practice.

How to Collect Ideas

First, set up a file to store your ideas. Choose the kind of file that works best for you.

- You might want to keep a notebook or a journal close by so you can write down ideas as you think of them.

- Maybe you want to save ticket stubs, special photos, cards from your friends, or other things that remind you of people and events. You'll need a box or folder that is big enough for all these things plus your lists and notes, too.

- A great place to keep a list of ideas is in a file on the computer. Your file can get as big as your ideas!

Then gather the ideas that interest you. Here are some tips.

1 Look and listen.

Keep your eyes and ears open. You'll be surprised at how many ideas you'll get!

- What are your friends talking about?

- Did you see something funny or amazing on TV?

- Did you find something interesting on the Internet? Do you want to know more about the topic?

- Is the weather really hot or really cold?

- Is it quiet outside or is it noisy? What do you see? What do you hear?

2 Read a lot!

When you read something you like, draw pictures or list details to tell about:

- your favorite characters
- interesting or unusual facts
- words and phrases that sound good
- topics that interest you

> roller hockey—
> "Dribble, pass, shoot, and score."

3 Make charts and lists.

List these headings in your file. Add examples to them throughout the year.

- Things I Wonder About
- What I'll Never Forget
- Things I Like to Do
- Funny Things That Have Happened to Me
- Places I'd Like to Go
- My Favorites
- When I Felt Proud
- The Most Beautiful Things I've Seen

> **Things I Wonder About**
>
> How our team will do in the roller hockey league
>
> If I'll get to play goalie this year
>
> How many teams will be in the league

4 Draw pictures.

Draw pictures to show what you are thinking. Sometimes the lines and shapes you draw can remind you of people, places, or things to write about. Try drawing a time line to show the events in your life. Look at your time line when you need a writing idea.

1995	1998	1999	2000
got my first skates	learned to skate backwards	started roller hockey	won first hockey tournament

Teach, continued:
For **How to Write for a Specific Purpose** or **Audience**, read aloud the introductory paragraphs and work through the pages. Elaborate on how the models meet the purpose for the writing or change depending upon the audience.

The Good Writer Guide, continued

How to Write for a Specific Purpose

Why are you writing? That's your **purpose**. Good writers change how and what they write to fit their purpose.

Purpose	Writing Examples	
To inform or to explain	You might give directions to explain how to do something. *If you want to stop on your in-line skates, have your brake foot in front. Then, bend your knees. Finally, put your brake down. If this doesn't work, hop onto some nearby grass!*	Or, you could write a paragraph that gives your readers important facts about a topic. *Safety equipment protects you when you skate. A hard helmet protects the head in case of a fall. Plastic knee and elbow pads keep knees and elbows from getting scraped.*
To describe	You could write a description that has lots of descriptive details to help your reader "see" what you are describing. *My new in-line skates are fantastic! They are a shiny blue with bright red trim.*	For a poem, use many colorful verbs to describe how something moves. *Clicking and Clacking* *Clicking and clacking over the concrete cracks, skates swish and slip by.*
To entertain	You could use a cartoon with a funny picture and words to make your readers laugh.	"They call this IN-LINE skating?"

Purpose	Writing Examples	
To persuade	In an advertisement, you can use persuasive words and phrases to convince someone to buy something.	In an editorial, give your opinion and use persuasive words to change the way things are.
	SKATE SALE! Check out the **HOTTEST** new colors of in-line skates. *They're guaranteed to help you skate better!*	Kids need a place to skate. We think that there should be special times for skaters to use the parking lot behind the school. Sign this paper to vote for an afternoon skating time.
To express	Write a journal entry to tell about your own personal thoughts and feelings.	
	Day June 30, 2001 I'm so excited about our club's in-line skating exhibit during the school fair tomorrow. Dennis, Ahn, and I are going to skate for the exhibition. I just hope that I	don't fall because that would be so embarrassing!
To learn	It helps to write things down when you are learning about a topic. That way you can see what you already know—and what you don't know.	
	In-line skating is good exercise. Now I want to know why and if it's good for everyone.	

How to Write for a Specific Audience

Who will read what you write? Your **audience**. Knowing who your audience is will help you decide what words to use and what kinds of details to include.

Audience	Writing Examples
Adults and people you don't know	Use formal language and details to help them understand what they might not know. My skating lesson was great. I learned how to cross my right foot over my left foot while making a turn. That's called a crossover.
Your friends	Use informal language because they'll probably understand exactly what you mean. My blading lesson was awesome! Now I can do crossovers like a pro.
Someone younger than you	Use simple language so they'll understand. My skating lesson was fun. Now I can make turns on my skates without stopping.

How to Make Your Writing Better

Teach, continued:
For **How to Make Your Writing Better**, read aloud the introduction and work through each improvement strategy. Then review each strategy by writing new models on the chalkboard and having students tell you how to make the sentences better.

Good writers work on their writing until it's the best it can be. Here are four important ways to make your writing spectacular!

1 Choose the right words.

Help your reader see what you are writing about by using just the right words.

Use **specific nouns** to tell exactly what you mean.

Use **colorful verbs** to give the best picture of the action.

Add **describing words** to tell what things are like.

Marcy got her things.

Marcy got her skates and helmet.

Marcy grabbed her skates and helmet.

Marcy grabbed her new skates and the blue helmet with the silver spots.

Sometimes you can find the right words to use in a **thesaurus**. A thesaurus is a book of words and their synonyms. Use alphabetical order to look up the entry word. Next to the entry word, you'll find a list of synonyms for it.

get *verb* **1.** ✦ acquire, catch, grab, grasp, pick up, obtain, take

2 Improve your sentences.

Combine Short Sentences

Whenever you have a lot of short sentences, try combining some of them.

Just OK

> Marcy loves to skate.
> Her friends love to skate.
> Marcy skates at the park.

Much Better

> Marcy and her friends
> love to skate at the park.

Break up Run-on Sentences

Sometimes a long sentence uses *and* too many times.
Break a sentence like this into two sentences.

Not OK

> Felicia loves to play roller hockey, and she practices every Tuesday after school, and she has a game every Saturday.

OK

> Felicia loves to play roller hockey. She practices every Tuesday after school, and she has a game every Saturday.

Start Sentences in Different Ways

If all your sentences start in the same way, your readers might get bored. Try changing the way some of your sentences begin.

Just OK

> Matt went skating for the first time yesterday. Matt fell forward on his knees as he was trying to stand up on his skates. Matt tried to stand up again and fell backward. Matt tried a third time. Matt finally rolled forward!

Much Better

> Yesterday, Matt went skating for the first time. As he tried to stand on his skates, Matt fell forward on his knees. When he tried to stand up again, Matt fell backward. He tried a third time. Finally, Matt rolled forward!

Start Off with a Great Sentence

A good beginning sentence will get your readers' attention. They'll want to read everything you have to say and to read it right away!

Just OK

This article is about Josie Rodríguez.

Much Better

"On your left," yelled Josie Rodríguez as she zipped by another skater on the bike path.

3 Add details.

Details make writing interesting to read.

Just OK

This article is about Josie Rodríguez. She has been skating for a long time. She really likes it. I talked to her for a long time.

Much Better

"On your left," yelled Josie Rodríguez as she zipped by another skater on the bike path. Josie arrived in front of her apartment just in time for our interview last week.

It was a thrill to meet Josie Rodríguez. She is a professional in-line skater who always has her skates on.

Include **dialogue**.

"I feel strange without them," she said. "I've been skating since I was two. I had to do something to keep up with my four older brothers."

For four hours Ms. Rodríguez shared her in-line skating experiences, including that she owns fifteen pairs of skates! This is a person who really loves what she does!

Include **your own thoughts**.

Add **specific details** that tell how, when, or where.

Add **examples**.

4 Show, don't tell.

You can just *tell* your readers about an event or a person. To give your readers the best picture, though, *show* them exactly what you mean!

■ Use details to show what something looks, sounds, tastes, smells, or feels like.

■ Use dialogue to show what a person is like.

This tells:

> Kristen likes in-line skating because it's great exercise. She skates for a long time after school.

This shows:

Kristen's words show that she thinks skating is good exercise.

> "If I didn't do in-line skating, I would probably be a couch potato," says Kristen, a very athletic fifth grader. As soon as Kristen gets home, she puts her books down, grabs her skates, and doesn't come back in the door until dinner.

Kristen's actions show how much she likes to skate.

The Good Writer Guide Practice: Encourage students to use the tips in **The Good Writer Guide** to help them revise their writing for Communication Projects 7–24 on pages 24T–95T. You may want to use students' writing as models for making revisions or have them complete the **Practice Book** pages and then revise their writing.

▶ **Practice Book pages 36, 37, 38, 39, and 40**

How to Evaluate Your Writing

Teach, continued:
In advance, prepare a portfolio of your own writing to use as a model as you work through **How to Evaluate Your Writing** with students. Display the portfolio as you read aloud the introduction. Then work through the rest of the page. Afterward, talk about the organization and contents of your portfolio and the kinds of writing you like to do. Then help students create their own portfolios.

Save everything you write! A collection of your writing is called a **portfolio**. It can be in a large folder or in a notebook. The writing in your portfolio will help you learn how you are doing as a writer.

Organize Your Portfolio

Organize your portfolio so you can find the writing you are looking for. You might want to:

- put all the writing you've done in order by date.

- make special sections in your portfolio to keep pieces you've written for the same purpose or the same audience.

- put all your stories together, all your reports together, and all your poems together. In other words, organize your portfolio by the kinds of writing you've done.

Look Over Your Writing

Look at your writing every now and then to see how you are doing.

- What is your favorite piece of writing?
- How is the first writing you did different from the last?
- What do you need to work on?
- What other kinds of writing do you want to try?

Think About How You Write

As you look over your writing, think about the words you like to use, the kinds of sentences you write, and what you like to write about. All of those things together are your writing **style**. That is what makes you a super writer with a style all your own!

I write with Style!

Grammar Made Graphic

it flies really ?

subject predicate

Pedro loves to fly kites. To tell about his kite, he is putting words together to make a sentence. Pedro makes sure to use the correct pronoun, verb, and adverbs so everyone can understand exactly what the kite does.

This chapter will help you make your writing clear, too. Here you'll find all the rules you need to know to write in English.

Sentences

Teach:
Read aloud the definition. Use the example to talk about how each part by itself doesn't give enough information: *The words* The kids *don't tell us what the kids do or what they are like. It's not a complete thought.* Repeat for "play in the park." Then read the sentence and ask students: *Is this a sentence? How do you know?* Then, work through pages 160–163, pausing at the end of each page to challenge students to generate more sentences of each type.

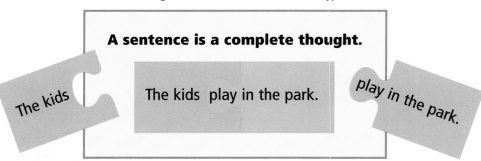

A sentence is a complete thought.

The kids

The kids play in the park.

play in the park.

Kinds of Sentences

■ **There are four kinds of sentences.**

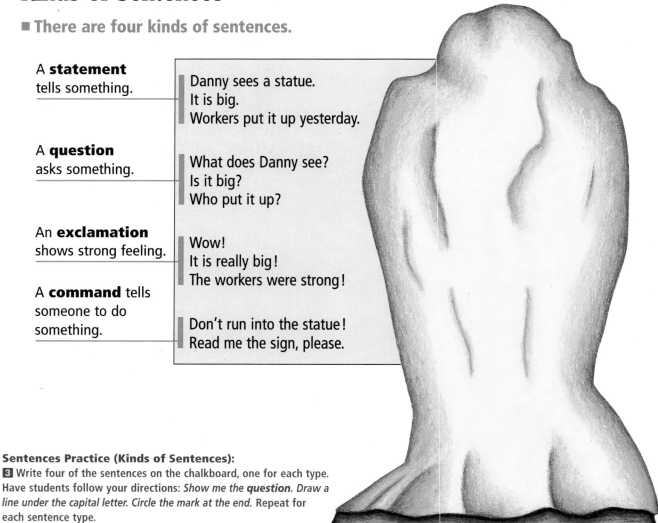

A **statement** tells something.

> Danny sees a statue.
> It is big.
> Workers put it up yesterday.

A **question** asks something.

> What does Danny see?
> Is it big?
> Who put it up?

An **exclamation** shows strong feeling.

> Wow!
> It is really big!
> The workers were strong!

A **command** tells someone to do something.

> Don't run into the statue!
> Read me the sign, please.

Sentences Practice (Kinds of Sentences):
3 Write four of the sentences on the chalkboard, one for each type. Have students follow your directions: *Show me the* **question**. *Draw a line under the capital letter. Circle the mark at the end.* Repeat for each sentence type.
4 Read aloud each sentence in random order and have students tell you what type it is and how they know.

5 Have partners write different kinds of sentences that relate to the statue on page 162.

■ Ask a question to get information.

Some questions ask for a "yes" or "no" answer.

Sentences Practice (Yes/No Questions):
3 Ask students the questions in the chart, and then reverse roles and have students ask you the questions.
4 Have partners take turns asking and answering yes/no questions about the statue and people on pages 160 and 161: *Do you see a statue? Yes, I do. Is the statue small? No, it isn't.*
5 Have students turn the statements on page 160 into questions and answers following the patterns on page 161: *Danny sees a statue. Does Danny see a statue? Yes, he does. Danny sees a statue, doesn't he? Yes, he does.*

▶ **Practice Book pages 42 and 43**

Question	Answer
1. **Is** the statue ready?	No, it isn't.
2. **Are** the workers finished?	No, they aren't.
3. **Have** you seen the statue?	Yes.
4. **Has** anyone else seen it?	No.
5. **Do** you like the statue?	Yes, I do.
6. **Does** it have a name?	Yes, it does.
7. **Would** you take the cover off?	No.
8. **Could** we peek under the cover?	No.
9. **Should** we come back tomorrow?	Yes.
10. **Will** you show us the statue then?	Sure.

You can also add a question to the end of a statement.

Examples: You are busy.
You are busy, aren't you?   Yes, I am.

You're not busy.
You're not busy, are you?   No, I'm not.

Kinds of Sentences, continued

When you want more information than just "yes" or "no," start your question with one of these words.

Sentences Practice (W-H Questions):

3 Ask each student to copy and illustrate one question and answer from the box.

4 Have groups of three use the questions and answers in the chart as they role-play the scene with the park worker and children.

5 Have partners read the story about Paul Bunyan on page 146. Ask one student to write three W-H questions using the details in the story and have the partner write the answers. Then partners can reverse roles.

▶ **Practice Book page 44**

Question	Answer
1. **When** did you uncover the statue?	This morning.
2. **How much** does the statue weigh?	I don't know. It's very heavy.
3. **Who** is it?	That's Paul Bunyan.
4. **What** did he do?	He was a lumberjack.
5. **Where** did he live?	He lived in Minnesota.
6. **How** big was he?	He was big enough to pick up railroad tracks.
7. **Why** is he famous?	Some stories say he made all the lakes in Minnesota.
8. **How many** lakes did he make?	More than 10,000!
9. **Which** story about Paul Bunyan is your favorite?	I like the stories about Paul and Babe, his blue ox.
10. **How** can we find out more about Paul Bunyan?	Use the computer at the library.

Go To ▶ Practices A and B on page 305.

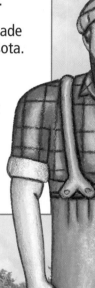

162

■ Some sentences mean "no."

Teach:
Read aloud the red rule. Then read the sentence and negative words as you use gestures for *no* such as shaking your head. Read the sentences on the computer screen and have students identify the negative words.

Use negative words like these to make a sentence say "no."

| **Examples:** | no | nothing | nobody | never |
| | not | none | no one | nowhere |

File   Edit   View   Label   Special   Thu 2:40 PM

document

Q: Why is Paul Bunyan famous?
A: He was as tall as a house—or taller. In fact, **nobody** was taller than Paul Bunyan.

Q: Did he have any famous friends?
A: Yes, his blue ox, Babe. Babe was so big he was **never** measured from nose to tail.

Q: What did Paul Bunyan do?
A: He was a lumberjack. He cleared all the land in North Dakota for farming. There were **no** trees left when he was done!

Ellen   **Danny**

Sentences Practice (Negative Sentences):
3 Say sentences with negative words. Ask students to identify the word(s) that make the sentence say "no."
4 5 Have partners read the story about Paul Bunyan on page 146 and then write five negative statements about him. Ask them to trade papers with another pair to check. Volunteers can read their sentences aloud to the class.

➤ **Practice Book page 45**

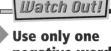

Watch Out!

▶ **Use only one negative word in a sentence.**

We have never
              a
seen ~~no~~ man as
tall as this!

I have not seen
        any
~~no~~ shoes as big
as his.

Go To ▶ Page 146 to read a story about Paul Bunyan.

Subject and Predicate

Teach:
Read aloud the definition and the example. Ask *Who read some books?* and confirm the answer: *The friends read some books.* The friends *is the subject of the sentence.* Repeat for the predicate. Then work through pages 164 and 165, calling on different students to identify the subjects or predicates in the sentences about Paul Bunyan.

Every sentence has two main parts.

The friends read some books.

subject   predicate

■ **The subject tells whom or what the sentence is about.**

The subject usually comes at the beginning of the sentence. It can have more than one word.

Paul Bunyan and Babe

10 TALL TALES

The complete subject includes all the words that tell about the subject.

Sentences Practice (Subject):
3 Point to the words in the subjects of the sentences and ask yes/no questions: *Does this tell whom the sentence is about? Is this the most important word in the subject? Is it the complete subject?*

Danny finds a book with tall tales.

It has stories about Paul Bunyan.

One funny **story** is about Babe, his ox.

This big, blue **ox** drank a lake every morning!

Danny and Ellen enjoy the tale.

They laugh and laugh.

The **simple subject** is the most important word in the subject.

A **compound subject** has two or more simple subjects. They are joined by **and** or **or**.

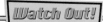
Watch Out!

▶ **Sometimes a subject comes at the end of a sentence.**

Here is my **book.**
There are many **books** to read.

▶ **Sometimes the subject is not named, but you can guess who the subject is!**

Don't talk in the library!
Please return your books here.

4 Write the sentences on the chalkboard. Have students circle the complete subject as they identify it: *This is the complete subject.* Then, have them underline the simple subject and identify it. Have them identify the sentence with a compound subject.

5 Have students write complete sentences to describe the scene on page 162. Have them underline the complete subject and circle the simple subject in each sentence. Encourage students to include at least one sentence with a compound subject.

3 Say each sentence and ask questions: *Who finds a book with tall tales? Is Danny the subject or the predicate? What does Danny do? Is finds a book with tall tales the subject or the predicate?*

■ **The predicate tells what the subject is, does, or has.**

The predicate usually comes at the end of a sentence.

4 Write sentences without subjects or without predicates. Point to each and ask *What's missing?* Have students tell what the subject or predicate should be to make a complete thought.

The complete predicate includes all the words in the predicate part of the sentence.

Danny **finds** a book with tall tales.

It **has** stories about Paul Bunyan.

One funny story **is** about Babe, his ox.

This big, blue ox **drank** a lake every morning!

Danny and Ellen **enjoy** the tale.

They **laugh and laugh**.

The **simple predicate** is the most important word in the predicate. It is the **verb**.

A **compound predicate** has two or more verbs that tell about the same subject.

5 Have students write complete sentences to tell about the Paul Bunyan Story on page 146. Encourage them to trade papers with a partner to check for verbs in the predicates. You may want students to save their sentences for the practice on page 166.

Watch Out! Practice:
Place classroom objects as you say a positive sentence following the pattern: *The book is on the chair.* Students use *not* to say the opposite as you remove the objects: *The book is not on the chair.*

➤ **Practice Book page 46**

Go To ▶ Practices C–F on page 306.

Watch Out!

▶ **Put the word *not* after the verb.**

That book **is** on the shelf.
That book **is not** on the shelf.

The stories about Paul Bunyan **are** in the book.
The stories about Paul Bunyan **are not** in this book.

Compound Sentences

Teach:
Read aloud the definition and talk about how writers join two sentences together to make their writing easier and more interesting to read. Then work through the page, elaborating on how the ideas are alike or different; or how they show a choice. Point out the placement of the comma and conjunction in each speech balloon.

Sentences Practice (Compound Sentences):
3 Write the sentence pairs. Have students point to or tell you where to add a comma and conjunction to make a compound sentence.

> You can put two sentences together to make a **compound sentence**. Just use a comma in front of:
>
> **and   but   or**

When you put two ideas that are alike together, use **and**.

Example:
Paul cut down many trees.
Babe carried the logs to the river.

Paul cut down many trees, **and** Babe carried the logs to the river.

4 5 Have students check the sentences they wrote about Paul Bunyan (see page 165). Help them join some of their sentences together to make compound sentences.

▶ **Practice Book page 47**

When you want to show a difference between two ideas, use **but**.

Example:
The farmers could not clear their land.
Paul did it overnight.

The farmers could not clear their land, **but** Paul did it overnight.

When you want to show a choice between two ideas, use **or**.

Example:
You can find books about Paul Bunyan in the library.
You can download stories from the Internet.

You can find books about Paul Bunyan in the library, **or** you can download stories from the Internet.

Watch Out!

▶ **If a sentence uses _and_ too many times, make two sentences.**

We saw the new statue of Paul Bunyan, and we asked a lot of questions and then we went to the library to find some books.

Go To ▶ Practice G on page 307.

Nouns

Teach:
Read aloud the definition and the examples. Use the picture to clarify the concept. Ask students for more names of people, places, or things as you categorize them in a chart. Point out that some nouns start with a capital letter and others do not. Then work through the page.

Noun Practice (Common and Proper):
3 **4** **5** Form heterogeneous groups. Help each group write a paragraph about a place they want to visit, who would go with them, and a particular landmark they want to see. Have groups check the nouns for correct capitalization.

> ### A **noun** is the name of a person, place, or thing.
>
> **Example:** Say hello to **Luisa**.
> She lives in **Galveston**.
> She rides a purple **bicycle**.

Common and Proper Nouns

- A common noun names any person, place, or thing.

- A proper noun names one particular person, place, or thing.

All the important words in a proper noun start with a capital letter.

▶ COMMON NOUNS	▶ PROPER NOUNS	
Any Person The **girl** rides her bike. A **runner** jogs by her.	**One Particular Person** **Luisa** rides her bike. **Max Medina** jogs by her.	
Any Place Our **state** has many cities. This **city** is pretty. We ride by the **bay**.	**One Particular Place** **Texas** has many cities. **Galveston** is pretty. We ride by **Galveston Bay**.	
Any Thing The **building** is historic. That **street** is famous. Luisa sees the **boat**.	**One Particular Thing** **Ashton Villa** is historic. **Hope Boulevard** is famous. Luisa sees **Tall Ship** *Elissa*.	

Go To ▶ Practice A on page 307.

Singular and Plural Nouns

A **singular noun** shows "one."
A **plural noun** shows "more than one."

Examples: He is flying one **kite**.   She is flying two **kites**.

My **kites** look like **boxes**.

My kite has **dots** on it.

Teach, continued:
Use classroom items to demonstrate nouns that can be counted, including irregular plurals such as *one child* and *three children*; and those that cannot be counted such as *homework* and *furniture*.

■ **Most nouns can be counted.**
  They have a singular and a plural form.

▶ PLURAL NOUNS

To make most nouns plural, add **-s** to the singular noun.	dot dot**s**	kite kite**s**	flower flower**s**		
If the noun ends in **x**, **ch**, **sh**, **s**, or **z**, add **-es**.	box box**es**	lunch lunch**es**	dish dish**es**	glass glass**es**	waltz waltz**es**
For most nouns that end in **y**, change the **y** to **i** and add **-es**.	story stor**ies**	sky sk**ies**			
For nouns that end in a **vowel** plus **y**, just add **-s**.	boy boy**s**	toy toy**s**	day day**s**	monkey monkey**s**	
For most nouns that end in **f** or **fe**, change the **f** to **v** and add **-es**. For some nouns that end in **f**, just add **-s**.	leaf lea**ves**	knife kni**ves**	roof roof**s**	cliff cliff**s**	

A few nouns change in different ways to show "more than one."

One	man	woman	foot	tooth	mouse	goose	child	person
More than One	men	women	feet	teeth	mice	geese	children	people

Nouns Practice (Singular and Plural):
3 Ask one student to point to something in the classroom and name it. Have the partner say the plural form: *girl/girls; desk/desks; window/windows.*
4 Have groups illustrate and label the spelling rules on chart paper. Display the charts in the Writing Center.
5 Help groups write limericks including as many irregular plurals as they can: *There once was a man with two **feet**, whose **mice** wanted something to eat; his **children** were nice; they found food for the mice; then they all sat down for a treat.*

➤ **Practice Book page 48**

Go To Practice B on page 308.

■ **Some nouns cannot be counted. They have only one form for "one" and "more than one."**

▶ NOUNS THAT CANNOT BE COUNTED		
Weather Words Many nouns that refer to weather cannot be counted. **Example: Thunder** and **lightning** scare my dog.	hail ice lightning rain	snow temperature thunder wind
Food Many food items cannot be counted unless you use a measurement word like **cup**, **slice**, or **head**. Make the measurement word plural to show "more than one." **Examples:** I love **lettuce**! Mom bought **two heads of lettuce**.	bread cereal cheese corn flour lettuce	meat milk rice soup sugar tea
Ideas and Feelings **Examples:** I need some **help**. What **information** do you need?	democracy fun health help happiness	homework information luck trouble work
Category Nouns These nouns name a group, or category. Some of the items within the category can be counted. **Example:** I have some **money** in my pocket. There are **four dollars** and **two dimes**.	equipment energy fruit furniture	machinery mail money time
Materials **Example:** Is the table made of **wood** or **metal**?	metal paper	water wood
Activities and Sports **Examples:** My mom and dad love to play **golf**. **Camping** is my favorite thing to do.	baseball camping dancing football	golf singing soccer swimming

Nouns Practice (Noncountable Nouns):

3 Role-play a school cafeteria scene with students. Help students ask and answer questions using the food words: *Do you want corn? Yes, I want corn/No, I do not want corn.*

4 Have students use nouns from the chart to write sentences about their weekend activities: *On Saturday I played soccer. On Sunday I did my homework.*

5 Have partners use as many noncountable nouns as they can to write a paragraph about the importance of exercising.

Watch Out! Practice:
Follow the example to write the two meanings for *volleyball* and *lunch*. Help students make up sentences for each meaning, using the correct form of the nouns.

➤ **Practice Book page 49**

Watch Out!

▶ **Some nouns have more than one meaning. Add -s for the plural only if the noun means something you can count.**

football
1. **a ball** *We need two **footballs** for the game.*
2. **a sport** *I like to watch **football**.*

Go To ▶ Practice C on page 308.

Grammar Made Graphic 169

Words that Signal Nouns

Teach:
Read aloud the definition and the examples. Then work through pages 170 and 171. Check students' understanding by having them generate examples using classroom objects.

> **Some words help identify a noun:**
>
> a   an   some   the   this   that   these   those
>
> **Examples:** I'd like to buy **a** shirt.
> How about **this** nice shirt?
> Do you like **the** collar?

■ Use *a, an,* or *some* to talk about something in general.

One	More than One
a hat **an umbrella**	**some hats** **some umbrellas**

Examples: I'll buy **a hat** for me and **an umbrella** for you.

Some hats are too fancy.

Some umbrellas are too expensive.

Watch Out!

▶ Use **an** before a noun that begins with a vowel like:

a in **a**nt, **a**pron, **a**mount
e in **e**lbow, **e**el, **e**lection
i in **i**nch, **i**dea
o in **o**tter, **o**cean, **o**wl
u in **u**mbrella

Don't forget to use **an** before a word with silent **h**: **an hour**

■ Use *the* to talk about something specific.

One	More than One
the pink hat **the large umbrella**	**the blue hats** **the small umbrellas**

Examples: I'll buy **the pink hat** for me and **the large umbrella** for you.

The blue hat is too fancy.

The small umbrellas are too expensive.

Nouns Practice (General and Specific Identifiers):

3 Have each student in a group put a shoe in a pile. One student says *I need a shoe*, picks up his or her shoe, and then says *The white shoe is mine*. Students continue until all the shoes are gone.

4 5 Have groups role-play shopping using students' school items such as lunch boxes, jackets, backpacks, and so on. Encourage students to use both general and specific identifiers as they buy and sell items. For example: Buyer—*I need a jacket.* Seller—*The blue jacket is very warm, but the purple jacket has more pockets.*

▶ **Practice Book pages 50 and 51**

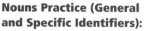

Here are some tips to help you use **a** and **the** correctly.

Never use **the** before the name of a:

Galveston is a city in **Texas**.

• city or state

Many people there speak **English** and **Spanish**.

• language
• day, month, or holiday

If you talk about the same thing a second time, use **the**.

We visited the city in **September** on **Labor Day**.

I found a great beach by the seawall.
The beach was nice and big.

Several of us played **volleyball**.

• sport or activity

When you compare three or more things, use **the**.

Then we went to lunch at **Joe's Cafe**.

• business

Joe serves **the** best hamburgers in the city.

Nouns Practice (*this, that, these,* and *those*):
3 4 5 Gather sets of classroom objects and arrange them in two areas in the classroom to simulate the scene at the bottom of the page. Then have groups role-play the scene using identifiers.

► **Practice Book page 52**

■ Use *this, that, these,* and *those* to talk about something specific.

	One	**More than One**
Close By	**this** T-shirt	**these** T-shirts
Far Away	**that** umbrella	**those** umbrellas

Do you like **these** pink T-shirts or **this** red one?

That purple umbrella is bigger than **those** green ones.

Go To Practices D and E on page 309.

Grammar Made Graphic 171

Teach:
Read aloud the definition and the examples. Point to the owner(s) in the picture to clarify the concept. Give more examples as you describe students' clothing: *Wilbur's shirt is red. Cynthia's dress is green.* Then work through the page.

Possessive Nouns

> **A possessive noun is the name of an owner. The name always has an apostrophe:** '
>
> **Example: Luisa's** T-shirt is from the Galveston Springfest.
> The **boys'** T-shirts are from the Flight Museum.

The placement of the apostrophe depends on whether there is one owner or more than one owner. Look at these examples.

Teach, continued:
Help students summarize: *If there is one owner, the name has an apostrophe and then an s. If there is more than one owner, the name has an s and then an apostrophe.*

One Owner	More Than One Owner
Martin's cap	the **boys'** caps
Mom's umbrella	my **parents'** umbrella
the **umbrella's** handle	the **umbrellas'** stripes
the **student's** T-shirt	the **students'** T-shirts

Nouns Practice (Possessive Nouns):
3 4 5 Have partners interview each other to find out his or her favorite color, animal, music, food, and so on. Students can use the information to draw and design a T-shirt for the partner. Depending on their proficiency levels, have students describe the drawings to the class: *Lisa's shirt. Green. Cats.* or *Tim's shirt is blue. It has a leopard.* or *This is Raul's shirt. The shirt's sleeves have baseballs on them because that is his favorite sport.*

▶ **Practice Book pages 53 and 54**

I just love **Galveston's** shops! This cap will look perfect with my **brother's** T-shirt.

But the **cap's** bill is torn. Maybe you would like this one.

 Practice F on page 310.

Using Nouns in Writing

Teach:
Read aloud the writing tip and the example. Point out that *parrots* is a specific noun—it tells what kind of birds flew around the restaurant. Use word webs to help students generate specific nouns for places and food. Then read "Time for Lunch." Ask students to name the specific nouns.

> Use **specific nouns** to help your reader see what you are writing about.
>
> **Example:** Two **birds** flew around the restaurant.
> Two **parrots** flew around the restaurant.

Nouns Practice (Specific Nouns):

3 Have one student in a group name a general category and other students in the group name a specific noun in that category. Students can switch roles and repeat.

4 Provide students with a similar paragraph: *The restaurant is a busy place. Many people like to eat there. The cook makes good food for lunch. Their desserts are the best!* Have students think about their favorite place to eat and rewrite the paragraph using specific nouns.

Time for Lunch

The ~~restaurant~~ Parrot Cafe is a busy place. Many people love to eat there. They serve tasty tacos all through the day. The chef's best dish is black beans and rice.

He also serves great pizza. Have you ever tried a tuna pizza? How about a pizza with apples and walnuts? Now there's a taste not to miss!

Don't forget to save room for ~~dessert~~ chocolate fudge cake. It's thick and rich. You shouldn't skip this two-napkin treat.

Are you hungry yet? Come right this way. Welcome to the Parrot Cafe, where your table is waiting.

The writer replaced **restaurant** with **Parrot Cafe** to let readers know exactly which restaurant it is.

Replacing **dessert** with **chocolate fudge cake** gives a much clearer picture of the treat. You can almost taste it!

5 Have students write and illustrate either an ad for their favorite restaurant or a review of one of the dishes from the menu on page 120. Encourage them to use specific nouns to persuade people to go there.

Practices G and H on page 310.

Pronouns

Teach:
Read aloud the definition and the example, using the picture to clarify the concept "takes the place of."
Have a student say a sentence that tells what someone in the class wears. Repeat the sentence substituting a pronoun. Then have the student say the sentence pair. Repeat several times. Next, work through pages 174–176, pointing out the examples in the dialogue and pronouns in the charts. Pause after reading each group of rules to ask questions: *When should you use the pronoun **it**? (When you talk about a thing.)*

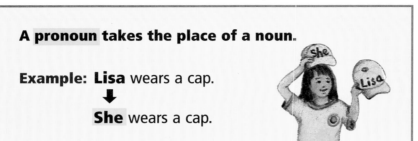

A **pronoun** takes the place of a noun.

Example: **Lisa** wears a cap.
➡
She wears a cap.

Using Different Kinds of Pronouns

■ **When you use a pronoun, be sure you are talking about the right person.**

1. For yourself, use **I**.

Hi! **I** am Mr. Brown.

2. When you speak to another person, use **you**.

Are **you** the coach?

Pronoun Practice (Gender):
3 Have students point to themselves and other people or objects in the classroom as they say *I, you, he, she,* or *it*.
4 Ask one student to pantomime an activity shown on the page such as holding a ball, pointing, and so on, while another student says a sentence: *He holds the ball. She is pointing.*
5 Students can write sentences about the people and objects in the classroom: *That's Felicia. She is wearing a blue dress. That's Jason. He has short hair and brown eyes. That's a pencil. It's red.* (Students may want to refer to **Describing Words** on pages 12–19.)

3. For a boy or a man, use **he**.

Yes! **He** is the coach.

Lisa

4. For a girl or a woman, use **she**.

That's Lisa. **She** is on the soccer team.

5. For a thing, use **it**.

Oh, the ball. Where is **it**?

■ **Be sure you are talking about the right number of people or things.**

One	More than One
I	**we**
you	**you**
he, she, it	**they**

1. When you speak to two or more people, use **you**.

2. For yourself and another person use **we**.

Are **you** ready?

Yes! **We** are going to beat the Bobcats.

Pronoun Practice (Singular/Plural):
3 Have students draw a picture of soccer players in action and use simple sentences with a verb and each pronoun to tell about it: *She runs, He runs, They run.*
4 Have students draw playground scenes and write captions: *Annie and Rebecca are friends. They jump rope. They swing.* Students can add speech balloons for the characters and write dialogue using the pronouns *I, you,* and *we.*

3. For other people, use **they**.

No, **they** won't! We will win!

5 Have partners write a short story based on their pictures of playground scenes: *I went to the playground with Marie. We played jacks with Paula and Liu. Liu didn't know how to play. We played slowly, and she learned the rules.* They can act out the story.

▶ **Practice Book page 56**

Tom

Joey

Lisa

■ **If you talk about a person twice in a sentence, use these pairs of pronouns.**

One		More than One	
I	**myself**	**we**	**ourselves**
you	**yourself**	**you**	**yourselves**
he	**himself**	**they**	**themselves**
she	**herself**		
it	**itself**		

Examples:

I hurt **myself**.
She found the ball **herself**.

Pronoun Practice (Reflexive):
3 4 5 Have the first student in a circle say a sentence using a reflexive: *I made this myself.* The next student changes the sentence using a different set of pronouns: *She made this herself,* and so on around the circle.

Grammar Made Graphic 175

Using Different Kinds of Pronouns, continued

■ **Be sure you use the right pronoun in the right place.**

Use these pronouns to tell who or what is doing something. They take the place of the subject in the sentence.

One	More than One
I	we
you	you
he, she, it	they

Examples:

Juan and Lisa are kicking the ball back and forth.
⬇
They are kicking the ball back and forth.

Juan kicks the ball up in the air.
⬇
He kicks the ball up in the air.

Lisa   Juan

Use these pronouns after a verb or a preposition.

One	More than One
me	us
you	you
him, her, it	them

Examples:

The ball flies past **Jasmine and Tom**.
⬇
The ball flies past **them**.

The goalie reaches for **the ball**.
⬇
The goalie reaches for **it**.

Pronoun Practice (Subject/Object):

3 Students sit in a circle and pass sports-related objects to each other. Help them make sentence pairs to describe the action: *Tim passes the ball to Sarah. He passes the ball to her.* Have students point to the person each pronoun stands for.

4 Have partners interview each other and report to the group: *Masaki told me that he gets up late on Saturday. He eats breakfast and then goes to soccer practice. After lunch, he plays with friends and watches TV. Do you have any questions for him?*

5 Students can draw pictures of safety equipment used for their favorite sport. Have them talk about the items using subject and object pronouns: *The catcher wears a face mask. It protects him from the ball. All players wear gloves to protect their hands.*

▶ **Practice Book page 57**

Tom

Jasmine

Go To Practice A on page 311.

Some pronouns tell who owns something.

Example: This is **Jasmine's** cap.
→
This is **her** cap.

This is **Jasmine's cap**.
→
This is **hers**.

These pronouns take the place of a person's name.

One	More than One
my	our
your	your
his, her, its	their

Pronoun Practice (Possessives):
3 Have each student draw a portrait of themselves dressed in a sport uniform and related equipment. They can show their portrait to another student and tell about their picture. Post students' pictures and ask questions: *Whose bat is this?*

1. Is this **Jasmine's** cap?
Lisa

2. No. I think **her** cap is red.
Joey

These pronouns take the place of a person's name and what the person owns.

One	More than One
mine	ours
yours	yours
his, hers	theirs

Hmm. Is this **my** cap?

Yes. It's **mine**.

4 Each student puts an item in a bag. The first student takes out one item and tries to remember to whom it belongs: *Tony, is this your pen?* or *Tony, is this yours?* Have the next student do the same. Continue to use third person pronouns, guiding students as necessary.
5 Have each student make a cluster (see **Clusters**, page 62) of items that belong to one person. Other students use complete sentences to help them guess who owns the items: *Juanita has a backpack. Could this red backpack be hers? No, hers is blue.*

Watch Out!

▶ **its** = pronoun
it's = it is

The dog is wearing **its** cap, too. I like the cap. **It's** cute!

Watch Out! Practice:
Divide students into two groups. Each group writes ten sentences using *its* or *it's* about items in the classroom. Groups exchange sentences to check.

➡ **Practice Book page 58**

Using Different Kinds of Pronouns, continued

When you don't name a specific person or thing, use one of these special pronouns.

anyone	someone	everyone
anybody	somebody	everybody
anything	something	everything

Example: Who left a cap on the table?
I don't know, but **someone** did.

Pronoun Practice (Indefinites):
3 **4** Have students write a card for each person at the party, using an indefinite pronoun in each sentence. For example, a card for Mr. Brown might say: *For Someone Special— Everyone knows you are a good coach. You lose something at every game!*
5 Divide students into two groups. Each group writes a mystery story starting with this sentence: *There's something under the napkin.* Encourage students to build suspense by using indefinite pronouns: *Does anyone know what it is?*

➤ **Practice Book page 59**

Go To Practice C on page 312.

Using Pronouns in Writing

Teach:
Read aloud the writing tip. Relate each pronoun in the example paragraph to the noun it agrees with. Then read aloud the sports column and discuss with students how the pronouns are used.

In a paragraph, each pronoun must agree with its noun.

Example:
  Mr. Brown wears **his** cap at every game. The players say the **cap** is lucky. One day, **it** was missing. Mr. Brown looked everywhere, and finally the players found it in his back pocket. He thanked them again and again.

By replacing **the Bobcats** ↓ with **they**, the writer makes this paragraph sound better.

Kicking Around!
Soccer Team Wins Again!
by Andy Thomas

  Let's hear it for our team! Yesterday the Bobcats won their match. *They* ~~The Bobcats~~ played hard against the Eagles and won by one goal. Lisa Anderson kicked the winning goal. Juan Chávez, her teammate, assisted on the goal.

  The team's record is now five wins and one loss—their best record in four years. Juan Silva and Jasmine Cummins also scored one goal each, and Joey Lee, the goalie, had six saves. Congratulations to them, too!

  After the game, everyone celebrated at the coach's house. He and his wife thanked all the people who helped organize the celebration.

  The players will go to Valley School next Wednesday. We hope they can win again!

The pronoun **them** agrees with ↓ **Juan Silva, Jasmine Cummins,** and **Joey Lee**.

Go To ▶ Practices D and E on page 313.

Pronoun Practice (Agreement):
3 Point out and say each pronoun in the sports column and ask students to tell you what noun each agrees with.
4 Have students rewrite the third paragraph of the sports column in as many ways as possible, substituting nouns for pronouns, and vice versa.
5 Have students write about a recent event at school. Then have them circle the pronouns they used and draw arrows to the nouns they agree with.

▶ **Practice Book page 60**

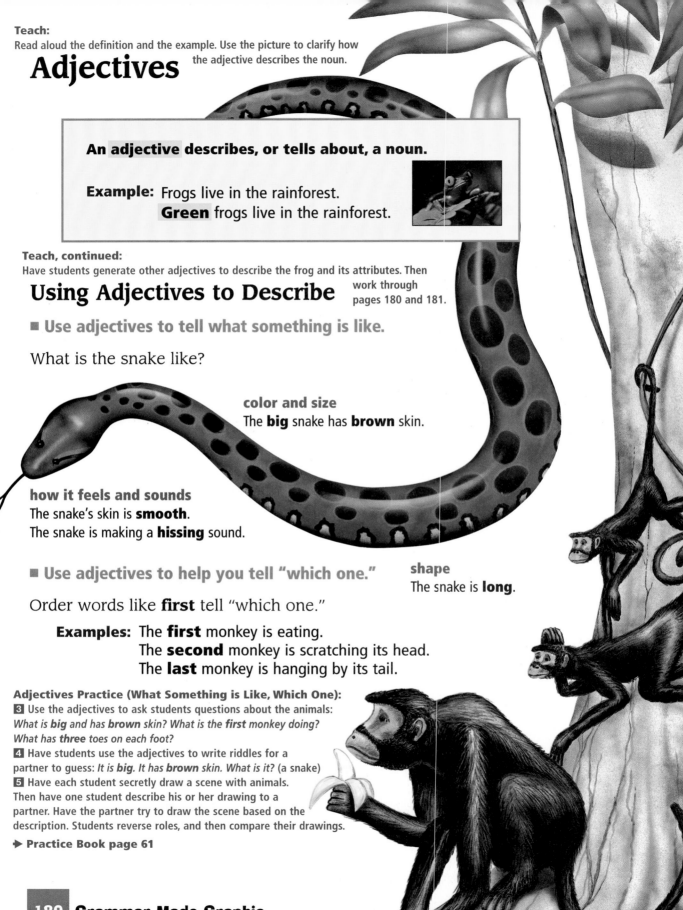

Adjectives

> ### An **adjective** describes, or tells about, a noun.
>
> **Example:** Frogs live in the rainforest.
> **Green** frogs live in the rainforest.

Using Adjectives to Describe

■ **Use adjectives to tell what something is like.**

What is the snake like?

color and size
The **big** snake has **brown** skin.

how it feels and sounds
The snake's skin is **smooth**.
The snake is making a **hissing** sound.

shape
The snake is **long**.

■ **Use adjectives to help you tell "which one."**

Order words like **first** tell "which one."

Examples: The **first** monkey is eating.
The **second** monkey is scratching its head.
The **last** monkey is hanging by its tail.

Adjectives Practice (What Something is Like, Which One):
3 Use the adjectives to ask students questions about the animals: *What is **big** and has **brown** skin? What is the **first** monkey doing? What has **three** toes on each foot?*
4 Have students use the adjectives to write riddles for a partner to guess: *It is **big**. It has **brown** skin. What is it?* (a snake)
5 Have each student secretly draw a scene with animals. Then have one student describe his or her drawing to a partner. Have the partner try to draw the scene based on the description. Students reverse roles, and then compare their drawings.

▶ **Practice Book page 61**

■ Use adjectives to help you tell "how many" or "how much."

Sometimes you know exactly how many things you see.
Use number words to describe them.

Examples: A sloth has **four** feet.
It has **three** toes on each foot.
A **dozen** sloths and **144** toes are in the tree.

If you don't know the exact number, use the words in this chart.

▶ MORE WAYS TO TELL "HOW MANY" OR "HOW MUCH"	
When you can count what you see, use these words.	**When you can't count what you see, use these words.**

many birds	**much** rain

a few birds **some** birds **several** birds **only a few** birds	**a little** rain **some** rain **not much** rain **only a little** rain

not any birds **no** birds	**not any** rain **no** rain

Adjectives Practice (How Many and How Much):

3 Redraw the illustrations of birds and rain to make picture cards. Place the cards face down in a pile. As you turn each card over, have students use an appropriate adjective to tell "how many" or "how much."

4 Have each student write three complete sentences to describe three of the pictures in the chart. Students trade sentences with a partner who reads each sentence aloud and finds the picture the sentence goes with.

5 Have students talk about the pictures on pages 180 and 181, and then write a paragraph about the rainforest and what it's like. Encourage students to use adjectives to describe whatever details they can about the animals and their habitat.

▶ **Practice Book page 62**

Go To ▶ Practices A and B on pages 313–314.

Using Adjectives to Compare

Teach:
Read aloud the definition and the example. Use the pictures to clarify the concept. Work through the pages, inviting students to use the adjectives to make comparisons.

small

smaller

Adjectives can help you make a comparison, to show how things are alike or different.

smallest

Example: This is a **small** bird.
This bird is **smaller** than that one.
This is the **smallest** bird of all.

■ **When you compare two things, add -er to the adjective.**

You'll probably use the word **than** in your sentence, too.

> **Example:** The parrot's beak is **long**.
> The motmot's beak is **longer than** the parrot's beak.

parrot

■ **When you compare three or more things, add -est to the adjective.**

Remember to use **the** before the adjective.

> **Example:** The toucan's beak is **the longest** of them all.

You may have to change the spelling of the adjective before you add **-er** or **-est**.

toucan   **motmot**

▶ SPELLING RULES		
For adjectives that end in a silent **e**, drop the **e** and add **-er** or **-est**.	larg~~e~~ larg**er** larg**est**	nic~~e~~ nic**er** nic**est**
For adjectives that end in **y**, change the **y** to **i** and add **-er** or **-est**.	pretty prett**ier** prett**iest**	sleepy sleep**ier** sleep**iest**
Does the adjective end in one vowel and one consonant? If so, double the final consonant and add **-er** or **-est**.	big big**ger** big**gest**	sad sad**der** sad**dest**

**Adjectives Practice
(Comparative/Superlative Adjectives):**

3 Give partners a set of three classroom objects such as pencils or scraps of paper. Have them arrange the objects in size or length order, point to each, and use adjectives to make comparisons: *This pencil is **long**. This pencil is **longer** than that one. This is the **longest** pencil.*

4 Have students use the adjective *tiny* to write sentences to compare the eyes of the birds at the top of the page, and *thin* or *long* to compare their tails.

5 Form groups of three. Have each student illustrate a bird (they can make one up) and label it. Display the drawings and have students write as many sentences as they can to compare the birds.

Go To Practice C on page 314.

Adjectives Practice (Irregular Adjectives):

3 Have students fold a paper into quarters and draw different numbers of a familiar object like a flower, heart, star, and so on, in each quarter to illustrate *more, most, less,* and *least.* Ask students to show their pictures and say phrases or sentences to compare them.

■ **If the adjective is a long word, do not add *-er* or *-est* to make a comparison.**

Adjectives with three or more syllables would be too hard to say if you added **-er** or **-est**. To make a comparison with these adjectives, use **more**, **most**, **less**, or **least** instead.

hummingbird   **motmot**   **macaw**

Examples:
The hummingbird is **colorful**.
The motmot is **more colorful** than the hummingbird.
The macaw is **the most colorful** bird of all.

4 Call on three volunteers to pantomime *surprised, more surprised,* and *most surprised.* Point to each student in turn as you make comparisons. Then have the volunteers pantomime a different emotion or feeling such as *sad, confused, embarrassed, enthusiastic,* or *afraid.* Have students follow your model to make comparisons.

5 Have groups debate the best ways to spend their free time. Students might discuss activities that are *important, more important, most important; good, better, best,* and so on.

▶ **Practice Book page 63**

Examples:
The first monkey was **frightened**.
The second monkey was **less frightened**.
The third monkey was the **least frightened** of all.

When you make a comparison, use either **-er** or **more**, but not both.

> The hummingbird is ~~more~~ smaller than the monkey.
>
> The macaw is ~~more~~ prettier than the motmot.

Watch Out!

▶ Some adjectives have special forms for comparing things.

good	bad
better	worse
best	worst
some	little
more	less
most	least

My photo of the toucan is the **best** picture of all those I took on my trip.

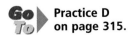 **Practice D on page 315.**

Grammar Made Graphic 183

Adding Adjectives to Sentences

> **Adjectives** can appear anywhere in a sentence.
>
> **Examples:** Look at that **big** jaguar.
> Its eyes are **big**, too.
> The **big** jaguar just looks back at me.

Usually, an adjective comes before the noun it tells about.

Examples: An **old** jaguar hides in the **green** leaves.

Its **spotted** coat makes the **big** jaguar hard to see.

Two or more adjectives can also come before a noun.
A comma usually comes between them.

Examples: The **wise, old** jaguar knows where to hide.

An adjective can come after words like **is**, **are**, **look**, **feel**, **smell**, and **taste**. The adjective describes the noun in the subject.

Examples: A rainforest is **beautiful**.

The air smells **clean**.

Each day in the rainforest feels **fresh**.

Adjectives Practice (Before a Noun):
3 Use the examples to make word cards. Have students put the words back together to make sentences.
4 Encourage students to choose an adjective to tell about the jaguar. Have them use the adjective in three different sentences and in a different place in each sentence.
5 Have each student in a group write an adjective on a notecard. Place the notecards in a pile in the middle of a circle. Students take turns selecting a notecard and making three sentences by placing the adjective in a different place in each sentence.

Adjectives Practice (After a Linking Verb):
3 4 5 List the words *feel, smell, taste, sound,* and *look* on the chalkboard. Select objects to pass around the room and have students use the verbs to generate sentences that follow the pattern: *The pencil looks blue.*

Using Adjectives in Writing

about. Call on different students to read aloud a paragraph from the article. Then ask students to find other nouns in the paragraph and suggest adjectives to tell about them.

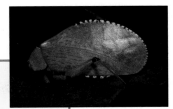

katydid

> **Use adjectives to help your reader "see" what you are writing about.**
>
> **Example:** The katydid chewed on the leaf.
> The **shiny** katydid chewed on the **green** leaf.

Adjectives Practice (Adding Descriptive Details):

3 Point to a picture of an animal on pages 180–185 and identify it: *Here is a snake.* Repeat the sentence, pausing to have students supply adjectives that give a better picture of the animal: *Here is <u>big, brown</u> snake.*

Animal Disguises

Some animals in the rainforest are hard to find. That's because their special colors help them hide. For example, a stick insect can look like a skinny, brown twig.

These two **adjectives** help you picture the insect.

Some katydids have bodies that look like green and brown leaves. One kind of katydid has wings with spots that look like big eyes. These two spots help them fool the animals that try to eat them.

Now you know how many spots are on the katydid's wings.

The black spots on jaguars make it easy for them to hide in the leaves. Then they can watch for animals on the ground without being seen.

This **adjective** helps you know which disguises.

These disguises protect animals from other animals, but sometimes they can help an animal sneak up on its own food. This is how rainforest creatures survive.

4 Have partners choose an animal from pages 180–185 and each write three or four sentences to describe it. Have them compare their sentences, find the adjectives, and decide which sentences give the best "pictures" of the animal.

5 Have students use an encyclopedia to research a rainforest animal like an anaconda or an iguana. Have students share what they learned with the class. Encourage them to use adjectives to help the class visualize the animal. Students can refer to pages 254–255 to find out how to find information in an encyclopedia.

▶ Practice Book page 64

katydid

stick insect

Go To Practices E and F on page 315.

Grammar Made Graphic 185

Verbs

Teach:
Read aloud the definition for action verbs. Ask a volunteer to read the example while another student demonstrates *float*. Have students pantomime other action verbs while the class guesses the verb. Then read the definition for linking verbs and the example. Have students use *are* to make up sentences about the clouds. Work through pages 186 and 187. Stop after reading each set of examples to have students name the verbs and tell what they do.

Some verbs show action:

> **Example:** The clouds **float** across the sky.

Some verbs link words in a sentence.

> **Example:** The sky **is** blue.

Action and Linking Verbs

■ **An action verb tells what the subject does.**

Most verbs are action verbs.

Some **action verbs** show action that you cannot see.

> The wind **blows** the clouds.
> The clouds **cover** the sun.
> Then the clouds **move** again.
>
> We **learn** about clouds in school.
> The class **enjoys** the lesson.

■ **A linking verb connects, or links, the subject of a sentence to a word in the predicate.**

The word in the predicate can describe the subject.

> **Examples:** Some clouds **look** fluffy on the top.

> They **are** flat on the bottom.

Or, the word in the predicate can name the subject in another way.

> **Example:** Those white streaks **are** clouds, too.

Verbs Practice (Action Verbs and Linking Verbs):
3 Have students use action and linking verbs to talk about the soccer scene on page 176.
4 Help students brainstorm details about the sun and write their responses in a word web. Have each student use the web to write four sentences about the sun: two with action verbs and two with linking verbs.
5 Ask these students to find the verbs in the story map about the hurricane on page 75. Have them imagine that they are the characters and make up their own sentences to tell about the event.

➤ **Practice Book pages 65 and 66**

▶ **LINKING VERBS**

Forms of the Verb *be*

am	was
are	were
is	

Other Linking Verbs

appear	seem
feel	taste
look	

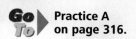
Go To Practice A on page 316.

Helping Verbs

■ **Some verbs are made up of more than one word.**

In these verbs, the last word is called the **main verb**.
The verbs that come before are called **helping verbs**.

The **helping verb** agrees with the subject. The **main verb** shows the action.

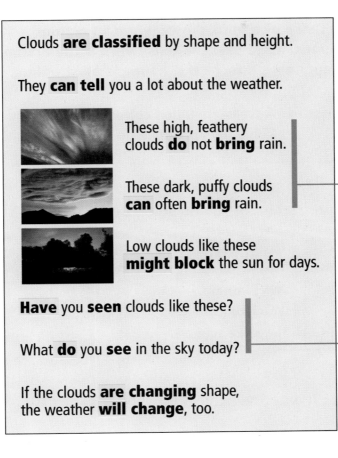

Clouds **are classified** by shape and height.

They **can tell** you a lot about the weather.

These high, feathery clouds **do** not **bring** rain.

These dark, puffy clouds **can** often **bring** rain.

Low clouds like these **might block** the sun for days.

Have you **seen** clouds like these?

What **do** you **see** in the sky today?

If the clouds **are changing** shape, the weather **will change**, too.

Words can come between a helping verb and a main verb. The word *not* always goes in between.

In questions, the subject comes between the helping verb and the main verb.

Here are some useful helping verbs.

▶ **HELPING VERBS**

Forms of the Verb *be*	Forms of the Verb *do*	Forms of the Verb *have*	Other Helping Verbs	
am	do	have	can	might
are	does	has	could	should
is	did	had	may	will
was			must	would
were				

Verbs Practice (Helping Verbs):
3 Read aloud each sentence as you write the verbs on the chalkboard. Point to each verb and have students complete your sentences: *The helping verb is (are). The main verb is (classified).* Then repeat the sentence and have students echo.
4 Make separate word cards for each kind of verb and distribute to partners. Write the sentences about clouds on the chalkboard without the verbs. Have students find the helping verb and main verb that finish the sentence and tape the verbs in place. Read the sentence aloud to confirm correct choices.
5 Have students talk about the current weather, and then use helping verbs and main verbs to write questions and sentences about it. Students can trade sentences with a partner who can check for correct placement.

➡ Practice Book page 67

Go To ▶ Practices B and C on page 316.

Present-Tense Verbs

Teach:
Talk about the graphic. Explain that verbs can tell about an action that happened before today, that happens right now, or that will happen tomorrow or the next day. Then read aloud the definition and the examples. Ask students to name the verb in each sentence, tell what tense it is, and describe when the action happens. Then work through pages 188–189. Call on volunteers to read aloud the example sentences in the charts.

Earlier	Now	Later
Past Tense	Present Tense	Future Tense

The tense of a verb shows when an action happens. Use a **present-tense verb** if the action is happening now or if it happens all the time.

Examples: A weather station **collects** information.
Computers **produce** maps of the weather.

■ **Some present-tense verbs end in -s, and some do not.**

One	More Than One
I like rain.	We like rain.
You like rain.	You like rain.
He, she, or it **likes** rain.	They like rain.

The use of **-s** depends on who the subject is.

Subjects	Present-Tense Verbs Ending in -s
She	The TV reporter **gives** the weather forecast for the day. She **gives** the weather forecast for the day. Sarita Pérez **gives** the weather forecast for the day.
He	The scientist **gathers** data on big storms. He **gathers** data on big storms. Mr. Taylor **gathers** data on big storms.
It	A newspaper **prints** weather stories. It **prints** weather stories.

Verbs Practice (Present Tense):
3 Write *watch*, *watches*, and *are watching* on the chalkboard. Say several sentences, pausing to have students supply the correct verb: *I (watch) the weather report. Dad (watches) the weather report. Mom and Dad (are watching) the weather report.* Repeat for other verbs.
4 Have each student draw a comic strip of someone getting caught in the rain. Students can use present-tense verbs to write sentences to describe the action. *The rain starts to fall. He opens his umbrella. A strong wind blows. He watches his umbrella fly away!*

5 Have students use the details and pictures on this page to write a description of a weather reporter's job. Ask them to use present-tense verbs in their sentences.
▶ **Practice Book pages 68 and 69**

 **Go To** Practice D on page 317.

Follow these rules to add -s or -es to a verb.

▶ **SPELLING RULES**

For most verbs, add **-s**.	**read**	My mother **reads** weather stories.
For verbs that end in **x**, **ch**, **sh**, **s**, or **z**, add **-es**.	**watch**	She **watches** weather reports.
For verbs that end in a consonant and **y**, change the **y** to **i** and add **-es**.	**study**	She **studies** weather patterns.
For verbs that end in a vowel and **y**, just add **-s**.	**say**	She **says** the weather is fascinating!

■ Some present-tense verbs tell about an action as it is happening.

These verbs have a helping verb and a main verb. The helping verb is am, is, or are. The main verb ends in -ing.

> Examples: **get** The clouds **are getting** darker.
> **start** The rain **is starting**.
> **run** I **am running** for cover.

Follow these rules to add -ing to a verb.

▶ **SPELLING RULES**

For most verbs, add **-ing**.	**fall** **fly** **look**	Big raindrops **are falling**. All the birds **are flying** home. A squirrel **is looking** for its hole.
For verbs that end in silent **e**, drop the **e** and add **-ing**.	**come** **make**	Now the rain **is coming** down harder. It **is making** so much noise!
Does the verb end in one vowel and one consonant? If so, double the final consonant and add **-ing**.	**tap** **clap**	The rain **is tapping** a beat on the roof. The thunder **is clapping** loudly. It likes the rain's music!

 Practices E and F on pages 317–318.

Past-Tense Verbs

Teach:
Use the graphic to briefly review present-tense verbs, and then read aloud the definition and the example. Talk about why *invented* is in the past tense. Help students generate other sentences that tell about the past. Then work through pages 190 and 191. Have students explain in their own words how the verbs change to show that the actions happened in the past.

Earlier Past Tense	Now Present Tense	Later Future Tense

The tense of a verb shows when an action happens. Use a past-tense verb if the action happened earlier, or in the past.

Example: Galileo Galilei **invented** the thermometer around 1600.

Verbs Practice (Regular Past-Tense Verbs):
3 Have one student say a present-tense verb. Have the partner say and write the past-tense form. Students reverse roles and repeat several times.
4 Write each present-tense verb on the chalkboard. Read aloud the spelling rule and ask students what you should do to make the verb tell about the past. Confirm responses as you write the past-tense verb and use it in a sentence.

■ **Many past-tense verbs end in -ed.**

These verbs are called **regular verbs**.

Example: measure Galileo's thermometer **measured** the air's temperature.

Galileo's thermometer

Follow these rules to add **-ed** to a verb.

5 Provide a paragraph with present-tense verbs for students to rewrite using past-tense verbs: *The temperature reaches 90 degrees. I try to cool off. I grab my swimsuit. Then I step into the water. Ah! The water saves me from the heat!*

▶ **Practice Book page 70**

▶ SPELLING RULES		
For most verbs, add **-ed**.	**launch**	Scientists **launched** the first weather satellite in 1960.
For verbs that end in silent **e**, drop the **e** and add **-ed**.	**circle**	It **circled** Earth every two hours.
Does the verb end in one vowel and one consonant? If so, double the final consonant and add **-ed**.	**snap**	It **snapped** pictures of the clouds around Earth.
For verbs that end in a consonant and **y**, change the **y** to **i** and add **-ed**.	**study**	Scientists **studied** the pictures to predict a heat wave.
For verbs that end in a vowel and **y**, just add **-ed**.	**stay**	The weather **stayed** hot for a few days, but then it changed!

Go To ▶ Practice G on page 318.

■ **Irregular verbs do not add *-ed* to show past tense.**

▶ IRREGULAR VERBS

Verb	Now–In the Present	Earlier–In the Past
be	Our family **is** in Arizona.	Our family **was** in Arizona.
	We **are** excited.	We **were** excited.
begin	Our desert vacation **begins**.	Our desert vacation **began**.
break	The temperature here **breaks** 100°.	The temperature **broke** 100°.
bring	My mom **brings** sunscreen.	My mom **brought** sunscreen.
buy	We **buy** special hats.	We **bought** special hats.
do	We **do** the same things every day.	We **did** the same things every day.
drink	We **drink** a lot of water.	We **drank** a lot of water.
eat	We **eat** very little.	We **ate** very little.
find	My sister and I **find** interesting rocks.	My sister and I **found** interesting rocks.
go	I **go** back to camp at noon.	I **went** back to camp at noon.
get	It **gets** even hotter at that time!	It **got** even hotter at that time!
give	The afternoon **gives** us time to rest.	The afternoon **gave** us time to rest.
hear	We **hear** a sound nearby.	We **heard** a sound nearby.
hide	Something **hides** by our tent.	Something **hid** by our tent.
hold	I **hold** my breath.	I **held** my breath.
keep	I **keep** listening.	I **kept** listening.
know	My dad **knows** it is a lizard.	My dad **knew** it was a lizard.
make	We **make** a drawing of the lizard.	We **made** a drawing of the lizard.
ride	In the evening, we **ride** horses.	In the evening, we **rode** horses.
run	Something **runs** by us.	Something **ran** by us.
say	"Look at that," I **say**.	"Look at that," I **said**.
see	We **see** a big roadrunner.	We **saw** a big roadrunner.
sing	At night, we **sing** together.	At night, we **sang** together.
take	I **take** photos of our family.	I **took** photos of our family.
think	Everyone **thinks** the trip was great.	Everyone **thought** the trip was great.
write	We **write** about our hot vacation in school, and I add my photos.	We **wrote** about our hot vacation in school, and I added my photos.

Verbs Practice (Irregular Past-Tense Verbs):

3 Say a verb and have students read aloud the sentence that uses its past-tense form. Repeat for several more verbs.

4 Have one student say a sentence using the present-tense of a verb. The partner repeats the sentence, but uses the past-tense: *I go to the store. I went to the store.* Students continue for four sentences, and then reverse roles for four more sentences.

5 Ask students to write a paragraph about a place that they visited and what they did there. Have them read aloud the paragraph to the class.

▶ **Practice Book pages 71 and 72**

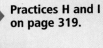
Practices H and I on page 319.

Future-Tense Verbs

Teach:
Use the graphic to briefly review present- and past-tense verbs. Then read aloud the definition and example. Talk about why the verbs are in the future tense. Work through the page, and help students generate more examples by having them finish these sentences: *Tomorrow I will ___. Next week I am going to ___. Tomorrow I won't ___.*

Earlier Past Tense	Now Present Tense	Later Future Tense

The tense of a verb shows when an action happens. Use a future-tense verb if the action will happen later, or in the future.

Example: **Will** the weather **be** windy next week?
Yes, next week it **will be** windy.

**Verbs Practice
(Will and Going to):**
3 Ask students yes/no questions. Encourage them to respond in complete sentences: *Will it rain tomorrow? Yes (No), it will (won't) rain tomorrow. Are you going to watch the weather report? Yes (No), I am going to (am not going to) watch the weather report.*
4 Have students role-play being weather reporters and use *will, going to,* and *won't* to tell what they will do the next day.

■ **There are two ways to show the future tense.**

1. Use the helping verb **will** along with a main verb.

2. Use the phrase **going to**.

Tomorrow I **am going to build** a weather vane, too.

Tomorrow I **will build** a weather vane.

The word **won't** also shows future tense. **Won't** is a contraction, or shortened form, of the words **will** and **not**.

We will check the wind direction every day.

I bet we **won't** get the same results.

5 Have students use future-tense verbs to write a script for a weather report for your area. Encourage volunteers to present the report to the class.

➤ **Practice Book page 73**

Go To Practice J on page 320.

Contractions with Verbs

Teach:
Read aloud the definition and examples. Write *Weather is* and *I would* on the chalkboard and verbalize as you demonstrate how to put the two words together to make a contraction. Then work through the charts. Have volunteers demonstrate making contractions and using each contraction in a sentence.

> You can put two words together to make a **contraction**.
> An apostrophe shows where one or more letters have been left out.
>
> Examples: **Weather is**   **Weather's** an interesting subject.
>   **I would**   **I'd** like to be a weather reporter.

In many contractions, the verb is shortened.

▶ CONTRACTIONS WITH VERBS

Verb	Phrase	Contraction	Verb	Phrase	Contraction
am	I am	I'm	have	I have	I've
				they have	they've
are	they are	they're			
			will	they will	they'll
is	he is	he's		we will	we'll
	it is	it's			
	where is	where's	would	she would	she'd
	what is	what's		you would	you'd

**Verbs Practice
(Verb Contractions):**
3 Make two sets of word cards: one set with the two words that make up a contraction and one set for contractions. Have partners match the two words to its contracted form.
4 Have each student interview two people about the kind of weather they like or don't like and why, and then report to the class: *Tina doesn't like rain. Her shoes always get wet.*

In contractions with a verb and **not**, the word **not** is shortened to **n't**.

▶ CONTRACTIONS WITH *not*

Verb	Phrase	Contraction	Verb	Phrase	Contraction
do	I do not	I don't	have	I have not	I haven't
does	he does not	he doesn't	could	you could not	you couldn't
did	we did not	we didn't	would	she would not	she wouldn't
are	you are not	you aren't	should	we should not	we shouldn't
is	he is not	he isn't			
was	she was not	she wasn't	**Exception**		
were	they were not	they weren't	can	you cannot	you can't

5 Have students use contractions to write and illustrate advertisements or posters for a place. Encourage them to include details about the climate: *Florida's the best place to visit! You'll love the warm weather. Won't you give Florida a try?*

➤ Practice Book page 74

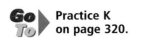 Practice K on page 320.

Using Verbs in Writing

Teach:
Read aloud the writing tip. Have students close their eyes as you read the example with appropriate sound effects. Ask them which verb gives a clearer picture. Discuss the meaning of colorful and how colorful verbs help the reader "see" and better understand the action. Then read the poem and have students identify the colorful verbs.

> **Use colorful verbs to help your reader see what you are talking about.**
>
> **Example:** An icicle **fell** to the ground.
> An icicle **crashed** to the ground.

Can you see what the skater is doing? The **verbs** tell you.

ICY

I slip and I slide
On the slippery ice;
I skid and I glide—
Oh, isn't it nice
To lie on your tummy
And slither and skim
On the slick crust of snow
Where you skid as you swim?

—*Rhoda W. Bacmeister*

Verbs Practice (Colorful Verbs):

3 Have each student draw a weather scene (for example, a rainy, windy, or snowy day). Help them make a list of verbs that tell what happens or what they would do on that day. Help students choose colorful verbs to write on their picture.

4 Give students sentences that tell about the weather: *The lightning started. The rain fell on the sidewalk.* Have students rewrite the sentences using colorful verbs: *The lightning flashed. The rain splashed on the sidewalk.*

5 Have students write and illustrate a weather concept poem using colorful verbs. Students can look on pages 134–137 for models of poems.

→ **Practice Book page 75**

Go To Practices L and M on page 320.

Adverbs

Teach:
Read aloud the definition and examples. Use the pictures of Ciara and Mariah to clarify how adverbs tell more about the action. Then work through pages 195 and 196, having students read aloud the examples and generate new sentences that tell about the gymnasts in the pictures.

Lu

Jason

Beto

Mariah

Ciara

> **An adverb tells "how," "where," or "when."**
>
> **Examples:** Ciara stretches **carefully**.
> Mariah stands **nearby**.
> She will stretch **later**.

Using Adverbs

■ **Adverbs usually tell more about a verb.**

An **adverb** can come before or after a **verb**.

Adverbs Practice (Types and Placement):
3 Read aloud each example, pausing to have students complete the sentence with the adverb.
4 Ask students how, where, or when questions and have them use the examples to answer: *Where are the gymnasts? (The gymnasts are everywhere.)*
5 Have students use these adverbs and others they know to write new sentences about the gymnasts Jason, Lu, or Beto.
▶ **Practice Book page 76**

These **adverbs** tell "where."

These **adverbs** tell "when."

Many **adverbs** tell "how." They usually end in **-ly**.

The gymnasts are **everywhere**.
The judges wait **outside**.

Each gymnast **always** tries to win.
Who won **yesterday**?

Mariah walks **carefully** across the beam.
Ciara tumbles **quickly** across the mat.

■ **Sometimes an adverb tells more about an adjective or another adverb.**

Mariah

Examples: This is **really** exciting.

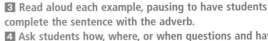

The audience claps **very** loudly.

Ciara

Using Adverbs to Compare

■ **You can use an adverb to compare actions.**

Lu jumps **high**.

Jason jumps **higher** than Lu.

Beto jumps **highest** of all.

1. Add **-er** to an adverb to compare two actions. You'll probably use the word **than** in your sentence, too.

2. Add **-est** to an adverb to compare three or more actions.

Ciara   Mariah

3. If the adverb ends in **-ly**, use **more**, **most**, **less**, or **least** to compare the actions.

   Examples: Ciara walks **more quickly** than Mariah.
   Both girls fall **less frequently** than other gymnasts.

Watch Out!

▶ **Don't use an adjective when you need an adverb.**

Everyone was sorry that the
gymnastics show ended so quick.
                                  ly
                                  ^
                       well
The girls performed good on the
                    ^
balance beam.

Adverbs Practice (Comparative/Superlative Adverbs):
3 Have groups of three say a word or phrase in varying degrees of loudness or softness. As each student speaks, use comparative adverbs to describe the action: *Joan speaks loudly/softly. Mark speaks louder/more softly than Jason. Lee speaks loudest/most softly of all.*
4 Have partners make up sentences to compare the actions of the gymnasts: *Mariah walks more carefully across the beam than Ciara. Jason tumbles faster than Beto.*
5 Have groups sit in a circle. One student makes a sentence and selects two other students to act out the sentence: *Karen stands up more slowly than Paola. Tonya speaks louder than Scott.*

Watch Out! Practice:
Provide additional sentences with errors. Have students find the adjective and tell you how to correct it: *The audience cheered happy* (happily). *Mariah smiled thankful* (thankfully) *when she got her trophy. She knew she had performed good* (well).

➤ **Practice Book page 77**

Go To ▶ Practice A on page 321.

Using Adverbs in Writing

Teach:
Read aloud the writing tip. Then read the example without the adverb. Read it again with the adverb. Ask students why the adverb makes the sentence clearer. Read the letter and talk about how adverbs help Mariah clearly describe the contest to her aunt.

> **Use adverbs to tell where, when, and how things happen. These important details will make your writing clear.**
>
> **Example:** Mariah walked **gracefully** across the balance beam.

Adverbs Practice (Using Adverbs for Detail):
3 Read aloud the letter, pausing to have students point to and say the adverbs.
4 Have students use adverbs to write several sentences about an experience they have had that was both exciting and scary.

Adding **very** shows just how scared Mariah was.

5 Have students write a friendly letter to tell a friend about a recent special event. Encourage them to use adverbs to make their writing clearer. Students can find a model of a letter on page 114.

▶ **Practice Book page 78**

1431 Oak Street
Los Angeles, CA 90015
March 4, 2001

Dear Aunt Ann,
    I was in an exciting contest! ^yesterday
I had a great time! I performed on the balance beam. It was the first time that I walked on the beam in front of an audience. It was ^very scary. I had to focus on staying on the beam.
    My friend Ciara was in the show, too. She can walk on the beam more quickly than anyone. The audience clapped loudly for her. I wish you could have seen her. She performed so ~~good~~ well that she won.
    Will you come to our next gymnastics show? I hope so.

                        Your niece,
                        Mariah

Yesterday is an important detail. It tells Aunt Ann when the contest happened.

Mariah is telling how Ciara performed, so she changed the adjective **good** to the adverb **well**.

Prepositions

Prepositions are small words. A prepositional phrase starts with a preposition and ends with a noun or pronoun.

Example: Can you make a fish kite **with** green paper?

Ways to Use Prepositions

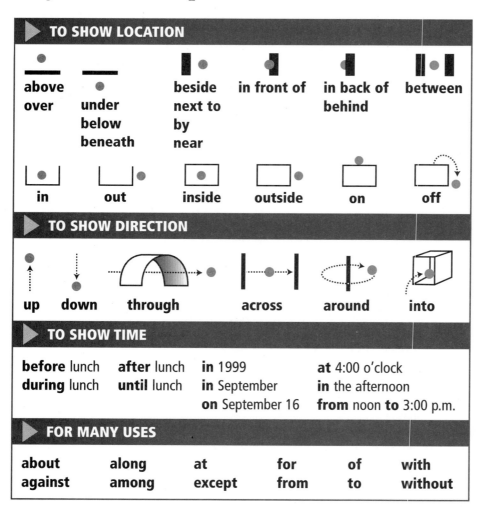

TO SHOW LOCATION

| above over | under below beneath | beside next to by near | in front of | in back of behind | between |

| in | out | inside | outside | on | off |

TO SHOW DIRECTION

| up | down | through | across | around | into |

TO SHOW TIME

before lunch	after lunch	in 1999	at 4:00 o'clock
during lunch	until lunch	in September	in the afternoon
		on September 16	from noon to 3:00 p.m.

FOR MANY USES

| about | along | at | for | of | with |
| against | among | except | from | to | without |

Teach:
Read aloud the definition and the example. As you work through the page, have volunteers generate sentences using prepositions that show location, direction, and time. Ask other students to act out the sentences.

Prepositions Practice (Location and Direction):
3 Have one student place an object like scissors in different locations around a table or desk. Have the partner use prepositional phrases to tell where it is. Then students reverse roles.
4 Groups can play "I Spy," using prepositional phrases for clues: *I spy something under the table/between the clock and the wall/next to the window.*
5 Have partners hide or select an object in the classroom. Have them write clues for another pair of students to find it: *Walk around the teacher's desk. Stop when you see the sign on the door. Look up,* and so on.

Prepositions Practice (Time):
3 4 5 Draw a time line for a school day on the chalkboard. Show "now" on the line. Ask students to name daily activities as you label them on the time line. Have students use prepositions to tell more about the activity and when it takes place: *recess—We have recess **before** lunch. **During** recess we play jump ball.*

▶ **Practice Book pages 79 and 80**

 Practices C, D, and E on pages 321–322.

Using Prepositions in Writing

Teach:
Discuss the writing tip and how prepositional phrases can be used to add descriptive details. Read through the instructions and help students identify the prepositions. Talk about how the prepositions make the instructions clear.

Prepositional phrases add details to your writing.

Example: I will decorate my fish kite.
I will decorate my fish kite **with red dots**.

The information in these **prepositional phrases** helps the reader put the kite together correctly.

Prepositions Practice (Prepositional Phrases):
3 Provide materials and work with students to make a fish kite. Before students complete each step, read aloud the specific task and ask questions to clarify: *Where should the glue go?* (near the straight edge of the paper)
4 **5** Have students follow the directions to make a fish kite. Afterward, encourage them to display their kites and use prepositional phrases to explain the steps in their own words.

▶ **Practice Book page 81**

How to Make a Fish Kite

1. Fold a piece of tissue like this. Do not press the fold. Then, cut the paper in this shape. Unfold the paper.

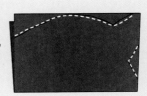

2. Add some glue in a line near the edge of the paper. Put a pipe cleaner by the glue and fold the paper over. Press it down.

3. Turn the paper over and decorate the fish.

4. Bend the pipe cleaner into a circle and twist the ends together.

5. Glue the bottom edges of the fish together, but be sure to leave the tail end open.

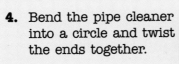

6. Tie a short string to the mouth like this.

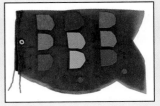

7. Tie the short string to a long string. Tie the long string to a long pole. Then take your fish outside and fly it!

Go To ▶ Practices F and G on page 322.

Grammar Made Graphic 199

Interjections

Teach:
Read aloud the definition. Read the example, emphasizing the interjection. Then have students say the sentence, with expression. Work through the explanation, and then invite students to use an interjection to create a class motto. For example: *Yes! We can do it!* or *Wow! What a team!* Each student can copy and decorate the motto to display in the classroom.

> **Use an interjection to show feelings, like surprise.**
>
> **Example: Wow!** That was a great catch.

An interjection can be a word or a phrase.

Examples: **Help!**   **Hooray!**   **Oh boy!**   **Wow!**
               Hey!   **Oh!**   **Oops!**   **Yikes!**

A comma follows the interjection if it is part of a sentence.
An exclamation point follows an interjection that stands alone.

Examples: **Hooray,** his catch saved a home run!
               Oh, boy! Now our team can win.

Conjunctions

Teach:
Read aloud the definition. Then read the example, emphasizing the conjunction. Work through the chart, elaborating on how the conjunctions are used. Create a chart with the headings "Alike (and)," "Difference (but)," and "Choice (or)." Have students generate sentences to write in each column. Discuss the differences among the sentences, pointing out those with compound subjects or compound predicates, and those that are compound sentences.

> **To connect words and sentences, use these conjunctions:**
>
> **and   but   or**
>
> **Example:** The Tigers **and** the Eagles are playing today.

▶ HOW TO USE CONJUNCTIONS

When you want to put two ideas that are alike together, use **and**.	Keith Morrow can hit **and** run well. He hit the ball, **and** then he scored a run.
When you want to show a difference between two ideas, use **but**.	Mom likes the Tigers, **but** I like the Eagles.
When you want to show a choice between two ideas, use **or**.	Either the Tigers **or** the Eagles will be in first place after this game. Mom will be happy, **or** I will be!

Using Conjunctions in Writing

Use **conjunctions** to avoid short, choppy sentences.

Example:

Should we leave now? Should we stay? It's been raining for twenty minutes. Maybe it will stop soon.

Should we leave now, **or** should we stay? It's been raining for twenty minutes, **but** maybe it will stop soon.

Conjunctions Practice:

3 Write each compound sentence from the postcard as two separate sentences on the chalkboard. Have students point to the compound sentence made from those two sentences, and tell what was added when the sentences were joined.

4 Have students write several sentences to tell about family members' favorite sports or teams. Help them identify any short, choppy sentences that could be combined with conjunctions, and have them rewrite those sentences.

5 Have students write a paragraph with compound sentences that describe the action in the soccer game pictured on page 176.

▶ **Practice Book**
page 82

By joining these two sentences with **or**, the choice is easier to see.

Dear Joey,
   The baseball game was very close! My mom is a Tigers fan, but my favorite team is the Eagles. In the bottom of the ninth inning, the score was tied 2-2. The Eagles had one man on base and Keith Morrow hit a fly into left field. Would it be a home run? or Would the Tigers' outfielder catch the ball?
   Can you guess? It was a home run and the Eagles won!
                    Your friend,
                    Junji

Joey Hosaka
998 Sunset Lane, Apt. 3D
San Francisco, CA 94610

USA
20
1996

Remember to use a comma before a conjunction in a compound sentence.

Go To ▶ Practices H and I
on page 323.

Grammar Made Graphic 201

Capital Letters

A word that begins with a **capital letter** is special in some way.

Example: **The** name of this boat is *Lucky Seas*.

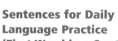

Ride on *Lucky Seas*!

Come with us and see big, beautiful whales. The boat leaves every day at 8:00 a.m.

Meet us at pier 9.

Teach:
Read aloud the first sentence in the box. Have students look at the capital letters as you read the example. Explain that each capital letter signals something special: *The capital T in **The** signals the start of the sentence.*

■ **A capital letter shows where a sentence begins.**

■ **When you talk about yourself, use the capital letter I.**

Oh, *I* see the boat.

Soon, you and *I* will be watching whales!

Teach, continued:
*The capital letters in **Lucky Seas** signal the name of a particular boat.* Work through pages 202–207. Pause after each section to point out a few examples and have students tell what the capital letter signals.

For daily language practice, form heterogeneous groups and give each group a copy of the Practice sentences. Have students discuss and collaborate to identify the errors in the sentences. Each student can then rewrite the sentences correctly.

Sentences for Daily Language Practice (First Word in a Sentence; I):

1. have you ever been whale-watching?
2. last year i went whale-watching with my sister.
3. she only saw one whale, but I saw two!
4. they were both humpback whales.
5. it was a fun trip, and i want to go again next year.

■ **The name of a person begins with a capital letter.**

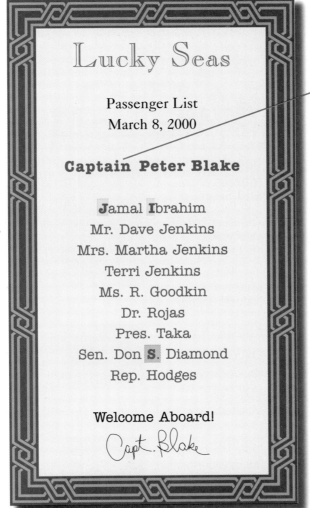

Lucky Seas

Passenger List
March 8, 2000

Captain Peter Blake

Jamal Ibrahim
Mr. Dave Jenkins
Mrs. Martha Jenkins
Terri Jenkins
Ms. R. Goodkin
Dr. Rojas
Pres. Taka
Sen. Don S. Diamond
Rep. Hodges

Welcome Aboard!

Capt. Blake

Begin all **first
and last names**
with a capital letter.

Capitalize an
initial in a name.

Capitalize a **title**
when it is used
with a name.

Sometimes the title is
abbreviated, or made
shorter. Use these
abbreviations:

Mr.	for a man
Mrs.	for a married woman
Ms.	for any woman
Dr.	for a doctor
Pres.	for the president of a country, a company, a club, or an organization
Sen.	for a member of the U.S. Senate
Rep.	for a member of the U.S. House of Representatives
Capt.	for the captain of a boat

**Sentences for
Daily Language Practice
(Names of People):**
1. My name is terri a. jenkins.
2. My best friend, jamal ibrahim, lives next door to me.
3. His parents, dr. and mrs. ibrahim, are always nice to me.
4. My other friend, j.j. price, lives across the street.
5. His dad is sen. phil price.

▶ **Practice Book page 83**

Watch Out!

▶ **Do not capitalize a title
when it is used without
a name.**

I'm Mike Hardin. I work
with the **captain.**

▶ **Capitalize words like *Mom*
and *Dad* when they are
used as names.**

Hey, **Mom**! Come meet Mike.
Mike, I'd like you to meet **my mom.**

 **Practice A
on page 323.**

Capital Letters, continued

■ **The important words in the name of a special place or thing begin with a capital letter.**

Where do you travel on the Lucky Seas?

We go out of San Francisco Bay to the Pacific Ocean.

NAMES OF SPECIAL PLACES AND THINGS

Streets and Roads
King Boulevard
Avenue M
First Street
Simmons Expressway

Cities

New York City
Houston
Los Angeles

States
New York
Texas
California

Countries
Vietnam
Ecuador
France

Continents
Asia
South America
Australia

Buildings, Monuments, and Ships

Statue of Liberty
Lucky Seas
Three Rivers Stadium
Museum of Natural History

Bodies of Water
Colorado River
Pacific Ocean
Lake Baikal
Mediterranean Sea

Landforms
Rocky Mountains
Sahara Desert
Grand Canyon

Public Spaces
Mesa Verde National Park
Central Park
Arapaho National Forest

Planets and Heavenly Bodies
Earth
Jupiter
Milky Way

Sentences for Daily Language Practice (Names of Places and Things):

1. We are going on the tour boat <u>mermaid</u>.
2. <u>mermaid</u> is docked in victoria harbor, near vancouver.
3. vancouver is in british columbia, canada.
4. The tour director, Mary Fine, is canadian.
5. Her family lives on vancouver island.

▶ **Practice Book page 84**

Watch Out!

▶ **Capitalize an adjective if it comes from the name of a special place.**

Mike is from **Canada**.
He is a **Canadian** sailor.

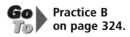 **Go To** Practice B on page 324.

When you write the abbreviation, or short form, of a place name, use a capital letter.

Dear Kim,

Hello from California. We went whale watching today. Did you know some gray whales are over 40 feet long? I really liked it when they came up for air— I could see their spouts. I'll show you some pictures when I get home.

Your friend,
Jamal

Kim Messina
10250 W. Fourth St.
Las Vegas, NV 89015

▶ ABBREVIATED PLACE NAMES

For State Names on Letters and Cards That Are Mailed

AL	Alabama	**MT**	Montana
AK	Alaska	**NE**	Nebraska
AZ	Arizona	**NV**	Nevada
AR	Arkansas	**NH**	New Hampshire
CA	California	**NJ**	New Jersey
CO	Colorado	**NM**	New Mexico
CT	Connecticut	**NY**	New York
DE	Delaware	**NC**	North Carolina
FL	Florida	**ND**	North Dakota
GA	Georgia	**OH**	Ohio
HI	Hawaii	**OK**	Oklahoma
ID	Idaho	**OR**	Oregon
IL	Illinois	**PA**	Pennsylvania
IN	Indiana	**RI**	Rhode Island
IA	Iowa	**SC**	South Carolina
KS	Kansas	**SD**	South Dakota
KY	Kentucky	**TN**	Tennessee
LA	Louisiana	**TX**	Texas
ME	Maine	**UT**	Utah
MD	Maryland	**VT**	Vermont
MA	Massachusetts	**VA**	Virginia
MI	Michigan	**WA**	Washington
MN	Minnesota	**WV**	West Virginia
MS	Mississippi	**WI**	Wisconsin
MO	Missouri	**WY**	Wyoming

For Words Used in Addresses

Ave.	Avenue
Blvd.	Boulevard
Ct.	Court
Dr.	Drive
E.	East
Hwy.	Highway
Ln.	Lane
N.	North
Pl.	Place
Rd.	Road
S.	South
Sq.	Square
St.	Street
W.	West

Sentences for Daily Language Practice (Abbreviated Place Names):
1. 944 w. Pine boulevard
2. Syracuse, ny
3. 501 n. Maple Square
4. Miami, fl
5. Seattle, wa

▶ **Practice Book page 85**

Capital Letters, continued

■ **The first word and all important words in the name of an organization begin with a capital letter.**

▶ NAMES OF ORGANIZATIONS

Clubs
Whale Watcher's Club
at Monterey Bay
Girl Scouts of America

World Organizations
International Whaling Commission
United Nations

Sports Teams
Los Angeles Dodgers
Seattle Supersonics

Professional Groups
American Medical Association
Professional Golfers' Association

Political Parties
Democratic Party
Republican Party

Businesses
Sal's Camera Shop
Little Taco House

© 1993 Sea World, Inc.

■ **Names of the months, days of the week, and special days and holidays begin with a capital letter.**

If you abbreviate one of these names, begin the abbreviation with a capital letter and end it with a period.

▶ MONTHS AND DAYS

Months of the Year		Days of the Week		Special Days and Holidays
January	Jan.	**Sunday**	Sun.	April Fool's Day
February	Feb.	**Monday**	Mon.	Christmas
March	Mar.	**Tuesday**	Tues.	Earth Day
April	Apr.	**Wednesday**	Wed.	Graduation Day
May	*These months*	**Thursday**	Thurs.	Hanukkah
June	*are never*	**Friday**	Fri.	Kwanzaa
July	*abbreviated.*	**Saturday**	Sat.	Labor Day
August	Aug.			New Year's Day
September	Sept.			Thanksgiving
October	Oct.			
November	Nov.			
December	Dec.			

Sentences for Daily Language Practice (Organizations, Months/Days):
1. I love Summer.
2. My boy scout troop is going to a baseball game.
3. It's on thursday, july 4.
4. independence day is my favorite holiday!
5. My favorite team, the chicago red sox, are playing.

▶ **Practice Book page 86**

Watch Out!

▶ The names of **seasons do not start with a capital letter.**

In **spring**, the whales go north.

In **fall**, they go south.

206 **Grammar Made Graphic**

Go To ▶ Practice C on page 324.

■ **The important words in a title begin with a capital letter.**

What has a title? Books, magazines, newspapers, and all kinds of written works have titles. So do multimedia works like movies, computer programs, TV shows, and videos. Stories, poems, and songs have titles, too.

Sentences for Daily Language Practice (Important Words in a Title, Person's Exact Words):
1. I read a book called <u>oceans of the world</u>.
2. The author said, "lots of whales live in the pacific ocean."
3. Then I watched the TV program "sea adventures with dr. pratt."
4. He said, "whales are mammals, not fish."
5. Now I'm going to write a report called "the most amazing mammals."

Little words like **a**, **an**, **the**, **in**, **at**, **of**, and **for** are not capitalized unless they are the first word in the **title**.

Meet a Majestic Sea Mammal

By Sarah O'Neal

Whales are gigantic animals that live in the oceans and seas of the world. Dr. Gregory Pratt knows. He has just published ***The Largest Mammals on the Planet***. In it, he explains that whales look like fish, but are really mammals. On a recent segment of the television show ***Nature Hour***, Dr. Pratt said, "Like other mammals, whales have well-developed brains. Unlike fish, whales are warm-blooded and their babies are born alive."

According to Dr. Pratt, the respiratory system of whales clearly makes them mammals. He said, "All mammals have lungs. Whales, therefore, must regularly come to the surface of the water to breathe. But, unlike humans, whales can go for 40 minutes or longer without breathing."

■ **When a person's exact words appear in print, the first word begins with a capital letter.**

Go To ▶ Practice D on page 325.

Punctuation Marks

After talking about each kind of punctuation, encourage students to talk about the pictures or the story; and then dictate new sentences that use the same punctuation.

For daily language practice, form heterogeneous groups and give each group a copy of the Practice sentences. Have students discuss and collaborate to identify the errors in the sentences. Each student can then rewrite the sentences correctly.

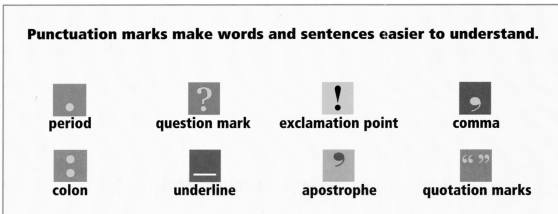

Punctuation marks make words and sentences easier to understand.

period	question mark	exclamation point	comma
colon	underline	apostrophe	quotation marks

Sentence Punctuation

■ **Always use a punctuation mark at the end of a sentence. It gives important information.**

Sentences for Daily Language Practice (Sentence Punctuation):

1. Do you read the newspaper
2. My dad reads it every morning
3. One day our dog chewed up the newspaper
4. Boy, was my dad mad
5. Has this ever happened to you

▶ **Practice Book page 87**

●	Use a **period** to show that you are making a statement or giving a polite command.	Aaron saw an ad in the newspaper.

FOR SALE
Used bicycle, good condition.
Call J.J. Davies, 555-1290.

Read it to me.

?	Use a **question mark** to show that you are asking a question.

Can I buy J.J.'s bike?

Have you saved enough money?

!	Use an **exclamation point** to show that you feel strongly about what you are saying.

Yes!

Then, that's a great idea!

Go To ▶ Practice A on page 325.

More Ways to Use a Period

●	Use a **period** after an initial or an abbreviation.	Aaron called J.J. Mrs. Davies answered the phone.
●	Use a **period** to separate dollars and cents. The period is the decimal point.	Mrs. Davies told Aaron the bike cost $55.00 and no less. Aaron had exactly $50.40 and no more.

The Comma

,	Use **commas** to separate three or more items in a series	Aaron needs 4 dollars, 2 quarters, and one dime after all. He could clean the kitchen, the closet, and the bathroom. He could take out the trash, walk some dogs, or sweep the steps.
,	Use **commas** when you write large numbers.	Aaron has taken out the trash 1,000,000 times, so he decides to walk Mrs. Romero's dog. It weighs 1,200 pounds!
,	**Commas** have important uses in a letter. How many can you find?	

177 North Avenue
New York, Ny 10033

October 3, 2000

Dear Mrs. Romero,
   I am saving money to buy a bicycle. Can I walk Brute for you? I know that most people pay $.25 to walk a dog, but Brute is big! Can you pay me $5.00?
   I will take good care of Brute. I like him even though he is bigger than I am!
   Thank you.

          Sincerely,

          Aaron

Use a comma:

- between the city and the state
- between the date and the year
- after the greeting, or "hello" part, of a friendly letter
- after the closing, or "good-bye" part, of the letter

Sentences for Daily Language Practice (Period, Comma):

1. This summer, Marc is going to visit Miami Florida.
2. He wants to buy PJ's skates so he can skate while he is there.
3. He has $20.00, but needs $200 more to buy them for $22.00.
4. He searched for money in his drawer his desk and even in his bed.
5. He found 1000 things that he had lost but no money.

▶ **Practice Book page 88**

The Comma, continued

Sentences for Daily Language Practice (Comma):
1. Marc really wants to buy P.J.'s shiny black skates.
2. He has some money but he doesn't have enough.
3. Marc needs to earn some money doesn't he?
4. His mom said "If you wash the car, I'll pay you $5.00."
5. Well that will give him more than enough money!
▶ **Practice Book page 89**

Use **commas** to set off certain words in a sentence.

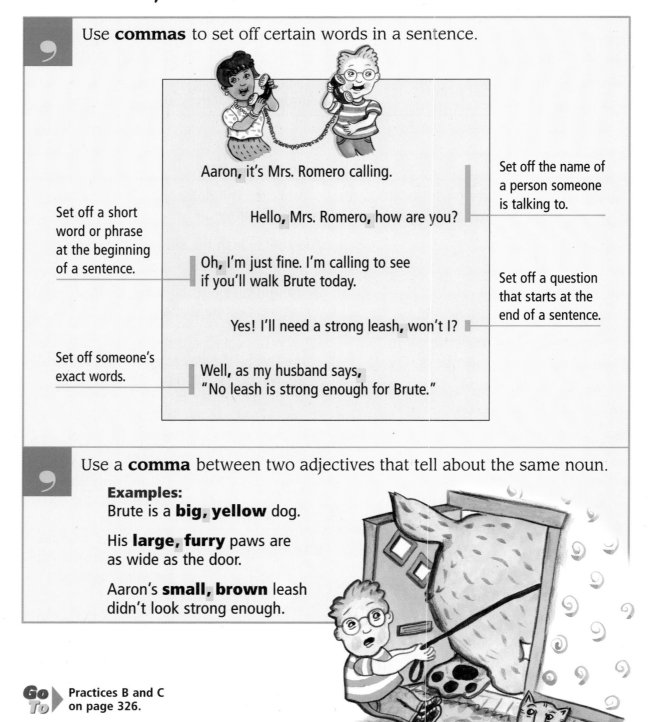

Aaron, it's Mrs. Romero calling.

Set off the name of a person someone is talking to.

Set off a short word or phrase at the beginning of a sentence.

Hello, Mrs. Romero, how are you?

Oh, I'm just fine. I'm calling to see if you'll walk Brute today.

Set off a question that starts at the end of a sentence.

Yes! I'll need a strong leash, won't I?

Set off someone's exact words.

Well, as my husband says, "No leash is strong enough for Brute."

Use a **comma** between two adjectives that tell about the same noun.

Examples:
Brute is a **big, yellow** dog.

His **large, furry** paws are as wide as the door.

Aaron's **small, brown** leash didn't look strong enough.

Go To ▶ Practices B and C on page 326.

, Use a **comma** before **and**, **but**, or **or** in a compound sentence.

Examples:

Brute was big**, and** Aaron could hardly control him.

Aaron tried to stop Brute**, but** he ran right into Mr. Sayeed's deli.

Boxes either flew out**, or** they got crushed.

Apples went everywhere**, and** a newspaper rack fell down.

Mr. Sayeed was calm**, but** he told Brute he was a bad dog.

The Colon

Use a **colon**:

- after the greeting in a business letter

- to separate hours and minutes

- to start a list

179 North Avenue
New York, NY 10033
October 4, 2002

Mr. Omar Sayeed
Sayeed Deli
686 Fifth Street
New York, NY 10033

Dear Mr. Sayeed:

Yesterday, at about 10:30, my neighbor Aaron Jackson took my dog Brute for a walk. Brute is a large dog, and Aaron had some trouble controlling him. Aaron told me that Brute did three bad things:

1. He ate two cartons of apples.
2. He stepped on a customer.
3. He knocked over one newspaper rack.

Aaron said that he apologized to the customer. How much do I owe you for the apples and the rack?

Please accept my apologies. Next time, I will have two boys walk Brute. Or, maybe three!

Sincerely,

Electra Romero

Electra Romero

Punctuation Marks, continued

Sentences for Daily Language Practice (Colon, Apostrophe):
1. Marc can finally buy P.J.s skates.
2. Hes so excited!
3. He is going to get them at 1000 this morning.
4. Its only 800 now.
5. He doesnt want to wait two hours, but he has to!

➤ **Practice Book page 90**

The Apostrophe

 In a contraction, or shortened form of two words, an **apostrophe** shows that one or more letters have been left out.

	Aaron got $5.00 for walking Brute.
He's = He is	**He's** happy now.
I'll = I will	"**I'll** go over to see J.J.," said Aaron.
hasn't = has not	"I hope he **hasn't** sold the bike."

 An **apostrophe** can also show that someone or something owns something.

Use **'s** when one person owns something.	Aaron and his dad look at each building**'s** number. Aaron**'s** heart is pounding.
Use **s'** to show that two or more people own something.	Two boys ride by. The boy**s'** bikes are neat!
If the plural noun does not end in **s**, use **'s**.	A girl rides by. All the children**'s** bikes are neat!

Go To Practice D on page 327.

212

Underline

 Underline the titles of books, magazines, and newspapers.

**Sentences for Daily Language Practice
(Underline, Quotation Marks):**
1. Marc was reading The Post Gazette newspaper.
2. He read an article called Skater Safety.
3. He said, I should buy a helmet.

▶ **Practice Book page 91**

> If J.J. has sold his bike, I'll look in **The Daily News** and find another bike for sale.

Quotation Marks

 Put **quotation marks** around the title of a:

- song, poem, or short story
- magazine article or newspaper article
- chapter from a book

Aaron sang "Let It Be Mine" as he walked up to J.J.'s apartment building.

Use **quotation marks** around words you copy from a book or other printed material.

The words in the ad were "used bicycle, good condition."

Use **quotation marks** to show a speaker's exact words.

A new paragraph begins each time the speaker changes.

Aaron knocked on J.J.'s door and said to his dad, "I hope the bike is in really good condition."

"We'll see," said his dad.

Just then a boy opened the door and said, "Hello, I'm J.J. How are you?"

"I'm great," Aaron said. "Can I see your bike? I brought enough money to buy it."

"Sure," J.J. said. "It's a cool bike."

"It sure is," Aaron said happily.

"We'll take it," his dad said. Aaron handed J.J. the money.

"Thank you and enjoy the bike!" J.J. shouted.

"I will! See you later, Dad!" Aaron yelled as he rode off to buy a cookie with the 40¢ he had left.

Go To ▶ Practice E on page 327.

Spelling

Teach:
Invite students to talk about the pictures on pages 214 and 215. Then read aloud each tip, pausing to have students demonstrate the tip by pointing to the word *aquarium*, saying the word out loud, and so on. Call on volunteers to restate each tip in their own words.

Here are some tips to help you spell words correctly.

1.

Look at the new word.

2.

Look again as you **say** the word out loud.

3.

Listen to the word as you say it again.

4.

Make a picture of the word in your head.

5.

a-q-u-a-r-i-u-m

Spell the word out loud several times.

6.

Write the word for practice. Write it five or ten times.

7.

Check the word. You can use a dictionary, a computer spell-check, or a word list.

8.

Hi, Mom. I saw a really neat **aquarium** today.

Make a sentence with the word to be sure that you understand what the word means.

Spelling Practice:

3 Write one of students' spelling words on the chalkboard, say it, and have students echo. Briefly review the spelling tips. Then erase the word. Say the word again and have students spell it out loud. Encourage students to use the word in a sentence. Repeat for several words.

4 5 Have each student use as many spelling words as possible to write a story. Encourage students to trade stories with a partner. The partner finds the spelling words and checks them against a word list or in a dictionary.

Follow these rules and your spelling will get better and better!

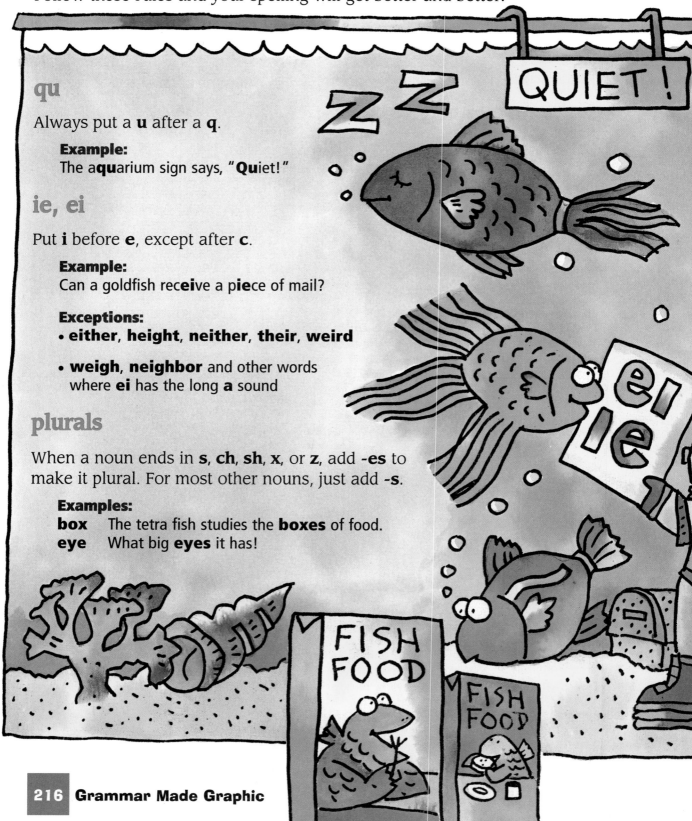

qu

Always put a **u** after a **q**.

Example:
The a**qu**arium sign says, "**Qu**iet!"

ie, ei

Put **i** before **e**, except after **c**.

Example:
Can a goldfish rec**ei**ve a p**ie**ce of mail?

Exceptions:
• **either**, **height**, **neither**, **their**, **weird**

• **weigh**, **neighbor** and other words where **ei** has the long **a** sound

plurals

When a noun ends in **s**, **ch**, **sh**, **x**, or **z**, add **-es** to make it plural. For most other nouns, just add **-s**.

Examples:
box   The tetra fish studies the **boxes** of food.
eye   What big **eyes** it has!

Spelling Practice:
3 Say a word and spell it out loud as you write it on the chalkboard. Point to the target letters. Say the rule and have students echo, and then have students spell the word aloud. Repeat for words that follow each rule.
4 Have groups use the headings **qu; ie, ei;** and so on, to make a spelling poster to display in the classroom. Each time students find or learn a word that follows each rule, they can add it to the poster.
5 Involve teams in a Spelling Bee using the words from pages 216 and 217 and others from students' spelling lists. For each correctly spelled word, teams score a point. The team with the most points wins.

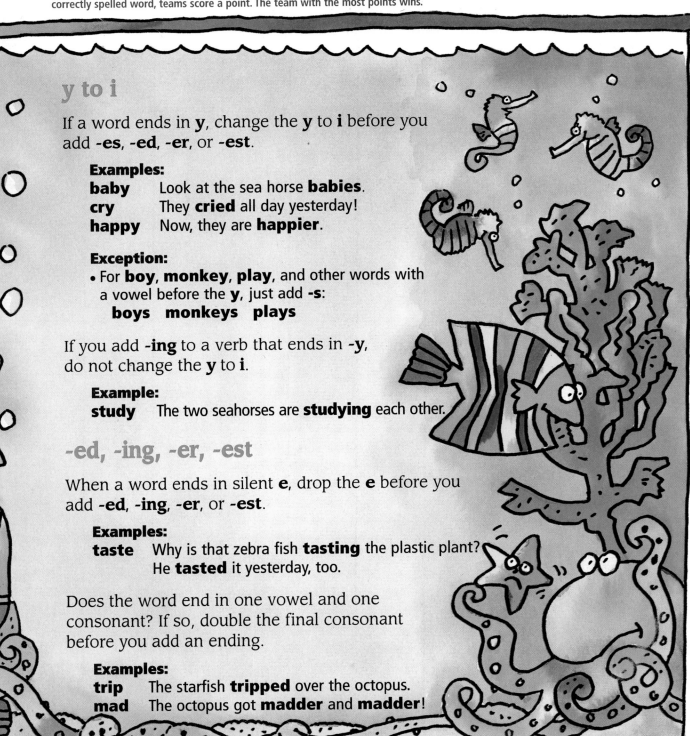

y to i

If a word ends in **y**, change the **y** to **i** before you add **-es**, **-ed**, **-er**, or **-est**.

Examples:
baby   Look at the sea horse **babies**.
cry   They **cried** all day yesterday!
happy   Now, they are **happier**.

Exception:
- For **boy**, **monkey**, **play**, and other words with a vowel before the **y**, just add **-s**:
  boys   monkeys   plays

If you add **-ing** to a verb that ends in **-y**, do not change the **y** to **i**.

Example:
study   The two seahorses are **studying** each other.

-ed, -ing, -er, -est

When a word ends in silent **e**, drop the **e** before you add **-ed**, **-ing**, **-er**, or **-est**.

Examples:
taste   Why is that zebra fish **tasting** the plastic plant?
            He **tasted** it yesterday, too.

Does the word end in one vowel and one consonant? If so, double the final consonant before you add an ending.

Examples:
trip   The starfish **tripped** over the octopus.
mad   The octopus got **madder** and **madder**!

Chapter 5
Look It Up!

File   Edit   Go   Favorites

Search

Back   Forward   Home   Reload   Stop   Print

Address   Hampton-Brown@txdirect.com

"Look It Up!"   Search

Jason wonders "Is there life on Mars?" Yolanda asks "What does *axis* mean?" Jason and Yolanda are using different resources to look up the answers to their questions. You can look up any kind of information, too, once you know where to begin. This chapter will show you how to start looking for information and do research. You'll also find out how to use all kinds of resources like an almanac, dictionary, globe, and the Internet.

The Research Process

When you **research**, you look up information about a topic. You can use the information you find to write a story, article, book, or research report.

STEP
1 Choose a Topic

Think of something you want to learn more about and something that interests you. That will be your research **topic**. Make sure you pick a topic that is not too general. A specific, or smaller, topic is easier to research and to write about. It is also more interesting to read about in a report.

Teach:
Depending on the proficiency levels of your students, allow several days to introduce **The Research Process**. You may want to plan one day to present an overview of the process and Steps 1–3, a day for **The Library**, and at least two days each for Steps 4, 5, and 6. To begin, read aloud the introduction and explain that going through the research process is like going up steps—each step takes you closer to your goal. Record the steps on the chalkboard and briefly discuss what happens during each step.
• Work through Step 1, using hand gestures to demonstrate moving from a large topic to a smaller, more specific one. Ask volunteers to suggest possible research topics and comment on whether they are too general and why.

Outer Space
This is a big topic! There are a lot of things in outer space: stars, suns, planets, moons, and black holes. That would be too much to research or write about in one report.

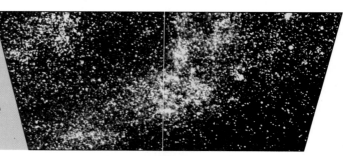

Planets
This topic is better, but it's still too big. There are nine planets in our solar system! You could do a report on the planet Mars. But what is it you want to know about Mars?

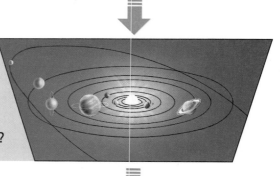

Life on Mars
The topic "Life on Mars" is more specific than "Mars." Finding out if Mars has water, plants, animals, or Martians could be VERY interesting!

3 Speech Emergence **4** Intermediate Fluency **5** Advanced Fluency/Fluent

Teach, continued:
• For Step 2, read aloud the paragraph and research questions. Explain that in most resources, words and phrases are listed in alphabetical order, so to find information you need to know the key words.

STEP 2 Decide What to Look Up

What do you want to know about your topic? Write down some questions. Look at the most important words in your questions. Those are **key words** you can look up when you start your research.

STEP 3 Locate Resources

Now that you know what to look up, you can go to different **resources** to find information about your topic. Resources can be people, such as librarians, teachers, and family members. Resources can also be books, magazines, newspapers, videos, or the Internet. You can find resources all around you.

Whatever your topic is, try exploring the library first. There you'll discover a world of information!

> Is there life on Mars?
>
> Is there water or oxygen on Mars?
>
> Can people, plants, or animals live on the surface of Mars?
>
> Have there been any space missions there?
>
> Did anyone find proof of Martian life forms?

Teach, continued:
• For Step 3, invite students to talk about the picture. Then read aloud the paragraph.

Practice:
3 Talk with students about the topics on page 220. Ask questions with embedded answers: *Are there more things to look up for the topic "outer space" or for the topic "planets?" Would it take longer to find out about nine planets or just one planet?*
4 Have students narrow down the topic "outer space" to a new topic such as the sun, the moon, or a different planet like Pluto or Neptune. Help them brainstorm and write three or four questions about their topic and identify the key words.
5 Have partners come up with a new topic related to outer space, write research questions, and circle the key words. Ask them what kinds of resources they think would be best for their research.

The Library

A **library** is a place full of books and other kinds of resources like videos, magazines, and newspapers. It's organized in a special way so you can find things easily.

Teach:
Ask students to share what they know about a library. Then read aloud the introduction and work through pages 222 and 223 as you point to and describe each section. Arrange for a tour of a library, and help students who don't have a library card obtain one.

Information Desk
If you can't find what you're looking for, you can ask a **librarian**. The librarian will usually be at the **Information Desk**.

Fiction
One section of the library has all of the **fiction** books. These are stories that are not true. If you're looking for facts about life on Mars, you won't find them here!

Nonfiction
In the **nonfiction** section, there are books that have **facts** about all kinds of topics.

Children's Room
The **children's room** is full of books and magazines especially for kids.

Reference Section
The **reference section** has lots of special resources. You can't check out reference books like these, but you can make copies of pages or articles.

Atlas

Reference Section

Information Desk

Fiction

Nonfiction

Children's Room

3 Speech Emergence 4 Intermediate Fluency 5 Advanced Fluency/Fluent

Almanac

Encyclopedia

Dictionary

Practice:

3 As you visit each section of the library, hold up a book and describe it; then ask students questions with embedded answers: *This is an almanac. It has lots of facts in it. Is it in the reference section or in the fiction section?*

4 Have students go to different sections of the library and pick out a book. When they return, have them define what kind of book it is and where they got it.

5 Have partners ask the reference librarian where to find information about Mars. Have them each find a different book or article on Mars. Encourage students to write down the title of the book or article and what they did to find it.

Checkout Desk

The **checkout desk** is where you check out books. You can get your library card here, too.

Periodicals

Magazines and newspapers are called **periodicals**. To find the most recent, or current, information about a topic, look for articles in periodicals.

Computers for the Internet

Some libraries have **computers** for looking up information on the **Internet**.

Card Catalog

The computer and **card catalogs** list all the books in the library.

In-illustration labels: Checkout Desk · Periodicals · Internet · Card Catalog

The Resources section on pages 234–262 to find out more about the library and special resources.

The Research Process, continued

Teach:
Plan to spend one session introducing **How to Find Information Quickly** and a separate session for **How to Take Notes**. For the first session, teach alphabetical order and skim and scan. To begin, read aloud the introduction. Explain that in order to look up key words, you need to know about alphabetical order. Ask volunteers to define alphabetical order. Then work through the page.

STEP 4 Gather Information

When you **gather information**, you find the best resources for your topic. You look up your key words to find facts about your topic. Then you take notes.

How to Find Information Quickly

■ **Use alphabetical order to look up words in a list.**

In many resources, the words, titles, and subjects are listed in **alphabetical order**.

Look at these words. They are in order by the **first** letter of each word.

> **a**steroid
> **m**oon
> **p**lanet
> **s**un

If the word you are looking up has the same first letter as other words in the list, look at the **second** letters.

> **Ma**rs
> **Me**rcury
> **mi**ssion
> **mo**on

If the word you are looking up has the same first <u>and</u> second letters as others in the list, look at the **third** letters.

> **mag**netic
> **ma**p
> **Ma**rs
> **ma**ss

Practice:
3 Write the first list of words on the chalkboard. Offer new words to add to the list such as *crater* or *orbit*. Have students tell where you should write the new words in alphabetical order. Repeat for the second and third lists: list 2, *mud*; list 3, *matter* or *maze*.
4 Make word cards for all the words in the lists and give teams 15 minutes to put them in alphabetical order. The first team to finish wins.
5 Have partners brainstorm more space words like *comet, crater, matter, meteor, orbit, Saturn, spacecraft,* and *star* to add to the lists. Ask them to write all the words in alphabetical order, add a title, and display their lists in the Writing Center.
▶ **Practice Book page 92**

3 Speech Emergence **4** Intermediate Fluency **5** Advanced Fluency/Fluent

Teach, continued:
Read aloud the introduction and work through the page. Pause after reading each caption to have volunteers read aloud the parts in the article that illustrate each characteristic.

■ **Skim and scan the text to decide if it is useful.**

When you **skim** and **scan**, you look at text quickly to see if it has the information you need. If it does, then you can take the time to read it more carefully. If it doesn't, you can go on to another source.

To Skim:

To Scan:

Read the **title** to see if the article is useful for your topic.

Read the **beginning** sentences and **headings** to find out more about an article's topic.

Skim the **ending**. It often sums up all the ideas in the article.

Look for **key words** or **details** in dark type or italics. If you find key words that go with your topic, you'll probably want to read the article.

PLANETS, STARS, AND SPACE TRAVEL

LOOKING FOR LIFE ELSEWHERE IN THE UNIVERSE

For years scientists have been trying to discover if there is life on other planets in our solar system or life elsewhere in the universe. Some scientists have been looking for evidence based on what is necessary for life on Earth—basics like water and proper temperature.

WHAT SCIENTISTS HAVE LEARNED SO FAR

Mars and Jupiter. In 1996, two teams of scientists examined two meteorites that may have come from **Mars** and found evidence that some form of life may have existed on Mars billions of years ago. In 1997, in photographs of Europa, a moon of **Jupiter**, scientists saw areas with icy ridges and areas without ice. It seemed that underneath the ice there might be water—one of the essentials of life.

New Planets. In 1996, astronomers believed they found several new planets traveling around stars very far away (many light-years away) from our sun. Scientists do not think life exists on these planets, because they are so close to their sun that they would be too hot. But scientists are hoping to find other stars with planets around them that might support life.

AND THE SEARCH CONTINUES

NASA (the National Aeronautics and Space Administration) has a program to look for life on Mars. Ten spacecraft are to be sent to Mars over the next ten years. Some will fly around Mars taking pictures, while others will land on Mars to study the soil and rocks and look for living things. The first two, *Mars Pathfinder* and *Mars Global Surveyor*, launched in 1996, were scheduled to reach Mars in 1997.

Another program that searches for life on other worlds is called **SETI**. SETI (an acronym for Search for Extraterrestrial Intelligence) uses powerful radio telescopes to look for life elsewhere in the universe.

Question: Is there life elsewhere in the universe? **Answer:** No one knows yet.

Practice:

3 Ask students yes/no questions: *When you skim and scan, do you read an article slowly and carefully? To find out if the article is useful for your topic, should you read every word? Will the headings help you decide whether to read the article?*

4 Display the research questions from page 221. Have partners skim and scan the article. Ask if the article answers any of the questions about Mars. Would they read this article more carefully?

5 Display the research questions from page 221. Give students 10 minutes to skim and scan the article on this page and the article on pages 244 and 245. Ask students which article they would take time to read more carefully and why.

The Research Process, continued

4 Gather Information, continued

How to Take Notes

Notes are important words, phrases, and ideas that you write while you are reading and researching. Your notes will help you remember **details**. They'll also help you remember the **source**. The source is where you got the information.

■ **Write notes in your own words.**

In this book it says: "Mars may look dry as dust, but water once flowed over the surface."

Okay. I'll write: Mars—dry now, used to have water

If you copy exactly what you read, put **quotation marks** around the words.

Is there water on Mars?

Mars by Seymour Simon, page 28

— "Mars may look dry as dust, but water once flowed over the surface"

Teach:
Read aloud the introduction. Hold up a notecard and explain why it is a good place for writing down notes. Then talk about how to write notes in your own words, asking students to suggest other ways to paraphrase the quotation: *Mars dusty—water used to be there; at one time Mars was wet, dry now.* Continue, pointing out the information on each notecard and how it's arranged.

3 Speech Emergence **4** Intermediate Fluency **5** Advanced Fluency/Fluent

■ **Set up your notecards like these so you can easily put your information in order when you write.**

Notecard for a Book

Include your **research question**.

Write down the **source** so you can remember where you found your facts. List the title, author, and page number.

> Is there life on Mars?
>
> <u>Mars</u> by Seymour Simon, page 27
>
> — <u>Viking</u> spacecraft supposed to find out if there's life
>
> — some think experiments showed there isn't
>
> — others believe experiments were the wrong kind; maybe scientists looked in wrong places

List **details** and **facts** in your own words.

Notecard for a Magazine or Newspaper

List the name, date, volume, and issue number of your **source**. Also write the name of the article in quotation marks.

> Is there life on Mars?
>
> <u>Time for Kids</u>, Sept. 13, 1996 Vol. 2, No. 1
>
> "Next stop: Mars"
>
> — maybe—Mars has some features like Earth.
>
>   "It has volcanoes and giant canyons."
>
> — hard to prove, but maybe space missions like <u>Pathfinder</u> can find something

Include your **research question**.

Use **quotation marks for exact words** you copy from a source.

Practice:
3 Display a blank notecard and have students help you complete it with the information for the book *Mars* on the first notecard. Ask students to point to or tell you where you should write the research question, the source, and the details.
4 Give students notecards. Have them take notes for the article on page 225. Provide the research question *Is there life on Mars?* and the source information: <u>The World Almanac for Kids 1998</u>, page 159. Remind students to use their own words or quotations if they copy exact words.
5 Display the research question *What were some U.S. space missions?* Then have students read and take notes on notecards from **Dateline U.S.A.** page 288.

The Research Process, continued

STEP
5 Organize Information

Make an Outline

Follow these steps to turn your notes into an outline.
Your outline will then help you write your report.

Teach:
Review Steps 1–4, and then read aloud the introduction for Step 5. Explain: *Making an outline before you write a report is a lot like making a frame before you build a house. For a house, you need to make a frame with wood so you know how to put the walls together. For a report, you need to make a frame with words so you know how to put sentences and paragraphs together.* Then work through each step. Point out elements on the cards and the outline, and elaborate on how the research questions change into main ideas and the notes into details and related details.

1 Put all the notecards with the same research question together.

> Is there life on Mars?
> <u>Mars</u> by Seymour Simon, page 27

> Is there life on Mars?
> <u>Time for Kids</u>, Sept. 13, 1996 Vol. 2, No. 1
> "Next stop: Mars"
> — maybe — Mars has some features like Earth.
>   "It has volcanoes and giant canyons."
> — hard to prove, but maybe space missions like
>   Pathfinder can find something

2 Turn your notes into an outline.

First, turn your question into a main idea.

Next, find details in your notes that go with the main idea. Add them to your outline.

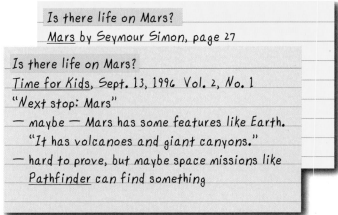

> I. Life on Mars
>   A. How Mars is like Earth
>   1. Volcanoes
>   2. Giant canyons
>   B. Fact-finding missions

3 Write a title for your outline.

> Mars: Is Anyone Up There?

Practice:
3 Have students read aloud the parts of the outline. Ask: *Tell me the **title** of the outline. Tell me the first **main idea**,* and so on.
4 Write the research question *Have there been any signs of life on Mars?* Then write the details and related details from section II of the outline out of order and without letters or numbers. Have students rewrite the section by turning the question into a main idea; putting the details and related details in order; and adding the missing Roman numeral, letters, and numbers.
5 Have students use the notecards they created for page 227 to write a section for an outline about U.S. space missions.

▶ **Practice Book pages 95 and 96**

Here's an outline for a research report about life on Mars.

Title
The title tells what your outline is all about. You can use it again when you write your report.

Main Idea
Each main idea follows a Roman numeral.

Details and **related details**.
Each detail follows a capital letter. Each related detail follows a number.

Mars: Is Anyone Up There?
  I. Life on Mars
        A. How Mars is like Earth
              1. Volcanoes
              2. Giant canyons
        B. Fact-finding missions
              1. <u>Viking</u>
              2. <u>Pathfinder</u>
 II. Signs of life on Mars
        A. Studied by David McKay's team
        B. Meteorite
              1. Contains bacteria fossils
              2. Found in Antarctica
              3. From Mars
III. Continued search for life on Mars
        A. Look underground
        B. More study
              1. Mission planned for 2005
              2. Gases in atmosphere
              3. What rocks are made of

The Research Process, continued

Teach:
You may want to teach Step 6 during two separate sessions. For pages 230–231, review Step 5 and work through the pages. For each set of examples, elaborate on how the words and phrases in the outline can be turned into complete sentences with subjects and verbs.

STEP 6 Write a Research Report

Once you've finished your outline, you're ready to write a **research report**. Turn the main ideas and details from your outline into sentences and paragraphs.

1 Write the title from your outline and an introduction.

The title and introduction should tell what your report is mostly about and should be interesting to your readers.

Outline

Mars: Is Anyone Up There?

Title and Introduction

Mars: Is Anyone Up There?

You've probably seen some pretty creepy outer space creatures in movies and TV. Do they really look like that? Are there really living beings up there?

2 Turn your first main idea into a topic sentence for the next paragraph.

Look at Roman numeral I on your outline. Turn the words into a sentence with a subject and a predicate. That sentence will be the topic sentence for your first paragraph.

Outline

I. Life on Mars

Topic Sentence

People have always wondered if there is life on any other planet, especially Mars.

3 Speech Emergence **4** Intermediate Fluency **5** Advanced Fluency/Fluent

3 Turn the details and related details into sentences.

Look at the letters and numbers on your outline. Turn those words into sentences that tell more about the main idea. Add them to your paragraph.

Outline

> I. Life on Mars
>   A. How Mars is like Earth
>   1. Volcanoes
>   2. Giant canyons
>   B. Fact-finding missions
>   1. Viking
>   2. Pathfinder

Topic Sentence and Supporting Details

> People have always wondered if there is life on any other planet, especially Mars. Because Mars is similar to Earth with features like volcanoes and giant canyons, it seems possible that there is life on Mars. There are lots of missions to Mars like the spacecrafts <u>Viking</u> and <u>Pathfinder</u>, so it seems like we might find out soon!

4 Follow steps 2 and 3 to write the other paragraphs for your report.

5 Write a conclusion to sum up your report.

Look back at all the main ideas on your outline. Write a sentence for each main idea to include in the last paragraph of your report. The last paragraph is a summary of the most important information about your topic.

Practice:
3 Point to and describe each part of the outline and its corresponding report section: *This is the **title** for the outline. Here is the **title** for the report. Here is the **introduction**,* and so on. Have students follow your model and repeat.
4 **5** Form heterogeneous groups. Display the outline on page 229 and have students follow steps 2 and 3 to write topic and detail sentences for sections II and III of the outline. You may want to have students compare their sentences to the finished report on pages 232 and 233.

Outline

> I. Life on Mars
>
> II. Signs of life on Mars
>
> III. Continued search for life on Mars

Conclusion

> Basically, no one knows if there is or isn't life on Mars. It is possible that life does or did exist there. Spacecraft that go to Mars in the future will give us more proof. Hopefully, the mystery will be solved soon for all of us!

The Research Process, continued

6 Write a Research Report, continued

A good **research report** gives facts about a topic in an organized and interesting way.

Teach, continued:
For pages 232–233, review how the main ideas and details on an outline are turned into sentences and paragraphs. Then read aloud the introduction and the captions for the report. Call on volunteers to read aloud the examples in the model that illustrate the title, introduction, and body of the report.

The **title** and introduction tell what your report is about. They get your reader interested.

The **body** of the report presents the facts you found. Each paragraph goes with one main idea from your outline.

Mars: Is Anyone Up There?

You've probably seen some pretty creepy outer space creatures in movies and TV. Do they really look like that? Are there really living beings up there?

People have always wondered if there is life on any other planet, especially Mars. Because Mars is similar to Earth with features like volcanoes and giant canyons, it seems possible that there is life on Mars. There are lots of missions to Mars like the spacecrafts Viking and Pathfinder, so it seems like we might find out soon!

Recently, David McKay and his team of scientists discovered possible signs of ancient Martian life. They found bacteria fossils in a meteorite that crashed into Antarctica thousands of years ago. They know the meteorite is from Mars because it has the same chemicals in it as the Martian atmosphere. They believe the fossils, which are a lot smaller than the width of a human hair, were alive on Mars from 3 to 4 billion years ago. At that time, there was water on the planet. Since the fossils were deep in the center of the meteorite, McKay's team feels that the fossils were definitely from Mars, and not from Earth.

Write a Research Report Practice:
Use Communication Project 18 on pages 68T–71T or Project 24 on pages 92T–95T to involve students in writing a report.

No one has seen a live Martian, but some scientists feel that we need to keep looking. Since no one has found water on the surface of Mars, maybe Martians live underground where there is water. A mission to look for Martian life and bring soil samples back to Earth is planned for 2005. Until then, scientists will continue to study other aspects of Mars like the gases in its atmosphere and what its rocks are made of.

Basically, no one knows if there is or isn't life on Mars. It is possible that life does or did exist there. Spacecraft that go to Mars in the future will give us more proof. Hopefully, the mystery will be solved soon for all of us!

Each paragraph in the **body** begins with a **topic sentence** that tells a main idea. The other sentences give **details** and **related details**.

The last paragraph is the **conclusion**. It sums up the report.

Remind students that going through the research process is like going up steps. Each step takes you closer to your goal. Ask students to summarize the steps in the research process.

STEP 6

STEP 5

The Resources

You can find information in books, periodicals, videos, on computers, and in many kinds of special resources.

Finding Information in Books

Card Catalog

Some libraries have a set of drawers called a **card catalog**. In the drawers are cards that tell what books are in the library and where to find them. Each card has:

■ a **book title** and **author**

■ **publishing information**

Here you will find:

- the book's edition number. When books are printed all at the same time, they have the same edition number (**1st ed.** means **first edition**).

- whether the book has a bibliography, or list of other books the author used to write the book (**bibl.** means **bibliography**)

- the city where the publisher is located and the publisher's name

- the copyright date (**c** means **copyright**)

- the number of pages in the book (**p.** means **pages**)

- if the book is illustrated or has photographs (**ill.** means **illustrated**)

- how tall the book is (**cm.** means **centimeters**)

■ **cross references** to other related subjects

```
          Are we moving to Mars?
J
620.4   Schraff, Anne.
Sch        Are we moving to Mars? / Anne Schraff.--
        1st ed.--Santa Fe: John Muir Publications.
        c1996. 32 p.: ill. (some color); 20 cm.

        ISBN 1-56261-310-3.


        1. Mars (Planet)--Surface--Juvenile literature
        2. Life on other planets--Juvenile literature
        3. Extraterrestrial (anthropology--Juvenile
        literature). I. Title.
```

Card Catalog Practice:
3 Ask students questions about the information on the cards: *Where is the book's* **title**? *What is the title? Show me where the* **publishing information** *is. Where was this book published?* and so on.
4 Have partners take turns asking and answering each other's questions about the information on the cards.
5 Have these students make up a title card for the book *Mars* by Elaine Landau using the information on the copyright page shown on page 240.

▶ **Practice Book page 97**

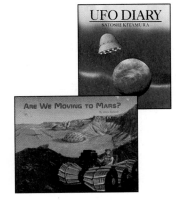

Each card also has a **call number** that tells you what section of the library the book is in. Call numbers with a **J** mean that the books are in the Juvenile, or children's, section of the library.

■ **Fiction books** are stories made up by an author. They are arranged on the library shelves in alphabetical order by the author's last name. Their call numbers usually show the first two or three **letters of the author's last name**.

```
J
KIT   Kitamura, Satoshi.
        UFO Diary / Satoshi Kitamura. --
      Farrar, Straus and Giroux, 1991.
      unpaged: color ill. ; 23cm.

        ISBN 0-374-48041-9
```

■ **Nonfiction books** contain facts about a subject. They are arranged on the library shelves by **call numbers**. These numbers stand for subject areas from the Dewey Decimal System:

```
          Are we moving to Mars?
J
620.4  Schraff, Anne.
Sch      Are we moving to Mars? / Anne S
       1st ed.--Santa Fe: John Muir Pub
       c1996. 32 p.: ill. (some color);

         ISBN 1-56261-310-3.
```

000–099 General Books
100–199 Philosophy
200–299 Religion
300–399 Social Sciences
400–499 Language

500–599 Pure Sciences
600–699 Technology
700–799 The Arts
800–899 Literature
900–999 History and Geography

Biographies are an exception. These nonfiction books give facts about people who really lived. Biographies are grouped on the shelves by the last name of the person the book is about.

Finding Information in Books, continued

The cards in a card catalog are in alphabetical order according to the first word or words on the card. Here are the three kinds of cards you'll find in a card catalog.

Card Catalog Practice:

3 Ask students yes/no questions about the information on the cards: *Is the call number on the **subject card**? Is the author's name listed first on the **title card**?* and so on.

4 Have students help you create the three kinds of cards that would appear for the book shown on page 240.

5 Ask students to bring in their favorite books or select some from the classroom. Have them write subject, title, and author cards for their books, using the copyright page for information. (Most new books will include the Dewey Decimal number.)

➤ **Practice Book page 98**

Subject Card

The **subject** of a book appears first on a subject card. Only nonfiction books have subject cards.

```
        MARS (PLANET)
J
620.4   Schraff, Anne.
Sch       Are we moving to Mars? / Anne Schraff.--
        1st ed.--Santa Fe: John Muir Publications.
        c1996. 32 p.: ill. (some color); 20 cm.

          ISBN 1-56261-310-3.


          1. Mars (Planet)--Surface--Juvenile literature.
          2. Life on other planets--Juvenile literature.
          3. Extraterrestrial (anthropology--Juvenile
          literature). I. Title.
```

Title Card

The **title** of a book appears first on a title card. If the first word is *A* or *The*, look up the next word in alphabetical order.

```
          Are we moving to Mars?
J
620.4   Schraff, Anne.
Sch       Are we moving to Mars? / Anne Schraff.--
        1st ed.--Santa Fe: John Muir Publications.
        c1996. 32 p.: ill. (some color); 20 cm.

          ISBN 1-56261-310-3.


          1. Mars (Planet)--Surface--Juvenile literature.
          2. Life on other planets--Juvenile literature.
          3. Extraterrestrial (anthropology--Juvenile
          literature). I. Title.
```

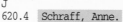

Author Card

The **author's name** appears first on an author card. The author's last name appears first. Look it up in alphabetical order.

```
J
620.4   Schraff, Anne.
Sch       Are we moving to Mars? / Anne Schraff.--
        1st ed.--Santa Fe: John Muir Publications.
        c1996. 32 p.: ill. (some color); 20 cm.

          ISBN 1-56261-310-3.


          1. Mars (Planet)--Surface--Juvenile literature.
          2. Life on other planets--Juvenile literature.
          3. Extraterrestrial (anthropology--Juvenile
          literature). I. Title.
```

Computerized Card Catalog

A **computerized card catalog** is a card catalog on the computer. It's a lot like the paper card catalog, but faster to use because the computer looks up a book for you.

Teach:
Plan time to demonstrate how to use the computerized card catalog or arrange a session with your school or public librarian. If you have access to the Internet, some on-line catalogs are the Harrison Memorial Library (www.hm-lib.org) and the LeRoy Collins Leon County Library (library.co.leon.fl.us/MARION).

Before the demonstration, have students share what they know about computerized card catalogs and work through pages 237–239.

Computerized catalogs are not all the same. Here's one example and the steps you might follow to find *Are We Moving to Mars?* by Anne Schraff.

1 **Read the instructions on the computer screen.**

The **instructions** will help you find the information you're looking for in the computer.

2 **Type a letter to start your search.**

To search for available information about a **subject**, you would type an **S**.

3 **Type in a word or words that name your subject and press return.**

For the subject Mars, type in **the planet mars** or just **mars**. It doesn't matter to the computer if you use capital letters or not.

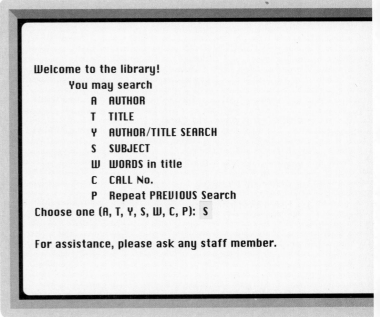

```
Welcome to the library!
      You may search
         A   AUTHOR
         T   TITLE
         Y   AUTHOR/TITLE SEARCH
         S   SUBJECT
         W   WORDS in title
         C   CALL No.
         P   Repeat PREVIOUS Search
Choose one (A, T, Y, S, W, C, P):  S

For assistance, please ask any staff member.
```

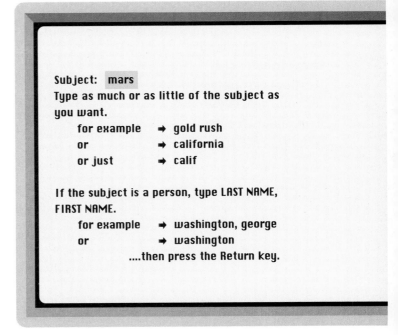

```
Subject:  mars
Type as much or as little of the subject as
you want.
      for example   →  gold rush
      or            →  california
      or just       →  calif

If the subject is a person, type LAST NAME,
FIRST NAME.
      for example   →  washington, george
      or            →  washington
            ....then press the Return key.
```

Finding Information in Books, continued

④ Look at the subjects that come up. Choose the ones you want.

For information about the planet Mars, press **④** on your keyboard.

This number shows how many **entries** there are for a subject. An entry can be a book, video, or a cassette tape.

You can press other keys to go to more entries or to start a new search.

You searched for the SUBJECT: mars
78 SUBJECTS found, with 144 entries; SUBJECTS 1-8 are:

```
1 Mars.............................................................1 entry
2 Mars Mines and Mineral Resources Fiction ...............1 entry
3 Mars Planet ➡ See also narrower term SPACE FLIGHT TO ..........1 entry
4 Mars Planet.................................................16 entries
5 Mars Colonization Forecasting............................1 entry
6 Mars Planet Drama .......................................1 entry
7 Mars Planet Exploration ➡ See Related Subjects .....................2 entries
8 Mars Planet Exploration .................................5 entries
```

Please type the NUMBER of the item you want to see, OR
F>Go FORWARD   A>ANOTHER search by SUBJECT
W>Same search as WORD search   P>PRINT
N>NEW search   +>ADDITIONAL options
Choose one [1-8, F, W, N, A, P, +]

---

⑤ Look at the entries that come up. Choose the ones you want.

Read the **titles** and **locations** to see which books are best for you. Press **③** to learn about *Are We Moving to Mars*?

You searched for the SUBJECT: mars
16 entries found, entries 1-8 are:

```
Mars Planet                                         LOCATION
1 Guide to Mars  ..............................ADULT NON-FICTION
2 The hunt for life on Mars ....................ADULT NON-FICTION
3 Are we moving to Mars? ......................YOUTH NON-FICTION
4 The inner planets: new light on the rocky worlds ...ADULT NON-FICTION
5 Mars and the inner planets ..................YOUTH NON-FICTION
6 Mars at last! ...............................ADULT NON-FICTION
7 Mars beckons ...............................ADULT NON-FICTION
8 Mars, the Red Planet ........................YOUTH NON-FICTION
```

Please type the NUMBER of the item you want to see, OR
F>Go FORWARD   A>ANOTHER search by SUBJECT
R>RETURN to Browsing   P>PRINT
N>NEW search   +>ADDITIONAL options
Choose one [1-8, F, R, N, A, P, +]

---

③ Speech Emergence **④** Intermediate Fluency **⑤** Advanced Fluency/Fluent

6 Read the information about the entry you chose.

Would you like to read this book? If so, use the information on the screen to help you find it in the library.

The **location** tells you if the book is in the Juvenile or Adult part of the library.

The **call number** will help you find the book on the shelves.

The **status** tells you if the book is currently in the library or if someone has checked it out.

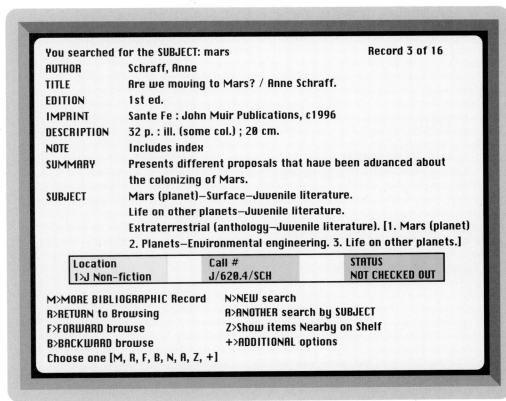

```
You searched for the SUBJECT: mars                    Record 3 of 16
AUTHOR       Schraff, Anne
TITLE        Are we moving to Mars? / Anne Schraff.
EDITION      1st ed.
IMPRINT      Sante Fe : John Muir Publications, c1996
DESCRIPTION  32 p. : ill. (some col.) ; 20 cm.
NOTE         Includes index
SUMMARY      Presents different proposals that have been advanced about
             the colonizing of Mars.
SUBJECT      Mars (planet)–Surface–Juvenile literature.
             Life on other planets–Juvenile literature.
             Extraterrestrial (anthology–Juvenile literature). [1. Mars (planet)
             2. Planets–Environmental engineering. 3. Life on other planets.]
```

Location	Call #	STATUS
1>J Non-fiction	J/620.4/SCH	NOT CHECKED OUT

```
M>MORE BIBLIOGRAPHIC Record      N>NEW search
R>RETURN to Browsing             A>ANOTHER search by SUBJECT
F>FORWARD browse                 Z>Show items Nearby on Shelf
B>BACKWARD browse                +>ADDITIONAL options
Choose one [M, R, F, B, N, A, Z, +]
```

7 Record the call number or press [P] to print out the information. Use it to look up your book.

```
You searched for the SUBJECT: mars              Record 3 of 16
AUTHOR       Schraff, Anne
TITLE        Are we moving to Mars? / Anne Schraff.
EDITION      1st ed.
IMPRINT      Sante Fe : John Muir Publications, c1996
DESCRIPTION  32 p. : ill. (some col.) ; 20 cm.
NOTE         Includes index
SUMMARY      Presents different proposals that have been
             advanced about the colonizing of Mars.
SUBJECT      Mars (planet)–Surface–Juvenile literature.
             Life on other planets–Juvenile literature.
             Extraterrestrial (anthology–Juvenile literature). [1. Mars (planet)
             2. Planets–Environmental engineering. 3. Life on other planets.]
```

Location	Call #	STATUS
1>J Non-fiction	J/620.4/SCH	NOT CHECKED OUT

Computerized Card Catalog Practice:
3 4 5 Form heterogeneous groups of four or five students. Have them use a computerized card catalog to locate books about Mars. When students find the resources they want, have them print out the information, find the books, and check them out.

Finding Information in Books, continued

Parts of a Book

Teach:
Have students look at pages 240–243. Ask where they might see these types of pages in a book. Then read aloud the introduction and the description for each type of page.

The pages at the front and back of a book help you know what the book is about and how it's organized. Look at these pages first to find out quickly if the book has the information you need for your research.

Title Page

The **title page** is usually the first page in a book.

It gives the **title** of the book and the **author**.

It tells the **publisher** and often names the cities where the publisher has offices.

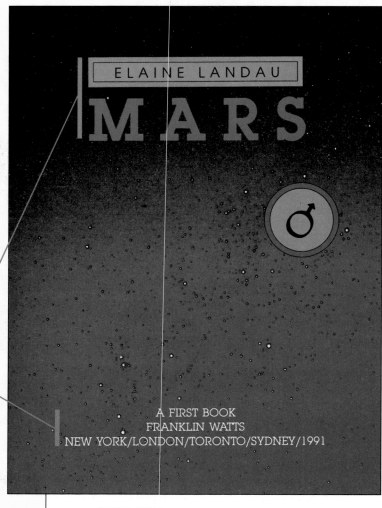

E L A I N E   L A N D A U

M A R S

A FIRST BOOK
FRANKLIN WATTS
NEW YORK/LONDON/TORONTO/SYDNEY/1991

Landau, Elaine.
    Mars / by Elaine Landau.
        p.   cm. — (First book)
    Includes bibliographical references and index.
    Summary: Uses photographs and other recent findings to describe the atmosphere and geographic features of Mars.
        ISBN 0-531-20012-4 (lib. bdg.)—ISBN 0-531-15773-3 (pbk.)
        1. Mars (Planet)—Juvenile literature. [1. Mars (Planet)]
    I. Title.   II. Series.
    QB641.L36 1991
    523.4'3—dc20   90-13097   CIP AC

Copyright © 1991 Elaine Landau
All rights reserved
Printed in the United States of America
6 5 4 3

Copyright Page

The **copyright** (©) **page** gives the date when the book was published.

Check the **copyright** to see how current the information is.

Table of Contents

The **table of contents** is in the front of a book.
It shows how many chapters, or parts, are in a book.
It tells the page numbers where those chapters begin.

CONTENTS

Title Page and Table of Contents Practice:

3 Have students finish your sentences as you point to each page: *This page is a (title page). This is the book's (author). Here is the book's (title).*

4 Have students write the headings "Title Page" and "Table of Contents," and then write sentences under the correct heading to tell about the information in the models.

• *Title Page*: The title of this book is <u>Mars</u>.
• *Contents*: There are four chapters in this book.

5 Have partners find and talk about the title page and table of contents for this **Handbook**. Students can ask and answer questions about the pages: *Who is the publisher? How many chapters are in the book? On which page does Look It Up! begin?* and so on.

▶ **Practice Book page 99**

The **chapter title** tells what the chapter is mostly about.

The **page number** tells where the chapter begins.

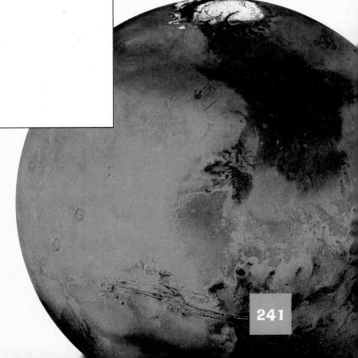

241

Finding Information in Books, continued

Index

The **index** is usually in the back of a book. It lists all the subjects in the book in alphabetical order. It gives page numbers where you can find information about those subjects.

Index Practice:

3 Have students use the index to find and tell you the page numbers for the subjects you name: *On which pages can you find information about **manned missions** to Mars?* and so on.

4 Provide a list of entries from the index in this **Handbook**. Have students use the index to find the entries, write the page numbers, turn to the pages, and tell where the information is on the page.

5 Give students a list of subjects to look up in a classroom textbook. Have them write the page numbers and then turn to the page and summarize the information they find about the subject. Students can find a model of a summary on page 145.

▶ **Practice Book page 100**

Names of people are listed in alphabetical order by their last names.

Related details are often listed for a subject.

INDEX

62

Sometimes page numbers are in *italics* to show that there is an illustration or photograph on that page.

Some indexes have words in **parentheses** that explain more about the subject. For example, these pages tell about the moons on Mars.

Glossary

A **glossary** is a short dictionary of important words used in the book. It appears at the back of the book. In a glossary, the words are listed in alphabetical order.

GLOSSARY

Astronomer—a scientist who studies the stars, planets, and all of outer space

Atmosphere—the various gases that surround a planet or other body in space

Axis—the invisible line through a planet's center around which it spins, or rotates

Crater—an irregular oval-shaped hole created through a collision with another object

Density—the compactness of materials

Equator—an imaginary circle around the center of the Earth, another planet, or the sun

Erosion—the process of being worn away by the action of wind, water, or other factors

55

Glossary Practice:
3 Ask questions with embedded answers: *Is a glossary at the front or at the back of a book? Does it give page numbers or definitions for words? Does crater come before or after axis in alphabetical order?*
4 **5** Pair Level 4 students with 5s and have them create pages for a glossary of unfamiliar words for **Dateline U.S.A.** They might begin by finding and listing the words in dark print and their definitions. Students can add more words as time permits. Level 4 students can help find and write the words in alphabetical order; Level 5 students can use a dictionary, if necessary, to look up and add the definitions.
▶ **Practice Book page 101**

Finding Information in Special Resources

Almanac

An **almanac** is a book filled with facts about things like inventions, animals, sports, science, movies, and TV. It's rewritten every year, so all the information is very up-to-date.

How to Use an Almanac

1 Look up your key words in the index.

2 Find those pages. Skim and scan to see if the pages have the information you are looking for.

INDEX
Soccer, 14, 207
Soil erosion, 94
Solar eclipse, 155
Solar system
    exploration of, 159
    facts about, 152-154
Solomon Islands, 58-59
    map, 76; flag, 80

PLANETS, STARS, AND SPACE TRAVEL

The SOLAR SYSTEM

Nine planets, including Earth, travel around the sun. These planets, together with the sun, form the **solar system**.

Look at the **titles** and **headings** for the main ideas.

THE SUN IS A STAR
Did you know that the sun is a star, like the other stars you see at night? However, astronomers have found that it is hotter, bigger, brighter, and more massive than most other stars. The diameter of the sun is 864,000 miles. The gravity of the sun is nearly 28 times the gravity of Earth.

How Hot Is the Sun? The temperature of the sun's surface is close to 11,000°F, and the inner core may reach temperatures near 35 million degrees! The sun provides enough light and heat energy to support all forms of life on our planet.

Look at the **key words** and **details** in dark print.

THE PLANETS ARE IN MOTION
The planets move around the sun along oval-shaped paths called **orbits**. Each planet travels in its own orbit. One complete path around the sun is called a **revolution**. Earth takes one year, or 365 days, to make one revolution around the sun. Planets that are farther away from the sun take longer. Some planets have one or more **moons**. A moon orbits a planet in much the same way that the planets orbit the sun.

Each planet also spins (or rotates) on its axis. An **axis** is an imaginary line running through the center of a planet. The time it takes for one rotation of the planet Earth on its axis equals one day. Below are some facts about the planets and the symbol for each planet.

Almanac Practice:

3 Have students find examples of each characteristic in the model and read them aloud: *Show me the **title** of this article. What does it say?*

4 Brainstorm topics with students and model looking them up using the index, skimming and scanning, and so on. Have students follow your model to look up the same topics and tell as many facts as they can about each topic.

5 Display the research questions from page 221 and give students an almanac. Have them follow the steps to look up the information about Mars. Encourage students to compare the articles they found and tell you which one they would use for research and why.

➤ **Practice Book pages 102 and 103**

③ If the information seems useful for your research, read the pages carefully and take notes.

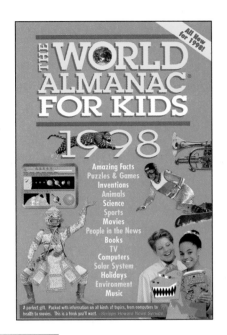

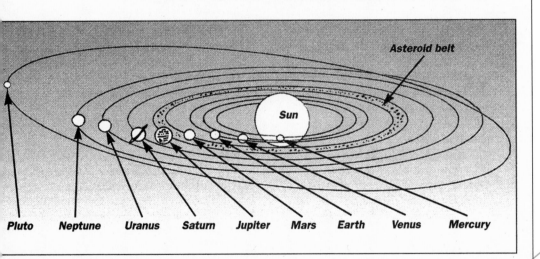

PLANETS, STARS, AND SPACE TRAVEL

Asteroid belt

Sun

Pluto   Neptune   Uranus   Saturn   Jupiter   Mars   Earth   Venus   Mercury

Sometimes **tables**, **lists**, and **diagrams** will give useful information for your report.

---

3. EARTH
Average distance from the sun:
  93 million miles
Diameter: 7,926 miles
Time to revolve around the sun:
  365 ¼ days
Time to rotate on its axis:
  23 hours, 56 minutes, 4.1 seconds
Number of moons: 1

DID YOU KNOW? Earth's path around the sun is nearly 600 million miles long. To make the trip in one year, Earth travels more than 66,000 miles per hour.

4. MARS
Average distance from the sun:
  142 million miles
Diameter: 4,220 miles
Time to revolve around the sun:
  687 days
Time to rotate on its axis:
  24 hours, 37 minutes, 26 seconds
Number of moons: 2

DID YOU KNOW? Mars is the home of Olympus Mons, the largest volcano found in the solar system. It stands about 17 miles high, with a crater 50 miles wide.

Special features like this one may give interesting facts.

Look It Up! 245

Atlas and Globe

An **atlas** is a book of maps. A **globe** is a round map that shows the curve of the earth.

Physical Map

A **physical map** shows features of a place like rivers, forests, mountains, lowlands, coastlines, or oceans.

Teach:
Display different kinds of maps like a road map, an atlas, a globe, and so on, and talk with students about how maps are useful. Then read aloud the introduction and work through pages 246–249.

Mountains look as if they are rising off the page.

Areas in blue are **lakes**.

The thin, blue lines are **rivers**.

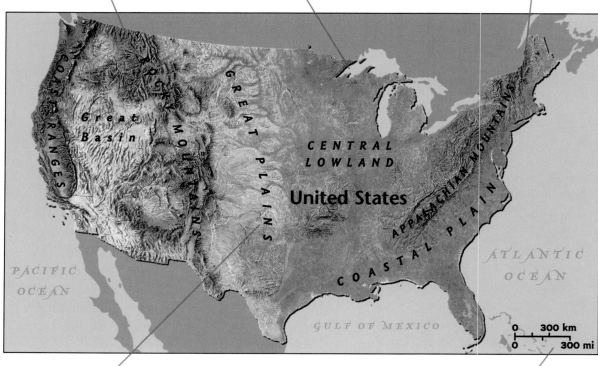

Sometimes there are labels for types of **landforms**.

The **scale** shows you that this distance on the map is equal to 300 miles on land.

Physical Map and Political Map Practice:

3 Ask students to point to and name the features they recognize on each map. Then have them show you the features you name:
Show me where the mountains are on this map.
Show me the state of Florida and so on.

4 Have students compare a physical and a political map by having them finish sentences: *To find out what landforms there are in the U.S., I would look at a (physical map). To find out where the city of Boston is, I would use a (political map).*

5 Bring in atlases with political maps in them. Give partners five cities to look up as you time them. Students should write the name of the city and the state. Then give them five more cities to look up to see if they can find the information more quickly.

 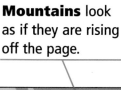

Political Map

A **political map** shows the boundaries between countries and states. It also shows the capitals and other major cities.

How to Find a Place on a Political Map

1 Use alphabetical order to look up the name of the place in the index.

In the index, you'll find the **page number** for the map. You might also find a special code, like **L-6** to help you find the exact **location** of the place on the map.

2 Look up the map and locate the place.

First turn to the page noted in the index. Then use the code **L-6** to find the place:

- Look for **L** on the side of the map.

Each letter is between two lines of **latitude**. Latitude lines are lines that go from east to west ⟷ around the earth.

- Look for **6** along the top or bottom of the map.

Each number is between two lines of **longitude**. Longitude lines are lines that go from north to south. ⇕

- Find the section where the lettered and numbered spaces meet. Then look for the name of the place.

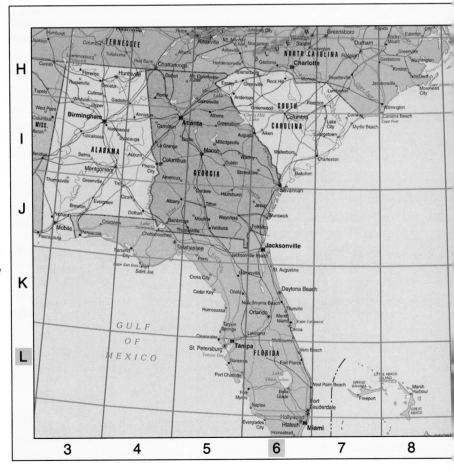

Atlas and Globe, continued

Historical Map

A **historical map** shows when and where certain events happened.

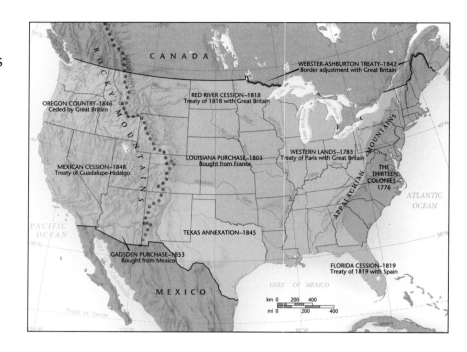

Product Map

A **product map** uses pictures and symbols to show where products come from.

A **compass rose** shows which directions are **north**, **south**, **east**, and **west** on the map.

A **legend** shows what each picture stands for.

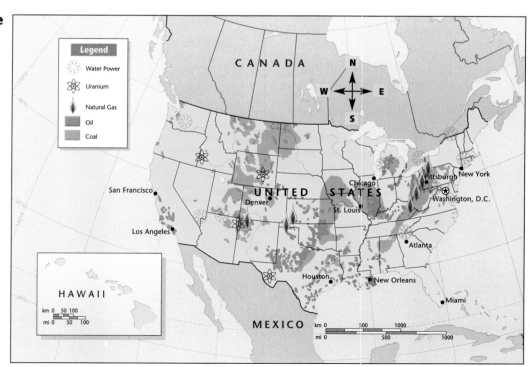

Globe Practice:
3 Have students look at a globe and find the equator, the North Pole, the South Pole and the axis. Ask yes/no questions: *Is Africa near the South Pole? Is Greenland near the North Pole?*
4 5 Pair up Level 4 and 5 students and have them use a globe to plan a trip around the world with stops on each continent. As Level 4 students talk about the trip and identify places on the globe, have Level 5s write a description of the trip to display for the class: *We would start our trip near the equator in Africa. Then we would go north to Egypt,* and so on.

Globe

A **globe** is a small model of the Earth. A globe has a round shape like the Earth does. It gives a better picture of Earth than a flat map does.

This is the **equator**. The equator is an imaginary line around the middle of the Earth. It divides the Earth into two parts, or **hemispheres**.

The **North Pole** is the point on Earth that is the farthest north.

The Earth spins around an imaginary straight line called an **axis**. A globe is made to spin the same way.

The **South Pole** is the point on Earth that is the farthest south.

Dictionary

Teach:
Hold up a dictionary and display some of its pages. Talk with students about when they might use a dictionary. Then work through pages 250–253, pausing to have volunteers read aloud guide words, entry words, definitions, and so on in the models.

A **dictionary** is a book filled with all kinds of information about words. It lists the words in alphabetical order from A to Z.

How to Look Up a Word

1 **Look at the beginning letter of your word and turn to the part of the dictionary it would be in.**

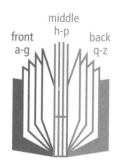

front
a-g

middle
h-p

back
q-z

Suppose you want to look up *spacesuit*. Words that begin with *S* are in the back part of a dictionary.

S **southwards > space shuttle**

ward slope of the mountain. Adjective.
south·ward (south′wərd) *adverb; adjective.*
southwards Another spelling of the adverb southward: *They drove southwards.* **south·wards** (south′wərdz) *adverb.*
southwest 1. The direction halfway between south and west. 2. The point of the compass showing this direction. 3. A region or place in this direction. 4. **the Southwest.** The region in the south and west of the United States. *Noun.*
  ° 1. Toward or in the southwest: *the southwest corner of the street.* 2. Coming from the southwest: *a southwest wind. Adjective.*
  ° Toward the southwest: *The ship sailed southwest. Adverb.*
south·west (south′west′) *noun; adjective; adverb.*
souvenir Something kept because it reminds one of a person, place, or event: *I bought a pennant as a souvenir of the baseball game.* **sou·ve·nir** (sü′və nîr′ *or* sü′və nîr′) *noun, plural* **souvenirs.**
sovereign A king or queen. *Noun.*
  ° 1. Having the greatest power or highest rank or authority: *The king and queen were the sovereign rulers of the country.* 2. Not controlled by others; independent: *Mexico is a sovereign nation. Adjective.*
sov·er·eign (sov′ər ən *or* sov′rən) *noun, plural* **sovereigns;** *adjective.*
Soviet Union Formerly, a large country in eastern Europe and northern Asia. It was composed of 15 republics and was also called the U.S.S.R. The largest and most important of the 15 republics was Russia.
sow[1] 1. To scatter seeds over the ground; plant: *The farmer will sow corn in this field.* 2. To spread or scatter: *The clown sowed happiness among the children.*
Other words that sound like this are **sew** and **so.**
sow (sō) *verb,* **sowed, sown** *or* **sowed, sowing.**
sow[2] An adult female pig. **sow** (sou) *noun, plural* **sows.**
soybean A seed rich in oil and protein and used as food. Soybeans grow in pods on bushy plants. **soy·bean** (soi′bēn′) *noun, plural* **soybeans.**
space 1. The area in which the whole universe exists. It has no limits. The planet earth is in space. 2. The region beyond the earth's atmosphere; outer space: *The rocket was launched into space.* 3. A distance or area between things: *There is not much space between our house and theirs.* 4. An area reserved or available for some purpose: *a parking space.* 5. A period of time: *Both jets landed in the space of ten minutes. Noun.*
  ° To put space in between: *The architect spaced the houses far apart. Verb.*
space (spās) *noun, plural* **spaces;** *verb,* **spaced, spacing.**
spacecraft A vehicle used for flight in outer space. This is also called a spaceship. **space·craft** (spās′kraft′) *noun, plural* **spacecraft.**
space shuttle A spacecraft that carries a crew into space and returns to land on earth. The same

space shuttle

flight deck and crew's quarters — orbiter
remote-control arm
container for experiments
rudder
booster nozzle
external fuel tank
tank for liquid oxygen
payload bay
solid-rocket booster
cargo bay door
satellite inside protective cocoon
wing

Dictionary Practice:

3 Write a word on the chalkboard. Ask students for its beginning letter. Then verbalize and restate the steps as you model looking up the word. Repeat the process. Have students follow your model to look up a different word.

4 Give partners a dictionary. Name a word and have them use the guide words and alphabetical order to find and point to the entry for the word. Have students tell where in the dictionary they found the page, name the guide words for the page, and name the words that come before and after the entry. Repeat for two more words.

② Use the guide words to help you find the page your word is on.

③ Look down the columns to find your entry word.

5 Have students use a dictionary to look up these words: *astronaut, flight, outer space*. Encourage them to write paragraphs that explain where and how they found the entry for each word.

▶ Practice Book page 105

---

space station ▸ Spanish ⑤

space shuttle can be used again. A space shuttle is also called a shuttle.

space station A spaceship that orbits around the earth like a satellite and on which a crew can live for long periods of time.

spacesuit Special clothing worn by an astronaut in space. A spacesuit covers an astronaut's entire body and has equipment to help the astronaut breathe. **space·suit** (spās'süt') *noun, plural* **spacesuits.**

Astronauts take spacewalks to repair satellites and vehicles.

spacewalk A period of activity during which an astronaut in space is outside a spacecraft. **space·walk** (spās'wôk') *noun, plural* **spacewalks.**

spacious Having a lot of space or room; roomy; large. —**spa·cious** *adjective* —**spaciousness** *noun.*

spade¹ A tool used for digging. It has a long handle and a flat blade that can be pressed into the ground with the foot. *Noun.*
○ To dig with a spade: *We spaded the garden and then raked it. Verb.*
spade (spād) *noun, plural* **spades;** *verb,* **spaded, spading.**

spade² 1. A playing card marked with one or more figures shaped like this. 2. spades. The suit of cards marked with this figure. **spade** (spād) *noun, plural* **spades.**

spaghetti A kind of pasta that looks like long,

thin strings. It is made of a mixture of flour and water. **spa·ghet·ti** (spə get'ē) *noun.*

WORD HISTORY

The word spaghetti comes from an Italian word meaning "strings" or "little cords." Spaghetti looks a bit like strings.

Spain A country in southwest Europe. **Spain** (spān) *noun.*

spamming The sending of the same message to large numbers of e-mail addresses or to many newsgroups at the same time. Spamming is often thought of as impolite behavior on the Internet. **spam·ming** (spa'ming) *noun.*

span 1. The distance or part between two supports: *The span of that bridge is very long.* 2. The full reach or length of anything: *Some people accomplish a great deal in the span of their lives. Noun.*
○ To extend over or across. *Verb.*
span (span) *noun, plural* **spans;** *verb,* **spanned, spanning.**

This bridge spans a wide river.

spaniel Any of various dogs of small to medium size with long, drooping ears, a silky, wavy coat, and short legs. The larger types are used in hunting. **span·iel** (span'yəl) *noun, plural* **spaniels.**

Spanish 1. The people of Spain. The word *Spanish* in this sense is used with a plural verb. 2. The language spoken in Spain. It is also spoken in many countries south of the United States as well as in parts of the U.S. *Noun.*
○ Of or having to do with Spain, its people, or the Spanish language. *Adjective.*
Span·ish (span'ish) *noun; adjective.*

The first **guide word** is *space station* because that word comes first on the page. The second guide word is *Spanish* because that word comes last. Your word will be on the page if it comes between the two guide words in alphabetical order.

Look at the **entry word** *spacesuit*. It's in alphabetical order on the page.

Look It Up! 251

Dictionary, continued

Each **entry** gives you important information about the word.

The **definition** tells you what the word means. If a word has more than one meaning, the definitions are numbered.

An entry may also give the **plural form** or **verb forms** of the word and how to spell them.

Some entries have a **sample sentence** to help you know how to use the word.

...be... A s... ...ch in o... ...and used as food. Soybeans grow in pods on bushy plants.
soy·bean (soi′bēn′) *noun, plural* **soybeans.**

space 1. The area in which the whole universe exists. It has no limits. The planet earth is in space. 2. The region beyond the earth's atmosphere; outer space: *The rocket was launched into space.* 3. A distance or area between things: *There is not much space between our house and theirs.* 4. An area reserved or available for some purpose: *a parking space.* 5. A period of time: *Both jets landed in the space of ten minutes. Noun.*
○ To put space in between: *The architect spaced the houses far apart. Verb.*
space (spās) *noun, plural* **spaces**; *verb,* **spaced, spacing.**

spacecraft A vehicle used for flight in outer space. This is also called a spaceship.
space·craft (spās′kraft′) *noun, plural* **spacecraft.**

space shuttle A spacecraft that carries a crew ...to space an... ...urns to land on earth. The sa...

This information tells you **how to pronounce** the word. You can look up the marks in the **pronunciation key**. The mark **ā** tells you to say the **a** the same way you would say the **a** in **āpe**. The mark ′ tells you to emphasize the first part of the word, **space**.

Pronunciation Key

PRONUNCIATION KEY:

at	āpe	fär	câre	end	mē	it	īce	pîerce	hot	ōld	sòng	fôrk
oil	out	up	ūse	rüle	pùll	tûrn	chin	sing	shop	thin	this	

hw in white; zh in treasure. The symbol ə stands for the unstressed vowel sound in about, taken, pencil, lemon, and circus.

252 **Look It Up!**

All entries include words like *noun*, or its abbreviation *n*, that tell the word's **part of speech**. A word's part of speech shows how the word can be used in a sentence.

Abbreviations for the parts of speech are:

adj	adjective
adv	adverb
conj	conjunction
interj	interjection
n	noun
prep	preposition
pron	pronoun
v	verb

for long periods of time.

spacesuit Special clothing worn by an astronaut in space. A spacesuit covers an astronaut's entire body and has equipment to help the astronaut breathe. **space•suit** (spās'süt') *noun*, *plural* **spacesuits.**

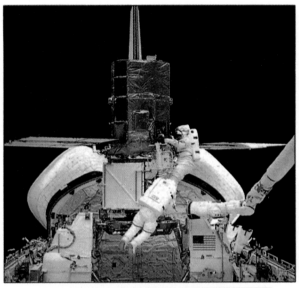

Astronauts take spacewalks to repair satellites and vehicles.

spacewalk A period of activity during which an astronaut in space is outside a spacecraft. **space•walk** (spās'wôk') *noun*, *plural* **spacewalks.**

spacious Having a lot of space or room; roomy; large. —**spa•cious** *adjective* —**spaciousness**

Some entries have a **picture** and a **caption**. They give you more information about a word and its meaning.

Dictionary Practice:

3 Have students answer questions with embedded answers and follow your directions to identify elements of an entry: *Show me the definition for* space. *Is* spacecraft *a noun or a verb?* and so on.

4 Have students write new sentences to illustrate the meanings for *space, spacesuit,* and *spacewalk.* Help them as necessary to use the correct plural form or verb forms for their sentences.

5 Have students choose and then look up three multiple-meaning words from pages 21–27. Have them use the pronunciation key to say the words, and then read the dictionary definition and the part of speech aloud.

▶ **Practice Book page 106**

Encyclopedia

An **encyclopedia** is a set of books. Each book is called a **volume**. Each volume has articles that give facts about many different topics. The volumes and articles in an encyclopedia are arranged in alphabetical order.

How to Find Information in an Encyclopedia

1 **Find the correct volume.**

What is the first letter of the word you plan to look up? Find the volume that has articles beginning with that letter.

Teach:
Remind students what they learned about the reference section of the library. Then read aloud the introduction and work through the page. Have students talk about the information in the article and ask volunteers to read aloud the parts in the article that illustrate the characteristics of an encyclopedia article.

An article about **M**ars would be in this volume.

This is where you would find information about **sp**ace travel.

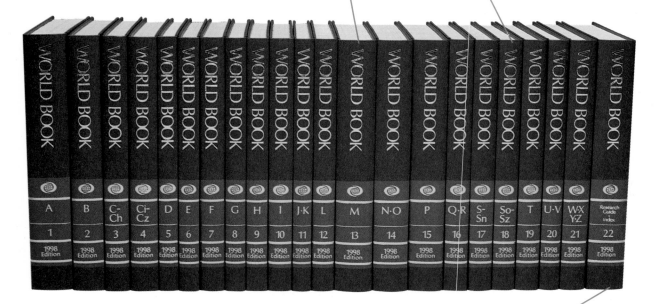

Most encyclopedias have a volume called an **Index**. The index lists other related subjects to look up.

3 Speech Emergence **4** Intermediate Fluency **5** Advanced Fluency/Fluent

❷ Use alphabetical order to find the article.

Flip through the pages looking just at the **guide words** to get to the page where the article appears. Then find the article on the page.

❸ Skim and scan the article to see if it has the information you need.

Encyclopedia Practice:
3 Name a subject and have students point to and say the volume letter and number that would contain articles about that subject. Repeat for other subjects.
4 Have students look up *Mars* in an encyclopedia and then skim and scan the article. Ask: *If you were researching "life on Mars," would you read this article more carefully and take notes. Why? Why not?*
5 Have students look up *Mars* in an encyclopedia Index volume. Then have them look up the articles listed. Ask them to skim and scan the articles and take notes on any information they find about "life on Mars." Refer students to **How to Take Notes** on pages 226 and 227 for help.

➤ **Practice Book page 107**

This is an **entry word**. It is the title of the article.

Headings tell what each section in the article is about.

Mars 223

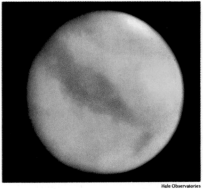

Hale Observatories   NASA

Mars's surface features are visible in a photograph taken from the earth, *left*. The earth's atmosphere makes the picture blurry. A series of canyons called the Valles Marineris (Mariner Valleys) make up the diagonal landform in the photo at the right, taken by the U.S. Viking 1 space probe. This landform is more than 2,500 miles (4,000 kilometers) long.

Mars is the only planet whose surface can be seen in detail from the earth. It is reddish in color, and was named Mars after the bloody-red god of war of the ancient Romans. Mars is the only planet other than the earth to produce evidence suggesting that it was once the home of living creatures. However, there is no evidence that life now exists on Mars.

Mars is the fourth closest planet to the sun, and the next planet beyond the earth. Its mean distance from the sun is 141,600,000 miles (227,900,000 kilometers), compared with about 93,000,000 miles (150,000,000 kilometers) for the earth. At its closest approach to the earth, Mars is 34,600,000 miles (55,700,000 kilometers) away. Venus is the only planet in the solar system that comes closer to the earth.

The diameter of Mars is 4,223 miles (6,796 kilometers), a little over half that of the earth. Pluto and Mercury are the only planets smaller than Mars.

Orbit and rotation

Mars travels around the sun in an *elliptical* (oval-shaped) orbit. Its distance from the sun varies from about 154,800,000 miles (249,200,000 kilometers) at its farthest point, to about 128,400,000 miles (206,600,000 kilometers) at its closest point. Mars takes about 687 earth-days to go around the sun.

As Mars orbits the sun, it spins on its *axis*, an imaginary line through its center. Mars's axis is not *perpendicular* (at an angle of 90°) to its path around the sun. The axis tilts at an angle of about 24° from the perpendicular position. For an illustration of the tilt of an axis, see **Planet** (The axes of the planets). Mars rotates once every 24 hours and 37 minutes. The earth rotates once every 23 hours and 56 minutes.

The contributor of this article is Hyron Spinrad, Professor of Astronomy at the University of California, Berkeley.

Mars at a glance

Mars, shown in blue in the diagram, is the next planet beyond the earth. The ancient symbol for Mars, *right*, is still used today.

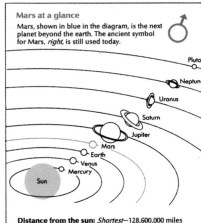

Distance from the sun: *Shortest*—128,600,000 miles (206,600,000 kilometers); *Greatest*—154,800,000 miles (249,200,000 kilometers); *Mean*—141,600,000 miles (227,900,000 kilometers).
Distance from the earth: *Shortest*—34,600,000 miles (55,700,000 kilometers); *Greatest*—248,000,000 miles (399,000,000 kilometers).
Diameter: 4,223 miles (6,796 kilometers).
Length of year: About 1 earth-year and 10½ months.
Rotation period: 24 hours and 37 minutes.
Temperature: −225 to 63 °F (−143 to 17 °C).
Atmosphere: Carbon dioxide, nitrogen, argon, oxygen, carbon monoxide, neon, krypton, xenon, and water vapor.
Number of satellites: 2.

❹ If the article has the information you need, read it and take notes.

Telephone Directory

Sometimes you need to make a phone call to set up an interview or to get information for a report. You can find the phone numbers you need in the **telephone directory**, or phone book.

White Pages

In the **white pages** you'll find telephone numbers for people and businesses. Names for people are listed in alphabetical order by their last names. Businesses are listed in alphabetical order by the first important word in their name.

Teach:
Talk with students about their experiences with the telephone: *How do you use a telephone? Whom do you call? What do you need to know in order to make a call?* Then read aloud the introduction and work through the different kinds of pages in a telephone directory.

Guide words show the first name and last name included on the page.

Some businesses will pay to have their names printed in **larger type**. The larger type makes the name stand out from the rest.

SANTOS–SETA

Santos Sally	555-1273
Santoso Rini	555-8924
Sarma Karan	555-5639
Sarma Sanjay	555-0956
Search for Extraterrestrial Intelligence (SETI)	
75 Atlantic	555-4563
Seguin G	555-5629
Serrano Aaron	555-1870
Serrano Anthony 51 Porter	555-0446
Serrano E 62 Falconcrest	555-0830
Serrano Nera 160 Devon	555-4974
Serrano Q	555-0223
Serre A	555-3856
Serre Francis	555-3847

SERVICE CENTER

199 Townsend	555-5833
Service Deli 111 East St	555-2446
Seta Elizabeth 1462 Zamora	555-9877

Sometimes people or businesses list their **addresses** as well as their telephone number.

Telephone Directory Practice:

3 Have students point to or tell you the answers to these questions: *What is Anthony Serrano's phone number? Where is the Service Center? What kind of business is Wilma dot Com?* and so on.

4 Give partners a telephone directory and have them look up their favorite stores. Encourage them to write down the name of the store and its telephone number. Partners can compare their lists with other students.

5 Encourage groups to use a telephone directory to find and list the names and telephone numbers of their favorite stores, places to visit, and so on. Have them add brief descriptions for each entry such as what the store sells or why the place is a good place to visit. Students can use the information to make a directory for the class or new students.

▶ Practice Book page 108

Yellow Pages

The **yellow pages** have names and telephone numbers for companies or businesses in your area.

The **guide words** name the kinds of businesses listed on the page in alphabetical order.

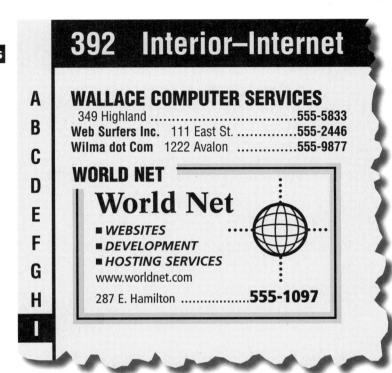

392 Interior–Internet

A
B
C
D
E
F
G
H
I

WALLACE COMPUTER SERVICES
349 Highland **555-5833**
Web Surfers Inc. 111 East St. **555-2446**
Wilma dot Com 1222 Avalon **555-9877**

WORLD NET

World Net
- **WEBSITES**
- **DEVELOPMENT**
- **HOSTING SERVICES**
www.worldnet.com

287 E. Hamilton **555-1097**

Many companies pay to have a **big advertisement** on the page.

Most yellow pages have **guide letters** to help you find a section easily.

Special Sections

Many telephone directories also have special sections that give information such as

- emergency telephone numbers for the fire and police department

- guidelines for first aid

- names and telephone numbers for government officials

- museums, parks, and other places to visit.

Look in the front pages of the directory to find out more about these special sections.

3. Customer Guide

Turn to the first page in each section for a complete table of contents.

Finding Information on the Internet

Teach:
Have students share any experiences they've had with the Internet. Talk about the advantages and disadvantages of using the Internet. If possible, arrange for a demonstration. Read aloud page 258, and then work through pages 259–262. Stop after each step to point out and identify the elements on the screen.

The **Internet** is an international network, or connection, of computers that share information with one another. The **World Wide Web** allows you to find, read, go through, and organize information. The Internet is like a giant library, and the World Wide Web is everything in the library including the books, the librarian, and the computer catalog.

The Internet is a *fast* way to get the most current information about your topic! You'll find resources like encyclopedias and dictionaries on the Internet and amazing pictures, movies, and sounds.

What You'll Need

To use the Internet, you need a computer with software that allows you to access it. You'll also need a modem connected to a telephone line.

How to Get Started

You can search on the Internet in many different ways. In fact, you'll probably find something new whenever you search on it. Don't be afraid to try something—you never know what you'll find!

Check with your teacher for how to access the Internet from your school. Usually you can just double click on the **icon**, or picture, to get access to the Internet and you're on your way!

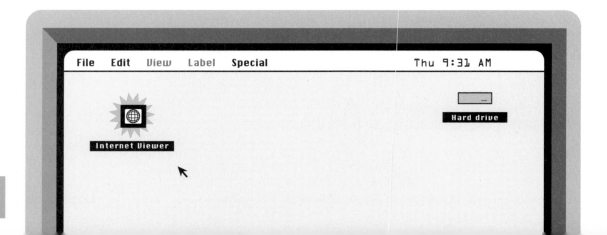

Doing the Research

Once the search page comes up, you can begin the research process. Just follow these steps.

1 Type your subject in the search box and then click on the Search button.

You'll always see a **toolbar** like this one at the top of the screen. Click on the pictures to do things like print the page.

This is where you type in your **subject**.

File   Edit   Go   Favorites

Search

Back   Forward   Home   Reload   Stop   Print

Address   http://search.com

"life on Mars"   Search

Try different ways to type in your subject. You'll get different results!

- If you type in **Mars**, you'll see all the sites that have the word *Mars* in them. This may give you too many categories and sites to look through!

- If you type in **"life on Mars"** you'll see all the sites with the exact phrase, or group of words, *life on Mars*.

- If you type in **+Mars +life** you'll see all the sites with the words *Mars* and *life* in them.

Finding Information on the Internet, continued

2 Read the search results.

All underlined, colored words are **links**, or connections, to other sites. They help you get from page to page quickly.

If you want to go directly to a **web page**, click on a **site**.

Click on a **category** to see more options for information related to your topic.

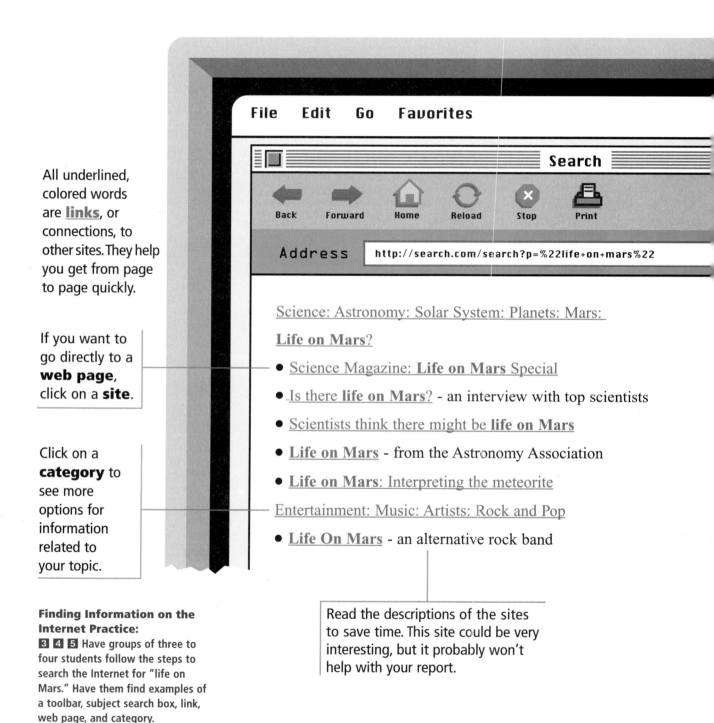

File   Edit   Go   Favorites

Search

Back   Forward   Home   Reload   Stop   Print

Address   http://search.com/search?p=%22life+on+mars%22

Science: Astronomy: Solar System: Planets: Mars:
Life on Mars?

● Science Magazine: **Life on Mars** Special

● Is there **life on Mars**? - an interview with top scientists

● Scientists think there might be **life on Mars**

● **Life on Mars** - from the Astronomy Association

● **Life on Mars**: Interpreting the meteorite

Entertainment: Music: Artists: Rock and Pop

● **Life On Mars** - an alternative rock band

Read the descriptions of the sites to save time. This site could be very interesting, but it probably won't help with your report.

Finding Information on the Internet Practice:
3 **4** **5** Have groups of three to four students follow the steps to search the Internet for "life on Mars." Have them find examples of a toolbar, subject search box, link, web page, and category.

3 Speech Emergence **4** Intermediate Fluency **5** Advanced Fluency/Fluent

3 Select a site, and read the article.

You might want to pick a new site or start a new search. If so, click on the **Back** arrow to go back a page to the search results.

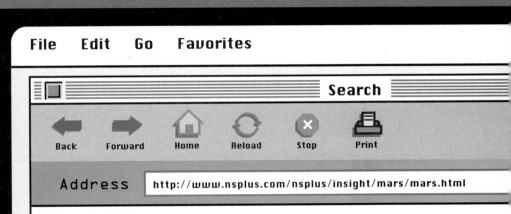

File   Edit   Go   **Favorites**

Search

| Back | Forward | Home | Reload | Stop | Print |

Address   http://www.nsplus.com/nsplus/insight/mars/mars.html

Mars

In this special section we bring you all the stories on the Mars probe landing, from New Scientist's award-winning team of reporters. We also offer an extensive archive of articles on NASA's earlier claim that Mars once supported life and a look at the search for life in space, as well as numerous web links. From the August 1996 heady excitement of that announcement--"life on Mars"--to the disappointing revelation-- "no, probably not", Planet Science was there.

If you want to go to another web page, click on a **link**.

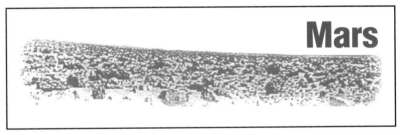

MORE ON MARS:

● <u>Mission to Mars makes do with robots</u>
THE US has formally abandoned its goal of landing astronauts on Mars by 2019. Instead, the new national space policy unveiled last week commits the nation to a permanent robot presence on the Red Planet starting no later than 2000. Human exploration might come later, depending on what the robots find.

MARS LATEST:

13 DEC 97: <u>Hop, skip and jump</u>
A little robot in a lab in Arizona is preparing to take several giant leaps for robotkind. If it reaches Mars in the next century, as its developers hope, it will produce its own fuel and be able to fly, hop and hover over the surface of the Red Planet.

12 NOV 97: <u>In the dark</u>
If life developed on ancient Mars, it got going in almost complete darkness, say scientists in the US and France. The newborn planet was shrouded in dense clouds of frozen carbon dioxide which acted like a mirror, they say, reflecting up to 95 percent of incident lighting. "In its early days, Mars was the white planet rather than the Red Planet".

4 Print the article if it is helpful for your research. Later on, you can use the article to take notes.

Finding Information on the Internet, continued

Locating More Resources

If you already know the **URL** (Uniform Resource Locator), or address, of a Web site, you can type it in the address box at the top of the screen.

Finding Information on the Internet Practice:
3 **4** **5** Have groups search the Internet for a topic of their choice from **Dateline U.S.A.** Have them print any articles that they would like to read in more depth later and note the URLs of interesting sites. Ask them to present any interesting information they find.

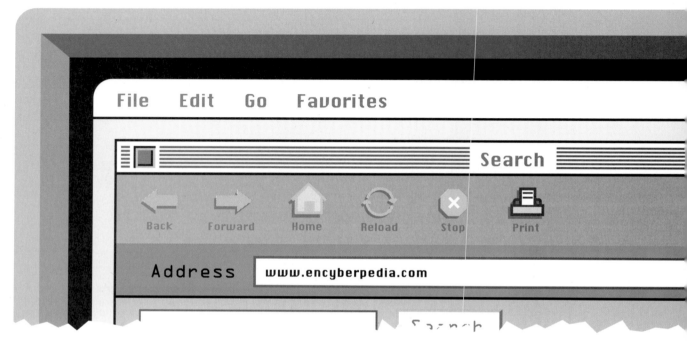

Here are a few good references to try. Because the Internet is always changing, these addresses might change. If you can't find a site, try searching by using its name.

Encyberpedia (Encyclopedia)
www.encyberpedia.com

Encyclopedia Britannica
www.eb.com

Grolier Encyclopedia
www.grolier.com

Kids Web Digital Library
www.kidsvista.com/index.html

Merriam Webster Dictionary
www.m-w.com

Old Farmer's Almanac
www.almanac.com

One Look Dictionary
www.onelook.com

The Virtual Reference Desk
thorplus.lib.purdue.edu/reference/

3 Speech Emergence **4** Intermediate Fluency **5** Advanced Fluency/Fluent

Dateline U.S.A.™

New Year's Day

On the Roman calendar, January 1 is the first day of the calendar year.

■ At the beginning of the new year, people often make **resolutions**, or promises to themselves, to stop bad habits like eating too much and to start good habits like exercising. On New Year's Day, people start trying to make their resolutions come true.

■ Many people watch parades like the Tournament of Roses Parade in Pasadena, California, or football games like the Cotton Bowl in Texas.

Martin Luther King, Jr., Day

The third Monday in January honors Martin Luther King, Jr., a courageous American. People celebrate by remembering his message of peace and what he did for our country.

■ Martin Luther King, Jr., was a minister who helped the sick and needy. He was a leader promoting **nonviolence** during the Civil Rights movement. He and many others helped end laws that were **discriminatory**, or unfair, because they treated different groups of people in different ways.

■ In the summer of 1963, Martin Luther King, Jr., gave a famous speech called "I Have a Dream." He said that his dream was for people to judge each other by the "content of their character." He thought people should see each other as individuals and not as groups separated by the color of their skin.

Inauguration Day

Every four years a president is elected to be the leader of the United States. The president's term officially begins on January 20. On that day, people across the nation listen to speeches by the president and invited guests. This ceremony is called an **inauguration**.

The president of the United States lives in the White House.

Who has been president of the United States?

	President	Term
1	George Washington	1789–1797
2	John Adams	1797–1801
3	Thomas Jefferson	1801–1809
4	James Madison	1809–1817
5	James Monroe	1817–1825
6	John Quincy Adams	1825–1829
7	Andrew Jackson	1829–1837
8	Martin Van Buren	1837–1841
9	William H. Harrison	1841
10	John Tyler	1841–1845
11	James Knox Polk	1845–1849
12	Zachary Taylor	1849–1850
13	Millard Fillmore	1850–1853
14	Franklin Pierce	1853–1857
15	James Buchanan	1857–1861
16	Abraham Lincoln	1861–1865
17	Andrew Johnson	1865–1869
18	Ulysses S. Grant	1869–1877
19	Rutherford B. Hayes	1877–1881
20	James A. Garfield	1881
21	Chester A. Arthur	1881–1885
22	Grover Cleveland	1885–1889
23	Benjamin Harrison	1889–1893

	President	Term
24	Grover Cleveland	1893–1897
25	William McKinley	1897–1901
26	Theodore Roosevelt	1901–1909
27	William Howard Taft	1909–1913
28	Woodrow Wilson	1913–1921
29	Warren G. Harding	1921–1923
30	Calvin Coolidge	1923–1929
31	Herbert Hoover	1929–1933
32	Franklin D. Roosevelt	1933–1945
33	Harry S. Truman	1945–1953
34	Dwight D. Eisenhower	1953–1961
35	John F. Kennedy	1961–1963
36	Lyndon B. Johnson	1963–1969
37	Richard M. Nixon	1969–1974
38	Gerald R. Ford	1974–1977
39	Jimmy Carter	1977–1981
40	Ronald Reagan	1981–1989
41	George Bush	1989–1993
42	William Jefferson Clinton	1993–

Chinese New Year

Many Americans celebrate the Chinese New Year, which begins in late January or early February.

- For about two weeks, families wish each other luck, health, happiness, and wealth for the coming year.

- During the celebrations, people set off fireworks and have feasts. They march in big parades, sometimes under a lion's head or a long, colorful dragon. It takes a lot of people to move a dragon down the street!

- The new year is a time of gift-giving, too. Adults give children red envelopes with money inside for good luck.

Where is one of the biggest Chinese New Year parades in the U.S.?

San Francisco

This is Chinatown in San Francisco, California. It has the largest Chinese community in the United States. Thousands of people go to see the Chinese New Year parade every year.

Tet

Tet is another new year's celebration. It occurs on the first three days of the Vietnamese calendar, usually in late January or early February.

- The first visitor to a home on the first morning of Tet is important. If the visitor is kind and honest, the family will have good fortune for the rest of the year.

- Red is considered to be a lucky color, so people eat red food, like dyed watermelon seeds which stain their hands and mouth.

- People also hang banners on their doors that have greetings like "compliments of the season."

Groundhog Day

An old legend says that a groundhog comes up from its winter nest on February 2.

- If the groundhog sees its own shadow, it means that there will be six more weeks of winter.

- If the groundhog does not see its shadow, it means that spring is about to begin.

Valentine's Day

- On February 14, people exchange cards, or valentines, to show they care about each other.

- Many valentines are decorated with red hearts and have messages written on them. Some show Cupid, a boy with wings, whose arrows make people fall in love.

Be My Valentine

Black History Month

African Americans have made significant contributions in many areas from science and mathematics to literature and the fine arts. In the month of February, we recognize their contributions and learn more about the experiences of African Americans throughout the history of the United States.

Who are some courageous African Americans who fought for freedom and civil rights in the U.S.?

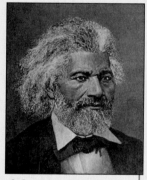

1841

Frederick Douglass spoke out against slavery.

Until the 1860s, African Americans were slaves, forced to work without pay. Frederick Douglass was born a slave but escaped to New England when he was 21. There Douglass began writing and speaking against slavery. He fought long and hard to stop slavery and to change the way African Americans were treated. ★

1850

Harriet Tubman helped slaves become free.

Harriet Tubman helped over 300 slaves leave the South for freedom in the North. She was a leader for the "Underground Railroad," a group of people who helped slaves by hiding them and moving them north in farm wagons. ★

1861–1865

African Americans fought in the Civil War.

During the Civil War, the Union army fought for the North who wanted to end slavery. About 180,000 African Americans fought with the Union army even though it did not treat them as equals and forced them to serve in all-black regiments. These regiments fought bravely and were important to winning the war and ending slavery. ★

★ **1840s**   ★ **1850s**   ★ **1860s**

My People

The night is beautiful,
So the faces of my people.

The stars are beautiful,
So the eyes of my people.

Beautiful, also, is the sun.
Beautiful, also, are the souls of my people.

— *Langston Hughes*

1947
Jackie Robinson joined the Brooklyn Dodgers.

Although many African Americans were playing baseball in the 1940s, they had to play in leagues that were separate from the major leagues. In 1947, Jackie Robinson became the first African American to play on a modern American major league team, the Brooklyn Dodgers. From then on, blacks and whites were able to play baseball in the same leagues. ★

1955
Rosa Parks inspired the Civil Rights movement.

Rosa Parks refused to give up her seat on a bus to a white person. Her protest inspired others to act against unfair laws. This was one event that helped get the Civil Rights movement started. **Civil rights** means that all people should be treated equally under the law. ★

1967
Thurgood Marshall joined the Supreme Court.

Thurgood Marshall presented the argument for **desegregation** of the public schools. Desegregation meant that African American students could go to the same schools as white children. Later, Marshall became the first African American Supreme Court justice. ★

★ **1940s**   ★ **1950s**   ★ **1960s**

Dateline U.S.A. 269

Presidents' Day

On the third Monday in February, Americans honor two great American presidents.

- **George Washington** became the first president of the United States in 1789. He is called the "Father of Our Country."

- **Abraham Lincoln,** the sixteenth president, was a great leader during difficult times. He helped to end the Civil War and slavery.

Both presidents were important leaders in the government of the United States.

How does the United States government work?

The Constitution of the United States of America

After the Revolutionary War, the American people needed a plan to help them organize the new government.

In 1787 several important leaders approved the United States **Constitution**. The Constitution is a written document that tells what the main laws of the country are and the powers and duties of each part of the government. It includes the **Bill of Rights** which protects the rights and freedoms of every citizen, such as freedom of religion, freedom of speech, and freedom of the press.

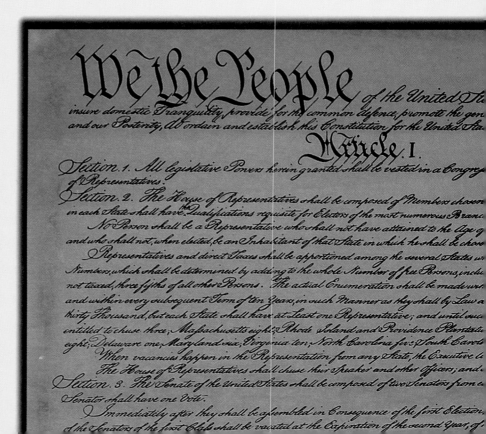

The Three Branches of Our Government

Legislative Branch

People who work in this branch write and pass new laws. This branch, also known as Congress, is made up of two parts: the House of Representatives and the Senate. Each state elects Representatives and Senators to work in Congress.

Executive Branch

People who work in the executive branch make sure that the laws of the country are obeyed. The president, the vice president, and other advisors to the president are the leaders in this branch of the government.

Judicial Branch

In the judicial branch, judges and justices listen to cases in court. They decide what the laws mean and if the laws are in agreement with the Constitution. The most important court is the United States Supreme Court.

U.S. Government

March

Saint Patrick's Day

On March 17, be sure to wear green or you might get pinched! Wearing green is a tradition on Saint Patrick's Day. You might also see lots of green decorations like three-leaf clovers called shamrocks and tiny elves called leprechauns.

This holiday began as a Catholic holiday in Ireland, a country with lots of green hills and valleys. It was a special day to honor the good works of a man named Saint Patrick. When Irish immigrants came to live in the United States in the 1700s, they brought this tradition with them and it has been celebrated here ever since.

What other groups of people have immigrated to the United States?

When	Who	About How Many
1840–1860	Irish	1,500,000
1840–1890	Germans	4,000,000
1870–1910	Danes, Norwegians, and Swedes	1,500,000
1880–1930	Eastern Europeans	3,500,000
	Austrians, Czechs, Hungarians, and Slovaks	4,000,000
	Italians	4,500,000
1910–1930	Mexicans	700,000
1950–1990	Mexicans	5,000,000
1960–1990	Cubans	700,000
1970–1990	Dominicans, Haitians, and Jamaicans	900,000
1970–1990	Vietnamese	500,000
1981–1996	Chinese	500,000
1981–1996	Filipinos	800,000

Statue of Liberty

When many immigrants came to the United States they arrived in New York. In New York Harbor, they were welcomed by this statue which stands for freedom and opportunity. The Statue of Liberty is still an important symbol today for all Americans.

Easter

Easter is a Christian holiday that occurs between March 22 and April 25. It is also a time when people celebrate new life and the coming of spring.

■ Some people wear new suits, dresses, and hats to church on Easter Sunday.

■ Children decorate hard-boiled eggs for an imaginary "Easter bunny" to hide, but it is really the parents who hide the eggs for children to find.

Passover

Jewish families celebrate Passover for eight days between March 27 and April 24. Passover is a time to celebrate freedom for all Jews and people everywhere.

■ During Passover, families clean house very carefully. This is a time when everything must be orderly and clean.

■ On the first night, families talk about their history. They also eat a traditional meal called a *Seder* that includes *matzo*, a flat bread, and other special foods.

Ramadan

Ramadan is a Muslim celebration in the ninth month of the Islamic calendar. It lasts almost thirty days.

■ At this time, Muslims follow directions from the *Koran*, a holy book, and eat only before sunrise and after sunset.

■ Ramadan ends with a festival called *Ed al-Fitr* which means "a festival of happiness and a time of great joy." That's when families exchange gifts and have a large meal, or **feast**.

April

National Library Week

You can find out anything you want to know in a library. During April, people honor all that libraries have to offer. They might celebrate by going to the library to read books or to listen to favorite stories.

American literature has lots of characters and heroes. Some of the characters are real, while others are made-up. Many of the heroes have become so popular that they are featured in movies and television shows.

Who are some of the well-known characters and people in American literature?

From Cartoon Strips:

Superman

Superman is a comic book super hero who was created by Jerry Siegel and Joe Shuster. Superman is "more powerful than a locomotive" and "able to leap tall buildings in a single bound." When he isn't rescuing someone, he disguises himself as Clark Kent, a reporter for the *Daily Planet* newspaper.

Charlie Brown and Snoopy

Charlie Brown and his dog, Snoopy, are characters in the comic strip "Peanuts" by Charles M. Schulz. Some of their friends are Linus, Lucy, and Peppermint Patty. They all enjoy things like baseball and going to summer camp.

Wonder Woman

William Moulton Marston created Wonder Woman, a quick and strong super hero who had been an Amazonian princess before coming to the United States. She helps others with her magic lasso and can dodge bullets with her magic bracelet. When not fighting off evil, she teaches a message of peace and equality.

From Tall Tales:

John Henry

John Henry built railroad tracks. He was so strong that he could pound steel faster and longer than a steam drill.

Pecos Bill

Pecos Bill was a cowboy who wasn't afraid to do anything. Stories about him tell how he rode a hurricane to shake the rain out of it and rounded up every steer in Texas for his ranch.

From the Wild West:

Annie Oakley

Annie Oakley was so good with a rifle that she could shoot a dime out of her husband's hand.

From Literature:

Laura Ingalls

Laura Ingalls Wilder was a real woman who wrote about growing up in the Midwest. She tells about traveling in a covered wagon and living in a log cabin. Her books are called the *Little House* books.

Dorothy

Dorothy is a girl in the series of books about the magical land of Oz by Frank L. Baum. There she meets creatures like a scarecrow, a tin man, and a lion.

Tom Sawyer and Huckleberry Finn

Tom Sawyer and Huckleberry Finn are two characters in books by Mark Twain. Tom and Huck often get into trouble but always have amazing adventures in their hometown near the Mississippi River.

April Fools' Day

On April 1, don't believe everything you see and hear! On this day, many people play tricks on each other. For example, a friend might tell you that your shoes are untied. When you look down and see that nothing's wrong, your friend will say "April Fools!"

Earth Day

Earth Day is a day to think about and appreciate the Earth. On April 22, people talk about ways to protect our resources and environment. It's important to care about the Earth because people need clean air, water, and land to live a healthy life.

What are some of the special environments to protect in the United States?

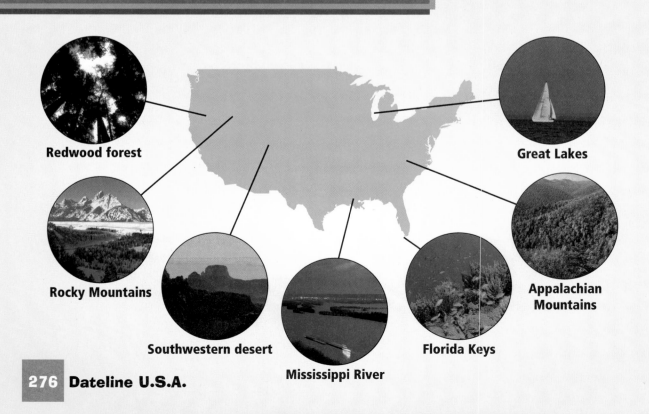

Redwood forest

Great Lakes

Rocky Mountains

Appalachian Mountains

Southwestern desert

Florida Keys

Mississippi River

Cinco de Mayo

On May 5th, 1862, the Mexican and French armies fought near Puebla, Mexico. The small Mexican army won the battle that day. Every year on May 5th, or *cinco de mayo* in Spanish, the people of Mexico celebrate this victory. Mexican immigrants brought this celebration with them when they came to the United States.

Today, people in many U.S. towns also celebrate *cinco de mayo*. Some people go to carnivals. Others enjoy watching parades and traditional Mexican dancing and listening to Mexican music.

May

Mother's Day

On the second Sunday in May, sons and daughters remind their mothers how much they love them.

- Many people give their moms cards, flowers, or chocolates, and an extra big hug!

- Some people also send greetings to other special women like their grandmothers, aunts, or close female friends.

Memorial Day

Memorial Day began as a way of honoring soldiers who died in the Civil War. Since then, the last Monday in May has become a day to remember all soldiers who have died fighting for the United States.

- On this day, people place flowers or flags on soldiers' graves.

- Some cities have military parades and other special programs.

- Because summer vacation begins on this day in many places, families often celebrate by having outdoor picnics and barbecues.

Flag Day

The United States flag is the most important symbol of our nation. On June 14, Americans pay respect to the flag and all it stands for by displaying it at their homes, schools, and businesses.

- The first flag had thirteen stars and thirteen stripes that stood for the number of original colonies.

- As the United States grew and more territories became states, the flag changed. Today there are still thirteen stripes, but there are fifty stars. Each star stands for a state.

The Flag of 1777

The United States Flag Today

How did the United States grow?

1803

The United States made the Louisiana Purchase.

In the 1700s, the western border of the United States was the Mississippi River. In 1803 the United States bought, or **purchased**, the land on the other side of the Mississippi from the French. This purchase made the United States twice as big! ★

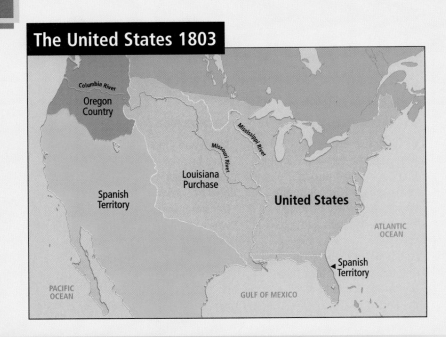

The United States 1803

★ **1800s**

The United States 1804–1836

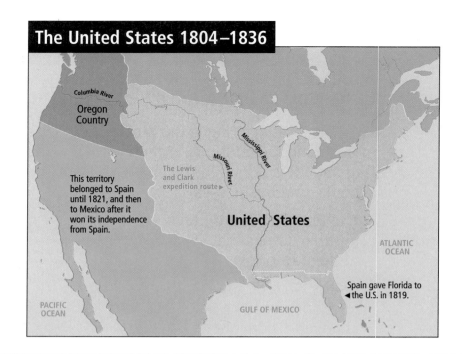

Oregon Country

Columbia River

This territory belonged to Spain until 1821, and then to Mexico after it won its independence from Spain.

The Lewis and Clark expedition route ▸

Missouri River

Mississippi River

United States

ATLANTIC OCEAN

Spain gave Florida to ◂ the U.S. in 1819.

PACIFIC OCEAN

GULF OF MEXICO

1804–1806
Lewis and Clark explored the West.

In 1804, two explorers, Meriwether Lewis and William Clark, journeyed through Louisiana and Oregon to the Pacific coast. They traveled along the Missouri and Columbia Rivers. As they explored, they created maps and took notes. It took them a year and a half to reach the Pacific. ★

Sacagawea

Lewis and Clark may not have been able to reach the Pacific Ocean without the help of Sacagawea, their translator and guide. She was a member of the Shoshone tribe. Sacagawea asked her relatives to help the explorers cross the Rocky Mountains before the winter snows. ★

1819
Florida became part of the United States.

Beginning in 1814, General Andrew Jackson lead American troops through Florida. They fought the Spanish until 1819 when the Spanish agreed to give Florida to the United States. ★

★ **1800s**

★ **1820s**

The United States 1845–1846

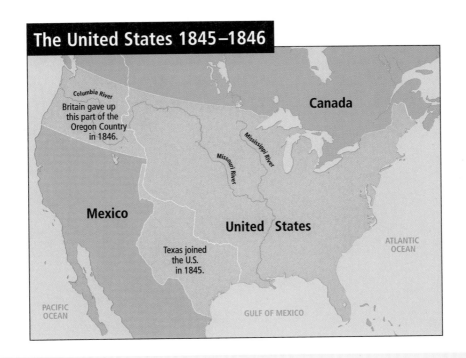

Columbia River
Britain gave up this part of the Oregon Country in 1846.

Canada

Mississippi River

Missouri River

Mexico

United States

ATLANTIC OCEAN

Texas joined the U.S. in 1845.

PACIFIC OCEAN

GULF OF MEXICO

1845
Texas became part of the United States.

So many Americans had moved to Texas that there were more American than Mexican citizens. People started fighting because of this. Sam Houston led a Texan army to victory in the Battle of San Jacinto. Mexico signed the Treaty of Velasco, which made Texas free from Mexico. Almost ten years later, the U.S. Congress offered to **annex**, or unite, Texas with the U.S. ★

1846
Britain gave up this part of the Oregon Country.

Many people had traveled by covered wagon across the U.S. to settle in the British-controlled Oregon Country. The settlers wanted the country to be a part of the United States. Because Great Britain did not want to go to war, they agreed to give up all the land south of the 49th parallel, which is now the Canadian border. ★

★1840s

The United States 1846–1848

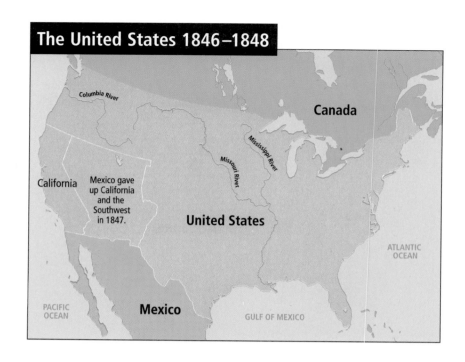

Columbia River

Canada

California

Mexico gave up California and the Southwest in 1847.

Mississippi River

Missouri River

United States

ATLANTIC OCEAN

PACIFIC OCEAN

Mexico

GULF OF MEXICO

CALIFORNIA REPUBLIC

Today's flag is based on the original flag.

1847

Mexico gave California and the Southwest to the U.S.

American settlers in the Mexican territory of California wanted to be free and become the Bear Flag Republic, named after the flag they designed. The United States sent armies and ships to help them. Mexico surrendered and signed the Treaty of Guadalupe Hidalgo, which gave the United States all of California and the Southwest. ★

1848

The California Gold Rush began.

Gold was discovered in California in 1848. As news spread about the discovery, thousands of Americans moved west to pan for gold. They were hoping to get rich. Very few people became rich, but many of them settled in California. ★

★1840s

★1850s

The United States 1862–1912

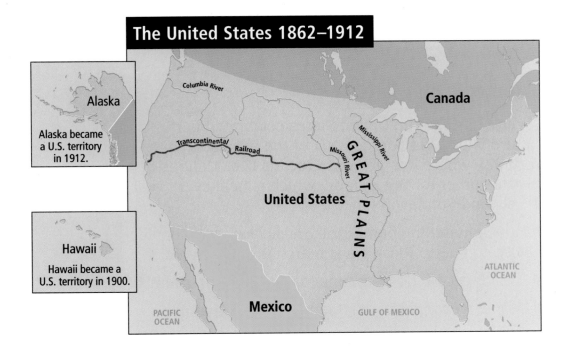

Alaska

Alaska became a U.S. territory in 1912.

Hawaii

Hawaii became a U.S. territory in 1900.

Columbia River

Transcontinental Railroad

Mississippi River

Missouri River

GREAT PLAINS

Canada

United States

ATLANTIC OCEAN

Mexico

PACIFIC OCEAN

GULF OF MEXICO

1862
Congress gave away free farmland with the Homestead Act.

By the mid-1800s, every part of the United States was settled except the Great Plains. The Homestead Act of 1862 was a law that said anyone who farmed on the Great Plains for five years could keep the land for free. Eventually, hard-working farmers turned the area into "America's breadbasket" and grew most of the food for the rest of the U.S. ★

1869
The first transcontinental railroad was finished.

In 1863, two companies began building railroads. One set of tracks went west from Nebraska; the other went east from California. In 1869, the two tracks joined in Promontory, Utah, to form a transcontinental railroad. This railroad made it possible for millions of people to travel west to establish farms and raise cattle. ★

★**1860s**

★**1870s**

June

Puerto Rican Day

Several cities in the United States celebrate Puerto Rican culture with a big parade. One of the biggest is in New York City where lots of Puerto Ricans live. Millions of people gather for this parade, which is held every year on the second Sunday in June.

- Floats, marching bands, folk musicians, and people waving Puerto Rican flags march up Fifth Avenue.

- Lots of people do traditional dances like the rhumba.

- People wear traditional Puerto Rican clothing like an embroidered *guayabera*, a long shirt for a man.

Father's Day

The third Sunday in June is a special day for fathers. That's when sons and daughters give their fathers gifts and cards to show their love.

- Father's Day is also a great time for children to go on a picnic, to a baseball game, or any place where they can be with their fathers.

- Often people send "Happy Father's Day" greetings to other men they respect like their uncles or grandfathers.

Dragon Boat Festival

In late June, on the fifth day of the fifth month of the Chinese lunar calendar, there are dragon boat races all over the world. These races are part of the Dragon Boat Festival, held in memory of an ancient Chinese poet named Qu Yuan.

When Qu Yuan was punished for saying bad things about his government, he jumped into a river and drowned. Today boat races are held in cities like Boston, New York City, and Honolulu to act out what his friends did to try to save Qu Yuan.

- Teams use boats that look like dragons. Since dragons are symbols of good luck, the boats are said to spread good luck as they race across the water.

- The teams race each other to a finish line. The team that wins shares the prize money.

July

Independence Day

Independence Day is the fourth of July. On this day, many Americans march in parades, wave the American flag, and watch fireworks at night. They are celebrating the time when America fought for and won its **independence**, or freedom, from Britain.

What events led to America's independence?

1773

The colonists took part in the Boston Tea Party.

In the 1700s, America belonged to Britain. The **colonists**, or the people living in colonial America, got tired of paying unfair British taxes on tea. They dressed as Mohawk Indians and protested by throwing the tea into the ocean. This was one of the events that led to the Revolutionary War. ★

1775

The Revolutionary War began.

On April 19, American soldiers fought against the British at Lexington and Concord in the first battle of the Revolutionary War. The soldiers were called "minutemen" because they were ready to fight "at a minute's notice." ★

★**1770s**

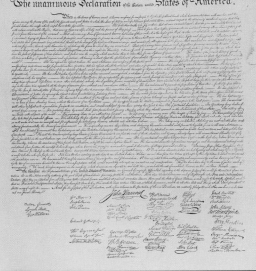

1781
The British surrended at Yorktown.

The last major battle of the Revolutionary War was fought in Yorktown, Virginia, in 1781. That's when the British surrendered to American General George Washington. ★

1776
The Declaration of Independence was signed.

On July 4, 1776, the American colonists signed the Declaration of Independence. This important paper stated that the thirteen American colonies were free from Britain. This meant that the colonies would no longer obey the laws of Great Britain or pay taxes to the British government. ★

1783
The Revolutionary War ended.

Benjamin Franklin, John Adams, John Jay, and Henry Laurens went to Paris to sign a peace treaty with the British. ★

★ **1780s**

Anniversary of the First Moon Walk

On July 20, 1969, the world watched as two American astronauts became the first human beings to walk on the moon.

- As astronaut Neil Armstrong stepped from the landing craft *Eagle*, he said, "That's one small step for a man, one giant leap for mankind."

- Armstrong and his partner, Edwin Aldrin, gathered samples of rocks and soil for over two and a half hours. Before they climbed back into the *Eagle*, they put an American flag in the ground.

Who are some other American astronauts? What did they do?

1961
Alan Shepard became the first American in space.

Alan Shepard traveled in space in *Freedom 7* for fifteen minutes. ★

1962
John Glenn, Jr., orbited the Earth.

John Glenn, Jr., was the first American to **orbit**, or go around, the Earth. His spacecraft, *Mercury 6*, flew around the Earth three times in a little over four and a half hours. ★

1965
Edward H. White II walked in space.

The first American to go outside the spacecraft while in space was Edward H. White II. He was on this spacewalk outside of *Gemini 4* for 21 minutes. ★

1983
Sally Ride became the first American woman in space.

Sally Ride and four other astronauts went on a six-day flight in the space shuttle, *Challenger*. ★

★ 1960s ★ 1970s ★ 1980s

Traditional dancing

Native American Powwows

From August 12–17 Native Americans get together for the Inter-Tribal Indian Ceremonial at Red Rock State Park in Gallup, New Mexico. This is just one of many powwows held by Native Americans across the United States throughout the year.

A powwow is a gathering of Native Americans to celebrate their culture and heritage.

■ Families and friends meet every year for reunions.

■ Some groups of people play drums and sing while others tape-record the traditional music. Later, people will use the tapes to practice singing and dancing.

■ Family members of all ages compete in dance contests. They can win prizes for traditional, fancy, grass, or jingle-dress dancing.

■ There are also special ceremonies. During an **introduction ceremony**, a family dances to introduce their child as a powwow dancer.

Jingle dress

Playing the drums

September

Labor Day

Americans honor working people on the first Monday in September. Many workers get this day off so they can rest and enjoy the holiday. Labor Day is usually the last day of summer vacation for many students, too! People arrange special events like parades, picnics, and concerts to celebrate the occasion.

Labor Day began during a period of time called the Industrial Revolution. That was a time when people invented many new products, businesses got bigger, more machines made more products, and more people moved to the cities to work in factories.

How did life change during the Industrial Revolution?

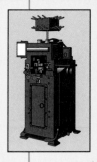

1882
Jan Matzeliger invented a shoe machine.

Jan Matzeliger invented the shoe-lasting machine to shape and then attach the top of a shoe to its sole. Shoes cost a lot less because this machine could do what had been done before by hand. ★

1876
Alexander Graham Bell invented the telephone.

Alexander Bell's first telephone was one-way, which meant that only one person could talk while the other listened. Within a year, Bell made a two-way telephone. As people started using this invention, communication became faster and easier for everyone around the world. ★

1879
Thomas Edison invented the electric light bulb.

Thomas Edison was one of America's greatest inventors. He is best known for inventing a practical light bulb, but he also invented many other things including the phonograph which recorded and replayed sounds. Edison's inventions were so useful that soon everyone had them in their homes. ★

★**1870s**

★**1880s**

Expanding Factories and New Inventions

From the mid-1800s to the early 1900s, many people started working in factories. At that time, they had to work twelve to sixteen hours a day for very little money. To improve the unfair working conditions, many workers formed groups called unions. The unions asked factory owners for better pay and safer workplaces.

This was also a time when many Americans thought of new things to make and new ways to do things. From those ideas and inventions, people began to make more and more products and new companies and businesses were formed.

1886

Samuel Gompers became a labor leader.

Samuel Gompers became an important leader of a large labor union. He worked hard to establish labor laws for all workers, including women and children. These laws led to improvements in working conditions and limited the number of hours people had to work. ★

1889

Jane Addams opened Hull House for workers.

During the late 1800s, many immigrants came to the city of Chicago to work. Jane Addams and another social worker created a special center called Hull House to help immigrants learn English and train for new jobs. With Addams's help, immigrants were able to demand fair working conditions. ★

1913

Henry Ford started the first modern assembly line.

Henry Ford created the modern assembly line, which made it faster and less expensive to build cars. Workers would do only one job such as tightening bolts as the cars moved past them on a conveyor belt. Because of the assembly line process, Ford was able to build the first car that many people could afford, the Model T. ★

★ **1890s**   ★ **1900s**   ★ **1910s**

Rosh Hashanah and Yom Kippur

In September in the Hebrew month *Tishri*, people celebrate the Jewish New Year.

Rosh Hashanah begins on the first day of *Tishri* and usually lasts for two days. *Rosh Hashanah* means "beginning (or head) of the year."

■ Some people give each other cards, greetings, and good wishes.

■ People fix a special treat made of apple slices dipped in honey. The honey stands for hope for a sweet new year!

Yom Kippur is from sunset on the ninth day of *Tishri* until three stars appear in the sky after the tenth day.

■ People do not work but go to their synagogue or temple to ask forgiveness and promise to make the new year a good one.

■ In order to concentrate on their religion, people do not eat or drink anything for twenty-four hours. Then they have a festive meal.

Citizenship Day

September 17 is Citizenship Day. It begins a week-long celebration called Constitution Week. People give speeches and display the American flag to show that they are proud to be American citizens.

In 1952, President Harry S. Truman established Citizenship Day to honor the date the United States Constitution was signed in 1787. Then in 1956, Congress established Constitution Week which lasts from September 17 through September 23. Congress did this because the Constitution is such an important document and symbol of freedom for all Americans.

What are some other symbols of the United States?

The Capitol

This building is located in Washington, D.C., the capital of the United States. It is where people in Congress work together to make laws. The Capitol stands for democracy. That's the kind of government that gives people the right to govern themselves.

The Great Seal of the United States

This **emblem**, or picture, is printed on official documents and on the one dollar bill. It shows an American bald eagle holding an olive branch and arrows. The olive branch is a symbol of peace. The arrows stand for strength. The paper, or scroll, in the eagle's beak says, *E pluribus unum.* That's Latin for "one (nation) out of many (states)."

Uncle Sam

Uncle Sam is a made-up man who stands for the United States. His name probably came from the initials U.S., the abbreviation for **U**nited **S**tates. You'll see Uncle Sam on posters and cartoons. You might also see him marching in a parade! He'll always be dressed in America's colors: red, white, and blue.

Columbus Day

On the second Monday in October, people remember Christopher Columbus's trip to the Americas in 1492. Columbus was an Italian sea captain who had been looking for a way to sail from Europe to China and India. He landed on an island in the Bahamas on October 12, 1492.

■ After Columbus, explorers from other countries sailed to the Americas. They were looking for gold, silver, spices, and other valuable things. They also wanted to conquer new lands for their countries.

■ Columbus and the other explorers called the land the "New World" because it was new to them. Native Americans had lived in the Americas for thousands of years before the explorers arrived.

Who were some of the explorers?

1492
Christopher Columbus landed in the Bahamas.

Christopher Columbus made four trips to the "New World." He explored the Bahamas, Puerto Rico, Cuba, the Dominican Republic, Jamaica, Trinidad, Venezuela, and Central America. ★

1497
John Cabot explored the northeastern American coast.

John Cabot, an Italian sea captain, made two trips to the northeastern American coast. His journeys began the exploration and settlement of North America. ★

1513
Juan Ponce de León landed in Florida.

Juan Ponce de León came from Spain. He was the first explorer to land in Florida. Some people say he was seeking the Fountain of Youth, a magical water that would keep him young forever. ★

★ **1490s**   ★ **1500s**   ★ **1510s**

Native North America

There were many different Native American tribes living in North America when the explorers arrived. Each tribe had its own language, culture, and way of life.

Some Native Americans were farmers who stayed in one place. Others were hunters who moved all year long, following the migrations of animals. One thing the tribes had in common was their deep respect for the land and close relationship with nature.

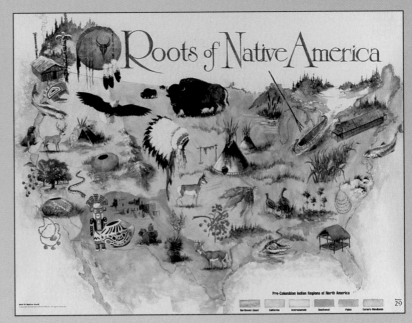

Native Americans taught explorers how to grow and prepare vegetables like tomatoes and corn. Europeans brought horses which the Native Americans used to follow and hunt migrating animals.

Sadly, Europeans brought diseases, and many Native Americans died. The explorers also thought they had the right to take whatever land they wanted. Many Native Americans died fighting for their homes.

1540–1542
Francisco de Coronado explored the Southwest.

Francisco Vázquez de Coronado of Spain traveled through much of the Southwest, including the villages of the Zuni tribes. ★

1565
Don Pedro Menéndez de Avilés established a fort in Florida.

Don Pedro Menéndez de Avilés also came from Spain. He established a settlement at St. Augustine, Florida, which is now the oldest city in the United States. ★

★ **1540s**   ★ **1550s**   ★ **1560s**

Halloween

On October 31, children and adults celebrate Halloween. It is a time to have fun and be creative.

- People put jack-o'-lanterns on their porches. A jack-o'-lantern is made from a hollow pumpkin with a face carved in it.

- Lots of children dress in costumes and masks and go to different houses in their neighborhoods. The children knock on the door and, when someone opens it, they say, "Trick or treat!" Then they get candy or other treats.

- Some families have Halloween parties instead of going out. One popular game at this kind of party is "bobbing for apples." A large tub is filled with water, and then apples are put in the water. Two players kneel next to the tub. Each player tries to bite an apple and take it out of the water. The first one to do this wins!

Day of the Dead

On November 1 and 2, for the Day of the Dead, people remember friends and relatives who have died.

- Families create an **altar**, or a memorial table, at home. These altars are decorated with candles, flowers, fruits, chocolate, and photographs of people who have died.

- People make skeleton figures and papier-mâché masks that look like skulls. They wear the masks as they walk to a cemetery to honor those who have died.

November

Veterans Day

On November 11, Americans honor veterans who have fought in wars for the United States. All over the country there are parades and speeches to thank veterans for their service to the United States and its people.

At the end of World War I, President Woodrow Wilson named November 11 Armistice Day. An **armistice** is an agreement between countries to stop fighting a war. It was a day to celebrate peace and the end of that war. Later on, the name was changed to Veterans Day to honor veterans of all American wars: World Wars I and II, the Korean War, the Vietnam War, and the Persian Gulf War.

What happened during World Wars I and II?

1914–1918
World War I

World War I was the first war involving countries from all over the world. Germany, Austria, Hungary, and Turkey formed a group called the Central Powers. They fought against Britain, France, the United States, and Russia, who were called the Allied Powers. The Allies won the war in 1918.★

1939–1945
World War II

In the late 1930s, **dictators** in Germany, Italy, and Japan (the Axis Powers) used their armies to invade their neighboring countries. A dictator is a ruler who has complete control over a country. Britain and France (the Allied forces) declared war on Germany. The United States joined the war in 1941, when the Japanese attacked Pearl Harbor, Hawaii, by surprise. Germany and Japan surrendered in 1945.★

★ **1910s** ★ **1920s** ★ **1930s** ★ **1940s**

Thanksgiving

The fourth Thursday in November is a very special day for Americans. Thanksgiving is a day when people give thanks for all the good things in their lives.

- Families and friends gather together for a large meal. Some traditional Thanksgiving dishes are baked turkey, sweet potatoes, cranberry sauce, and pumpkin pie.

- Before eating, someone may give thanks for the food on the table and for being together.

The celebration of Thanksgiving began when settlers arrived in North America. The first Thanksgiving meal took place when some of those settlers gave thanks for a good harvest after a difficult winter.

When did English settlers arrive in North America? What was their life like?

1585
The first English settlers arrived in North America.

The settlers arrived on what is now Roanoke Island off the coast of North Carolina. They tried to start a colony there, but living in an unfamiliar place was too hard so they returned to England. ★

1607
Jamestown became the first permanent English colony.

The settlers in colonies like Jamestown survived because they learned how to make their own supplies and grow their own food. At first the settlers lived in homes in holes in the ground with bark roofs. Later, they used lumber to build wooden houses. They learned how to fish and dig for clams on the beaches. They hunted for deer, geese, ducks, and wild turkeys in the woods. Many settlers became farmers and grew corn, potatoes, beans, wheat, rye, and oats. ★

★ **1580s**   ★ **1590s**   ★ **1600s**

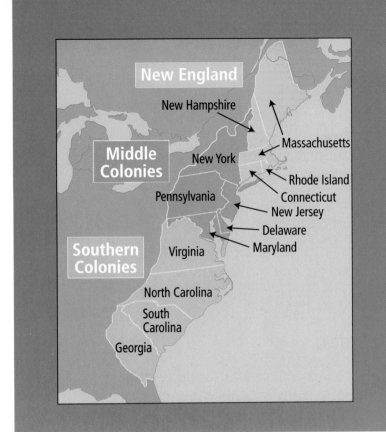

The Thirteen Original Colonies

The settlers sold things to each other and to other countries like England. Settlers in New England sold fur and lumber. People in the Middle Colonies made glass, leather, and iron tools. Farmers in the Southern Colonies sold tobacco which people said was worth its weight in silver.

1620
The Pilgrims wrote the Mayflower Compact.

Many of the settlers wanted to govern themselves. The Pilgrims who settled in Massachusetts wrote and signed the Mayflower Compact, an agreement to make and follow fair and equal laws. The United States government is based on some of the same ideas that these settlers had.★

1621
The event which is now called Thanksgiving was celebrated in the Plymouth Colony.

In 1621, the Pilgrims in Plymouth Colony had survived a very difficult winter because a member of a Native American tribe, the Wampanoag, had taught them to fish, hunt, and plant corn. To celebrate their first harvest, the settlers had a three day celebration and invited the Wampanoag. ★

1630
The Massachusetts Bay Colony formed.

In England in the 1600s, people called Puritans formed the Massachusetts Bay Company. That company sent lots of families to New England. The Puritans took everything they would need such as farm animals, tools and clothing. They first settled in Boston, Massachusetts.★

★**1620s**

★**1630s**

Hanukkah

For eight days in December, families celebrate the Jewish Festival of Lights, Hanukkah.

■ People light a candle each night of the holiday on a special nine-branched candleholder called a *menorah*.

■ Children often play a game with a *dreidl*. A *dreidl* is a spinning top with Hebrew letters on it.

Christmas

December 25 is a Christian holiday that celebrates the birth of Jesus Christ.

■ During the Christmas season, many people like to sing songs called Christmas carols.

■ Families and friends give each other gifts and often put them under decorated trees. Children believe that a character named Santa Claus brings them gifts if they are good.

Kwanzaa

African Americans celebrate Kwanzaa from December 26 through January 1.

■ On each day, someone lights a candle in a *kinara*, a special candleholder. Each candle represents a value like unity or creativity.

■ Families have a feast called *karamu*. During *karamu*, people wear traditional African clothes, play music, and dance.

New Year's Eve

On the Roman calendar, December 31 is the last day of the year. On this day, many people stay up until midnight. That's when the new year officially begins. At midnight, they throw confetti, blow horns, and wish each other "Happy New Year!"

If you want to be part of a great New Year's Eve celebration, where should you go?

Go to New York City!

One of the biggest New Year's Eve celebrations in the United States takes place in Times Square. A ball of lights slowly drops from the top of a tower just before midnight. When the ball reaches the bottom, at exactly midnight, thousands of people cheer loudly to welcome the new year.

New York City

Facts

■ Over 7 million people live in New York City. It is the most populated city in the United States.

■ The Empire State Building, one of the tallest skyscrapers in the world, is in this city.

■ Many of the world's largest banks are here, too. That's why New York City is often called the "financial center of the world"... and it's a great place to celebrate the new year.

U.S.A. Time Line

Up to the 1400s

Native America

Native Americans lived in America thousands of years before the first Europeans arrived. Each Native American tribe had its own language, culture, and way of life. ★

1500s

Europeans Explore North America

From the late 1400s through the 1600s, many explorers sailed to America from Europe. They came to find land and claim it for their countries. ★

1600s

Settlers Form Colonies

Groups of European settlers like the Puritans and the Pilgrims moved to America to build villages and towns called colonies. The colonists sold products to each other and to other countries. ★

1700s

American Revolution

By the 1760s, there were thirteen colonies that belonged to Britain. The colonists fought to be free because they wanted their own laws. They won their independence in 1783. ★

1800s

Westward Expansion

At first, most of the people settled in the East, but starting in the 1800s, the U.S. bought and fought for more land. Soon people called *pioneers* moved into the open spaces in the Midwest and the West. ★

Civil War

The people in the northern and southern parts of the United States led very different lifestyles. They disagreed so strongly about slavery and their ways of life that they fought the Civil War. The war and slavery ended in 1865 when the North won the Civil War. ★

Industrial Revolution

From the 1860s to the 1900s, many companies started using machines to make products faster. It was also a time when new inventions like the light bulb and the telephone made people's lives easier. ★

Becoming a World Leader
By the 1900s, the U.S. was greatly respected for its fine products and ability to defend itself. It had become a strong influence in the world.★

World War I (1914–1918)

The Great Depression
When many people lost money in the stock market crash of 1929, they were left without homes or jobs. A horrible drought in the Midwest called the Dust Bowl made things even worse. The depression lasted for many years.★

World War II (1941–1945)

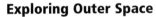

Exploring Outer Space
In the 1960s, American astronauts began journeys into outer space. The space program continues today as the astronauts help build an international laboratory in space and plan new missions.★

Civil Rights Movement
Beginning in the 1960s, many Americans marched and demonstrated for equal rights for black Americans. Several laws were passed that helped stop discrimination.★

Information Age
Today many Americans use computers to give and receive information. With programs like electronic mail and the Internet, people around the world are able to quickly and easily communicate with each other.★

2000s

Grammar Practice

Sentences

A. Choose an ending from the box to finish each sentence. Write the sentence.

mighty arms!	he do?
a strong man.	is Paul Bunyan.
amaze you!	he?
appearance.	famous lumberjack.

1. **statement**   The statue shows ____a strong man.____

2. **exclamation**   Wow, he has ____mighty arms!____

3. **question**   Who is ____he?____

4. **statement**   His name ____is Paul Bunyan.____

5. **command**   Describe his ____appearance.____

6. **question**   What did ____he do?____

7. **command**   Listen to the story of this ____famous lumberjack.____

8. **exclamation**   The story of Paul Bunyan will ____amaze you!____

B. Make up questions about this picture. Write them down. Then trade papers with a partner and answer the questions.

Answers will vary.

1. Is _____?
2. Who _____?
3. When _____?
4. Can _____?
5. Why _____?
6. How _____?
7. Are _____?
8. Will _____?
9. What _____?
10. Does _____?

C. Work with a partner to add a subject. Write the sentences.

Answers will vary.

1.

	worked with Paul Bunyan.
subject	**predicate**

3.

	cleared trees from the land.
subject	**predicate**

2.

	was a lumberjack.
subject	**predicate**

4.

	watched Paul Bunyan.
subject	**predicate**

D. Work with a partner to add a predicate. Write the sentences.

Answers will vary.

1.

Paul and Babe	
subject	**predicate**

3.

North Dakota	
subject	**predicate**

2.

Stories about Paul	
subject	**predicate**

4.

Every morning, Babe	
subject	**predicate**

E. Make each sentence you wrote in C and D into a question.

Example: Did your grandfather work with Paul Bunyan? Answers will vary.

F. Make each sentence you wrote in C and D into a negative sentence.

Example: My grandfather did **not** work with Paul Bunyan. Answers will vary.

G. Choose *and*, *but*, or *or* to join each pair of sentences. Write the compound sentences.

1. There were no more trees to cut down in North Dakota. Paul Bunyan wanted to keep working. (**but**)/ or

There were no more trees to cut down in North Dakota, but Paul Bunyan wanted to keep working.

2. Paul could stay in North Dakota and be bored. He could go west to find more trees. but /(**or**)

Paul could stay in North Dakota and be bored, or he could go west and find more trees.

3. Paul and Babe decided to go west. They said good-bye to their friends. but /(**and**)

Paul and Babe decided to go west, and they said good-bye to their friends.

4. On the way, Paul's sharp pole made the Grand Canyon. Babe's footsteps made paths through the Cascade Mountains. or /(**and**)

On the way, Paul's sharp pole made the Grand Canyon, and Babe's footsteps made paths through the Cascade Mountains.

5. At first, the West was full of trees. Paul and Babe cut them down quickly. (**but**)/ or

At first, the West was full of trees, but Paul and Babe cut them down quickly.

6. Now Paul and Babe could quit working. They could go to find more trees. (**or**)/ and

Now Paul and Babe could quit working, or they could go to find more trees.

Nouns

A. Write these sentences. Add the correct noun.

Gold Room	room	Galveston	corner
man	Broadway	James M. Brown	museum

1. Luisa went on a tour of this house in ____Galveston____.

2. Its address is 2328 ____Broadway____.

3. It is on the ____corner____ of the street.

4. The house is now a ____museum____ in Galveston.

5. Luisa read about the ____man____ who built Ashton Villa.

6. His name was ____James M. Brown____.

7. One room in Ashton Villa is named the ____Gold Room____.

8. Luisa thought it was the most beautiful ____room____ in the house.

B. Write the plural of each noun. Then copy the paragraph and add the new words.

1. beach   **3.** child   **5.** roof   **7.** wave

2. shell   **4.** city   **6.** half   **7.** foot

      Galveston is one of the best __cities__ to visit. It has many places that are fun for parents and their __children__. People can visit the sandy __beaches__. They can pick up colorful __shells__, too. One beach is Stewart Beach. It is behind a seawall that is 17 __feet__ high. At this beach, kids can play in the __waves__, or they can fly kites over the __roofs__ of nearby homes. Some visitors walk through a life-size maze called "Amaze'N Texas." At the end, they make sure that both __halves__ of their group made it through!

C. Write these sentences, adding the red word to the blank. Make the red word plural if you need to.

kind
1. There are many __kinds__ of vehicles to see in Galveston.

equipment
2. People go to Seawolf Park to see military __equipment__ like a real World War II submarine.

information
3. At the Lone Star Flight Museum there is __information__ on more than 40 restored planes.

lunch
4. Some people ride the Galveston Island Trolley car to the beach to eat the __lunches__ they've packed.

time
5. Others ride on the *Colonel* paddle boat and imagine going back in __time__ to the 1800s.

water
6. Many people tour the Tall Ship *Elissa* which sits in the __water__ in the Galveston port.

group
7. The displays in the Railroad Museum are popular with __groups__ of people who visit the city.

lunch
8. These visitors often eat __lunch__ at the Santa Fe Choo Choo Diner there.

D. Write these sentences. Add the correct word.

1. Look at ___(these)/ a___ pictures I took at Moody Gardens.

2. I went to ___(the)/ some___ Rainforest Pyramid there.

walking stick

3. Inside there is ___(a)/ some___ special place to watch caterpillars turn into butterflies.

4. I got to watch ___a /(some)___ butterflies form!

5. This picture shows ___some /(an)___ insect called a walking stick.

6. I spent over ___(an)/ a___ hour looking at all the insects.

7. ___(That)/ An___ walking stick was my favorite insect in the Rainforest Pyramid.

8. This is a picture of ___(a)/ an___ macaw I saw sitting in a tree.

macaw

9. ___(The)/ Some___ macaw was very colorful.

10. It was very safe in ___a /(the)___ tall trees.

11. ___(Those)/ That___ trees were over 55 feet tall!

bat

12. ___An /(This)___ picture shows one of the bats.

13. Later, I saw ___(a)/ the___ fruit bat, too.

14. I had ___a /(an)___ interesting day at Moody Gardens!

E. Write this paragraph. Add *the* where there is a blank only if you need to.

In _____ April, we went to Galveston's Grand KIDS Festival. There were lots of arts and crafts booths. My favorite booth was ___the___ Swedish woodcarving one. ___The___ woman at ___the___ booth even spoke _____ Swedish! We ate lots of food, including burritos from _____ Rita's Tacos. On the way home, we stopped at _____ Stewart Beach and went _____ swimming.

F. Write these sentences.
Add the correct possessive noun.

1. _(Luisa Rafael's) / Luisa Rafaels'_ house is near the water.

2. In the front yard is her _dads' / (dad's)_ boat.

3. Today, her family is going on a fishing trip near one of _Galvestons' / (Galveston's)_ jetties.

4. All of the family is going, including _(Luisa's) / Luisas'_ two older brothers.

5. Catching crabs is her _(brothers') / brother's_ favorite thing to do.

6. The boys have learned how to take crabs off their lines so that they don't get pinched by the _crab's / (crabs')_ claws!

7. Luisa likes to fish for trout with her _(mom's) / moms'_ fishing pole.

8. She drops the line into the _bays' / (bay's)_ warm water.

9. The fish start nibbling at the bait on the _(hook's) / hooks'_ sharp point.

10. At the end of the day, the _(boys') / boy's_ bucket is full of crabs.

11. The five fish Luisa caught flop around on the _(boat's) / boats'_ deck.

12. For dinner tonight, the Rafaels will be eating the _(world's) / worlds'_ best seafood!

G. Write the paragraph. Replace the underlined words with specific nouns about a city you know. Answers will vary.

Take a stroll down <u>the street</u>. Delicious smells come from <u>the café</u>. You can almost taste <u>the food</u>. Pause to look in the store windows. Look at <u>all the things</u> displayed there. Listen, can you hear <u>music</u> playing? It's coming from <u>the shop</u>. Have fun visiting <u>this city</u>!

H. Write a paragraph about a place you have visited. Use specific nouns. Answers will vary.

Pronouns

Lisa   Jasmine   Tom

A. **Write these sentences.**
Add the correct pronoun.

1. One day at practice, a bee buzzed Lisa. "It might sting <u>(me)/ he</u>, " she said.

2. "Just stand still," Tom said to <u>she /(her)</u>.

3. Lisa stood very still, but the bee kept buzzing <u>him /(her)</u>.

4. <u>I /(It)</u> buzzed around her ears and her eyes.

5. Jasmine said, "<u>They /(You)</u> will be okay in a minute."

6. Then the bee left as fast as <u>you /(it)</u> came!

7. "Whew," said Lisa. "<u>He /(I)</u> really don't like bees."

8. "But <u>it /(they)</u> are not as scary as snakes," said Jasmine.

9. "Snakes?" asked Tom. "<u>We /(They)</u> aren't scary at all!"

10. "Are you sure <u>(you)/ I</u> aren't afraid of snakes?" the girls asked.

11. "<u>(I)/ She</u> am sure," said Tom.

12. The girls didn't believe <u>(him)/ we</u>.

13. "<u>(We)/ Us</u> will see," they said to each other.

14. The girls knew a little snake was crawling toward <u>they /(them)</u>.

15. Tom jumped. <u>(He)/ She</u> was scared!

16. "That snake is coming right at <u>we /(us)</u>!" yelled Tom.

17. "Just stand still," Lisa said to <u>he /(him)</u>.

18. "<u>(You)/ Him</u> will be okay in a minute," Jasmine said.

One	More Than One
I	we
you	you
he, she, it	they

One	More Than One
me	us
you	you
him, her, it	them

Lisa

Juan

Tom

Jasmine

Coach

B. Write these sentences. Add the correct pronoun.

1. Tom and his friends were at _(their)/ theirs_ soccer practice. Tom and Lisa found a backpack.

2. They asked Juan, "Is this backpack _(yours)/ your_ ?"

3. Juan said, "No. Ask Jasmine. Maybe it's _(hers)/ theirs_ ."

4. "I've got _my /(mine)_ ," Jasmine said.

5. "Coach! Someone left a backpack on the field. Our friends say it isn't _their /(theirs)_ ."

6. "Oh! That's _(my)/ yours_ backpack," said the coach. "I've been looking everywhere for it!"

One	More Than One
my	our
your	your
his, her, its	their

One	More Than One
mine	ours
yours	yours
his, hers	theirs

C. Write these sentences. Add the correct pronoun.

1. Oh good, _anything /(someone)_ brought juice.

2. Has _(anyone)/ something_ seen my soda?

3. _Everything /(Somebody)_ put a napkin over it!

4. Did _(everyone)/ someone_ get enough to eat?

D. Write this paragraph. Add a pronoun from the box for each blank.

he	him	his
it	us	their

   Mr. Brown is our soccer coach. All of the Bobcat players like

___him___. We practice hard, but Mr. Brown is always fair.

___He___ lets everyone have a chance to play during the games.

When we win a game, he celebrates with ___us___. He and his

wife had a party for us after we beat the Eagles. They invited all

the players and the fans to ___their___ house. It was fun!

Sometimes Mr. Brown loses things. One time he lost ___his___

lucky cap. We found ___it___ right there in his pocket!

E. Write a paragraph about your favorite coach or teacher.
Answers will vary.

Adjectives

A. Write these sentences. Add the correct adjective from the box.

1. Just ___one___ berry isn't enough for the toucan.

2. This ___hungry___ bird gobbles up all the berries.

3. The toucan uses its ___sharp___ beak to pick them from the tree.

4. It loves berries and other kinds of ___ripe___ fruit.

| hungry |
| one |
| ripe |
| sharp |

5. The toucan is always squawking. It is very ___noisy___!

6. The toucan lives in the ___hot___ rainforest.

7. Its nest is in a ___hollow___ trunk of a tree.

8. The toucan likes to sit on the ___top___ branches of a tree.

| noisy |
| hot |
| top |
| hollow |

B. Write these sentences. Add the correct adjective.

1. There are __(many)/ much__ different kinds of flowers in the rainforest.

2. Some flowers are very colorful, but others have __(only a little)/ only a few__ color.

3. The hibiscus does not have __many /(much)__ smell, but it is very colorful.

4. The water lily has __much /(many)__ petals. It smells like butterscotch and pineapple.

5. __(Many)/ Much__ people do not like the horrible smell of the arum lily.

6. Some orchids have __(several)/ not much__ spots on their petals.

7. Most orchids have __only a little /(only a few)__ leaves on them.

8. The different flowers add so __(much)/ many__ beauty to the rainforest.

C. Write these sentences. Add *-er* or *-est* to the red adjective to make a comparison.

wet **1.** Monkeys and sloths both live in the ___wettest___ place in the world. Yet, these animals have many differences.

slow **2.** Of the two animals, the sloth is ___slower___.

small **3.** A sloth's tail is ___smaller___ than a monkey's tail.

big **4.** A monkey has one of the ___biggest___ and most useful tails in the animal world.

large **5.** A sloth has ___larger___ claws than a monkey.

sloth

hungry **6.** A monkey eats all day and is always ___hungrier___ than a sloth.

quiet **7.** The sloth doesn't make much noise; it is ___quieter___ than a monkey.

noisy **8.** A monkey is one of the ___noisiest___ animals in the rainforest!

D. Write these sentences. Add the correct word.

1. Ms. Steinberg's class went to the rainforest exhibit. They talked about what they liked the ___more / (most)___ .

2. Nina said the jaguar had a ___(good) / best___ disguise.

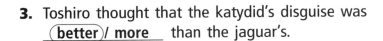

katydid

3. Toshiro thought that the katydid's disguise was ___(better) / more___ than the jaguar's.

4. They both agreed that the walking stick had the ___better / (best)___ disguise of all.

walking stick

5. Rita thought that the spotted, brown snake was the ___some / (most)___ frightening snake.

6. Tony felt that the long, green snake was ___some / (more)___ frightening than the brown one.

7. Everyone agreed that the sloth was the ___less / (least)___ active animal there!

8. The toucan was pretty ___(bad) / worse___ at keeping quiet.

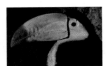

9. The monkey was ___(worse) / worst___ , though!

toucan

10. Everyone said that their ___little / (least)___ favorite thing was going home!

E. Write this paragraph. Add an adjective to each sentence.

Answers will vary.

Our zoo has a _____ rainforest exhibit. Inside, the air feels _____ . There are _____ vines hanging from the trees. _____ spiders crawl on the ground. You can see _____ butterflies fluttering through the air. Hanging from the branches are _____ monkeys. In the background, you can hear a _____ waterfall. This exhibit is _____ !

monkey

F. Write a description of an animal that lives in the rainforest. Use adjectives to help your readers picture the animal clearly.

Answers will vary.

Verbs

A. Write each sentence and add the verb.

1. At first the sky ___is___ clear.

2. Then the clouds ___roll___ in.

3. They ___look___ almost black.

4. Something ___flashes___ across the sky.

is
flashes
roll
look

5. It ___is___ lightning!

6. I ___hear___ the loud thunder.

7. Then the rain ___falls___ from the sky.

8. The raindrops ___are___ very cold and wet.

is
are
falls
hear

B. Write each sentence and add the verb. Then circle each helping verb.

1. The weather reporter says it ___(will) turn___ warmer today.

2. We ___(can) wear___ our T-shirts and shorts.

3. The weather ___(is) changing___ .

can wear
is changing
will turn

4. The flowers ___(should) bloom___ now.

5. The birds ___(might) return___ .

6. Spring ___(has) arrived___ !

might return
has arrived
should bloom

C. Write each sentence in Exercise B again. Add the word not.

1. The weather reporter says it will not turn warmer today.
2. We cannot wear our T-shirts and shorts.
3. The weather is not changing.
4. The flowers should not bloom now.
5. The birds might not return.
6. Spring has not arrived!

D. Write each sentence and add the verb.

1. In winter, the sun __rise / (rises)__ later in the morning.

2. The sky __get / (gets)__ dark early, too.

3. Some people __(want) / wants__ winter to end.

4. They __(like) / likes__ the long days of summer.

5. I __(prefer) / perfers__ winter, though.

6. To me, cold air __seem / (seems)__ fresher than hot air.

7. My favorite sport __begin / (begins)__ in winter, too.

8. I __(see) / sees__ all the hockey games on TV.

9. I also __(play) / plays__ hockey every afternoon.

10. It __keep / (keeps)__ me in shape!

E. Write each sentence and add the correct form of the red verb.

say   1. The weather reporter ___says___ it will hail this morning.

love   2. My sister ___loves___ the hail.

stay   3. She never ___stays___ inside when it is hailing.

watch   4. She always ___watches___ it from the front porch.

fly   5. She likes how the hail ___flies___ through the air.

bounce   6. She giggles as it ___bounces___ off the street.

play   7. She even ___plays___ in it if the hail stones are small.

try   8. She ___tries___ to catch the hail in her hands.

catch   9. Sometimes she ___catches___ a few.

miss   10. Most of the time, though, she ___misses___!

F. **Add *-ing* to each red verb. Then write each sentence and add the verb.**

watch   **1.** I am ____watching____ the 6:00 p.m. TV weather report.

describe   **2.** The reporter is ____describing____ weather around the country.

form   **3.** Hurricanes are ____forming____ off the coast of Florida.

rise   **4.** Some rivers are ____rising____ in the Midwest.

drop   **5.** The temperature is ____dropping____ in Maine.

fall   **6.** Hail is ____falling____ on North Dakota.

come   **7.** Storms are ____coming____ to the Southwest.

get   **8.** California is ____getting____ lots of rain.

shine   **9.** The sun is ____shining____ in Texas.

hope   **10.** We are ____hoping____ for a warm day tomorrow.

G. **Add *-ed* to each red verb to make it tell about an action that happened in the past. Then write each sentence and add the verb.**

visit   **1.** A TV weather reporter ____visited____ our class yesterday.

stay   **2.** She ____stayed____ for two hours.

show   **3.** She ____showed____ us different thermometers.

measure   **4.** Everyone ____measured____ the air temperature.

study   **5.** Then we ____studied____ a poster with different clouds on it.

try   **6.** We ____tried____ to draw pictures of each kind.

create   **7.** The reporter ____created____ a cloud inside a jar.

clap   **8.** The whole class ____clapped____. It was amazing!

play   **9.** Before the reporter left, we ____played____ a guessing game about the weather.

plan   **10.** We also ____planned____ a time for her to come back again.

H. Write each sentence. Change the underlined verb to make it tell about an action that happened in the past. Use the chart on page 191 to help you.

1. In the morning, Mr. Cruz <u>sees</u> dark clouds. saw

2. He <u>finds</u> the weather report in the newspaper. found

3. The forecast <u>is</u> for a sunny day. was

4. Mr. Cruz <u>does</u> not believe it. did

5. He <u>takes</u> his umbrella just in case. took

6. The sky <u>gets</u> very dark at about 4:00 p.m. got

7. Mr. Cruz <u>hears</u> thunder. heard

8. Before long, there <u>are</u> raindrops coming down. were

9. On his way home, Mr. Cruz <u>keeps</u> his umbrella over his head. kept

10. He finally <u>runs</u> for a taxi to get out of the rain. ran

I. Write each sentence. Change the underlined verb to make it tell about an action that happened in the past.

1. Lihn <u>listens</u> to a story about a snowy day. listened

2. She <u>thinks</u> about snow. thought

3. She <u>finds</u> a picture of snow. found

4. It <u>looks</u> so white and pretty. looked

5. Lihn <u>wonders</u> about snowflakes. wondered

6. She <u>writes</u> a poem about snow. wrote

7. In her poem, Lihn <u>says</u> that it is cold and wet. said

8. She <u>names</u> her poem, "Does Snow Feel Soft?" named

9. She <u>brings</u> her poem to her teacher. brought

10. "Does Snow Feel Soft?" <u>makes</u> the teacher smile. made

J. Write this paragraph to tell about an action that will happen in the future.

will bring	is going to
am going to	are going to go

Tomorrow ___is going to___ be hot because it will be the first day in July. We ___are going to go___ to the lake. Mom and Dad ___will bring___ their rafts, but I ___am going to___ swim.

K. Write each sentence, using a contraction for the underlined words.

1. Tomorrow <u>we are</u> going to do weather projects. we're

2. <u>I would</u> like to make something to measure the amount of rain. I'd

3. It <u>should not</u> be hard to do. shouldn't

4. First <u>I will</u> cut off the top of a plastic bottle. I'll

5. Then <u>I am</u> going to mark the sides of the bottle. I'm

6. It <u>will not</u> work unless I put it outside! won't

7. I <u>cannot</u> forget to empty the bottle after it rains. can't

8. Otherwise, the measurement <u>would not</u> be right the next time it rains. wouldn't

L. Write the paragraph. Replace each underlined verb with a verb that is more colorful. Answers will vary.

The hot sun <u>was</u> directly overhead. Freddie <u>went</u> to the pool. Some people <u>were</u> in the wading pool. Freddie <u>looked</u> at the water. He <u>got</u> into the pool. "Aaah, I'm finally cool," he <u>said</u>.

M. Write a paragraph about something you did when the weather was *hot, cold, wet,* or *dry*. Use colorful verbs.
Answers will vary.

Adverbs

A. Write these sentences. Add the correct word.

1. The gymnasts are practicing (everywhere)/ nowhere in the gym.

2. Beto always performs good /(well) on the mat.

Mariah

3. Today he jumped (higher)/ highest than he has ever jumped before!

4. Beto's muscles are getting real /(really) strong.

5. Mariah tumbled smooth /(smoothly) on the balance beam.

6. Then she stood perfect /(perfectly) still.

7. She stepped more quick /(quickly) than usual across the beam, too.

8. The gymnasts improve when they practice (often)/ most often .

B. Write a paragraph about a sport. Use adverbs to describe how the players move and act. Answers will vary.

Prepositions

C. Where is the red dot? Write the correct answer.

1. The red dot is under /(in front of) the line.

2. The red dot is off /(in) the box.

3. The red dot is inside /(outside) the box.

4. The red dot is going around /(through) the tunnel.

D. Make more drawings of the line and the red dot. Trade papers with a partner and tell where the red dot is. Answers will vary.

E. Write each sentence and add the correct preposition.

1. My brother Tito and I were excited about the kite-flying contest __on /(in)__ March.

2. It was __(on)/ in__ the first Saturday in March.

3. __During /(After)__ breakfast that morning, we hurried to Grant Park.

4. The contest did not begin __(until)/ on__ noon.

5. Tito and I wanted to practice __on /(before)__ the contest.

6. We got our kite ready __(at)/ in__ 11:00 o'clock.

7. Tito flew the kite __after /(from)__ 11:00 to 12:00.

8. The wind blew nicely all morning __(before)/ in__ the start of the contest.

9. __During /(At)__ 12:00 o'clock, there was hardly any wind at all!

10. Our kite did not fly high __(during)/ on__ the contest, but we did win the "best design" award!

F. Write this paragraph. Add a phrase from the box for each blank.

around the kite	with a blue head	in his hand
for his birthday	to the beach	into the air

Daniel's uncle gave him a kite that looks like a red bird __with a blue head__. It was a gift __for his birthday__. Daniel and his uncle took the kite over __to the beach__. His uncle tossed the kite __into the air__ while Daniel held the string __in his hand__. The sea gulls circled __around the kite__ because they were very interested in the strange, new bird!

G. Write a paragraph about a kite or something else that flies. Include prepositions to tell about time, location, and direction.
Answers will vary.

Conjunctions

H. Write these paragraphs. Use conjunctions from the box to combine some sentences.

and	but	or

1. Jungi never misses an Eagles' baseball game. He'll go to the stadium. He'll watch the game on TV. The Eagles lost their last game. They won all the games before that.

1. Jungi never misses an Eagles' baseball game. He'll go to the stadium, or he'll watch the game on TV. The Eagles lost their last game, but they won all the games before that.

2. Robert Pérez is Jungi's favorite player. Robert is the pitcher. He is one of the best in the league. Robert could not play in the last game. Jungi thinks that is why the Eagles lost.

2. Robert Pérez is Jungi's favorite player. Robert is the pitcher, and he is one of the best in the league. Robert could not play in the last game, and Jungi thinks that is why the Eagles lost.

I. Write a paragraph about a team you like. Use the words *and*, *but*, and *or* at least once. Answers will vary.

Capital Letters

A. Write each sentence. Use capital letters correctly. Words to be capitalized are underscored in blue.

1. Today i am going on a whale-watching trip.
2. My friend richard yee will join me.
3. His mother, mrs. yee, might come, too.
4. Mr. ernie vega owns the boat.
5. His helper is Alice c. Beck.
6. she is a scientist who studies whales.
7. we will learn about whales from dr. Beck.
8. dr. Beck and i will watch for whales from the top of the boat.
9. last time Mr. Vega was the first to see a whale.
10. This time i hope that i am!

B. Write these sentences. Use capital letters correctly. Words to be capitalized are underscored in blue.

1. There is a great whale-watching boat in <u>boston</u>.

2. It is near <u>seaview</u> boulevard.

3. It's across from <u>central</u> <u>park</u>.

4. The boat is called *deep dreamer*.

5. Its captain has sailed all over the <u>atlantic</u> and <u>pacific</u> oceans.

6. He used to work for a <u>british</u> company.

7. He often sailed around the tip of <u>africa</u>.

8. He has even been to the <u>great</u> <u>barrier</u> <u>reef</u>.

9. In fact, he has sailed most of <u>earth's</u> oceans.

10. Now, he doesn't go far from the <u>massachusetts</u> coast.

C. Write this letter. Use abbreviations for the underlined words.

472 Lincoln <u>Avenue</u>   Ave.
Chicago, <u>Illinois</u> 60643   Il.
<u>Friday</u>, <u>October</u> 29, 2002   Fri., Oct.

Captain Boris Davidov
9 <u>East</u> 15th <u>Street</u>   E., St.
Boston, <u>Massachusetts</u> 02101   MA

Dear Captain Davidov,

My family and I wanted to go on a whale-watching trip next weekend: <u>Saturday</u>, <u>November</u> 6 or <u>Sunday</u>, <u>November</u> 7. Do you have room on your boat for four people on one of those days?   Sat., Nov., Sun., Nov.

Sincerely,

Claude Delors

D. Write each sentence. Use capital letters correctly. Words to be capitalized are underscored in blue.

1. The <u>boy</u> <u>scouts</u> are planning a whale-watching trip.

2. They're going during the first weekend in <u>september</u>.

3. It will be <u>labor</u> <u>day</u> weekend.

4. The scoutmaster told the boys, "<u>we</u> might see some gray whales."

5. He showed them a video, <u>the great whales</u>.

6. It was made by the <u>national</u> <u>geographic</u> <u>society</u>.

7. He also read them an article called "<u>protecting</u> the <u>gray</u> <u>whales</u>."

8. The boys could hardly wait for that <u>saturday</u>.

Punctuation

A. Write each sentence. Add the correct punctuation at the end of what each person says.

period

question mark

exclamation point

Aaron
1. Please show me the newspaper.

Dad
2. Would you like to see the ads?

3. Here is an ad for a used bike.

Aaron
4. Wow, it sounds great!

5. What is the price?

Dad
6. Call the number to find out.

Aaron
7. How much can I spend?

8. I've been dreaming about a bike forever!

B. Write each sentence. Add commas where they are needed.

comma

Aaron

Romero, it's

1. Mrs. Romero it's Aaron calling.

2. I wanted you to know that I can walk Brute

Friday,   Saturday, or Sunday.

Friday Saturday or Sunday.

Mrs. Romero

Oh, Saturday

3. Oh Saturday should be fine!

Saturday, isn't

4. But, wait, your school fair is Saturday isn't it?

Aaron

says, "You

5. As Dad always says "You have to be flexible."

big, gentle

6. I'm willing to take your big gentle dog for a walk anytime.

Mrs. Romero

1,000,000

7. I have 1000000 things to do on Saturday anyway.

warm, sunny

8. Plus, Sunday is supposed to be a warm sunny day.

Aaron

OK, I'll

9. OK I'll take Brute on Sunday.

Sunday, Mrs.

10. I'll see you Sunday Mrs. Romero.

C. Write this friendly letter. Add commas where they belong.

251 Ramos Drive

Tucson, AZ Tucson AZ 85737

3, 1999 April 3 1999

Sanchez,
Dear Mr. and Mrs. Sanchez

My mother said that you are looking for helpers for your garage sale. Can I help you set up? I can also help sell things. Please let me know if you want my help. Thank you.

neighbor,
Your neighbor

Jaime

D. **Write this business letter. Add commas, colons, and apostrophes where they are needed.**

248 Ramos Drive
Tucson, AZ Tucson AZ 85737
12, 1999 June 12 1999

comma

Ms. Ella Jefferson
ABC Publishers
12 Brown Avenue
Sunset NJ 07109 Sunset, NJ

colon

Dear Ms. Jefferson Jefferson:

Money, and
I read your book *Kids Make Money* and I learned a lot from it.
ideas: walking   neighbor's dog, helping
I tried these ideas walking my neighbors dog helping at
sales,
garage sales and delivering newspapers every morning from
5:30   7:00
530 to 700. I would like to buy your other book *Kids Make More*
Money, but   can't   it's
Money but I cant find it. Can you please tell me where its sold?
yours,
Sincerely yours

Jaime Santiago
Jaime Santiago

apostrophe

E. **Write each sentence. Add quotation marks and underlining where they are needed.**

underline

"How   money?"
1. How can I earn some money? Aaron asked his dad.

"Teenagers   Clean-up."
2. His dad had seen a sign that said, Teenagers Wanted for Garage Clean-up.

Dollars
3. His dad also told him to look in the magazine Dollars.

Times-Press
4. There was an ad for delivering the Times-Press newspaper.

quotation marks

"Kids   Business."
5. There was also an article called Kids Can Run a Business.

Earning Money After School
6. It talked about a book called Earning Money After School.

"How $5"
7. The chapter called How to Quickly Earn $5 sounded interesting.

"Can   book?"
8. Aaron asked his dad, Can I borrow some money to buy this book?

Index

A

Abbreviations, 96, 119, 205–206
Addresses
    abbreviations in, 205
    electronic mail, 115
    in advertisements, 95
    in letters, 114, 116–118
    in postcards, 109
    of web sites, 262
Adjectives, 180–185
    kinds of, 180–183
    placement in a sentence, 184
    that compare (comparative/superlative), 182–183
    using in writing, 185
    See also Antonyms; Describing words; Grammar practice; Multiple-meaning words; Synonyms
Adverbs, 195–197
    that compare, 196
    using in writing, 197
    See also Grammar practice
Advice column, 94
Almanac, 244–245
Alphabetical order, 224
Announcements and advertisements, 95–96
Antonyms, 38–39
Apostrophe, 172, 193, 212
Articles
    See Nouns, words that signal nouns
Atlas and globe, 246–249
    globe, 249
    historical map, 248
    physical map, 246
    political map, 247
    product map, 248
Audience for writing, 86, 152
Autobiography, 96

B

Biography, 97
Book, parts of a, 240–243
    copyright page, 240
    glossary, 243
    index, 242
    table of contents, 241
    title page, 240
Book review, 98
Books, finding information in, 234–243
    card catalog, 234–236
    computerized card catalog, 237–239
    parts of a book, 240–243
Business letters, 116–118
    of complaint, 117
    of request, 116
    persuasive, 118

C

Call number, 235, 239
Capital letters, 202–207
    abbreviations, 205–206
    beginning of a sentence, 202
    days of the week, 206
    months, 206
    pronoun *I*, 202
    proper nouns, 203–206
    special days and holidays, 206
    titles, 207
    See also Grammar practice
Card catalog, 234–239
    author card, 236
    call number, 235, 239
    computerized, 237–239
    Dewey Decimal System, 235
    fiction books, 235
    information on cards, 234–236
    nonfiction books, 235–236
    subject card, 236
    title card, 236
Cards, greeting, 108
Cartoons and comic strips, 99
Cause-and-effect chart, 79
Cause-and-effect paragraphs, 127
Character
    map, 62
    sketch, 100
    See also Story, parts of a
Charts
    See Tables and charts

Dialog
in a play, 133
in a story, 140, 141
punctuation of, 210, 213
Diary
See Journal entry
Dictionary, 250–253
Directions, 102–103
for a game, 102
for making something, 103
to a place, 102
Drafting, 88

E

Editing marks, 91
Editorial, 104
Electronic mail, 115
Encyclopedia, 254–255
Envelope, 119
Exclamation point, 208

F

Fable, 105
Facts and opinions, 104, 118, 121, 130,
139, 232, 235, 244, 254
Fairy tale, 107
Fantasy, 143
Feeling words, 18
Floor plan, 65
Flow chart, 81
Folk tale, 106
Formal language, 20, 152
Friendly letter, 114
Future-tense verbs, 192

G

Globe
See Atlas and globe
Good Writer Guide, 148–157
adding details, 155
collecting ideas, 148–149
evaluating your writing, 157

interesting beginning sentence, 155
sentence combining, 154
show, don't tell, 156
word choice, 153
writing for a specific audience, 152
writing for a specific purpose, 150–151
Grammar practice, 305–327
adjectives, 313–315
adverbs, 321
capital letters, 323–325
conjunctions, 323
nouns, 307–310
prepositions, 321–322
pronouns, 311–313
punctuation, 325–327
sentences, 305–307
verbs, 316–320
Graphic organizers, 62–83
clusters, 62–64
diagrams, 65–67
graphs, 68–69
outlines, 70
story maps, 71–77
tables and charts, 78–81
time lines, 82–83
Graphs, 68–69
bar, 68
line, 69
pie, 69
Greetings (writing), 108–109
cards, 108
postcards, 109
Greetings and good-byes, 20

H

Historical fiction, 142
Holidays
See Dateline U.S.A.
Homophones
See Sound-alike words

I

Idioms, 50–53
Informal language, 20, 152
Interjections, 200
Internet, how to find information on,
258–262

P

Paragraphs
cause-and-effect, 127
main idea, 98, 125, 126, 138, 233
persuasive, 130
that compare, 128
that contrast, 129
topic sentence, 100, 101, 125–130, 138,
230–231, 233
with examples, 126
Parts diagram, 66
Parts of speech
defined, 253
See also Adjectives; Adverbs;
Conjunctions; Interjections; Nouns;
Prepositions; Pronouns; Verbs
Past-tense verbs, 190–191
irregular, 191
regular, 190
spelling rules, 190
Peer Conference, 90
Period, 208–209
as decimal points, 209
in abbreviations, 209
in sentences, 208
Personal narrative, 131
Play, 132–133
script for, 133
Plot
See Story, parts of a
Poems, 134–137
cinquain, 134
concrete poem, 135
diamante, 134
haiku, 136
poem in free verse, 136
rhyming poem, 137
Portfolio, writing, 157
Postcards, 109
Predicate, 165
complete, 165
compound, 165
simple, 165
Prefixes, 48–49
Prepositions, 198–199
prepositional phrases, 199
using in writing, 199
ways to use (chart), 198
See also Describing words, words that tell
where; Grammar practice

Present-tense verbs, 188–189
spelling rules, 189
Prewriting, 86–87
See also Graphic organizers
Pronouns
different kinds (subject, object, reflexive,
possessive, indefinite), 174–178
using in writing (agreement), 179
See also Grammar practice
Proofreading, 92
Proofreading marks, 92
Publishing, 93
Punctuation marks, 208–213
See also Apostrophe; Colon; Comma;
Exclamation point; Grammar practice;
Period; Question mark; Quotation
marks; Underline
Purpose for writing, 86, 150–151

Q

Question mark, 208
Questions, 160–162
at the end of a statement (tag
questions), 161
W-H, 162
yes/no, 162
Quotation marks
around exact words, 213, 226–227
for titles, 213

R

Realistic fiction, 141
Recipe, 103
Report, 138–139, 230–233
Research process, 220–233
alphabetical order, 224
choose a topic, 220
decide what to look up, 221
gather information, 224–227
locate resources, 221–223
organize information, 228–229
outline, 228–229
research question, 221, 227, 228
skim and scan, 225
taking notes, 226–227
write a research report, 230–233
See also Report

Two-word verbs, 54–59

Acknowledgments, continued

pp218, **223**, and **250–253**, Reprinted with the permission of Simon & Schuster Books for Young Readers, an imprint of Simon & Schuster Children's Publishing Division from MACMILLAN DICTIONARY FOR CHILDREN, Revised by Robert B. Costello, Editor in Chief. Copyright © 1997 Simon & Schuster. Photos, pp251 and 253, courtesy of NASA. Photo of Pennybacker Bridge, p. 251, courtesy of Texas Department of Transportation.

pp222 and **235**, Cover illustration from UFO DIARY by Satoshi Kitamura. Copyright © 1989 by Satoshi Kitamura. Reprinted by permission of Farrar, Straus & Giroux, Inc.

pp222, **240**, **241**, and **243**, As in original. Cover photo courtesy of NASA.

p223, © 1996 Time Inc. Reprinted by permission.

pp223 and **254–255**, From THE WORLD BOOK ENCYCLOPEDIA. © 1998 World Book, Inc. By permission of the publisher.

pp235 and **239**, ARE WE MOVING TO MARS? by Anne Schraff. Copyright © 1996 by John Muir Publications, Santa Fe, NM 87505.

pp237–239, Used by permission of Innovative Interfaces, Inc., Emeryville, California.

p246, NGS MAPS/NGS Image Sales.

p248, Maps by GeoSystems from BUILD OUR NATION in WE THE PEOPLE by Hartoonian, et al. Copyright © 1997 by Houghton Mifflin Company. Reprinted by permission of Houghton Mifflin Company. All rights reserved.

p261, "Mars" downloaded from NEW SCIENTIST web site http://www.newscientist.com. Produced 1998 by Reed Elsevier Group, RBI Limited, London. Used by permission.

p269, From COLLECTED POEMS by Langston Hughes. Copyright © 1994 by the Estate of Langston Hughes. Reprinted by permission of Alfred A Knopf Inc.

p271, Robbie Short.

p274, PEANUTS © United Features Syndicate, Inc.

p274, Superman is a trademark of DC Comics © 1998. All rights reserved. Used with permission.

p274, Wonder Woman is a trademark of DC Comics © 1998. All rights reserved. Used with permission.

p275, Cover illustration from THE WIZARD OF OZ by L. Frank Baum. Published by Apple Classics, an imprint of Scholastic Inc. Cover copyright © by Scholastic Inc. Reprinted by permission.

p275, Jacket art by Garth Williams. Jacket design by Charles Krelloff. Jacket copyright 1994 by Harpercollins Publishers. Little House is a trademark of Harpercollins Publishers, used by permission of Harpercollins.

p295, Barry Mullins.

Illustrations:

Cover Illustration: Steven Durke
American Girl Magazine: p94
Doug Bekke: pp128-129 (alligator, crocodile) pp180-183 and p315 (rainforest animal art) p190 (Galileo's thermometer) p220 (planets) p314 (monkey)
Lisa Berret: p23 (suitcase) p25 (dartboard) p28 (ice, pancake, bird, feather, pea pod) p32 (hands cutting apple) p42 (bowl, oven, cake) pp45-46 (lighthouse, coats) p48 (girl with cars)
Liz Callen: p108 (get well dog)
Chi Chung: pp190-191 (sun, desert)
Darius Detwiler: p275 (John Henry, Pecos Bill)
Steven Durke: pp10–11, pp60–61, pp84–85, pp158–159, and pp218–219 (openers)
Ray Godfrey: p40 (clocks) p66 (lifecycle) pp68-69 (raffle, rubber duck, medal) p79 (volcano) p120 (menu) p201 (baseball flyer)
Pauline Howard: p43 (boy on scale)

Beatrice Lebreton: p108 (Kwanzaa cards) p290 (Jan Matzeliger)
Claude Martinot: p65 (kites) p72 (apartment, moon) p74 (spider) p81 (sewing materials) p82 (first place) p102 (hands) p131 (hearts) pp216-217, p267, p272 (Leprechaun) p273 (Passover plate) p278 (card) p285 (gift) p296 (jack-o'-lantern) p300 (Christmas tree) p301 (confetti)
Russell Nemec: p41 (Times of the Day) p266, p276, pp279-283 (maps) p290 (shoe lasting machine) p299, p301 (maps)
Barbara Johansen Newman: p29, pp33-37 and p320, pp50-53, p147, p202 (Lucky Seas), p204 (kid and captain) pp208-213 and pp325-326, p221, p224, p226, p229, p230, p233
Winifred Barnum-Newman: pp106-107 (Stone Soup, Cinderella) p132 (the Jade Emperor) p280 (Sacagawea)
Donna Perrone: p160, p162, p320 (Paul Bunyan) p164, p165, and p305 (Babe) p168 (kites) p170 (table) p171 (umbrellas) p172 (illustrations) p173
Thom Ricks: p275 (Tom Sawyer and Huckleberry Finn)
Mary Rojas: p22 (compass) p108 (birthday card) p135 (oak) p135 (dragon) p137(dragon)
Roni Shepard: p22 (fair)
Robbie Short: pp 222-223 (library)
Camille Venti: p40 (calendar)
Elizabeth Wolf: p19 (basketball art) p140, pp174-178 and pp311-312, pp195-196 and p321 (gymnastics) p200 (baseball game)

Photographs:

Animals Animals: p182 (parrot: John Chellman, toucan: Michael Dick, motmot: Paul Freed) p183 (motmot: Ken Cole) p184 (jaguar: John Chellman, jaguar in jungle: Partridge Productions) p185 (katydid: Patti Murray, stick insect: C. McLaughlin, katydid on leaf: Michael Fogden) p205 (whale: Donna Ikenberry), p309 (stick insect: C. McLaughlin)

Credits

Design and Production: Andrea Carter, Command P, Darius Detwiler, Jeri Gibson, Curtis Spitler, Alicia Sternberg, Andrea Pastrano-Tamez, Edward Tamez, Teri Wilson, ZeitGraph, Inc.

Editorial: Janine Boylan, Fredrick Ignacio, Dawn Liseth, Sheron Long, Sharon Ursino

Permissions Staff: Barbara Mathewson

Index